Senator James Murray Mason

Senator James Murray Mason

Defender of the Old South

Robert W. Young

♦♦♦

The University of Tennessee Press / Knoxville

The paper in this book meets the minimum requirements of the
American National Standard for Permanence of Paper for Printed
Library Materials. The binding materials have been chosen
for strength and durability. ∞ ✪   Printed on recycled paper.

Library of Congress Cataloging-in-Publication Data

Young, Robert W., 1959–
    Senator James Murray Mason : defender of the old South / Robert
W. Young. — 1st ed.
        p. cm.
    Includes bibliographical references and index.
    ISBN 0-87049-998-X (cloth : alk. paper)
1. Mason, J. M. (James Murray), 1798–1871. 2. Legislators—United
States—Biography. 3. Diplomats—Confederate States of America—
Biography. 4. United States. Congress. Senate—Biography.
5. Virginia—Politics and government—1775–1865. 6. Confederate
States of America—Foreign relations. 7. Confederate States of
America—Politics and government. I. Title.
    E415.9.M2Y68 1998
    973.7'21'092—dc21
    [B]   97-21073

For Lisa—My love, my friend, my all

✦✦✦ Contents ✦✦✦

◆◆◆ Acknowledgments ◆◆◆

Attempting to put together the pieces of James Murray Mason's life has been an almost steady preoccupation of mine for this entire decade. It began as my dissertation topic at the University of Maryland, College Park. But while the research and writing for that ended in 1993, the quest to improve the manuscript has continued ever since. The process of re-editing the text and making important changes recommended by various readers has meant that Mason's life story has remained constantly present. It has also convinced me that a manuscript is only truly finished when the author says it is finished; otherwise, tinkering with it can continue forever.

Now that it is finished, there are a number of people and institutions I must gratefully acknowledge for helping me along the way. Most helpful in doing my research were the staffs at the Alderman Library of the University of Virginia, at the Gunston Hall Library, and at the Handley Library in Winchester, Virginia. I would like to particularly thank Anne Baker, librarian at Gunston Hall, who made a young researcher not only feel welcome but believe for the first time that his work was valued outside the University of Maryland.

At other libraries and archives whose materials contributed to this work, countless staff members provided their valuable time and effort. Those institutions include the Library of Congress, the National Archives, the Boston Public Library, the Massachusetts Historical Society, the New-York Historical Society, the William R. Perkins Library at Duke University, the Pierpont Morgan Library, and in Richmond, the Virginia Historical Society and the Virginia State Library and Archives. This work would not have been completed without them.

Special thanks go to various people at the University of Maryland. The words of advice given by Professors George H. Callcott, George O. Kent, and Whitman H. Ridgway are greatly appreciated, not only for helping to improve this work but to better my overall skills as a historian, always urging me to reach further. Their comments and criticisms have made this a better work than when I first presented it to them as my Ph.D. dissertation. I also wish to thank the staff at McKeldin Library, where I spent many long hours studying and photocopying pages and pages of the Congressional Globe and Hansard's Parliamentary Debates, as well as numerous other texts.

But no thanks or appreciation is greater than that I reserve for my advisor at the University of Maryland, Professor Wayne S. Cole. He has inspired me from the first weeks of his "Readings in the History of American Foreign Policy" class I took over ten years ago right through to the present. He drew out my interest in foreign affairs but allowed me to find my own focus rather than pushing me towards his specialty, the Franklin D. Roosevelt era. His strong hand guided me every step of the way. His ability to instill confidence in his students kept me going through many disheartening moments. I will always be proud and grateful to be his last Ph.D. historian before his retirement. He is a special gentleman whose inspiration will stay with me always.

And last, but certainly not least, I could not have done any of this without the support of family and friends. I particularly wish to express all the love and gratitude I have for my parents, who while not always understanding why I do certain things, nonetheless have always supported me and given me everything they could to help make me a better person and a success in life. More than anyone else, however, I must thank the most important person in my life; my wife Lisa. Her hard work to support us while I continued my education is something I can only hope to repay someday. But more than that, she has been my constant companion, sharing all the highs and lows with me, and always reminding me that home is wherever we are together. She is the love of my life, my one and only. To her this book is proudly dedicated.

Robert W. Young
April 22, 1997

♦♦♦ Introduction ♦♦♦

In her Civil War diary, Mary Boykin Chesnut referred to many famous politicians. James Murray Mason was included among them—but not because she held him in high esteem. Mrs. Chesnut wrote, "Mr. Mason is a high and mighty Virginian. He brooks no opposition to his will. . . . Whatever a Mason does is right in his own eyes. He is above law."[1] Although she intended no compliment, her words capture the essence of the man, a Virginia aristocrat born to privilege and determined to preserve his vision of southern society for future generations. He was the quintessential southerner, the embodiment of stereotypes, now long discarded, concerning the people of his country, the "Old South."

At the time when Mrs. Chesnut made those entries in her diary, that "Old South" stood beleaguered and defiant before the world. Dominated by conservative thinking, its leaders fought to keep southern society unchanged amid a changing world. As much as any southern politician, Mason espoused such thoughts. With the United States, and particularly the North, more and more becoming a democracy, he sought to preserve the republic of his youth. With the Constitution being interpreted ever more loosely as the country grew and expanded, he attempted to enforce a strict interpretation of the document to preserve powers for the states that were being usurped by the burgeoning federal government. And with the civilized world turning against the institution of chattel slavery, he continued to see it as a cornerstone of southern society, beneficial to both blacks and whites.

For the better part of three decades, Mason strode across the national and international stage, championing southern rights with aggressive fervor and rarely taking a neutral stand on any key issue. He either angered or pleased almost everybody; few could remain dispassionate about him. Mason managed to earn the respect and admiration of southerners, as well as the disdain and hatred of northerners.[2] When seen on the floor of the U.S. Senate, his figure made a strong impression. Mason carried himself in a dignified manner tinged with pomposity. A tall, big-boned man, the Virginian had a large head with a receding hairline and long salt-and-pepper hair that could give him a disheveled look when it stuck out at the sides. Under bushy brows, his blue eyes and tightly closed mouth could convey a stern scowl of insistent determination, or they could be open and friendly, depending upon his mood and his company.[3]

Contemporary critics regularly attempted to ridicule and discredit Mason by referring to his "shabby dress" (for frugality and simplicity, he tended to wear homespun clothes) and his seemingly incessant chewing of tobacco.[4] But many of those same critics took the man seriously, despite their caricatures.

An heir to Virginia's storied political tradition, Mason embodied the pride of his state, a vanity that had been nurtured by having generations of its leaders serve in top posts in the national government. That pride could at times become arrogance, when Virginians appeared to claim some special right to govern or particular skill in governing. When a Virginia aristocrat spoke, others needed to pay attention. Seeing themselves as "cavaliers" descended from upper-class English stock, such Virginians believed that they were more qualified to rule than others, particularly northerners.[5] Mason and others like him reveled in possessing the kinds of privileges that Mrs. Chesnut decried.

That storybook image of a "cavalier" South contrasted with a "Puritan" North, it has been shown, ignored the realities of America's ethnic texture.[6] James Murray Mason, however, played the role of cavalier that had been handed down from his ancestors. Born and reared in Virginia, he had lived most of his life there. He descended from true English cavaliers, officers in the armies of King Charles I.[7] A grandson of George Mason of Gunston Hall, he studied law at the College of William and Mary and set up practice in the Shenandoah Valley at Winchester. Mason participated in politics as early as 1826, when supporters elected him to the Virginia House of Delegates, where members of his family for generations had represented Virginians. That put the young lawyer in a circle where he could meet and converse with the leading politicians of the day, including John Randolph of Roanoke, who labeled James "a worthy son of worthy sires."[8]

A member of the Virginia convention of 1829–30 that revised the state constitution, Mason served in the U.S. House of Representatives from 1837 to 1839. In 1847, the Virginia legislature elected him to the U.S. Senate. There he remained until the fateful year of 1861. In the Senate he became a leader of the South, advocating southern rights on a wide range of issues, including slavery. A disciple of John C. Calhoun, Mason read the South Carolinian's last speech to his fellow legislators during the 1850 crisis. It was Mason who drafted the Fugitive Slave Law that became part of the compromise of that year. It was Mason who opposed all legislation that would increase the powers of the federal government in domestic affairs. And it was Mason who chaired the Senate committee that investigated the events surrounding John Brown's attack on the federal arsenal at Harpers Ferry in 1859. Those examples illustrate two of the three key themes running through his life and career: strict interpretation of the Constitution, and defense of the institution of slavery.

The third key theme was foreign affairs. Serving as chairman of the Senate Foreign Relations Committee from 1851 to 1861, Mason played a key role in any foreign policy issue that came before Congress. Dealing directly with the State Department as well as the president, Mason influenced American foreign policy as it emanated from the top. Although this role did not provide him with diplomatic experience abroad, those ten years left Mason well versed in the foreign policy concerns of the period, ranging from the Crimean War through trade with the Far East to myriad issues involving Latin America. Usually foreign affairs provided a nationalistic respite from the sectional politics of the time. But when foreign policy related to national expansion, policy makers proved unable or unwilling to keep the domestic debate over slavery separate. Thus, in the simmering cauldron of the 1850s, foreign and domestic affairs became intertwined.

That cauldron boiled over in 1860 and 1861, when eleven southern states seceded from the union and formed the Confederate States of America. When the "Old Dominion" seceded, Mason, loyal first to Virginia, resigned from the U.S. Senate and became a member of the Confederate Congress. Shortly thereafter, to make optimal use of

Mason's foreign policy experience, Jefferson Davis appointed him to be the Confederacy's diplomatic envoy to Great Britain. Mason sailed for Europe along with the southern envoy to France, Louisiana's John Slidell. But in the *Trent* affair, both were captured.

The *Trent* affair is the one part of Mason's life that has been examined thoroughly by historians. The focus on that three-month period has obscured Mason's seventy-plus other years. Moreover, the sheer quantity of writing about that episode has made the phrase "Mason and Slidell" a unit in the minds of historians. In the process, the two commissioners have been reduced to mere supporting characters in the diplomatic impasse between Washington and London. They appear inseparable, almost indistinguishable, to students of the Civil War era. The beginning of this unfortunate development occurred during the war itself. Northern newspapers wrote of "Mason and Slidell" so often that, when federal soldiers occupying Winchester found Mason's home, they assumed that Slidell owned and lived in the house next door.[9] Although Slidell served on Mason's Senate Foreign Relations Committee, the two men were not particularly close before the war and were quite different in personalities and styles. The South was not a monolithic unit. States of the Upper and the Lower South had different interests and priorities;[10] Mason tended to associate with those closest to him geographically and ideologically.

The *Trent* affair has been overemphasized, not only in comparison with Mason's years in the Senate, but also in comparison with those he spent in England. Although the appointment was the culmination of his political career, the years Mason spent as a diplomat were years of frustration. He suffered the indignity and humiliation of being rebuffed continually by the British government after he arrived in London. Confederate efforts to gain diplomatic recognition from Europe's great powers failed miserably, due to a combination of mistakes, miscalculations, and misfortunes.

In the Senate, Mason always had asserted that foreign affairs were the province of the executive. Therefore, as a diplomat, he tried to take his cues from Jefferson Davis in Richmond. Davis stressed the legality of secession and the illegality of the federal blockade. He saw diplomatic recognition as something deserved rather than something to be sought.[11] Mason's agreement with those perspectives assured that his diplomatic efforts would tend to be quite passive. Most of the time, he needed to be prodded into action. Secretary of State Judah P. Benjamin pushed him at various times, but with communication across the Atlantic less than speedy, Mason depended more upon British supporters of the Confederacy for advice and guidance. Those advisors usually urged caution, and this reinforced Mason's tendency to sit and await events rather than try to make things happen.

With the South's defeat, Mason became a citizen of the world but not a citizen of any particular country. He remained in Britain for an entire year after Appomattox. He then spent three years in Canada before reluctantly returning to a changed Virginia. By that time, at age seventy-one, he had less than two years to live. Those two years constituted a short epilogue to his long political career, which included over twenty years spent near the center of the key events of his day.

Mason died six years after the South's military defeat completed the destruction of the world he spent his life defending. The "second American Revolution" overthrew the southern aristocracy's hold on federal power and shifted it to northerners.[12] In the process, the war destroyed the institution of slavery.[13] The social structure of Mason's South had as its foundation the enslaving of blacks. Eliminating the basis of the southern social order meant that what replaced it could bear only a passing resemblance to its predecessor. The war hastened the ruination of the "Old South" that Mason, Davis, and others wanted to preserve. While struggling for independence much as their forefathers had, Confederate leaders tried to keep the forces of change from corrupting their romanticized image of the South.[14] The leaders of the Confederacy had resolved to swim against the tides of change in an effort to preserve southern society as they saw it. They failed.

Mason spent his long career fighting against change. That left him hopelessly outdated as the United States moved past the mid-century mark. He was an anachronism, a throwback to the eighteenth-century age of "gentleman freeholders," when the upper classes had ruled in a world of limited suffrage, with few real limits upon their political power.[15] For Mason, expanding democracy in the North and increased centralization of power in the hands of the federal government threatened that world. He wanted the Constitution to be interpreted strictly, to prevent both trends from encroaching upon the rights of southerners. He enunciated those beliefs concisely on July 28, 1856, when he exclaimed in the Senate that the South had "no security but in the Constitution. The Constitution was framed to secure the rights of the minority. The Constitution was framed to chain down the popular will, and thereby to make that in substance, which the Constitution says shall be in form, a Republic—not an unbridled irresponsible Democracy."[16] He wanted to preserve the "standard of old Virginia republicanism, as distinguished from wild northern democracy,"[17] while maintaining the states "as sovereign communities" and "the best judges of their own interests and their own policy."[18] According to Mason, the founding fathers intended the federal government to take responsibility for foreign affairs, with domestic affairs to be left in state hands.[19]

Such rigid constitutional rhetoric can be used to portray a Virginia statesman trying to be true to the ideals of his forefathers, particularly those of his grandfather. The Mason family coat of arms bore the motto *Pro Republica Semper* (for the republic always). George Mason of Gunston Hall had those words engraved on the family silver in the 1780s,[20] enabling those words to live on as the treasure passed from generation to generation. Since preservation of the republic served as the prime motivation behind his grandson's political career, the family motto sums up with great precision James Murray Mason the politician, as well as James Murray Mason the man. Whether he was a U.S. senator or a diplomat for the Confederacy, the words "for the republic always" guided the Virginian's actions.

But any portrait of Mason that omits southern slavery is incomplete. A firm believer that slavery uplifted both races, he asked his fellow senators in 1852 "what would have been the condition of these three millions of negroes, had not their ancestors been brought to this country? Would they not, by degradation and starvation, have gone out of existence?"[21] His belief in the benevolence of slavery led him to write in 1857 that "the condition of slavery, in the Southern States, . . . is now in truth, a patriarchal form of society, resulting from the social tendencies of our race."[22]

Mason had a paternalistic relationship with the few slaves whom he owned, and he made the mistake of assuming that kindness and generosity were the norm for southern slave holders. For the Virginia patrician, black slaves stood at the bottom of the South's social hierarchy and needed to remain there. Such a position could seem to conflict with his commitment to freedom from federal government interference for southern whites. But Mason saw no contradiction in his stance, and, as Edmund S. Morgan has shown, in Virginia the strange marriage of slavery and freedom developed in the colonial period, where the two became intertwined in both rhetoric and reality.[23] Perpetuating that society served as Mason's raison d'être, and its demise left him an empty and unfulfilled man whom neither friends nor family truly could cheer.

In "A Tribute to this Exalted Patriot," which appeared in the *Richmond Enquirer* after Mason's death, Virginia's former governor,

Henry A. Wise, used the words "a gentleman, in the highest sense of that much abused term." He lamented that critics saw Mason as haughty, arguing that "there was a geniality mixed with a hauteur uncongenial; a hearty laugh contrasted with the sternest frown; a brusqueness with a reticent and commanding dignity; a John Bull bluffness with a French-like air of finished politeness; a Virginian old-plantation way with marked attention to niceties; a jealous regard for conventional forms, and yet he would violate them imperiously."[24] One historian tried to sum up Mason the man by referring to him as "the stock Southern aristocrat of legend, without of course performing as a cabin Casanova, or showing any addiction to the whip and the bottle. He was devoutly and contentedly a family man in the best sense of the word."[25] Such words delineate him accurately as a man of great personal integrity. As the quintessential southerner and the carrier of Virginia's political torch, however, he was much more.

Mason had the admirable quality of always being true to his principles. He lived his life without deviating from a core set of beliefs that exalted the triumvirate of the Constitution, southern slavery, and Virginia. With the strong sense of pride and honor that predominated among antebellum southern politicians, he opposed all that would injure any of those three things. Such consistency helps make Mason's life an excellent model for understanding the world in which he lived. Learning why Mason acted as he did, one gains insight into why southern leaders as a group acted as they did, both before and during the national tragedy of the 1860s. His story is one of a good and decent man drawn to the exciting yet hazardous arena of high-stakes power politics.

While southerners celebrated him, northerners reviled him. Critics may accuse him of seeking to perpetuate a society built upon oppression. But within his own frame of reference, Mason fought for freedom just as much as his eighteenth-century predecessors had. The rallying cry of "state rights" meant more to Mason than simply planter and elite control, or protection of slavery. To him it meant freedom—a freedom from any central government interference with the liberties of the people. That had to be preserved at all cost, by those entrusted with the power to do so. As a Virginia "cavalier" from a family steeped in government service, Mason believed that it was his patriotic duty to serve his state. But in Mason's case, the state was the "Old Dominion" and not the federal Union; *Pro Republica Semper.*

♦♦♦ **Chapter 1** ♦♦♦

1798–1832

Heritage, Family, and Education

The state of Virginia had a long tradition of providing, from its upper classes, leaders for the American government. Virginians bearing names such as Washington, Jefferson, Lee, Randolph, Madison, and Monroe rose to positions of national leadership. Some, hungry for power, considered national prominence their birthright. Others saw it as a patriotic duty.

As the nineteenth century proceeded, however, the United States increased in size. As new states, particularly the more populous states of the North, were added to the Union, Virginia's share of political power decreased. By the 1850s, too, the Cotton Belt had replaced Tidewater Virginia as the center of the South's economic power. Nonetheless, Virginians did not lose their pride or their sense of honor. That pride "burned as fiercely in the breast of Virginia statesmen in 1850 as in 1789."[1] And that pride glowed brightly in the breast of United States Sen. James Murray Mason.

The name Mason had long been associated with the Virginia aristocracy. James Murray Mason's family had a considerable history of public service in both America and England, and he was deeply proud of his lineage. In 1857, he used his grandfather's papers to detail his paternal ancestry in a letter to a good friend, William C. Rives.[2] Mason traced the story back to George Mason of Staffordshire, England, a member of the House of Commons during the reign of King Charles I.[3] George sided with his king in the English Civil War and commanded a regiment of cavalry in the royal army, but after Charles's defeat, Mason left England, escaped to America, and landed at Norfolk, Virginia, in 1651. His family soon followed, and he set up a plantation in what is now Stafford County, Virginia, "named after the native shire of Col. Mason in England."[4] In America, George maintained his commitment to public service, being a member of the House of Burgesses, in addition to holding positions in the county government. The next three generations of George Masons continued this pattern; each held all the varied political offices filled by the first George Mason.[5]

The fourth George Mason "settled on a plantation in 'Doeg Neck' [afterwards the Gunston estate], then in Stafford, now Fairfax County."[6] In 1735, he drowned in the Potomac River, and the estate passed to his eldest son,[7] who would become the most famous George Mason—the builder of Gunston Hall. Less than twenty miles from Alexandria, the mansion was built a half-mile from the Potomac on an estate that originally covered six thousand acres.[8] Today the house still stands on what is known as Mason Neck Peninsula. One of the eighteenth-century gentlemen planters called to service by his fellow Virginians,[9] George Mason's political achievements included, in 1776, writing the Virginia Declaration of Rights and being the main author of the Virginia Constitution. He also can be viewed as the architect of the Bill of Rights because he refused to sign the U.S. Constitution without guarantees for individual freedom like those specified in his Declaration of Rights.[10] Large numbers of children were the rule in the Mason family, and George Mason of Gunston Hall was no exception. He fathered eight children. Similarly, the fourth of his five sons, John, born in 1766, had ten children, six boys and four girls. John Mason's second son, born in 1798, was James Murray Mason.[11]

John Mason's extensive resume included activities as merchant, farmer, ferry business owner, councilman, banker, foundryman, brigadier general of militia, domestic and foreign shipper and trader, canal company president, superintendent of Indian trade, and U.S. commissary general of prisoners in the War of 1812.[12] He married Anna Maria Murray of Annapolis, Maryland, who was described by one contemporary as "a charming woman—not so much in the face as in her whole deportment. Her face, tho' quite pretty enough with charming eyes and fine teeth—plays delightfully and sings really sweetly."[13] On land inherited from his father, John Mason built his home,

Clermont. Located on Analostan Island (today Theodore Roosevelt Island) in the Potomac River, Clermont was where the Masons spent the warm-weather months, while in winter they lived in Georgetown.[14] The mansion stood near the southern end of the island and had a view of Washington that included both the White House and the Capitol. In Georgetown, about a block away from the river and near Georgetown University, John Mason owned a town house.[15] It was there, on November 3, 1798, that his second child, James Murray Mason, was born.[16]

Very little evidence survives to give us details of the subject's privileged boyhood. He loved horses, becoming over the years a skillful rider,[17] and he attended school in Georgetown. He enjoyed a rich family and social life, growing up with five brothers and four sisters in and around the nation's capital. According to Mason's daughter, Virginia, the siblings were "as happy and as free from care as it was possible for indulgent parents possessed of large wealth to have made them; but they were, at the same time, trained to habits of ready obedience and of never failing respect, so much so, that to the end of their lives every one of the sons and daughters would quote the opinions of 'My Father,' or 'My Mother,' as might have been done in childhood when, as a matter of course, those opinions were admitted to be final and infallible."[18] His childhood days at Clermont, as well as the frequent trips down the river to Gunston Hall for hours of riding and hunting,[19] provided such happiness for James that in later years he would compare any pleasurable time with those orchestrated by his beloved parents.

His father's varied occupations and acquaintances exposed his son to politics at an early age. As a young boy, James often accompanied his father on trips to the Capitol, where he paid close attention to the debates in Congress.[20] During the War of 1812, as U.S. commissary general of prisoners, John Mason took his son on his regular rounds to see the captured British soldiers. On one occasion, James was particularly disturbed by the pale, emaciated condition of one of the British officers. He begged his mother to prepare some delicacies that he then could take to the prisoner. Charmed by her son's compassion, she relented, and James began bringing both food and books to the prison. Fifty years later, while representing the Confederacy in England, Mason was the guest of a British nobleman at a social gathering. Another guest at the event introduced himself as one of the British prisoners to whom the young boy had shown such kindness many years before.[21]

In addition to such practical education, Mason was also schooled

in more traditional pursuits, becoming an avid reader.[22] All this prepared him for the day in 1815, when, armed with his Georgetown
education and the best wishes of his parents, he journeyed to Philadelphia to attend the University of Pennsylvania. He first stayed with
relatives on his mother's side of the family, but he also boarded for a
time with a French family, who taught him to speak French fluently.
In three years he earned his bachelor's degree, and in 1819 he went
to Williamsburg, Virginia, to study law at the College of William and
Mary. Perhaps more significant than any of those developments in
young Mason's education was the fact that, in Philadelphia, he met
the love of his life, Eliza Margaretta Chew.[23]

Like James, Eliza traced her ancestry to an Englishman who came
to Virginia in the 1600s. Over time, members of the family gradually
migrated northward,[24] and in 1761 Eliza's grandfather built the country home that would be her birthplace—Cliveden, in Germantown,
Pennsylvania.[25] She was born into one of Philadelphia's elite families
just fifteen days after James. When both were sixteen years of age, a
seven-year courtship began. James was a schoolmate of Eliza's brothers and accepted their invitations to spend weekends and holidays at
Cliveden; but before long it became apparent that the main reason
for the young man's eagerness to visit was Eliza.[26]

He had found the perfect companion. Their relationship grew
throughout James's years in Philadelphia, as the young Virginian
developed a habit "of confiding to Eliza Chew all of his hopes and
aspirations, consulting her judgement in every question that arose,
seeking her advice and sympathy in all the perplexities and troubles
of his life, and claiming her congratulations and commendation in
every success that he achieved."[27] Their bond proved to be even stronger when his education took him away to William and Mary. In 1819,
while at Williamsburg, Mason received a letter from Eliza's sister,
Anne. She wrote that, after initial skepticism about whether the relationship could survive at such a long distance, she now saw that the
couple's interest in each other was as strong as ever. She thought that
his going to Williamsburg might have been a good thing after all,
"since it has been the test of your power and must have convinced
you, upon how firm a basis your affections were reposed. Your confidence after this trial, can never waver."[28]

The two waited patiently for over three more years. Mason completed his studies at William and Mary and in 1820 moved to Richmond, where he studied law under Benjamin Watkins Leigh and
gained admission to the bar.[29] Both family members and friends expected him to settle somewhere either in the traditional Tidewater

area or in one of the rising, bustling centers of power in the "Era of Good Feelings." Mason instead chose to pack his belongings and set off to start a legal practice in Winchester, Virginia, a Shenandoah Valley town which in 1820 had an almost frontier atmosphere, in sharp contrast to the familiar society and politics of Philadelphia, Washington, or Richmond.[30]

In later years, Mason often recalled that June afternoon in 1820 when his memorable journey on horseback from Analostan Island ended at Winchester's tavern, where the townfolk's initial suspiciousness of the stranger in their midst soon gave way to conversation and the beginnings of friendships. His daughter Virginia later wrote that, in his old age, her father's "eyes filled and his voice faltered whenever allusion was made to those happy days, or to the dear friends of his early manhood in Winchester."[31]

Despite providing happy memories later, the first few years in Winchester were difficult for a young man away from his family and struggling to establish his fledgling law practice. A year later, James hoped to be "getting some little more name and foothold in the county. At our last Superior Court, . . . I had an opportunity of making two speeches, both in cases of some little importance and was fortunate enough to succeed in both."[32] The young man's greatest problem was being almost perpetually short of cash. Mason strove to establish his independence from his father, but, like many a modern college student away from home, he often wrote his parents asking for funds. In 1821, he wrote: "My dear Father, . . . I had intended that the money you were good enough to give me, should have lasted a much longer time than to this date—nor should I have been disappointed and constrained to ask of you more at this time, but that my Land Lady some days ago made a demand that I could not well resist and has left me completely out of pocket. I sincerely trust that in a short time, I shall be sufficiently in practice to prevent at least the frequent calls I am now obliged to make on you for small sums to keep afloat."[33] He then asked his father for forty dollars. That ritual continued at least through 1823.[34] Indeed, in September of that year, Mason, knowing that his father was away, wrote his older brother that his fund was "exhausted" and that he had no "prospect hereabout of its being replenished." He asked for fifty dollars, assuming that John Mason, Jr., had "command of the Treasury, in the Interregnum."[35]

By 1823, any cash shortage had become all the more critical, because, on July 25, 1822, Mason finally married his beloved Eliza.[36] The wedding united the two in a gala affair held at Cliveden, and the

Chew family welcomed the young groom wholeheartedly. Earlier that month, Eliza's father, Benjamin, wrote James that, with the time approaching when the "very dear and valued object of a Parent's affections" was to be given away in marriage, "I cannot but meet you . . . with peculiar sensibility and a tenderness naturally resulting from the contemplated adoption of whom the future happiness of my child in this life must essentially depend."[37] The Chews and Masons kept the doors of Cliveden and Clermont open to the newlyweds; but, for James and Eliza, home lay beyond those aristocratic spheres, at Winchester.

The couple seemed to adjust well to the town's lack of ostentation. Eliza wrote her sister later in 1822 that Winchester was "the place for the enjoyment of society without display," and she detailed the active social calendar that the Masons kept, along with the other major families of the town.[38] Married life clearly agreed with the young bride. She found her husband to possess "the most cheerful, buoyant, and excellent temper I have ever known,"[39] being "always ready to read, play, talk or walk as my inclination may dictate." Being at home delighted James, who "often said that he does not know why every other place appears inferior unless because his wife has more taste and neatness than anybody else."[40]

James's law practice kept them apart many days, however, and Eliza wrote of his riding one hundred miles in the rain to keep a particular court date.[41] But such separations made their evenings alone all the more special. In late 1824, she gave her sister a description of their long evenings together: "We generally commence the evening by playing two or three games of chess, as Mr. Mason is extravagantly fond of the game; then we practise together for a little while, and afterwards he reads to me, while I sew, till eleven o'clock; as we have tea very early, we thus accomplish a great deal before bedtime."[42] In 1825, their evenings became even fuller, with the birth of their first child, a daughter named Anna Maria.[43] A shortage of cash would have been devastating then, but no letters to father were necessary, for James's legal career had begun to blossom.

Evidence regarding Mason's early career at Winchester is sparse, but it is clear that, from the start, a major portion of his income was derived from handling various legal affairs related to his father's vast business concerns.[44] By 1825, however, such an arrangement had become more beneficial to John Mason than to his son. James's reputation had grown steadily throughout the Shenandoah Valley, enabling him to achieve what he had lacked in his first years there: independence from his father. The following year, that new freedom from financial constraints allowed Mason to follow in the footsteps of his ancestors and enter the hallowed world of Virginia politics.

For years James had followed politics closely, as any Mason would have been expected to do. He read the Congressional Globe voraciously and followed the debates in the state legislature with great interest. Even in Winchester, far from the Tidewater, the name "Mason" had a certain magical ring, suggesting excellence and giving rise to a presumption that he would enter politics and demonstrate great talent for it.[45] Thus it should have surprised no one when, in the spring of 1826, James was elected to represent Frederick County in the Virginia House of Delegates.[46] That summer, as their representative and an honored citizen, he was the featured speaker at Winchester's Fourth of July celebration.[47] On July 15, he gave the oration after a funeral procession honoring the late presidents, Adams and Jefferson.[48] Chosen by his peers to serve them in Richmond, Mason had come far from that day six years earlier when he had ridden into town a total stranger.

In December, Mason arrived in Richmond as a freshman representative. He served on the Committee of Finance and the Committee for Courts of Justice. The session for the most part lacked any real drama; but in February 1827, Mason found himself in the middle of the recurring debate over the role of the federal government in building roads, canals, and other elements of the growing American infrastructure. As early as 1816, with the creation of a board of internal improvements, Virginia's leaders had sought to meet the growing need to build transportation systems connecting the East with the West.[49] Under President John Quincy Adams, the federal government's involvement in such activities increased dramatically. Discussions became heated over the constitutionality of using federal money to pay for what were essentially local improvement projects, deepening the growing rift between supporters of President Adams and those of his political rival, Gen. Andrew Jackson.[50]

Improvement projects involving canal and road building particularly benefited the western part of Virginia, an area that depended much more on trade over the Appalachian Mountains than the Tidewater did. Voters there undoubtedly expected Mason to back those interests. Instead, he aggressively supported resolutions introduced in the House of Delegates by William B. Giles,[51] a Jacksonian, protesting against "the claim or exercise of any power whatever, on the part of the General Government, to make internal improvements within the limits and jurisdiction of the several States, and particularly within the State of Virginia."[52] Mason was a member of the committee that reported those resolutions to the House of Delegates,[53] and his stance supporting Giles placed him squarely in opposition to the position held by many of his constituents.

He found that out personally upon his return to Winchester after the legislative session ended. He already had the political awareness to know that his prospects for reelection had dimmed. His position on the Giles resolutions had offset any positive impact of his introduction and support of various other measures beneficial to his part of Virginia.[54] Thus he deemed it necessary, both for his own vindication as well as to "correct misapprehension," for the subject of the Giles resolutions to be "exposed and canvassed" before the election.

Mason wrote an open letter to the "Freeholders of Frederick County" to explain and defend his actions. At the tender age of twenty-eight, he argued for a strict construction of the U.S. Constitution with the calm assurance of a more seasoned politician. Mason asserted that "the extension of Federal power tends to consolidation, from which, when once established, there is no alternative between despotism or civil war." Holding those "solemn and deliberate convictions, . . . and sworn to support the Constitution," he had voted for the resolutions. He had voted his conscience, rather than simply voting the way his constituents told him, which would have dishonored both himself and his office. Mason believed that "a representative is bound, by every obligation, to discard all personal considerations, and to express by his vote, the convictions of his best judgement." He knew the damage that probably had been done to his career, but he remained certain that he had acted correctly. He added, "If by my vote upon these resolutions, my political fate is to turn, let it be so. I have done my duty, according to the honest dictates of my best judgement, and I wish not to evade the test. There is no man who esteems your favour, or appreciates your confidence, more than I do, but I should be unworthy of either, were I meanly to solicit its continuance, by the suppression of my opinion, or the sacrifice of my principles."[55] Mason suffered defeat in the 1827 election, receiving less than 22 percent of the vote in a four-man contest.[56]

James lost despite the fact that the Giles resolutions also protested against protective tariffs, a position that supported agricultural interests and was favored by his constituents. Defending his actions regarding the tariff, Mason wrote that a tariff "for the protection of domestic manufactures" is "unwarranted by the Constitution as in practice it has been found oppressive and calamitous to our agricultural interests."[57]

But any support Mason won for his position on the tariff was

more than offset by voters' anger at his protest against federal fund-
ing of internal improvements. For his constituents, his reading of the
law of the land was too strict on that issue, and therefore his interpretation of the Constitution—one of those three themes that charac-
terize his life—led to a disappointing defeat at the polls.

For the rest of the year, he returned to being a Winchester lawyer
and a devoted father. Family matters took up a great deal of his time
in the summer, when the entire Mason clan converged on Analostan
Island for the weddings of James's sister, Sarah Maria Mason, and of
his older brother, John Mason, Jr. The combined celebration lasted
almost two weeks.[58] James seemed to enjoy spending time at home as
much as ever, particularly relishing such simple household chores as
tending a garden and chopping wood.[59]

But the world of politics still stirred his mind. He refused to sulk
over the voters' rejection, and throughout the year he continued to
defend his vote on the Giles resolutions, slowly but surely winning
converts to his way of thinking. In January 1828, Mason was appointed to serve as a delegate to the state convention for Andrew
Jackson.[60] In March, the Jacksonians once again nominated him for
the House of Delegates.[61] In a five-man race, Mason finished second,
but since the top two finishers went to Richmond, he still could claim
a redemptive comeback victory.[62] The venerable John Randolph of
Roanoke congratulated him, writing: "Frederick County has redeemed
nobly her errors and expiated her offences. She has one representative . . . worthy of the largest, richest and most populous county in
the State."[63]

Mason's political recovery continued in 1829, with his reelection to the House of Delegates.[64] He also was nominated for the
Virginia Constitutional Convention,[65] but in that voting, where four
delegates were to be chosen, Mason finished fifth, a mere fourteen
votes behind Hierome Opie.[66] Nonetheless, Mason still got to the
convention when he was chosen as the replacement for Opie, who on
December 15 resigned his seat for personal reasons.[67] The convention had begun meeting on October 5. Thus James missed the first
two months, but, as he was in Richmond for the legislative session,
he was able to make up for lost time quickly. He plunged into the
constitutional debates almost immediately after his selection.

Virginia's constitution of 1776 had been under attack for decades, with none other than Thomas Jefferson as its leading critic.
Largely a perpetuation of the colonial government structure, the
document had become less and less satisfactory as time passed and
the state's population grew and shifted. Conservatives, recognizing

that a constitutional convention most likely would focus upon the issue of representation, for years had resisted the calls of reformers. When they finally relented in the face of increasing popular pressure, the convention debates, just as they had feared, focused on representation and the question of who exactly constituted the population of Virginia.[68] The sides generally divided along sectional lines, with the Tidewater area wanting slaves counted, as they were in allocating representatives to the federal Congress. The West, having fewer slaves, wanted representation allocated on the basis of the white population, a system that would take power away from the planter elite and move Virginia closer to becoming a true democracy.

James Murray Mason cast his first votes in the convention on December 16[69] and made his first major speech on December 19. He began quietly by admitting that he was only the "humble successor" to the people's choice because of the "kind estimate of those who are now my colleagues," and then he recounted the history of the convention. He claimed to speak for the entire western part of the state, which he saw as a majority held in chains by the minority power of the eastern part. Mason viewed the issue in broad terms, proclaiming it "one of those fearful contests . . . in which the *Government* is on one side, and the *people* are on the other."[70]

Mason had used a similar argument in the House of Delegates almost a year earlier, when he stressed to his colleagues that "the people of Virginia, and not the slaves of that people, are those who wield the political power."[71] Therefore, slave numbers should be irrelevant in deciding representation. Ironically, that stance placed him in direct opposition to his own mentor, Benjamin Watkins Leigh, who championed the conservative Tidewater position, asserting that easterners would never agree to put "the power of controlling the wealth of the State into hands different from those which hold that wealth."[72]

But Mason wanted to end the Tidewater oligarchy that Leigh defended, particularly since he believed that to do otherwise "would be to abandon the whole purpose of reform—and in such abandonment to recognize and establish the very principle we condemn."[73] At the convention, Mason's side offered a compromise, whereby representation in the Virginia Senate would be decided by the numbers that included slaves, while the House of delegates would be based solely on the white population. To Mason, "the popular branch must be pure"; he thought of the compromise as a "concession" on the part of the western region. As he did with regard to internal improvements, Mason acted in accord with his own conscience. Stating that, given the distance between himself and his constituents, he could not be certain they would approve his course, he nonetheless proclaimed willingness to assume responsibility for his actions. If he had erred, he looked for "acquittal in that generous confidence, on which the Representative principle is founded."[74]

Despite the efforts of reformers, the compromise that emerged made few significant changes. On January 14, 1830, unhappy with the end product, Mason voted against the constitution, which passed by a vote of fifty-five to forty.[75] His own Frederick County approved the document by a narrow margin of thirteen votes, and it gained approval in the entire state, receiving almost 63 percent of the vote.[76]

Perhaps he was able to be philosophical about the consequences his vote might have on his political future, because of his increasing dislike for spending so much time away from his wife and children. With James's career and family growing, the Masons needed a larger house. On June 1, 1829, they purchased Selma, which would be their home for the next thirty-two years.[77] His daughter Virginia described her birthplace as "an unpretending, though substantial and comfortable, stone dwelling" located about a mile west of Winchester, toward the Blue Ridge Mountains, with an excellent view of the town.[78] The legislative sessions of the House of Delegates took place in the winter months, and for the first few years Mason's family spent those months with his parents at Clermont or with Eliza's parents at Cliveden. Now there was a bigger household to run, and, with three children, travel had become more difficult. Eliza faced the winter of 1830 at Selma, without her husband and without her parents.[79] On the eve of his journey to Richmond, she wrote to her sister that she was "already shrinking from the prospect of spending three months in solitude."[80] Mason hated leaving her and also regretted interrupting his law practice for three to four months each year. Despite such feelings, at the urging of friends and supporters he stood for reelection again in 1830,[81] serving one last term in the House of Delegates.[82]

Mason did not run for reelection in 1831 because those same friends and supporters convinced him that the time had come to aim for a larger prize. Running for Congress against the incumbent, Robert Allen, he overwhelmingly won Frederick County, but the vote in the rest of the congressional district went against him.[83] Refusing to dwell on the negative result, both James and Eliza almost felt a sense of relief in the defeat. The loss meant that he had more time to devote to both his family and his law practice. Each had continued to expand. The Masons then had four children, and the law practice extended farther and farther beyond Winchester and Frederick County.[84] Over the next few years, James's only genuine political responsibility came in 1832, when he was appointed an elector for President Jackson.[85]

Meanwhile, the politics of the day continued to unfold. In 1832, echoes of the nullification movement in South Carolina reverberated throughout the South. Ostensibly an economic protest against high tariffs, but with concern over slavery lurking in the background, nullification reached to the heart of the debate regarding the Constitution and the nature of the Union.[86]

James Murray Mason could not escape such a volatile issue, even though he was far from Richmond. Before year's end, the disruptive national debate had spread to the Shenandoah Valley. On December 31, 1832, citizens of Frederick County met at Winchester to discuss nullification. A committee of seven was formed, and it adopted resolutions approving the course of action taken by President Jackson. Mason was one of three, however, who submitted a minority report that more clearly articulated the rights of the states and the idea of secession from the Union.[87]

Mason was not "a nullifier," as some opponents charged. The trio's report, while defending the idea of secession as a right, supported the president. Secession was to be used only in extreme circumstances; and in 1832, the tariff policies of the federal government, while somewhat oppressive, were no grounds for any secessionist position. The minority report stressed veneration of "the Union of the States as the palladium of our liberty, the source of our dignity and influence abroad, and of our tranquility and prosperity at home"; but it also warned that "the portentous crisis of affairs in S. Carolina, loudly calls for the deep consideration of every citizen who regards the prosperity of that state, or values the repose and welfare of the Union."[88] Mason's thoughts were best expressed by a resolution he offered and argued for that was voted down by the committee: "*Resolved*, That we hail with peculiar satisfaction the disposition evinced by Congress to reduce the duties upon imports to the standard of revenue alone. Viewing our taxes as nothing more than the contribution paid by the citizen for the support of the government, which protects him in the enjoyment of civil liberty, we regard the present tariff, avowedly imposed for other purposes, as a departure from the meaning of the Constitution and repugnant to the character of our institutions."[89] With Virginia still reeling from the trauma of Nat Turner's rebellion,[90] Mason would have supported nullification if he thought the issue in question to be slavery, but not for a relatively minor grievance such as the tariff. He wanted to save such a potent constitutional defense mechanism for a bigger crisis.

Mason's position fit with his stance earlier in his career supporting the Giles resolutions, which he had defended by explaining: "The States are parties to the Constitution in their sovereign capacity. . . . As to the general doctrine of these resolutions upon the points which they involve of constitutional law, they express . . . the uniform policy of the Democratic Party, amongst whom I was born and bred, from whom my earliest impressions were received, and from whose doctrines, sanctioned by maturer years, I have never deviated, and never can."[91] In 1832, at the still-young age of thirty-four, he possessed an ideology. It was rooted in his heritage, in his family, and in the education he had gained from his school years, from serving as a legislator, and from life itself. While he supported President Jackson, Mason was no Jacksonian Democrat. While he wanted more political power for western Virginia, he did so in the *Pro Republica Semper* spirit of his grandfather. His efforts to preserve an older world showed in his calls for a strict interpretation of the Constitution. He would take positions contrary to the opinion of the majority but would not deviate from his core beliefs. He had taken admirable positions, but a politician often walks a fine line between consistency and rigidity, between purposefulness and obstinacy, and ultimately between success and failure. James Murray Mason was positioned for both these latter eventualities.

Chapter 2

1832–1847

Steps toward the Grand Arena

James Murray Mason spent much less time on politics after the nullification crisis faded away. He continued to follow the issues of the day with great interest but devoted his next five years to full-time pursuit of his legal career. The varied tasks of a country lawyer may have been less glamorous than those of a Virginia legislator, but they certainly kept him busy. Mason's caseload ranged from handling lawsuits jointly with his brother Eilbeck,[1] to providing legal services regarding unsurveyed land in the Shenandoah Valley.[2] His practice prospered, and, in working twelve months a year in and around Winchester, he gained the additional benefit of being able to spend more time at Selma, "the only spot on earth where, when one enters, he knows that suspicion, distrust, and jealousy do not attend him."[3] There his family provided Mason with the "domestic delight" he truly cherished.[4]

James and Eliza's fifth child, a daughter whom they named Virginia, was born on December 12, 1833. Many years later, she recalled her childhood with great affection. Generally, sons and daughters have memories of their parents that mix the wonderful with the far less than perfect. Mason must have provided her with both, but Virginia chose to skip over the bad moments and portrayed her father as being a nearly perfect parent and husband. She remembered

him as being at his best when he was at home with his family or
neighbors. There he exhibited a "uniformly cheerful, buoyant tem-
perament" and a "fondness for social life . . . making his presence
essential to the full enjoyment of any amusement." The children ea-
gerly anticipated their father's return from his office, when "his bright,
joyous voice and hearty laugh" would announce his homecoming.[5]
Spending more time in Winchester enabled Mason to participate directly in the raising of his family. He liked to read them stories on
cold winter evenings. He took them for walks and drives in the country, and when he worked in the garden or chopped wood for a fire,
they usually followed him, convincing themselves, as only children
can, that they were "helping" their father.[6]

Mason ran the household with a firm but gentle hand. Carrying
himself with the sort of dignity befitting a Virginia aristocrat, he believed in self-control, self-discipline, and self-respect; and he sought
to instill each of those traits in his offspring without resorting to fear
and punishment. He exhibited endless patience, and instead of raising his voice harshly, James would make every effort to speak positively in a calm attempt to change "the current of his thoughts" and
strengthen the child's character. Of course, Eliza was a partner in this
child-rearing, and she made her husband's role easier by teaching the
children that everything should be as pleasant as possible for their
father when he got home.[7] Perhaps because James's career required
him to be away for long periods of time, absence made the heart
grow fonder, and such modern parenting techniques succeeded.

During that period, with the children more and more important
in his life, Mason's interest in public service broadened to include the
arena of education. He became a trustee at the Winchester Acad-
emy,[8] and in July 1833 he accepted a commission "as one of the
Visitors of the University of Virginia."[9] He took that responsibility
seriously and made it a special point to attend all the board meetings.
He held the position for eighteen years, giving it up only when his
duties in the U.S. Senate made it impossible for him to attend regularly.[10]

Throughout those years, his correspondence, and especially letters to fellow visitor William Cabell Rives, contained references to
university business.[11] Usually the topic involved miscellaneous financial matters[12] or department chair vacancies.[13] But one issue is of particular interest because it illustrates so well the man's beliefs regarding governmental powers and responsibilities.

In 1835, Professor George Tucker, chair of the faculty, sought
the support of the various visitors for the construction of a chapel at

the university. The faculty gained enough support to build it,[14] but a dissenting voice belonged to James Murray Mason. He wrote Tucker that he found it necessary to "respectfully, though very decidedly, refuse my consent to the measures contemplated by the Faculty."[15] He questioned construction, with or without state funds, of such a building at "an institution belonging to the State." He argued that, even if purely private sources were involved, the chapel should not be built, because the charter did not allow any other group to build on university grounds. Both the doctrine of separation of church and state, and the desire to hold strictly to the university's charter, decided the issue for Mason. While he remained willing to discuss and debate the issue with his colleagues,[16] his vote was no. Whether the subject involved the U.S. Constitution or merely a state university charter, Mason was a strict constructionist.

Until late 1836, Mason remained on the political sidelines, taking care of legal business, university business, and his family. Then friends and supporters again urged him to run for Congress. The magic of his surname had kept him on Frederick County's short list of potential candidates year after year, as aristocrats of famous lineage continued to dominate Virginia politics. In the Old Dominion, political parties as we know them remained embryonic at best. The rituals of political courtship had changed little since the days of Mason's grandfather. Privately, a few prominent men got together to decide upon their candidate for the legislature.[17]

James enjoyed having extra time at home with his family, but the rough-and-tumble world of politics remained a strong temptation. He enjoyed being the center of attention, and his political suitors charmed him until he agreed to become the Democratic congressional candidate. On February 18, 1837, he responded to questions regarding various critical issues. First Mason discussed slavery, writing that his "opinion decidedly is, that it [Congress] has no power whatever over the subject," because any violation of private property by the federal government is forbidden "save in the single exigency of the necessities of public use." He also reiterated his opposition to the use of federal funds for internal improvements, stressing that "a more baleful influence . . . could not be brought to operate upon the community, than the control of the public purse for such purposes."[18]

Such arguments sprang from his strict construction of the Constitution, and so did his policy stance toward the Bank of the United States. Mason asserted that Congress had no power to charter such a bank; he wrote that he believed "the creation of such a corporation, is not only in derogation of the rights of the States, but that its existence is fraught with danger to the institutions and to the liberties of the country."[19]

His support for Andrew Jackson glowed brightly, particularly when he supported the president's removal of federal deposits from the Bank of the United States by calling it "the wisest and most patriotic move of the current administration."[20] Mason accepted the Democratic nomination for Congress on February 25[21] and a week later confidently predicted victory in a letter to Rives, writing that, "from the complexion of the District, to say nothing of the *merits* of the *nominee*, my election will follow *of course* upon the nomination—and from appearances, without opposition."[22]

Mason's political forecasting proved correct when, in April, he won the election, receiving almost 63 percent of the vote.[23] His friend Rives served in the U.S. Senate at the time, and in May he accepted the senator's offer that the two of them "confer freely and fully . . . knowing that I shall realize in that intercourse the counsels of the older and the better soldier."[24] Rives's experiences encompassed political warfare in both Washington and Richmond, as well as time in Paris as President Jackson's envoy to France. Carrying the credentials of conservative Jacksonian from the Old Dominion, he had garnered a great deal of support for the vice-presidency in 1836.[25] It certainly could not hurt the freshman congressman to have such an older hand as his patron, particularly since Mason had to enter what he labeled "the grand arena" months sooner than he expected.

President Martin Van Buren called a special session of Congress to meet in September to deal with the financial crisis known as the "Panic of 1837."[26] Economic pressures lingering from the Jackson years had exploded under the new president. Inflation and high interest rates helped spawn everything from riots in the streets to bank failures. In May, banks all over the country suspended specie payments for the face value of their deposits and outstanding notes.[27] After using the summer months to prepare, the Van Buren administration proposed, as a cure for the economy's problems, the creation of an independent Treasury to take in and disburse the public money on a specie basis. Senator Rives opposed the idea,[28] and so did Representative Mason.

On October 11, Mason argued against the president's proposal in his first major speech in the House of Representatives. He began by posing the question, "What is the currency of the country?" The Virginia freshman answered himself by asserting that it consisted solely "of irredeemable bank paper . . . that has been issued by the State banks, and which they no longer redeem with gold or silver." Those metals had "passed entirely out of circulation." He warned that "this condition of the currency, is the true and great evil of the times."[29]

To Mason that was the real problem, and establishing an independent Treasury would only aggravate the situation and keep the currency in its debased condition. As usual, he expressed his ideas in the idiom of a strict constructionist seeking to limit the size and scope of the federal government. He stressed that the measure's "sole effect will be to enrich the office-holders, and all who feed upon the public crib, at the expense of the rest of the community." He said he sided with the taxpayers rather than the tax gatherers.[30] In contrast to Democrats who supported the president, Mason saw the danger of a national bank returning if the proposal gained approval. Strong belief in that danger hardened his opposition to the administration. In his speech he reaffirmed his status as "an uncompromising foe to any such institution," expressing his belief that "the existence of such a bank is inconsistent with the purity, and dangerous to the safety, of popular government." He confidently asserted that "it has no sanction, either in the spirit or the letter of the constitution."[31]

The entire speech marked a potentially controversial entrance into national politics, because Mason had plunged into the heart of the debates regarding the American economy and had disagreed with President Van Buren and the majority of the Democratic Party. He had charted a course surprising for a freshman congressman. In a letter to Rives, Mason expressed confidence that his stance would not doom him to repeat what had happened ten years earlier when he supported the Giles resolutions. He saw no problem for himself with the voters of his district.[32]

Mason remained sure of himself in the knowledge that he had devoted most of his time to other issues of concern to his constituents. As a representative from rural western Virginia, legislation regarding post routes[33] and railroads[34] dominated his efforts. In many ways, his term in the House resembled that of most first-term legislators. He struggled to do the best he could to make a positive impact for his supporters and rarely made a major splash in the legislative waters, except for the battle over financial matters and the independent Treasury.

Those debates seemed to have no end. The House Committee on Ways and Means spent months dealing with a wide range of proposals to stimulate the economy and provide the federal government with needed revenue. On May 12, 1838, Mason spoke regarding the resulting bill, which authorized issuance of $10 million in Treasury notes for current revenue. He once more argued that the government should not interfere with the economy. He would support an issue of Treasury paper only to cover immediate needs, preferring loans for any other necessary funds. Mason pointed out that, in comparison to the previous year, "money is once more abundant, and to be had at the lowest rates."[35] The situation had changed. The American economy indeed had entered a short-lived period of recovery,[36] and the Virginian particularly rejoiced at the performance of the state banks, defending them as "cherished institutions." He said, "I rejoice that they present so formidable an obstacle in the way of Federal usurpation. I rejoice that they are to be found firmly planted on the soil of every State, like bulwarks to protect State rights and State supremacy against the aggressions of Federal power. . . . I wish to see our financial affairs conducted as they have always been, without the aid of any of this new machinery, either of Sub-Treasuries or Treasury 'regulators.'"[37] His arguments again had a strict constructionist foundation, and once more they placed the Virginian in opposition to the economic policies of the Van Buren administration.

In his opposition to the president, Mason was not alone. Martin Van Buren perpetually faced the problem of lackluster support in the South. Even before he entered the oval office, most southerners viewed Van Buren as the most ruthless, devious politician of a new and seemingly dishonorable era. Known as a master of political intrigue in both Albany and Washington, the New Yorker had an undignified image with southern aristocrats that could not be polished even by election to the presidency. Such a reputation made it very difficult for Democratic Party leaders to sell Van Buren to skeptical southern voters who wanted the ideals of honor, virtue, and trustworthiness to be the hallmark of their elected representatives.[38]

In his private letters, Mason's criticism of the president could get quite personal. In October, while mentioning to Rives that Van Buren had visited western Virginia on a trip to the springs, Mason commented that he did not "look for any improvement in him from the association."[39] A few months later, he described to his sister-in-law the details of a particular "grand levee" in Washington that he attended. The president hosted the event, and to Mason he appeared "very gracious, and trying all he knew to appear the gentleman" which was "rather a difficult task . . . for one who has not caught the manner in the natural way."[40]

Such an attitude led some to charge Mason and other southern Democrats with forming an alliance with the Whig Party. James issued a vigorous denial in a speech to the House on January 30, 1839. Speaking for himself, he insisted that, while his differences with the

Democratic leadership over banking issues had isolated him some-what, he disagreed just as strongly with the entire Whig program, including the National Bank, the tariff, and internal improvements.[41] With his renomination soon to be decided, Mason clung to his seat as a man at odds with his own party's leadership.

In his own words, Mason summed up what happened next: "At the close of this Congress, the Democratic Convention for the district treating me as *heretic*, refused to renominate me, and did nominate William Lucas . . . who was elected, I voting for him."[42] His support from Senator Rives did him no good. Mason had deviated from the party line, and the Democrats rejected him for a second term.[43]

Mason could not adjust to the new demands of loyalty that underpinned the second American party system. Even in Virginia, the politics of the past were fading.[44] As times changed, Mason's principles seemed increasingly anachronistic. He remained wedded to eighteenth-century models of behavior. He could not do as Rives did and switch to the Whig Party to preserve his political career.[45] Mason's overall principles made him a Democrat, yet he refused to compromise anything he believed in merely for the sake of party unity.

As had happened before with the Giles resolutions, Mason's promising political career came to a halt because he held fast to his core beliefs. But the events of 1839 unfolded differently from those of 1827. Then the *voters* rejected him because of his position on financial issues; now the *Democratic Party* rejected him. The voters—many of whom would have seen him as displaying virtue and honor in the tradition of his grandfather and other hallowed Virginians by taking such an anti-party stand—never had the opportunity to pass final judgment.

Once more James Murray Mason returned to Winchester to take up the tasks involved in being a full-time country lawyer and father. Again he felt glad to be home. The two years spent in Washington had done little to endear the capital city to him. Eliza often visited him there, usually bringing the children with her to Clermont. In a letter detailing one of her visits, Mason expressed how he enjoyed spending time with her but also stated his amazement at her desire "to amuse herself in this dissipated metropolis."[46] He hated the pomp and circumstance that surrounded events in Washington, and he particularly ridiculed foreign diplomats who strove "each with the other to excel in the profusion of gold lace, and gold bands."[47] Getting back to the simplicity of Winchester suited Mason just fine.

He settled into the routine of being a successful lawyer, with a practice that soon covered ten to twelve superior courts throughout western Virginia. For Mason, politics became relatively unimportant, and he rejected continuous overtures from friends who wanted him to return to the Virginia House of Delegates.[48] He enjoyed visits from friends left behind in Washington, but primarily for their social character. In 1840, for example, Mason invited Rives and his wife to Selma. He pledged to arrange his schedule to be able to "receive you from the hands of the Philistines," but he warned: "Not a word about politics, except that I will not vote for Harrison."[49] Except for his becoming chief prosecutor for Frederick and Hardy counties in 1844,[50] Mason's career rolled along with little fanfare and even less politics.

In 1841, Eliza gave birth to their final child, a son named John.[51] Given the ages of both parents, they viewed him as a particular blessing. Such a joyous event can be seen as a symbol of just how happy and genuinely rewarding family life remained for Mason and his wife. Despite some ups and downs regarding politics, the two had known little in the way of personal sorrow. They continued to visit both Cliveden and Clermont regularly, often as a family, taking the children to see their aging grandparents. They especially enjoyed Cliveden, where Eliza's father regularly touted the therapeutic nature of the air as a remedy for any bouts of ill health.

Soon after John's birth, Eliza planned to visit Philadelphia, and her father asked James if that visit could be extended another month or two.[52] He agreed, and Eliza spent over three months at Cliveden. The couple missed each other terribly, much as newly-weds might. Responding to a letter from her lonely man, she wrote, "Your letter my beloved husband, came as the balm of Giliad to my anxious heart. . . . As you already know, how immediately, and entirely my happiness depends upon your well being—I need not express the many solicitudes I have felt, since we parted. Even though surrounded by Father, Mother, Brother, and Sisters, I dare not permit myself to think of the distance which divides me from my best and dearest friend, and the recollection of your comfortless solitude."[53] The Masons spent many winters apart, with Eliza and the children away at Cliveden or Clermont and James left behind at Selma.[54] In December 1842, Mason wrote from Philadelphia, "I brought Mrs. Mason and her flock here . . . on a visit to her . . . parents, where she will remain for the winter—I return home the last of this week."[55] Such extended visits came to an end in 1844, with the death of old Benjamin Chew.

The death of Eliza's father brought grief to her husband as well as to her. Ever since those early days when young James arrived in

Philadelphia for schooling, Benjamin had treated him as a son. Dissolving the family estate at Cliveden marked the end of an era for the Masons.[56] Losing both a dear loved one and a place where so many happy times had been spent caused them great sorrow. In addition, James began to devote a great deal of his time to legal matters surrounding the Chew estate, as one of its executors.[57] Such responsibilities, added to those of his own legal practice, kept him even busier than he had been when he sat in Congress.

Even the simplest family commitments became difficult to fulfill. In December 1845, after returning to Selma from Philadelphia, he apologized to his father for not being able to keep his promise and spend Christmas at Clermont, complaining that "latterly it has seemed as impossible for me to control my own movements, as if I had become the bondsman of others." He lamented "this most provoking business in Philadelphia, has made such heavy demands on my time, that my utmost efforts heroly avail, to keep me afloat."[58] By the end of 1846, Mason also had become president of the Farmer's Bank at Winchester and prosecutor in three counties.[59] He certainly had little time for politics.

Nonetheless, Mason followed the politics of the 1840s as closely as he could, and occasionally he commented on the subject. He specifically made references to South Carolina's John C. Calhoun. During Mason's term in the House of Representatives, the two men had shared accommodations in Washington with several other members of Congress.[60] From the very beginning, Calhoun made a great impression on the Virginian. Mason wrote in 1839 that "nature has given him a mind of the very highest order . . . cultivated and improved to the uttermost extent of acquirement and profound study."[61]

He also found aspects of the South Carolinian's personality troublesome, however. Mason saw in Calhoun "a vein of hallucination pervading, which unsettles the whole, and renders him worse than useless to the country he seems born to have controlled. I talk with him a great deal, for he has a passion for arguing every one into that belief which happens to be his own for the time being. His mind is like a crucible where the most perplexed theories are melted down at once, and resolved back into their elements. It is in the combination afterwards, that his great genius leads him astray."[62] Since they agreed on most of the critical issues, Mason favored Calhoun for the Democratic presidential nomination throughout the 1840s. Simultaneously, however, he recognized that to be a practical impossibility. In 1842, viewing the party in disarray and wishing "to lend a hand, to save the true republican party of the older time," he wrote to Rives that he knew "of no leader at the present juncture who would be likely to rally its disciples better than Mr. Calhoun."[63] Despite holding such an opinion, Mason could envision nothing that would get the nomination for Calhoun in the face of certain opposition from the North,[64] particularly because "these northern men are so deep in the chicaneries of caucus management."[65]

At the same time Mason wrote of politics, he longed for the day when he would be "rich enough to indulge in farming."[66] By 1846, his legal career, though very successful, seemed increasingly unrewarding. He had always reveled in the excitement of open debate, either in court or in Congress, but dealing with the tangled family legal affairs of Benjamin Chew's estate proved to be merely monotonous. In addition, he handled more and more of his own father's responsibilities. John Mason, even at age eighty, had wide-ranging interests; and for years he relied upon James regarding the family businesses.[67] Such work more and more contrasted drearily with the intensity and rich intellectual stimulation he had experienced in Congress.

The personal joy he derived from his family life also began to diminish. A fatal illness struck his eldest son, Benjamin Chew Mason. He first became ill at the age of eighteen, in late 1844. A year later, a dispirited Mason reported to his father that "Ben, I am sorry to say[,] is again seriously threatened with another attack of the character which confined him all last winter." James reported that he planned to take the boy to Philadelphia "in the hope that the prescriptions of the wise men there, may ward it off."[68]

Such hopes went unfulfilled. A year after the trip to Pennsylvania, Ben lay dying, "prostrate in bed" from the "inexorable disease that has so long preyed upon him."[69] His son's death came as a heavy blow. Father and son had shared many interests through the years, including Ben's plans to join the legal profession.[70] In spite of his deep sorrow, by 1847 Mason's responsibilities allowed little time for personal despair. Several months before his son's death, Mason had resumed his political career.

During the 1840s, Mason's friends and supporters repeatedly had urged him to return to politics. Just as repeatedly, he had turned them down. But by the end of 1846, circumstances had changed. His life had become more frustrating and less fulfilling. And Mason recognized that politics could take him out of the increasingly monotonous world of being a country lawyer with an overburdened work schedule. It could return him to a position of leadership, which as a Virginia aristocrat, he saw as his birthright. At age forty-eight, if handed the right opportunity, Mason would think about taking it.

In December, he traveled to Richmond because the court of appeals there shortly would be handling one of his cases.[71] In January 1847, Virginia's Sen. Isaac Pennybacker died in Washington after a short illness. Speculation as to a successor fell quickly upon Mason. To take advantage of Mason's presence in Richmond, supporters arranged a dinner at which the candidate might meet some of the members of the legislature who were less familiar with him. But clinging to the decorum of the eighteenth century, Mason refused to appear at such an exhibition. When he found out that his name would be placed in nomination, Mason left Richmond for Clermont, so as "to avoid all suspicion or intimation of soliciting the appointment."[72]

But James did want it. Having discouraged earlier attempts to get him to run again for office, the prospective candidate, with a single word, certainly could have stopped efforts to place him in the Senate. Instead, he sat at his father's home to await the election results. While the election debate raged in the capitol, the *Winchester Virginian* heartily endorsed the candidacy, labeling it "utterly superfluous to state in detail the claims and qualifications of Col. Mason" and asserting that he had "attained and sustained a place among the first men and the first Statesmen of our good old Commonwealth." The newspaper continued: "To a mind of high order, we were going to say of the highest order, he superadds a most perfect and polished early education—high professional attainments and eminent qualifications as a Statesman. As a debater he is calm, courteous and convincing. Neither in the public area, nor in private intercourse has he ever gratuitously inflicted a wound. . . . It is this cast of his character which is preeminently adapted to the dignity, decorum, and composure of the National Senate Chamber."[73] On the evening of January 21, Virginia legislators elected Mason to the U.S. Senate. The *Richmond Enquirer* termed it an "exciting election" and reported that Mason had received "the largest majority given for any individual as United States Senator from Virginia within our recollection." The paper predicted that the new senator would serve Virginia well and become a member of "high standing in that body."[74] The magic of the Mason name, "a symbol of Virginia's past and the yearning of Virginians for a revival," had sent him back to Washington.[75]

Upon hearing the news, Mason returned to Richmond. He attended as best he could to the legal business that had called him there in the first place, and then he made the journey to the nation's capital.[76] On the morning of January 25, 1847, Vice-President George M. Dallas administered the oath of office, and Mason took his seat in the Senate.[77] Back on the national stage, he wrote to Rives that "things are mixed up and compounded in this grand cauldron of Washington," saying that he did not know whether "either of us can do much more than to keep an eye on . . . our dear old commonwealth."[78]

Mason did not return to Selma until March, when the session ended. There, with Ben lying near death, he temporarily returned to taking care of family business matters.[79] But, little by little, he cleared his schedule so that he could devote as much time as possible to his new position of responsibility. Upon his election, he resigned his positions as bank president and county prosecutor, and he soon would find "that a country practice could not be maintained, along with a seat in the Senate."[80] Although he still would cherish times spent at home with his family, Mason increasingly became wedded to the job of being a Virginia senator, enjoying politics and debates as never before. In many ways, his first forty-eight years had served merely as a prelude and a preparation for Mason's entrance into what would prove to be his grandest arena of all—the floor of the U.S. Senate. The young boy who had watched proceedings from the chamber's balconies now stood at center stage.

Chapter 3

1847–1859

Defender of the Constitution

James Murray Mason made his first major speech in the United States Senate on February 13, 1847. It dealt with a resolution to expel *Washington Union* reporters from the Senate galleries because of libel charges. The new Virginia senator stood up and argued strongly against the resolution. He pointed out that the measure trespassed upon the freedom of the press and stated that the consequences would be similar to reenacting the Sedition Law of 1798. "I can counsel nothing which will have even a tendency to impair the freedom of the press. I should deplore the hour when it would be found the policy of this Government to exercise any power which it may possess in such a way as even to tend to the abridgement of the freedom of the press. Sir, *it is* the 'bulwark of liberty!' It is the only hope of the American people. If their liberties ever are stricken down by the corrupting processes of the Government, or by an autocrat, it will be only when the press is manacled and dares not speak."[1] Those words reflected his firmly held opinions regarding the proper relationship between the citizens and their government. The powers of the federal government had to be limited, because, if left unchecked, the government would take away the liberty of the people.

Mason based his arguments upon a rigid interpretation of the U.S. Constitution. He had spoken as a strict constructionist as early as 1827, in the debate over the Giles resolutions,[2] and he continued to do so through the nullification[3] and national bank crises of the 1830s[4] and into his Senate years. Perhaps Mason's constitutional opinions can be traced back to his grandfather George Mason, who throughout the Constitutional Convention argued against enlarging the federal government.[5] Both thought it unwise for Americans to give up too much of their freedoms simply to provide the central government with more authority. Unwavering adherence to that philosophy characterized Mason's entire Senate career and governed his thinking on a variety of issues.

According to James Mason, the founding fathers designed the federal government primarily for the administration of foreign affairs. He vigorously opposed extending federal power beyond the letter of the Constitution. In 1849, the Senate debated a bill to create "a new Executive Department of the United States to be called the Department of the Interior." Mason fought it inch by inch, first by trying to have the bill laid on the table and then by amending it. Possessing "a deep and settled distrust of every measure which tends to strengthen the arm of Federal power," Mason asserted his firm conviction "that the State governments are to administer in our domestic relations; and that the operations of our Federal Government were intended chiefly for the regulation and administration of our exterior and foreign relations." Having been "formed to take charge of our exterior relations," Congress "should not extend its power to our interior relations any further than was absolutely necessary."[6]

The bill passed despite his objections, but he never changed his opinion of the Interior Department. He thought it an unnecessary extension of the federal government's power. Ten years later, he continued to express his opposition by denouncing the Interior Department's "enormous expenditures," saying that it had grown from "a cloud in the horizon hardly bigger than a man's hand" into something that "overshadows the whole land in its embrace." The Interior Department's expenditures had no benefits but had become merely "alms to the people," to such an extent that "you have taught the people almost to expect that they are to be fed by the crumbs which fall from the table of the Federal Government."[7]

To Mason, Interior Department spending corrupted the government unconstitutionally. He viewed additional expenditures as the certain path to unlimited federal power, in clear contradiction to the wishes of the founding fathers. His strict-constructionist position led him to oppose most spending proposals. Such a stance gave him the appearance of a fiscal conservative, but he based his reasoning primarily upon the Constitution and not on economic ideology. In 1856, during a debate over the recurring issue of internal improvements, he lamented that senators rarely referred to the Constitution, "unless it be to derogate from it." He opposed exposing the Treasury to a mad scramble in which "the most depraved, the most active, or the wealthiest, would be most successful; in which the public money would be made corrupting funds throughout the country, and wasted, extravagantly wasted, without limit."[8]

Mason's ire fell fastest upon proposals to involve the federal government in internal improvements. In the 1850s, the Congress debated a number of bills requiring the central government to spend money on the nation's rivers and harbors. Mason numbered among the opposition in every case. In 1851, he fought an amendment to a River and Harbor Bill that involved building a dry dock in California. He characterized it as a call for the government to go deep into debt merely to carry on these improvements.[9] He lost that skirmish; on the same day, his amendment to limit government expenditures for the removal of obstructions in the Rio Grande also went down to defeat.[10]

One or two setbacks did not mean that he gave up the war. In Mason's eyes, the Constitution needed at all times to be protected from predators, and the supporters of internal improvements had to be stopped before they inflicted irreparable damage upon the sacred document. A year later, another River and Harbor Bill involved the federal government in canal building. Mason believed that it proposed spending federal money on something not authorized by the Constitution. He queried, "Where is the power in the Constitution to give the General Government the right to acquire property in a State, whether the State assents or not?"[11]

As the debate continued, Mason stated that it did not matter if any amendments to the bill were approved, because "it cannot be presented in such a form that I shall vote for it in any event."[12] He criticized senators who maintained that the improvements had national purposes, while continually demanding larger appropriations for their own states.[13] Mason supported the 1852 Democratic Party platform that explicitly denied the federal government any jurisdiction over implementing internal improvements.[14] He viewed the River and Harbor Bill as merely "a scramble for the public money to be expended for local purposes, improvidently."[15] In 1854, regarding another River and Harbor Bill, he stated that, if President Franklin Pierce vetoed it, "he will transmit to posterity the reputation of a statesman" determined to preserve the Union. Mason warned that if the Senate continued to legislate "in utter ignorance of what we are doing, in order to expend the public treasure, these republics ought not to remain, and I apprehend will not remain, confederated together."[16] The Virginian took the issue of unconstitutional federal government spending for local improvements that seriously.

He spoke in even stronger tones in 1856. A bill for internal improvements on the Mississippi River had been vetoed by Pierce, and its supporters attempted an override. The veto heartened Mason, and, while tracing the history of the internal improvement issue, he pronounced it to be as dead as the protective tariff and the Bank of the United States. He claimed that those three issues of the Jacksonian era had been "ultimately frowned into oblivion, if not disgrace, by the intelligence of the American people."[17] Mason viewed the states as "independent and sovereign communities," and he warned that "it will be an evil day for this country, and for the people of this country, when any portion of that sovereignty shall be delegated to the Federal arm." Mason defended his views with pages of the Constitution, which he described as "the only shield between a powerless minority and an irresponsible majority." Therefore, he claimed that southerners "have nothing to look to but the Constitution, especially standing, as we do, in a minority, existing, and very likely to continue."[18] Again his arguments came to naught, as the Senate voted thirty-one to twelve to override the veto.[19]

According to Mason, "The less government men have, the more responsible they become."[20] He called upon his colleagues to bring spending down "to the lowest and most narrow limits of an economical administration," for then it would be virtually impossible for the government to oppress the people. He warned, however, that if Congress continued along its current path of reckless spending, establishing "leaks in the Treasury for the expenditure of countless millions on sources and demands utterly irresponsible to the country . . . you must, of necessity, have not only a corrupt, but a corrupting Government."[21] He spoke for the "Old Dominion," a state that "from the earliest days of this Republic . . . set her face decidedly against appropriations of this character," and he stressed that if he ever voted for such legislation he would face repudiation for abandoning "the faith of our fathers, and the established construction of the Federal compact amongst us."[22]

His strict interpretation of the Constitution had the strong support of most Virginians. In 1856, the *Richmond Enquirer*, reporting the recent Senate debates, complimented Mason in an unabashedly glowing manner, stating: "Foremost among the moving minds of that august body, representing the conservative element of government, was Mr. Mason. It certainly gives a man a better opinion of his country and confirms his confidence in the constitutional vitality of the Federation, to listen to this Senator. The dignity of simplicity, the earnest force of conscious rectitude, the finish of the high-toned gentleman, the glow and ardor of true patriotism and genuine love of country, combine to make Mr. Mason one of the ablest defenders of the Constitution in the Senate."[23] Of course, the ultimate show of approval for his actions was his being reelected twice. In 1850, Mason trounced his nearest opponent three to one, and in 1855 he outpolled his rivals two to one.[24]

Railroad construction also gained Mason's disapproval, because the bills proposed conflicted with his interpretation of the Constitution. In February 1853, the Senate debated a bill to construct a railroad from the Mississippi River to the Pacific Ocean. Mason refused to concede the federal government any power either to survey the necessary land or to build the road. He stressed that the Constitution gave the federal government power to survey only for post routes.[25] He criticized opening up the Treasury without assurances that the road definitely could be built. Mason declared that, if the bill became law, "the whole character of the Government will be changed . . . never to be reclaimed; and it will have been done by gold, and, worse than all, by gold out of the public Treasury."[26] With his penchant for rhetorical flourish, he sternly warned that, if Congress passed the railroad bill, "the Constitution will be gone . . . and the Government will be one of unlimited power."[27]

Mason did not oppose the *idea* of a transcontinental railroad, but he preferred to build it across southern Mexico at Tehuantepec. He thought that route best, even though the railroad would be outside the country's borders. He foresaw it as "a highway between nations . . . subject of no exclusive jurisdiction." Additionally, Mason asserted that, in such a project, the federal government would be involved with the railroad builders only to the extent of protecting "its own citizens against spoilation by a foreign Power."[28] Its greater practicality and, above all, the fact that it did not conflict with his strict constructionist position meant that Tehuantepec appealed to Mason as no other proposed route could.

Throughout the decade, with three routes across the United States suggested, he continued to ridicule supporters of the railway as being ignorant of whether one could be built at all, and of what such an endeavor would cost.[29] He did not play favorites with a southern or northern route, as other senators did. He opposed them all, stating that, even if a proposal called for beginning the railroad "on the James river, or the Potomac river, in Virginia, . . . I should feel myself bound to vote against it. Begin where it may, and end where it may, I cannot vote for it."[30]

Supporters of the road viewed it as a project of great national importance, but Mason pointed out astutely that their bitter sectional division over where it would go proved his point that the railroad provided only local benefits, which rendered it unconstitutional. He reiterated that he saw nothing in the Constitution that gave Congress authority regarding such a railroad.[31] He foresaw only disaster from the project, lamenting that, if the road ever were constructed, it would be built by the U.S. Treasury, with "all that immense system of contracts, and of patronage, and of frauds, which must be ever attendant upon a work of this character in the hands of the Government."[32] Even to those who wanted to build the railroad to improve the military's ability to defend California, he responded that, rather than build it and thus "change and destroy the fabric of this Government . . . I should be constrained to say it [California] must go."[33]

According to Mason, the federal government could not spend money simply for commercial purposes related to private enterprise. Even if he had deemed it constitutional, the Virginia senator still would have opposed building a transcontinental railroad, because he believed that it would benefit only speculators and monopolists.[34] He believed strongly in competitive markets, and he thought that governments should refrain from interfering in them. He opposed a bill that called for an appropriation of federal money to begin a steam mail route from San Francisco to Shanghai, because, in his view, its real purpose involved commerce. Mason supported Commodore Matthew C. Perry's expedition to Japan, but he "certainly never dreamed that the consequence of it would be that we should be asked for an appropriation from the Treasury of $500,000 a year to promote a correspondence, either with Japan or China."[35] As usual, his strict position put him on the losing side of the debate, and the bill passed by a margin of twenty-two to thirteen.[36]

Mason's opposition to reckless government spending applied even to the Capitol itself. In 1859, the Senate debated an appropriation to purchase new furniture for the committee rooms. The frugal Virginian rose and asserted that he saw no reason why they could not be content with the old furniture. He claimed that, in twelve years, he had ordered only one piece of furniture, a case to hold committee papers, that cost only fifteen dollars. For the room of the Foreign Relations Committee, all he required was "some very plain pine shelves to put books on," at a cost of ten dollars, and "painted in order to preserve them."[37] He did not want to burden the Treasury with such spending, and he got into a rousing argument with Sen. Jefferson Davis of Mississippi regarding the paintings and sculpture in the corridors. Mason remarked, "If the gentleman has a taste that approves these works of art, let him indulge it at his own expense; but not at the expense of the country. . . . I recognize no proper expenditure from the public Treasury but that which will facilitate the dispatch of the public business; and in making these buildings, I would go to any extent that was necessary to make them ample enough and durable enough, but no further."[38] While Davis wanted the government to purchase "furniture appropriate to the room and appropriate to the Senate of the United States,"[39] Mason came out firmly against the practice "which obtains in some parts of the country, where there is accumulated a redundant and exulting wealth, that would destroy an old fabric—destroy old furniture—that they may get new fashions."[40] The Senate rejected his attempts to limit the appropriation to $10,000,[41] but he did get a $50,000 limit approved.[42]

In contrast, Mason did approve of the construction of the Capitol dome. Mason supported it, regardless of the dollar amount, because the Constitution sanctioned it. He did, however, use the occasion to criticize the "unconstitutional appropriations" Congress "corruptingly lavished and wasted money on" and stated that he thought it best to spend funds "for public purposes" before others spend it "to corrupt the popular mind."[43]

Mason believed that the more money the federal government possessed, the greater the potential for corruption. He regularly opposed high tariffs, particularly when the country had a "redundant and overflowing" Treasury. He wished to leave money not needed by the government with the people, to prevent the Treasury from becoming "a corrupting fund" that "debauches the public morals."[44]

The resulting corruption took the form of all the spending bills which Mason saw as unconstitutional. But to the Virginian, none of them posed as serious a threat to the nation's values as did the various land bills debated in the Senate throughout the 1850s. In March 1854, a bill passed the House allowing settlers to secure 160 acres of public land by occupying and cultivating it for five years. Southern senators believed that passage of such a bill would injure the South by encouraging an expansion of the North's population and by leading to the creation of more free states. They opposed the proposal as being corrupting and unconstitutional, and insisted that some form of payment be required for the land.[45]

Mason exclaimed that he saw nothing in the Constitution that gave Congress power to give away public property. The Virginian believed that government should encourage the American people to become "independent by their own labor and own exertion, and yet the policy of the bill is to paralyze the arm of labor, to make the people dependent on the bounty of the Government."[46] Mason offered an amendment exempting from the Homestead Bill land that Virginia had ceded to the federal government under the Articles of Confederation. He doubted that, "far-seeing and sagacious as our ancestors were, . . . they ever contemplated a day when Congress would assume to give away the public property."[47] The Senate debated his amendment for two days before voting it down, thirty-three to seventeen.[48]

For similar reasons he opposed the Agricultural Colleges Bill in 1859. Once more, Mason fought an unconstitutional distribution of the public lands. He labeled it "one of the most extraordinary engines of mischief, under the guise of gratuities and donations, that I could conceive would originate in the Senate," because it attempted to use public lands to control the state legislatures. He believed that, if the bill passed, eventually agricultural interests would be taken out of state hands, enabling the federal government to either promote or depress each region as it saw fit. He labeled the bill a misuse of the country's property "in the worst and insidious form—by bribery, direct bribery, and bribery of the worst kind; for it is an unconstitutional robbing of the Treasury for the purpose of bribing the States." The state that refused to accept such alms from the federal government would be the one that "will go upon the page of history as one that was true to its constitutional duties and to its constitutional faith."[49] Such constitutional arguments had potency, but lurking behind Mason's stance lay strong convictions regarding immigration and education.

Mason concluded that, along with lazy Americans, the primary beneficiaries of homestead legislation would be immigrants, "individuals who may come here from every quarter, totally unconnected with our institutions."[50] He stereotyped those newcomers as Europeans sent by contract, "with their tickets, treated like bales of merchandise on the way, . . . dying in large numbers" of cholera in railroad cars bound for Minnesota or Ohio. But rather than show compassion to such people, Mason sarcastically remarked, "That is the class of people whom we are to invite over to our shores, suddenly to be converted into American citizens, by giving them a proprietary right in the soil." He denied bearing any animosity to foreigners, but he believed that holding out a bounty to them in advance, and bringing them here "by an *exodus*, . . . depopulating the old countries, and generally of the worst of their population, in order to populate ours, is a policy which, I for one, confess that I more than dislike."[51]

His rhetoric mimicked the words of the Know-Nothing Party, but Mason's position sprang from southern elitism and not northern nativism. While not hating immigrants outright, Mason certainly looked down his upper-class nose at them. Any lower-class person whom he viewed as lazy he also saw as unworthy to benefit from the U.S. Constitution. In criticizing the Homestead Bill, he emphasized that there existed "no American citizen, no man with an American tone, with that feeling of independence . . . who would not feel himself humiliated in receiving this bounty at the hands of the Government."[52] Those willing to accept it needed to be educated to improve their morality and self-esteem instead.

Education, however, remained the preserve of the states.[53] And, while Mason might speak rhetorically of the federal government's educating the people, he never meant it literally. In fighting against the Agricultural Colleges Bill, he wondered whether, if that bill passed, federal legislation to establish federally mandated schools in each state would not follow shortly thereafter. He pledged vigorously to oppose any attempt by a majority in the Congress to force upon the South the system of free schools that prevailed in New England. Such schools "would tend, I will not say to demoralize, but to destroy that peculiar character which I am happy to believe belongs to the great mass of the southern people."[54]

To Mason and other southerners, the U.S. Constitution had become the ultimate safeguard of their virtuous society in the increasingly bitter debates with corrupted northerners. The southern partisans saw legislation the North sought related to public lands or public education as potentially harmful to the South's way of life. To prevent such bills from becoming law, southern leaders repeatedly fell back upon the Constitution as a last defense. But they did so most fervently when northern legislation targeted the cherished institution of southern slavery.

Mason discussed slavery and the Constitution in the Senate for the first time in July 1848. Referring to the territory of Oregon's recent prohibition of slavery, he exclaimed that, if Congress allowed that law to stand, it would be contrary to both the letter and spirit of the Constitution. The Virginian proceeded to detail the clauses in the Constitution that recognized and protected slavery. He pointed out that many concessions and compromises had gone into making the document, and he denounced northerners for their use of the term *slave power* as a label for what in reality was nothing more than "the representative weight which is assigned by the Constitution to this species of population, or property." Therefore, southerners only asked "that the Constitution shall be observed in good faith."[55]

Mason believed so strongly that the North had a duty to uphold the slavery clauses of the Constitution, that he suggested disunion if Congress failed to follow the strict southern interpretation. He asked rhetorically whether any senator believed that Virginia would have ratified the Constitution, if part of it had forbidden "an extension of any part of her population to any territory that might hereafter become the property of the United States?" More ominously, he added that, if his state always considered such an extension to be a constitutional right, could anyone believe "that she, or any of her southern sister States, can remain in the Confederacy, when the barriers that had been erected for their protection have been ruthlessly broken down and disregarded?"[56]

Over twelve years before secession became a reality, Mason voiced the South's discontent and its willingness to leave the Union to defend its interpretation of the Constitution. A major crisis loomed on the horizon, and it came to pass less than two years later, when California requested statehood under a constitution that prohibited slavery. Grievances of both southerners and northerners poured forth in the spirited debates that ensued, tying additional issues to California statehood. Involving much of the territory acquired from Mexico in the recent war, including Texas, those discussions ultimately led to the Compromise of 1850.[57]

The word "compromise" is perhaps a misnomer; although the settlement included something for everybody, only a few found it totally satisfactory.[58] The proposals did not pass in a package. Henry Clay tried that path with his omnibus bill,[59] but only when split into separate pieces of legislation could the individual parts be approved by a series of shifting coalitions. Historian David M. Potter more accurately labeled the result, when he wrote of "the Armistice of 1850."[60]

James Murray Mason's role in the compromise began before Clay's legislation, with his introduction of a new Fugitive Slave Bill on January 4. In Virginia, the issue of recovering runaway slaves from free states had increased in importance as northern attacks on slavery escalated. Being close to the Mason-Dixon Line left the Old Dominion more vulnerable to the loss of its slave property than states in the

Deep South. No slavery-related issue touched Mason and his constituents more. Therefore he drew up new legislation to make recovery of such fugitives easier. The Senate Judiciary Committee, chaired by South Carolina's Andrew P. Butler, reported the bill favorably on the sixteenth, and debate began.[61]

The bill targeted the personal liberty laws of the North, which Mason saw as encouraging northerners in "depredation" of southern property. He wanted them to live up to their constitutional obligations and penned the bill in an attempt to gain proper enforcement of those responsibilities. He vigorously defended it but had no illusions as to the prospects for success, fearing "that the disease is seated too deeply to be reached by ordinary legislation" and "that the legislative bodies of the nonslaveholding States, and the spirit of their people, have inflicted a wound upon the Constitution."[62]

The next day Clay introduced his resolutions. Attempting to resolve all the most pressing concerns of both sides, the key points included California becoming a free state, Utah and New Mexico being organized as territories without reference to slavery, passage of a new and effective fugitive slave law, establishing the old boundary of New Mexico while compensating Texas for territorial losses, and prohibition of the slave trade in the District of Columbia.[63] Among several southern senators who responded immediately, Mason, while glad to have the Fugitive Slave Bill included, only could express willingness to vote for *some* of the resolutions, if they were considered separately.[64]

For six weeks, debates on Clay's proposals enlivened Congress, but Mason made no major speech. During that time he worked behind the scenes, while remaining entrenched as a confident member of a southern voting block that refused to compromise its interpretation of the Constitution. He received a pamphlet from a man named Robert Hubard defending the three-fifths provision counting slaves to determine southern representation. Mason thanked him for sending it "in opportune time to furnish valuable suggestions and materials for the great questions now pending in our council," and suggested the names of eleven receptive northern senators to whom it also should be sent.[65]

Mason implored his southern brethren to stand together in defense of their constitutional rights. He expressed total confidence that "nothing can lose the day for us, but treachery or folly in our own ranks."[66] He saw supporters of the "so called" Wilmot Proviso, prohibiting slavery in the territories, as "shrinking from the brink—under the conviction, that whether right, or whether wrong, the southern states have determined upon that issue to stake the union of the states."[67] Southerners "presented so determined a front as at least to satisfy those meddlers, that they would have to choose between separation or backing out, and were fast preparing for the latter."[68]

South Carolina's John C. Calhoun remained the embodiment of the southern will to defend that region's interpretation of the Constitution, but by 1850, severe illness left him a drawn and haggard shadow of his former self. Nonetheless, opposing Clay's resolutions, he spent the last days of February dictating what would be his final major speech.[69] Too weak to deliver it himself, he assigned to a fellow southerner, his friend and supporter James Murray Mason, the task of reading that historic speech.[70]

Having been somewhat in awe of Calhoun for years, Mason had to feel the importance of the moment. On March 4, the galleries filled to witness the drama, and all listened in silence while, standing directly behind the seated figure of the dying statesman, Mason read the speech.[71] Calhoun believed that the nation's balance of power had shifted to the North; short of leaving the Union, the South had only states' rights as a defense. His words offered nothing particularly new, just a deep sense of cynical gloom.[72] The speech conveyed his true feelings. Speaking to Mason not long before his death, Calhoun exhibited a knack for accurate forecasting when he declared that "the Union is doomed to dissolution, there is no mistaking the signs." He believed that, "even were the questions which now agitate Congress settled to the satisfaction and with the concurrence of the Southern States, it would not avert, or materially delay, the catastrophe." Calhoun predicted disunion "within twelve years or three Presidential terms," acknowledging that, while Mason and others would live to see it, he would not. He could not foretell "the mode by which it will be done . . . it may be brought about in a manner that none now foresee. But the probability is, it will explode in a Presidential election."[73]

On March 31, the great man died. Three days later, Mason introduced a resolution for a committee of senators to accompany Calhoun's body to South Carolina. He himself was selected as "chairman of the committee to superintend the funeral solemnities."[74] Despite the seriousness of such duties, the occasion provided an opportunity for southern aristocrats to congregate and celebrate the virtuousness of their section. Virginia Sen. Robert M. T. Hunter predicted that "Mason will have a grand reception in Charleston. I have no doubt but that he will be delighted with the trip."[75]

Upon the committee's return, the slavery debates resumed. Clay chaired a committee of thirteen set up to consider his resolutions.[76] On May 8, he presented the resulting omnibus bill lumping together his earlier proposals.[77] The committee's own members began attacking the product that same day, and it quickly became apparent that, only if the Kentuckian's points were separated from one another, would the Senate possibly pass them.

Mason split his votes. He voted for organizing the Utah and New Mexico territories without reference to slavery.[78] Of course, he served as the prime defender of his own Fugitive Slave Bill.[79] If the federal government failed to protect the property of slaveholders in the border slave states of Virginia, Kentucky, and Maryland, they believed themselves entitled to indemnification for their losses. Mason's estimates put the annual loss in slaveholders' property at more than $100,000 in Virginia. He called it an "invasion" that the states "had not the power to repel" and stressed that "it is asking too much of humanity, it is putting too grievous a burden upon the people of the slaveholding States, to require them to submit to the loss of hundreds of thousands of dollars yearly," just because the federal government "either will not or dare not carry into effect the provisions of the Constitution." For his fellow Virginians, such losses "have become too onerous and too heavy to be borne, and are increasing from year to year."[80]

Throughout August, Mason, as the quintessential southerner standing at the center of the grand arena, defended his bill with proslavery, strict-constructionist rhetoric. On August 19, he introduced a substitute for his original legislation.[81] It embodied a number of amendments that had been suggested since its first introduction in January, but he fought any attempts to modify it that would assign to Congress an authority over slavery "nowhere vested in that body by the Constitution."[82] On August 23, with twenty-one senators not voting (many absent on purpose, to avoid being counted), the bill passed by a margin of twenty-seven to twelve.[83]

Mason opposed the other pieces of the original omnibus without success. On August 9, the bill regarding Texas's boundary with New Mexico passed in the Senate, over his strong objections.[84] In June, he argued that to detach a large piece of Texas and give it to New Mexico would "falsify the action of this Government" when it rose to defend Texas from the Mexican invaders who started the late war.[85] During July, he failed in attempts to amend the bill in Texas's favor.[86] He tried one last time on the day the legislation passed, believing that his amendment "was best calculated to dissipate the cloud of civil war, which it is said is now impending on the horizon."[87] Again his proposal was rejected.

His arguments against the bill to abolish the slave trade in the District of Columbia also proved fruitless. The Commonwealth of Virginia had a particularly strong interest in that measure, as it bordered the nation's capital. Mason told the Senate that the citizens of his state opposed the bill, not because their rights would be affected but because Congress "will have legislated upon a subject which they consider forbidden; because Congress will have legislated upon a subject dangerous to her safety, as it is dangerous to the safety of the slaveholding States." Mason had no fondness for the slave trade; still, while condemning it "as an odious traffic," he felt that it was "necessarily incident to the institution of slavery," and therefore Congress had no power under the Constitution to abolish it.[88] But it did, as the measure gained approval in the Senate on September 16, by a margin of thirty-three to nineteen. All the nay votes came from the South.[89]

California's desire to become a free state precipitated the crisis and remained the centerpiece of debate. Mason fought it using all his customary constitutional rhetoric. On April 5, he expressed willingness to make California a state, but not if that meant derogating southern rights. He stated that territories are the property of all the sovereign states; therefore, as long as the southern states are constituents in the Union, their people "have the right to go into that territory, to reside there with their property, and to enjoy it under the protection of the Constitution." He also once more hinted at disunion, warning that southerners "would not regard the Constitution as worth the parchment on which it is impressed, if it is to be maintained at the expense of rights which they intended it to secure." He maintained that "as cordially as they came into this Union, so will they go out of it when they are satisfied that the bonds of Union are regarded by the majority only for the purpose of oppression."[90]

Mason did not want a peace "purchased by the surrender on the part of all the southern States of their right to equality with the other States of this Union."[91] He gestured toward peace, however, when in May he suggested that extending the Missouri Compromise line to the Pacific Ocean, splitting California into two parts, would be acceptable to the South. If northerners found that unpalatable, however, he feared they would find nothing satisfactory "but terms that import ruin to the South."[92]

Mason understood the seriousness of the situation, and in his heart he believed that he had done his utmost to prevent disaster. A committee of citizens in New Market, Virginia, invited him to address a mass meeting there on July 27, but because of his busy schedule, he declined. In apologizing for his inability to attend, he wrote, "Our glorious and once happy Union is brought into serious danger by the perverse and wicked counsels of those who seek to destroy the equality of the States, and to break up the social organization of our Southern institutions." Confident that his own actions were taken in the interest of peace, Mason exclaimed, "In the present unhappy dissensions which divide the country . . . I can only say that no one is prepared to go farther than I in efforts to compose and settle them forever."[93] Just over a year later, he penned a memorandum entitled "The Slave Question and the Disposition Made of It by the 31st Congress, 1850." In it he expressed complete satisfaction in "knowing that my judgement never wavered, or recognized one doubt as to the line of duty, an opposition from the beginning to the close of the disgusting drama, with a protest when it ended."[94]

On August 2, 1850, Mason and nine other southern senators caucused and presented to the Senate a "Protest Against the Passage of the Bill Admitting California as a State," concisely detailing their reasons for opposing the measure.[95] They also issued a signed statement avowing: "We will avail ourselves of any and every means . . . to prevent the admission of California as a State unless her southern boundary be reduced" to the Missouri Compromise line.[96] But none of those actions succeeded; on August 13, the Senate approved California statehood by a vote of thirty-four to eighteen.[97]

The "compromise" measures all passed. The Union had been preserved, as the sections agreed for the moment to disagree quietly. Few came away satisfied, and Mason left Washington quite displeased. To him, the South had given up all of California and a huge chunk of Texas for only a vague assurance of no Wilmot Proviso in Utah and New Mexico.[98] The new Fugitive Slave Law merely attempted to enforce what already existed as a constitutional right, and Congress had made inroads into legislating against slavery, by abolishing the slave trade in the capital. Mason did not feel like celebrating such a package.[99]

On October 2, Senators Mason and Hunter attended a dinner at Warrenton, Virginia, held to honor them for their conduct in the debates.[100] Six weeks later, Mason spoke to the citizens of nearby Jefferson County. There he clearly expressed his disdain for the final outcome. He stressed that, in the continuing struggle, as one of the state's "honored representatives and most devoted sons," he would "occupy whatever position her wisdom may assign to me," while stating that Virginia's "bugle note was sounded to rally the whole South for the maintenance of the Constitution, and the preservation of the Union, if it could be preserved, and for their own preservation if it could not. Unfortunately her voice was not heeded. Measures have been ultimately adopted, directly affecting the integrity of those institutions, upon the sole care of which, by the States where they are found, necessarily depends their safety and welfare. It rests with them to determine what remains on their part to be done to arrest the progress of the evil or to redress the wrongs that have been inflicted."[101] His reelection to the Senate came less than a month later, and Hunter wrote that "Mason's election has given us great gratification."[102] Mason saw his substantial triumph as a reflection of the Virginia legislature's "decided approbation of my course in the Senate, on the slavery questions, arising out of the acquisition of California and New Mexico."[103]

Many of the constitutional issues involved in California statehood reappeared later in the decade, when Minnesota sought admission to the Union as a free state. By March 1858, that territory, anticipating the approval of statehood, already had elected representatives. In the way, of course, stood Senator Mason. He condemned as a great irregularity electing congressmen while still a territory, particularly since the people of Minnesota had done so without checking a census to ascertain how many they should have. The census figures fell just short of giving the proposed state two members in the House. Mason moved to limit them to a single House member, because doing otherwise would be "in flagrant disregard both of the Constitution and the laws of the land."[104]

Mason claimed no intention of denying Minnesota statehood, but he wanted the representation to be fair to the other states. He argued that if Congress arbitrarily assigned "three members in the House of Representatives to Minnesota, what earthly security have we that under an excitement which may exist in the country, actuating a majority here to carry a political act, they would not assign to a new State ten or twenty members to attain a political object?" Arguing that the letter of the law had to be enforced, Mason exclaimed that there was "no curb but the Constitution, and if you depart from that, we have not the guarantee of a day for the stability of this Government."[105]

Some suggested that Minnesota's population grew daily, with laborers who eventually would bring their families along; therefore, soon they would deserve at least two House members. Mason disagreed, stating that most were single males with no dependents. Regardless of which picture was correct, however, he asked if something as important as dividing political power among the states should be decided unconstitutionally, based "upon wild and reckless conjecture."[106]

The times again had become troubled, mainly due to the ongoing agitation over "Bleeding Kansas," where abolitionists and slavery supporters had been fighting their own civil war for months.[107] Mason disapproved of pushing the Minnesota bill through quickly while the Kansas situation festered. Initially, he tried to delay consideration of the legislation "until every question connected with the Territory of Kansas has been matured."[108] He again based his arguments upon strict observance of the Constitution, but his rigidity could be selective and displayed a bias toward the South.

While ignoring voting irregularities in Kansas, a territory he believed "would take its place" as a state "recognizing and cherishing the condition of African Slavery,"[109] Mason found irregularities in Minnesota, a potential free state, to be quite serious. He expressed strong disapproval of Minnesota's practice of allowing foreigners to vote before they became U.S. citizens. His intense feelings regarding immigrants appeared when he alleged their inadequate knowledge of American institutions and character. Mason wondered how it could be possible for foreigners accustomed to governments "as unlike to ours as one thing can be to another," suddenly to be considered "upon their arrival here, enlightened, informed, considerate, thoughtful, and more than all, regardful of the true spirit of American liberty?"[110]

Seeing the odds stacked against him, Mason became willing to concede two House members to Minnesota, without taking another census. He came to the conclusion that, "from the character of that population, judging from . . . their entire ignorance of the Constitution and the laws of the country, or their utter disregard of them," no matter how many censuses were taken, the result would be "the same doubts and the same charges of a denial of justice that we have now."[111] After weeks of fighting it, in the end Mason voted yes on Minnesota statehood.[112]

Mason worried about a government "in an absolute state of decrepitude and decay" because of its disregard for the Constitution. He lamented that "political expediency" increasingly decided issues of constitutional law.[113] In contrast, he saw the 1857 Supreme Court decision in the Dred Scott case as perhaps the last time the federal government followed the document with precision.[114] In essence, the court ruled that no African American could be a U.S. citizen or, for that matter, a citizen of any individual state, "within the meaning of the Constitution."[115] Additionally, the justices decided that Congress had no power to keep slavery out of the territories and proclaimed the Missouri Compromise line unconstitutional.[116] Mason believed that the correct interpretation of the Constitution had been clearly and "rightfully expounded" in the court's opinion.[117]

At least the opinion rightfully expounded the Constitution as interpreted by James Murray Mason. The decision came down on the correct side of the slavery debate, holding the federal government to the strict meaning of the seventy-year-old document. Mason wrote to George Bancroft that he understood that Chief Justice Taney's opinion might be "too strong for stomachs debilitated by the sickly sensibilities of a depraved morality," but nonetheless he felt "content to let the opinion vindicate itself as the true law of the Constitution."[118]

Mason spent his entire senatorial career seeking to maintain that "true law." He saw himself as in many ways the keeper of the flame handed down from his grandfather. Times had changed, but to a Virginian holding to the ideals embodied in the words *Pro Republica Semper*, the basic need to limit the powers of the federal government had not altered a whit. James used George Mason's name and words from time to time in his letters of the late 1850s,[119] and always he seemed quite eager to discuss the origins of the federal republic. He took great pleasure in providing others with information about his grandfather and the history of the Constitutional Convention.[120]

Mason admired his grandfather for defending "the reserved rights of the respective States."[121] Nonetheless, while he sought to emulate his grandfather by working to keep the central government from becoming too powerful, James conveniently ignored the fact that George Mason, himself a slaveholder, loathed southern slavery. He had stunned southern delegates at the Constitutional Convention with a stirringly prophetic speech against the institution. Struggling to end the slave trade and prevent any expansion of slavery westward, he warned that "every master of slaves is born a petty tyrant. They bring the judgment of heaven upon a country. As nations cannot be rewarded or punished in the next world they must be in this. By an inevitable chain of causes and effects providence punished national sins by national calamities, I hold it essential to every point of view that the General Government have power to prevent the increase of slavery."[122] George Mason believed slavery to be bad economics, an inhumane practice, and a system that weakened the "morals and manners of our people."[123]

Over sixty years later, James Murray Mason asked, if the current controversies led to a fragmentation of the Union, "who would hesitate for one instant . . . when the choice is put to him between a dissolution of this Union and submission to a government of unlimited power?" Answering for himself, he said, "In that case, the Constitution would not only not be worth the parchment upon which it is written, but every son of the South would be truant to his fathers and his blood, who would regard it for one instant."[124]

But Mason's actions and rhetoric rendered *himself* truant to his own blood. While he used the Constitution as a strict blueprint to limit federal government power, he most often used it to defend southern slavery. His grandfather probably would not have considered that issue a proper focus of such cherished constitutional principles.

Chapter 4

1847–1859

Senator Mason and Slavery

Mason fought the slavery battles in Congress with rhetoric that combined proslavery arguments with strict constitutionalism, but his personal characterizations of the institution provide the philosophical background for his thinking. As with his interpretation of the Constitution, throughout his life Mason held steadfastly to his beliefs about slavery. In his early years, however, those thoughts rarely found public expression, except for a legalistic, matter-of-fact denial that Congress had any authority to tamper with it.[1] He did reveal a more personal attitude toward African Americans when he wrote to his sister-in-law about "two strapping negroes" who arrived for a dinner at the White House as aides to a Russian diplomat. Mason caricatured them as "the most ridiculous figures . . . with coats, etc., of Russian cut and make, manifestly, bedizened all over with gold cords and tassels, and each surmounted by an immense chapeau and feather." He further assumed "that his excellency could get no white man to play the ape so broadly, and it suited Sambo's taste finely."[2]

Those words must have sprung from the Virginia senator's paternalistic relationship with his own slaves. Despite mounting vigorous defenses of southern slavery, however, James Murray Mason never held a major stake in the system. He did not become a slaveholder until after he purchased Selma; and, while the number of slaves he owned fluctuated, at any given time he owned, on average, fewer than ten.[3] That number was barely enough to staff the household of a Virginia gentleman and added little to any family fortune. In actuality, Mason probably would have been better off, from a financial standpoint, if slavery had been abolished, since then he no longer would have had to support the one or two elderly slaves usually in his care.[4]

Perhaps because he had approximately equal numbers of both groups, Mason treated his slaves or servants much as he did his children, attempting to teach them all respect and obedience by offering a strong example rather than a strong hand. Eliza wrote to her mother that she often heard her husband say that "nothing seemed to him more cowardly and cruel than an unnecessary and tyrannical exercise of power over servants." Claiming that she always treated their slaves kindly, even though "they often test my patience," she nonetheless found them to be "so much less capable, careful, or industrious than white servants." In the same letter, however, Eliza also described them with such adjectives as "obedient, faithful, and affectionate."[5] Such a caricature reverberates with the stereotypical image of the docile, ignorant, childlike, submissive Sambo.[6] Whether such a description was or was not accurate, James and Eliza saw the slaves that way. This helps to explain why both used the same tactics to handle their slaves and to raise their children.

Their daughter, Virginia, gave another example of how her father interacted with African Americans. Perhaps out of gratitude for Mason's relative kindness, a "negro band" in Winchester, made up of both slaves and free Negroes, had the custom of "giving Marster a serenade" the night after he returned home from a long trip. One of his own slaves would arrange the festivities; in return, Mason gave hearty thanks and whiskey to all. The story illustrates his relationship with the local black population, but probably it also shows that Winchester's African Americans knew just what they needed to do to get some free whiskey![7]

Mason seems seldom to have referred to African Americans or to slavery before he entered the U.S. Senate. Throughout his Senate career, though, Mason championed the southern political platform. And slavery, another of the three themes that most affected his life, lay at the core of that political ideology.[8] Both his public pronouncements and his private remarks upon the subject spoke for him vividly, leaving no doubt about the man's true thoughts.

Mason had the habit of writing down his thinking about issues in personal memoranda. Sometimes they consisted of sentences and paragraphs, while at other times they amounted merely to a written record of his train of thought, without punctuation. Few of those are extant, primarily because the bulk of his pre-1862 papers were destroyed by Union soldiers who occupied Winchester. But one memorandum that Mason penned around 1860 survives. In it, he dealt with the topic of slavery in Virginia, attempting to analyze all possible answers to the question, "What will become of the negroes?"

Mason cheered the great "change in feeling, and sentiment" that he saw in Virginia "since that day when the house was almost equally divided, when slavery was thought an evil, but the evil was palliated and excused by being termed a necessity." He wrote that now a proposition to abolish slavery in Virginia would "meet with universal ridicule, and my word for it, would not receive a single solitary vote. . . . *Today*, slavery is called a blessing, and finds none to spurn it as a curse, none to shun it as an evil." Mason predicted that slavery would be perpetual and stressed that he found it "essential to the very existence of the nation."[9] He and other Virginians believed not only that "the condition of African bondage in their midst was the best condition to which the African race had ever been subjected; but [also] that it had the effect of ennobling both races, the white and the black."[10]

In his defenses of slavery, Mason consistently returned to the legal argument that slavery was a *condition* and not an *institution*. As early as the 1848 Oregon debates, Mason had asserted that Africans "brought to the shores of North America in bondage, and sold to the inhabitants as bondsmen, brought slavery as their condition from the shores of Africa." Therefore American laws did not institute it but simply recognized it.[11]

That reasoning reappeared in his rhetoric, as tensions between North and South increased in the late 1850s. In the Senate, Mason declared slavery to be merely a condition of property brought from Africa and "recognized by the common law of this country." American laws did not make Africans property, but they remained "property ever afterwards" unless some new legislation outlawed the condition.[12] Mason claimed that slavery no more required positive law to create it "than it required law to create slavery in an ox."[13]

Mason believed that many of the harsh images northerners had of southern slavery would disappear "if it were accepted there in its true and real character, of a *Condition* and not an *Institution*." To the Virginian's mind, the word *institution* implied that slavery existed as a positive creation of American law, when in reality the "condition of property in the form of servitude for life, had attached to the subject, in the Country from whence it was brought."[14]

Viewing slavery as beneficial to both whites and blacks, James regularly pointed to the plight of free blacks either in the North or in Africa. In 1848, he attacked northerners for exhibiting contradictory behavior in insisting that blacks go into the new territories only as freemen, and simultaneously greeting with violence free blacks coming to their own states. Claiming that there was no difference between the relationship of slave and owner and that of master and apprentice (except for time of service), he described reports about how African Americans fared as freemen in New York. First he asserted that "the black population in a state of freedom dwindles and diminishes, and would soon become extinct. It is incident to their race. They do not multiply, in a state of freedom, on our continent." Then, looking northward, he asked his colleagues to "see the rivalry, jealousy, and hatred, that is engendered there between the white population and the free blacks; and see that race, the subject of so much commiseration here, because they are in slavery, dying and rotting in nakedness and filth, in the cellars and dens of your northern cities." If, in Mason's mind, that picture was suspended alongside his image of the happy "Sambo" slaves of Winchester, it should come as no surprise that he took a dim view of abolitionists. Seeing such misery as the fate of free blacks in the North, Mason concluded grimly that "this matter of abolition is destitute of every savor of humanity."[15]

He knew "no race of men upon the earth whose original normal condition was that of slavery, but the African." In every land, at every time, they existed in bondage, sold by their own race. In the South, however, the African came in contact with a civilization that "has elevated him very far beyond the uttermost conceptions of his ancestors in the scale of being." When he compared southern slaves to blacks in Africa, Mason saw the difference between "a high grade of civilization and the lowest grade of the savage."[16]

He also found southern slaves more civilized than free blacks in the North. Admitting the existence of only rare exceptions, Mason contended that "the negro free is the most worthless population that can be conceived of, and not worthless alone, but contaminating, vicious, depraved, unprincipled, without any recognition of any moral law, or moral obligation."[17] Mason mocked northerners for hypocritically wanting the slaves freed while not allowing the freemen to move to their states. Both the free states and Canada rejected freed blacks; and, because they found freedom so difficult, increasing numbers of freemen asked the Commonwealth of Virginia to return them to bondage. Mason claimed that free blacks had learned the painful lesson that in slavery their condition was elevated and improved every day, while in freedom "they are despised, loathed, not tolerated in a society that professes to tolerate them, and their residences are found always in destitution and poverty."[18]

Having ruled out altruism as the cause of northern actions toward slavery, and claiming that climate alone "extinguished it in their section," Mason concluded that practical political reasons and not humanitarianism caused abolitionist agitation. He condemned their stance as rooted in resistance to the clauses of the Constitution that made slavery an element of political power, arguing that, if you took that resistance away, "there will be no more clamor on the subject of slavery."[19]

He did not dismiss the *idea* of abolishing slavery without giving the possibility some thought, albeit only for a brief moment. In that memorandum in which he asked, "What will become of the negroes?" Mason pondered whether there existed any practical method of emancipation for Virginia. The legislature already had decided that freed blacks could not stay in the state. Therefore they had to go elsewhere. Additionally, from the example of Haiti, Mason concluded that freed slaves would not work. Therefore the freemen could not move to the North, as he doubted that "our Northern Brethren" would be willing to receive with open arms a large group of unrestrained freemen. Such a mass would be "more licentious on account of the unmerited freedom, . . . men of an inferior race, degraded and despised, . . . without any means of subsistence, who must live by plunder or charity." He labeled the idea "ridiculous."[20]

That logic left Mason only with the option of deporting the freemen to Africa. He then concluded that he had proved emancipation to be "impracticable," because the owners needed to be compensated and the state government could get such a large amount of money only by raising taxes significantly.[21] The federal government could not provide such compensation, because, as he earlier had claimed in the Senate, Congress did not possess "constitutionally the right to make appropriations for the deportation of that class of the population of the United States."[22] Mason saw "no power in the Government of the United States, in any form, directly or indirectly, to provide for the emancipation of slaves,"[23] and thus he reasoned that manumission needed to be rejected out of hand.

Eliminating every alternative supported Mason's inclination to be a staunch defender of slavery as a positive aspect of southern society. Such defense had become particularly important because of per-

ceived northern encroachments. The spread or containment of slavery in the 1840s and 1850s translated into shifting amounts of political clout for one part of the country or another. Mason's firmness
drew strength from southern unity in the face of northern hostility.
In 1850, during the compromise debates, he wrote to his friend Rives,
then serving as minister to France, that the question of Congress's
interference with southern slavery "has become the touchstone of
party in the South." He asserted that, because of public pressure,
even "the Southern Whigs would vote for no more of their own party,
who would not produce a clean bill of health on that subject."[24] In
August 1850, Mason warned "that the slaveholding States of this
Union have made up their minds irrevocably to admit no further
trenching upon what they believe to be their rights."[25] He spoke
particularly for Virginia, whose legislature had approved resolutions
regarding the Wilmot Proviso and any other attempts by Congress to
interfere with southern slavery, stressing that it viewed such legislation "as a direct attack upon the institutions of the southern States,
to be resisted at every hazard."[26]

Mason believed that unity increased when southerners compre-
hended the depth of the North's hostility toward them. Northern
senators often presented petitions from their states condemning slavery. Most southern senators attempted to reject them without consideration, but Mason generally pushed for them to be printed and
disseminated. Responding to resolutions from the New York Legislature in 1849, he stressed that "whenever one of the States of this
Confederacy addresses the Senate of the United States, she has the
right to be heard."[27] But Mason's sentiments did not spring from
concerns about free speech. Instead, they originated from his "desire
that these resolutions, and all others of kindred stock, which come
from States where slavery now no longer exists, should be reported
to the southern States in the language in which they are uttered." He
believed that the time had come when the two sections should "understand each other. Nothing should be suppressed—nothing. If they
speak of the domestic institutions of other sister States in terms of
indignity and contumely, those other States should know it."[28] A year
later, regarding resolutions from Vermont, Mason insisted the Senate records show that one state had called another's domestic institution "a crime." He wanted it spread among the southern people, to
show "that such vituperative language has been heaped upon us day
after day, not by fanatics only, but, I regret to say, by sovereign States
upon this floor."[29]

Such a response may have helped unite southerners, but it also served to inflame the enmity of average citizens in the free states, making the process of recovering runaway slaves increasingly difficult. During the debates on his Fugitive Slave Bill, Mason detailed the hindrances under which slaveholders labored when they attempted to retrieve their property. He claimed that, in trying to capture a runaway slave in one of the free states, "you may as well go down to the sea, and recover a fish which has escaped you, as expect to recover such fugitive."[30] Mason referred specifically to Pennsylvania and Ohio when he claimed that "it is just as impossible to recover a fugitive slave now in either of those States as it would be to bring him up from the depths of the sea."[31]

Indeed, Mason claimed, if the owner made a successful capture, afterwards the costs continued to mount. Having recaptured a fugitive, the owner, "probably in nineteen cases out of twenty at least," had to sell the slave. The paternalistic relationship had been damaged irreparably; therefore "he cannot be kept at home; he cannot be put on the plantation to mix again with his associates; he cannot be trusted; he has forfeited the confidence of his master."[32] Such instances had become more frequent because of northern attitudes. Mason warned that "these acts are forcing the people of the South to believe that we cannot exist together under one common Government."[33]

Even while fighting for his Fugitive Slave Bill, Mason admitted that he saw little prospect of getting northerners to live up to their constitutional responsibilities, without some change in their disposition towards the South.[34] Mason recognized that, for the law to succeed, it had to be enforced zealously and executed by northerners. They had to "aid, and assist, and countenance, and encourage those who go there to recover their property, and must not throw all sorts of resistance, difficulties, and obstacles in their way."[35]

In January 1851, Mason gave examples of slaveholders who went to Massachusetts and Pennsylvania to try to bring back their property, only to end up with increased financial hardship. He announced in the Senate, "So far as I am informed . . . the law of the last session intended to require the fulfillment of this obligation, if not a dead letter, has not answered the ends for which it was designed."[36] That picture differed from the truth, however; in reality, only a small percentage of fugitive slave cases did not result in the slave's being remanded to bondage.[37] But appearances were more important than reality, as Mason and other southerners viewed northern propaganda as encouraging slaves to attempt a run to freedom. That fact alone served to undermine the effectiveness of Mason's Law.[38]

By 1851, Mason found not only the enforcement of his Fugitive

Slave Law wanting, but the entire "pseudo compromise of the slave question." He wrote that it will "in its consequences, be found fatal, either to the Union of the States, or to the institution of slavery."[39] He believed emphatically that "the safety and integrity of the Southern States (to say nothing of their dignity and honor) are indissolubly bound up with domestic slavery" and that the federal government had been committed to its overthrow.[40]

The compromise measures of 1850 did buy time for the Union, and in general, agitation over slavery declined over the next few years. Attempting to keep things quiet, Mason opposed a December 1851 resolution declaring the Compromise of 1850 as having terminated "all questions arising out of the institution of slavery," because he believed the measure only could lead to renewed problems. He asserted that "the public mind has become to some extent tranquilized. The people of the Southern States who felt themselves aggrieved, . . . if not reconciled, are disposed to acquiesce."

He disagreed with many of the measures passed but "never counseled, and never shall counsel, my people to further resistance on account of these laws." Ever believing in the idea of honor, Mason hoped that if southerners could acquiesce, even though treated unjustly, impressed northerners also would behave honorably and live up to their constitutional obligations, so that the Union could be kept safe.[41] Mason pledged Virginia's loyalty and criticized those who continued to speak loudly for disunion. But he warned that it "must continue to be a Union under the Constitution." If it did not, and if the Union became one of "force, or a Union in which . . . the rights of the minority are violated, her past history shows she will be the first to repudiate and to disown."[42] The resolution never came to a vote.

In July 1852, Mason again attempted to prevent discussion of the topic. He chastised Sen. Charles Sumner of Massachusetts[43] for trying to rehash debates over the Fugitive Slave Law so late in the session. Mason believed that only harm could come from such a reopening of old wounds,[44] particularly in a presidential election year.[45] For the sake of both the South and the Union, he desired to keep the politics of slavery deep in the background if possible.

In the two years from late 1851 to late 1853, only rarely did Mason discuss slavery. One noteworthy exception came in August 1852, when he debated the subject with Sen. Horace Mann of Massachusetts. Mason declared that the "negroes in the United States who are slaves, are in a better condition, physically and morally, than any . . . of the African race that have existed since we have any authentic accounts of them." He did not wish to be misunderstood "as being an enemy of the African race," but he saw them as "an entirely different people." In explaining why they had not become more civilized, he claimed that the reason could be found "in the nature of the black man, as made by his Creator." Mason stressed that only as slaves could Africans be civilized; had their ancestors not been brought to the United States, they would have "gone out of existence . . . by degradation and starvation."[46]

Not until 1854 would slavery return to the center of congressional debate. The new dispute surrounded the Kansas-Nebraska Bill, introduced by Sen. Stephen A. Douglas of Illinois, chairman of the Senate Committee on Territories.[47] With both settlers and railroaders impatient to move west of Iowa and Missouri, Douglas saw a potential to score political points for himself and his party by organizing the Territory of Nebraska. One thing hampered the idea, however: that land lay above the Missouri Compromise line. Slavery could not be extended there. Southern representatives would not support any more free territories. And, lacking their support, the bill stood no chance of passing. Therefore the territories needed to be organized as Utah and New Mexico had been, without reference to slavery. The people could decide later. Popular sovereignty would rule.[48]

To get his bill through the Congress, Douglas wanted and needed a broad base of support. He desired particularly the support of President Franklin Pierce. Pierce did not want the slavery issue reopened by any direct attempt to repeal the Missouri Compromise, but Douglas hoped that he would accept the idea of Congress's declaring it "inoperative" there. In January, fearing that his legislation was doomed without White House support, Douglas asked Secretary of War Jefferson Davis for an appointment with the president. Pierce hated to be disturbed on a Sunday, but Davis prevailed upon him to see Douglas and his entourage of five congressional colleagues.[49]

Those five included Sen. David R. Atchison of Missouri, Sen. Robert M. T. Hunter of Virginia, and James Murray Mason. At that time, the three lived together in a house on F Street, along with Sen. Andrew P. Butler of South Carolina. The group has been labeled the "F Street Mess." Mason, chairman of the Senate Foreign Relations Committee; Hunter, chairman of the Senate Finance Committee; and Atchison, the Senate's president *pro tempore*, constituted as influential a trio of southerners as existed in the Thirty-third Congress.[50] They saw in Douglas's bill an opportunity to flex the muscles of the South after a series of setbacks, as well as to test loyalty toward their way of thinking within the Democratic Party.[51]

Pierce agreed with the proposal's aim, yet he worried about the risks involved. But when the powerful legislators finished their arguments, the president reluctantly assented to Douglas's new bill incorporating the idea of making the Missouri Compromise "inoperative" in what would be two territories, Kansas and Nebraska. Pierce did request, however, that the senators consult with Secretary of State William L. Marcy first,[52] warning them that they were "entering on a serious undertaking, and the ground should be well surveyed before the first step is taken."[53]

Marcy, a New Yorker, numbered among the conservatives in Pierce's cabinet. He had the same concerns about stirring up trouble as the president. As Pierce had requested, Douglas, Mason, and the others called on the secretary that afternoon, but they found him not at home.[54] The group did not try again. They had the approval they wanted, in writing, from the easily influenced President Pierce.

The next day, Douglas introduced his new Kansas-Nebraska Bill. A week later, formal debates began. They lasted over a month, as the bill's critics lambasted Douglas for attempting to open free territory to the possibility of allowing slavery.[55] Mason did not enter the debates until early March. Then he stated his belief that, if the bill passed, agitation would stop and conciliation would result. Unlike earlier slavery-related measures that had characteristics of aggressive hatred, Mason saw the quiet of peace in the Kansas-Nebraska Bill.[56]

In the same speech, he denounced northern abolitionist senators, and particularly Ohio's Salmon P. Chase, for attempting to "destroy and defeat" Douglas's efforts at peacemaking. Mason asserted that such actions meant those "incendiaries" could not stand the thought of a peaceful solution to the slavery question. The Virginian reasoned that, without abolitionism, "the last plank in the shipwreck of their political fortunes will be taken from them, and they will expire, as they deserve to expire, howling—howling like fiends attempting to destroy this country." Mason himself found the bill flawed because it did not *guarantee* southerners their constitutional rights in the new territories. But he believed southern honor had been saved, and he viewed the legislation as an "olive branch from the North" that he could take home to the people of Virginia.[57]

For once, Mason stood on the winning side. Two days later, on March 4, Douglas's bill passed the Senate by a margin of thirty-seven to fourteen,[58] with most of the opposition coming from northern Whigs.[59] Supporters faced an even greater task in the House, but the measure gained approval there on May 22, by only thirteen votes, and President Pierce signed the bill into law.[60]

New England continued to protest, and clergymen there asked Senator Sumner to present their petition against the bill's passage. Whereas he usually championed the rights of petitioners, even if they espoused an abolitionist point of view, in the case of the New England clergy, Senator Mason's voice rose in loud disapproval. He refused to consider hearing the petition because it came "from a class who have put aside their character of citizens . . . a class who style themselves in the petition ministers of the Gospel, and not citizens." Those ministers denounced the Senate for passing the Kansas-Nebraska Bill and, according to Mason, had the effrontery to invoke "the vengeance of the Almighty, whom they profess to serve, against us."[61]

The petition struck Mason as a blatant affront to the principle of separation of church and state. He labeled ministers as a body "the most encroaching . . . arrogant class of men"[62] and condemned the New England clergy for presenting themselves to Congress as "a third estate." The Virginian called their purposes "unchristian" and stated that they had "prostituted" their once sacred offices. He exulted in declaring that the southern church was "yet pure in its great and holy mission." He rejoiced that the churches planned to separate into northern and southern branches; if northern clergymen dared set "aside the character of American citizens, and come here profaning their office, profaning the name of the Almighty, for the purpose of political alliances, they are unworthy of their associates in the church."[63]

Weeks later, Mason again sparred with Sumner over a Massachusetts petition. It demanded that Congress repeal the Fugitive Slave Law. He censured his opponent for rudely assailing "the dignity of the American Senate" as well as the dignity "of the whole people." The Virginia aristocrat had been deeply offended when Sumner "denounced a gentleman from Virginia who goes under the protection of the Constitution, and the sanction of the law into his State, to reclaim his property . . . as a 'slave-hunter from Virginia.'" According to Mason, Sumner's "use of such vulgar language here, betrays the vulgarity of his associations at home," and he asked whether the Senate would tolerate it.[64]

Passions in the Congress cooled temporarily, and for almost two years Mason and the other senators devoted most of their time to concerns unrelated to slavery. By 1856, however, many of the slavery issues faced by the Senate during the debates on California statehood resurfaced. The situation in "Bleeding Kansas" had deteriorated into virtual civil war. Allowing Kansas to decide its status with regard to slavery on the basis of "popular sovereignty" had created a situation in which northern abolitionists and southern slaveholders poured into the territory and brutally attacked each other in an effort to gain the upper hand.[65]

An assembly of free-soil Kansans gathered at Topeka in response to the proslavery assembly at Lecompton. Each claimed to be a genuine reflection of the territory's popular sentiment. Proposals that Kansas become a free state predictably drew Mason's fire. He stressed that the Lecompton legislature represented Kansas and that those at Topeka who claimed to be the true representatives of the people were merely a group of "certain residents, occupants of the public lands belonging to the whole country, in utter disregard of the authority of the Congress of the United States, and in contempt of that authority."[66] Labeling the Topekans "a body of men who are in rebellion against the laws of the country and in disrespect . . . of its institutions," Mason sternly warned abolitionists and their "emigrant aid societies" that "the country will learn who are the people that have been sent as hirelings by the emigrant aid societies to preoccupy territory and keep others out, and who are to be sustained by the priesthood in New England by contributions to purchase Sharpe's rifles. They will see what sort of people they are."[67] Mason's rhetoric reflected a level of passion shared by most of his colleagues. Southern senators and abolitionist northern senators finally had locked horns in a slavery debate where no compromise solution appeared to be available.

In May 1856, the violence of the Kansan frontier spilled over into the halls of Congress. Legislators on both sides stretched the limits of congressional propriety. On May 20, Senator Sumner rose and gave a vitriolic speech entitled "The Crime Against Kansas," in which he castigated southern slaveholders, reserving particularly scathing words for Senators Stephen Douglas, James Murray Mason, and Andrew Butler.[68]

Sumner claimed that God had aligned himself against Douglas, calling him one of the "mad spirits who would endanger and degrade the Republic, while they betray all the cherished sentiments of the Fathers and the spirit of the Constitution, in order to give new spread to slavery." He labeled Mason a representative of the other Virginia, "where human beings are bred as cattle for the shambles, and where a dungeon rewards the pious matron who teaches little children to relieve their bondage by reading the Book of Life," the Virginia "from which Washington and Jefferson now avert their faces." But Sumner saved his cruelest words for Butler, a white-haired old man and a

respected legislator. The Massachusetts senator assailed him for having made "the harlot, slavery" his mistress, and ridiculed a recent
speech by the South Carolinian, in which the latter had "overflowed
with rage," spoken in "incoherent phrases," and "discharged loose
expectoration."[69]

Senators, including Mason, rushed to respond. In an unexpur-
gated speech, Mason detailed his feelings about the abolitionist senators with whom he shared the Senate floor. He lamented that
southerners, out of political necessity, were forced "into relations and
associations, which, beyond the walls of this Chamber, we are enabled to avoid—associations here, whose presence elsewhere is dishonor, and the touch of whose hand would be a disgrace."[70] He
expressed despair at being constrained to hear, day in and day out,
"depravity, vice in its most odious form uncoiled in this presence,
exhibiting its loathsome deformities in accusation and vilification
against the quarter of the country from which I come."[71]

He aimed his comments particularly at Sumner and at Sen. William H. Seward of New York, because they denounced but refused to
define what they meant by "the slave power." He stated that they
could not be referring to the South's wealth, because Sumner himself
boasted that Massachusetts produced three times that of the cotton
states. They could not mean any sort of numerical strength, because
the South clearly had a population lower than that of the North.
Mason asked rhetorically, what could they mean by "slave power"?[72]

He answered that northern abolitionists feared the South's "moral
power of truth and justice . . . which recognizes the obligations of a
compact." The Virginian exclaimed that, when northerners attacked
the slave power, they involuntarily paid tribute to slavery as an inte-
gral element of southern society. Mason charged that Sumner showed
ingratitude toward the South, which enriched New England with
cotton for its factories and dollars in payment for its finished goods.
Whatever wealth New England had, Mason said, was "the creature"
of the federal confederation; "let them be separated from it, and they
would dwindle, and decay, and die."[73] Sumner could only counter
"that hard words are not argument; frowns not reasons; nor do scowls
belong to the proper arsenal of parliamentary debate."[74]

Mason's retort possessed only a fraction of the emotional intensity exhibited by Senator Butler's nephew, Rep. Preston Brooks of
South Carolina. Two days after Sumner's speech, Brooks entered a
nearly empty Senate chamber shortly after adjournment. Standing
over Sumner, he declared that the Massachusetts senator had libeled
both his uncle and the entire state of South Carolina. Brooks then

beat him on the head with his cane until restrained by others and until Sumner fell bloodied to the floor.[75]

Southerners and northerners predictably rallied to the two men's defense. Sumner's injuries became an exaggerated testimony to southern brutality, while Brooks's actions became a metaphor for the South's anger at abolitionist attacks.[76] Despite this disruption, the Senate debates resumed. In June, Mason fought against a resolution to send Gen. Winfield Scott with troops to quell the trouble in Kansas. He saw it as an interference with President Pierce's authority as commander-in-chief and claimed "that everything has been done which the occasion called for, or which propriety would allow, to bring that unfortunate condition of things to a close."[77]

Mason's appraisal could be called inaccurate at best, but it derived from his firm support for the Lecompton government and its proslavery laws. He saw others' acceptance of them as the surest way to peace. He denounced the House of Representatives for attempting to "ingraft legislation . . . to the people of Kansas." He understood that some of the Lecompton laws paralleled laws in the southern states that shocked northern sensibilities because "they trench upon human rights and human liberty," but he claimed that "there is not one of the southern people who is not perfectly satisfied that such laws are not only just but expedient and wise, and tend to the best ends of the promotion and furtherance of civilization."[78] That same southern people did not want northern laws forced upon them, "because we consider that they would convert man into a mere machine, make his understanding and will subservient . . . and breed up the worst race of men that were ever bred up under free institutions."[79]

Despite rhetoric emphasizing their differences, Mason still held out hope "that there is a public sentiment at the North yet remaining which unites with the South in the desire to perpetuate the Union and that, by the aid of that public sentiment . . . the Union will be preserved." He expressed his "earnest and anxious hope" that, in spite of the serious differences between the two sections, somehow "a fabric of Government which has had no predecessor in the world, which, if honestly and legitimately administered, would make us the greatest people that has ever yet existed, both in moral and physical power, should be preserved and perpetuated." Nonetheless, the Virginian warned that "the constant and obstinate agitation of questions connected with the institution of slavery" had brought southerners "to the conviction that the preservation of that institution rests with themselves and themselves only."[80]

He voiced those words in the Senate while defending President

Pierce's final annual message. Instead of focusing on the achieve-ments of his administration, Pierce had used the occasion aggres-sively, to blame northerners for the troubles in Kansas, and succeeded in only stirring passions once more.[81] Mason proclaimed that, when the emotions of the day subsided, the greatness of the man's words would become apparent to all. He hoped that Pierce's thoughts would reach northerners' minds and "that they will unite, in a common, patriotic interest and purpose, to come back to the Constitution which our fathers framed . . . and to administer it legitimately," giving each section, including the South, that to which it was entitled.[82]

But in 1857, the Kansas problem deepened. It came to a head on December 8, when President James Buchanan, in his first annual message, urged that the territory be made a slave state under the Lecompton Constitution.[83] Mason quickly applauded the president and voiced his agreement that the people of Kansas had spoken in favor of slavery.[84] He always had expected Kansas, because of its prox-imity to Arkansas and Missouri, to become a slave state. Mason had counted on fair competition under popular sovereignty to put it into the southern column, but he had failed to anticipate "*unfair* compe-tition" in the form of "extraordinary and unscrupulous efforts of Northern Abolitionists to force a population there."[85] Therefore the Virginia senator believed that his president had come down on the correct and fair side of the debate.

Stephen Douglas disagreed. The next day, the Illinois senator attacked Buchanan's position in a stirring three-hour speech that, at its conclusion, brought those in the galleries to their feet in rousing applause.[86] Ever the Senate's spokesman for order, James Murray Mason immediately demanded that the galleries be cleared. Denying that he had made his motion for partisan reasons, Mason labeled it necessary "to preserve the decorum and propriety of the Senate."[87] Convinced to withdraw the motion, he changed his target to Douglas's speech itself. While admitting that it certainly had power, he decried it for what he viewed as fallacious arguments.[88]

The debates seemed to go on forever. In March 1858, Mason quarreled with Sen. Lafayette Foster of Connecticut over the Lecompton Constitution.[89] He objected to a petition from Maine because it used language that charged "perfidy upon Congress, false-hood upon the President, and infamy upon the judiciary."[90] Mason jeered at northerners who longed for a return of the unconstitutional Missouri Compromise to Kansas, because those same people had opposed southern efforts in 1850 to extend that line all the way to the Pacific. Mason again blamed abolitionist senators and their sup-

porters for the turmoil, stating that the ink barely had dried on the
Kansas-Nebraska Law when they invited and encouraged their people
to emigrate there. He held them "responsible for the bloodshed, and
rapine, and murder, and the utter destitution of every moral principle, which have disgraced that Territory ever since," because they
stirred up the northern populace "to induce them to contribute money
and fire-arms to be used in Kansas against their fellow-countrymen."[91]

Kansas, Mason argued, needed to become a slave state for the
sake of slavery itself and, incidentally, for the benefit of the African
race. While the Kansas debates raged, Mason wrote to J. H. Clifford
that southerners knew with confidence that slavery would "not only
bear the most free and unrestrained discussion, but that the better it
is understood in its relations both social and political, the more it will
be cherished by those, amongst whom it is found." He wrote that
slavery had become "a patriarchal form of society, resulting from the
social tendencies of our race," arguing that "it would be dangerous
for the law to interfere with or regulate the relations of Master and
slave, as it would be to interfere with any other purely family relation.
To preserve the peace and repose the whole family, as well as to en-
gender and foster affection and confidence throughout all its ramifi-
cations, the Master must be the supreme head, and sole Lawgiver, in
everything that pertains to such family relation."[92] Those words were
consonant with the paternalistic relationship he had always maintained
with his own slaves. But Mason continued to commit the fallacy of
composition by making the assumption that the actions of all southern slaveholders matched his own treatment of African Americans.

Over a year passed and little changed, except that Stephen
Douglas's "Freeport Doctrine" struck another blow against Mason's
idea of southern rights. In his 1858 debates with Abraham Lincoln,
Douglas declared that slavery could be kept out of a territory if its
citizens did not pass a "slave code" to deal with the commonplace
necessities of the institution.[93] Any application of such a theory would
overturn what proslavery forces saw as their victories in the Kansas-
Nebraska Act and the Dred Scott decision.

On February 23, 1859, Mason rose to recount that, when the
Kansas-Nebraska Bill passed, he had thought Congress had "established a system of legislation which would quiet once and for all, the
distracting question of slavery." He had believed so "sincerely and
honestly," but he had been mistaken. When the Supreme Court issued the Dred Scott decision, Mason also had judged the question
settled, "but it seems not."[94]

Mason then reproved Douglas for his treatment of southerners.

Addressing the Illinois senator directly, he declared, "You promised us bread, and you have given us stone; you promised us a fish, and you have given us a serpent; we thought you had given us a substantial right, and you have given us the most evanescent shadow and delusion." According to Mason, the Freeport Doctrine acknowledged that the people of a territory had "power to contravene and to nullify and destroy . . . the Constitution of the United States . . . as interpreted by the Supreme Court."[95] Mason could never accede to such an idea. Instead, he warned Douglas, if any future presidential candidate made the Freeport Doctrine his rallying point, southerners "would be truant and recreant to themselves and to their safety and honor, if they should cast for him a single vote . . . and if it is to be the dissolution of the party, let it be dissolved, and the sooner the better."[96]

By the end of his first twelve years in the Senate, the slavery issue had come to dominate most of Mason's speeches. Almost every one referred to the country's division over that peculiar aspect of southern society. He repeated again and again his previously expressed defenses of southern slavery. On January 3, 1860, still characterizing the latter as something positive, he confidently stood in the Senate and emphasized that "the opinion once entertained, certainly in my own State by able and distinguished men and patriots, that the condition of African slavery was one more to be deplored than to be fostered, has undergone a change, and that the uniform—I might almost say universal—sentiment in my own State upon the subject of African bondage is, that it is a blessing to both races, one to be encouraged, cherished, and fostered."[97] He also believed that, if those who earlier thought otherwise had lived until 1860, their opinions too would have changed. George Mason's grandson had become the embodiment of all southerners who defiantly defended slavery in the face of increased abolitionist pressure.[98]

Mason's struggle to enforce the South's rights by the means of his strict interpretation of the Constitution seeped into debates regarding virtually any question. In the 1850s, however, one set of issues remained that those on both sides of the Mason-Dixon Line could discuss in relative harmony. But sometimes even in the area of foreign affairs, where Mason reigned as chairman of the Senate Foreign Relations Committee, nationalistic sentiments could not avoid taking on a strong sectional flavor.

Chapter 5

1847–1859

Mason and United States
Foreign Relations

On March 3, 1849, during Senate debates regarding establishing a Department of the Interior, James Murray Mason described the purpose of the original departments of the federal government. He stated that "the War and Navy Departments . . . manage our foreign relations; for the military power has reference to foreign relations alone." He pointed out that "the State Department is to manage our foreign relations within the sphere of peaceful government relations." Even the Treasury Department's main source of revenue came from tariffs on foreign goods. Therefore, reasoned the Virginia senator, the founding fathers designed the federal government for the management of foreign affairs.[1] If the heroic statesmen who crafted the United States Constitution believed foreign affairs to be that important, it stood to reason that a strict constructionist such as Mason would think the same.

Mason commented on foreign affairs in the Senate more times than on any other issue, including slavery. Most of his remarks dealt with minor concerns, but their sheer quantity suggests that foreign policy issues were as significant in Mason's life and career as constitutional or slavery-related issues. Foreign relations grew to be his power base in the Congress after December 1851, when he became chairman of the Senate Foreign Relations Committee.[2] One of the most important chairs in the Senate, it traditionally went to a Virginian. The Old Dominion held it almost 60 percent of the time in the antebellum period,[3] and Mason occupied that position for almost ten years, working with three presidents and five secretaries of state.[4] The job gave him influence far beyond what he would have had without it, as a wide range of foreign policy items passed through his southern hands.

Mason's foreign policy convictions reflected a rigid legalism akin to the strict-constructionist position he adopted on constitutional issues. He held the sanctity of treaties to be extremely important, and he never failed to criticize governments for not living up to the terms of diplomatic agreements.[5] Similarly, he believed that American foreign policy needed to continue to follow precedents established by earlier generations. In 1852, Mason asserted on the Senate floor that "the foundations of our foreign policy," which were laid out in Washington's farewell address, have "guided us thus far to honor, dignity, and strength. Under them the country is prosperous at home and respected abroad." He warned that "to abandon them now, would be in the very wantonness of power, to hazard in speculative philanthropy, the peace and welfare of a whole people."[6]

American foreign policy also rested to some extent upon the pillar of the Monroe Doctrine. Mason admitted that the doctrine contained some vague and undefined aspects,[7] and he stressed that it "was made in the most circumspect and guarded manner, and confined to a single purpose."[8] Nonetheless he characterized the measure as "a deliberate declaration . . . boldly and wisely done," one that had led the United States to a position of "proud eminence."[9] He found it to be a potent policy even thirty years after its declaration.[10]

Mason had one glaring inadequacy when it came to foreign relations: his experiences did not include travel abroad. The Virginia senator recognized that weakness, confessing on the Senate floor that he had "very limited knowledge of the practices of Governments in their relations towards each other." But he claimed modestly to have at least "some knowledge of human affairs and human conduct in the relations of the world."[11] Therefore, to compensate for any provincial tendencies, Mason applied his own frame of reference to diplomatic relations. He did not seek to direct foreign policy from his Senate seat. Instead, he supported the executive's wishes in most foreign policy matters. Mason did so out of a firm commitment to the notion that the Constitution "devolved upon the President the duty of regulating our intercourse with foreign nations."[12] Mason's strict constructionism demanded that he not overstep his bounds and tread upon areas delegated to the executive.

As chairman of the Foreign Relations Committee, Mason's day-to-day work seldom made headlines. He spent a great deal of time sifting through myriad petitions for compensation, from foreigners as well as U.S. citizens.[13] Examples of the wide range of claims that passed through his committee's hands include a claim by the Spanish consul at New Orleans for compensation for injuries to his person and property during riots there,[14] and payment to Commodore Matthew C. Perry for diplomatic services rendered during his trip to Japan.[15] Not all the petitions related to recent events, however; some dated all the way back to the War of 1812![16]

Most of the claims lacked controversy beyond the question of their legitimacy. A notable exception was the *Amistad* case. In 1839, some fifty Africans bound for slavery took control of that Spanish vessel and, after arriving in an American port, won their freedom in court. Abolitionists cheered the verdict. The Spanish government, however, demanded compensation, despite the court's ruling that the Africans had been kidnapped illegally.[17] Throughout his years in the Senate, Mason pressed for action on those Spanish claims.[18] In 1851[19] and 1852,[20] he introduced resolutions to inquire into the propriety of paying them but got nowhere. In 1853, Mason spoke to both President Franklin Pierce and Secretary of State William L. Marcy about it. He pointed out that, in speaking to the Spanish minister, he learned that "the sensibilities of his government and his people had been deeply wounded." The legalistic Virginian argued "that it rests finally on treaty obligations, and were it presented by a stronger power, I am mortified in saying that this government would long since have found it expedient to discharge it."[21] He could have saved his breath. Regardless of any support from the administration, the claims had no prospect of gaining approval from a Congress increasingly hostile to anything connected with the issue of slavery.

Another minor area of diplomacy on which Mason spent time involved receptions honoring foreign dignitaries. As a Virginia aristocrat, Mason always had been concerned about honor and decorum in social matters, and that principle transferred easily to foreign affairs. He believed that the United States should treat foreign visitors in a polite, dignified manner. Such conduct not only was proper, but also it was a simple way to cultivate good relations. For example, in 1853, he urged the Senate to appropriate $20,000 for receiving a visiting warship from Turkey.[22] Five years later, Mason similarly fought for a joint resolution to make special arrangements for welcoming

Mehmed Pasha, vice-admiral of the Turkish navy. He wisely recognized "that courtesies and hospitalities of this kind are very highly appreciated, and lead to very useful results."[23]

Mason had his eye on increased trade, thinking that "a civility of this kind will bear abundant fruits, by opening new intercourses and new relations between our people and the remote people belonging to that eastern country."[24] Thoughts of trade guided his support for Commodore Perry's endeavors in Japan, as well as diplomatic efforts with other distant lands. He urged the United States not to allow opportunities to open new commercial channels with countries such as Persia to pass into European hands.[25] Even if the trade in question would not yield direct advantages to Virginia, Mason recognized that "the wealth of a nation depends on her commerce." He believed that all Americans benefited from expanded international trade.[26]

Such comments reflected Mason's nationalism in foreign affairs. His support for the *Amistad* claims may have hinted at a southern bias in his conduct of diplomatic relations, but it would be a mistake to generalize from that example. During his tenure he pushed for a number of diplomatic measures in addition to trade bills that provided benefits primarily to other sections of the country. He sought to diffuse tension between Britain and the United States that could prevent settlement in the Territory of Washington,[27] and he wanted the boundaries with both Mexico[28] and Canada clearly measured to prevent disputes.[29] Perhaps most surprising of all, given his continual skirmishes with senators from New England, Mason strongly supported the rights of that region's citizens in the ongoing controversy with Britain regarding the fisheries of Canada's coastal waters.

The fisheries problem had been a bone of contention between New Englanders and the British at least since the American Revolution. Both John Adams and John Quincy Adams had fought successfully for the rights of those fishermen,[30] but, increasingly, colonial parliaments in Canada restricted American access to their coastal waters.[31] To Americans, it seemed that the British interpretation of the 1818 treaty had changed. In 1852, Mason announced in the Senate that "suddenly, without notice of any kind, we are informed . . . that a very large British naval force has been ordered into those seas for the purpose of enforcing, at the mouth of the cannon, the construction which Great Britain has now determined to place on that convention." The Virginia senator saw Britain's actions "as a far higher offense than a breach of national courtesy" and, indeed, "as one of insult and indignity to the American people."[32] Beyond the livelihood of New England fishermen, Mason believed that the honor and reputation of the nation were at stake. He urged President Millard Fillmore to send a naval force to those waters to protect the fishermen, stating boldly that he would not "exchange one word, or write one line on the subject of these fisheries" until the British government withdrew its ships and stopped trying to make America "negotiate under duress."[33]

Mason reiterated those statements three weeks later,[34] and his rhetoric did not go unnoticed by those directly affected by the crisis. Earlier in the year he had received a letter from a feisty New Englander, asserting that the Virginian's "conduct in the Senate excites the warmest approbation along the coast" and expressing "gratification that you should so promptly tread in the steps of the illustrious Jefferson (your countryman) in vindicating that child of his policy, the nursery of American seamen."[35]

The dispute lingered for two years. Secretary of State Edward Everett worked on a treaty with the British minister to the United States, but it never reached fruition.[36] Marcy picked up where his predecessor left off, and in the summer of 1854, negotiations culminated with a treaty that gave Americans full use of the fisheries. In exchange, the United States allowed Britain free trade in most natural products between the two countries.[37] The treaty passed in the Senate with Mason's wholehearted approval.[38]

Mason also fought to reform the U.S. diplomatic and consular systems. In 1855, a House bill to remodel the systems came up for debate in the Senate. The bill simplified compensation amounts by fixing salaries and doing away with commissions, to "rid the Government of that dangerous and increasing source of wasteful expenditure which is experienced by the country" and streamline the conduct of foreign relations. Additionally, it barred foreigners from holding diplomatic or consular appointments and prohibited ministers from being absent from their post without the president's permission.[39] Mason, after first consulting with Marcy, urged his colleagues to pass the House bill without amendment.[40] The Virginian believed that the urgent need for reform required the bill's immediate approval and that problems with details could be worked out later.[41] The measure passed in less than a week.

A year later, on behalf of the Foreign Relations Committee, he presented a joint resolution to clear up some continuing inequities in the area of compensation, and the Senate approved it.[42] As usual, Mason's efforts aimed at supporting the president's power in foreign affairs. He believed that "a part of executive power is supreme control, free from the intervention of legislation, over the diplomatic service." Therefore he helped to push through a bill that left "discretionary with the President" both "the grade of ministers abroad" and the "appropriate salary" for each appointment.[43]

Issues such as consular reform, claims for compensation, and receiving foreign dignitaries rarely elicited the levels of emotion evoked when foreign affairs involved war and peace. When Mason joined the ranks of U.S. senators, no foreign policy concern had greater importance than diplomacy concerning the War with Mexico.[44] On May 13, 1846, the United States had declared war. Victory after victory on the battlefield brought huge tracts of Mexican territory under U.S. control,[45] but the unstable, unpredictable character of Mexican politics rendered peacemaking difficult. After months of irregular negotiations, President James K. Polk presented the Treaty of Guadalupe-Hidalgo to the Senate. With opposition coming only from those who wanted to acquire either all of Mexico or none of Mexico, the Senate approved it on March 10, 1848.[46]

Mason, a party to neither extreme position, voted for the treaty. He supported the war wholeheartedly, placing the blame for starting it on Mexico. In the Senate he labeled the war "just and necessary," seeing it as one that "could not have been avoided without dishonor," because "it was commenced by Mexico in the invasion of one of the States of this Confederacy." He hailed "the whole conduct and management of the war" for spreading across the country "honor in everything, not only in the unparalleled victories obtained by our arms, but in the dignity and the forbearance uniformly shown by this Republic to deluded, infatuated Mexico."[47]

Those words reflected the Virginia patrician's condescension toward America's southern neighbors. This attitude permeated Mason's foreign policy positions involving that part of the globe. The Mexican War reinforced the negative opinions he held of all Latin American governments. Five days after the peace treaty gained Senate approval but before Mexican ratification, Mason argued in favor of continuing to apply military pressure. He stressed that Americans had "learned that Mexico is a wily and faithless foe," and he asked, "Do we not know that if Mexico be brought to listen to the terms of peace, it will be because she has been prostrated and rendered powerless by the force of our arms? Do we not know that up to a very late period, with a perfect consciousness that it must be madness to resist any longer, the spirit of every party in Mexico was averse to peace? A spirit of infatuation seemed to pervade them to the last moment, when they were forced to submit to the stern lesson of inferiority."[48] Almost five years later, Mason exclaimed that "Mexico is no fit adver-

sary for such a people as ours." He deplored its "weakness" and refused to allow the United States to "be impeded in its great career by
the mere imbecility of Mexico."[49] Nonetheless he maintained that,
despite their feebleness, the United States had recognized Mexico
and the other Latin American governments "as sovereign and independent states." They had been recognized "as equals . . . before the
world," and Mason later fought attempts by Sen. Sam Houston of
Texas to inquire into the expediency of establishing protectorates over
those countries, believing that to do so would constitute an unjust
indignity toward them.[50]

Many Americans in Mason's time believed that expansion fueled
that "great career" of the United States. They thought it the nation's
"manifest destiny" to spread the benefits of its freedom over more and
more territory to more and more people.[51] Indeed, since 1800 the
republic's borders had moved farther westward and southward. Often
the most aggressive expansionists came from below the Mason-Dixon
Line, as southerners envisioned U.S. expansion into the Caribbean. Then
slavery could be extended, and their political power base in the Senate
could remain intact despite northern gains in the House.[52]

More than any other territory, those expansionists desired the
pearl of the Caribbean, the island of Cuba. They believed that the
United States had a vested interest in the island's independence from
Spain. President Franklin Pierce, an avowed expansionist, hoped that
the Cubans would launch a successful revolution and then request
admission to the Union, as Texas had.[53]

In 1854, the situation heated up, as talk of U.S. interference
and intervention contributed to the seizing of the American
steamer *Black Warrior*. Asserting that the captain had failed to
report to customs that his ship had cargo in transit (a technicality
often ignored), Spanish authorities captured it.[54] Pierce responded
quickly. On March 15, 1854, just two weeks after the seizure, he
reported to Congress that official complaints had been registered
and that he had warned Spain not to "expect that a series of unfriendly acts infringing our commercial rights and the adoption
of a policy threatening the honor and security of these States can
long consist with peaceful relations."[55]

Many southerners, hoping for a pretext to seize Cuba, anticipated a violent disruption of Spanish-American relations. Not James
Murray Mason, however. He frowned upon any scheme to take the
island by force. Instead of using violence, Mason preferred to await
the natural course of events. On the Senate floor in 1852, he expressed contentment that the island should remain under Spanish

control, "unless it can be acquired from her by voluntary cession on her part, or unless the people of Cuba, by their own act, shall sever all political connection with their European mother, and voluntarily propose annexation."[56]

Mason believed that peaceful relations could continue as long as the relatively weak government of Spain, rather than a stronger power such as Britain or France, controlled the island. Mason viewed the island as Spanish property, exactly as Oregon or New Mexico belonged to the United States. He did, however, believe it was inevitable that Cuba would become a part of the United States. He asserted that, before too long, "the fruit will ripen, and fall from the parent stem. . . . The geographical position of Cuba, with the increasing growth of this country, will determine all the rest."[57]

Finding force unnecessary, Mason opposed filibustering efforts to stir up revolution in Latin America.[58] Stressing the inherent illegality of such conduct, he maintained "that the honor of our country, as well as its safety, is deeply interested in preventing these marauding expeditions from leaving our shores with a view to commit depredations upon foreign powers."[59] Such views triumphed during the *Black Warrior* crisis, when President Pierce came out against American filibustering expeditions to Cuba by demanding strict observance of neutrality laws.[60] Shunning military options, the United States instead sought an indemnity of $300,000 and the disavowal by the Spanish government of the customs officers involved in the seizure.[61]

That summer, the Senate passed a Mason resolution asking the administration to provide up-to-date information on the diplomatic crisis.[62] Pierce responded quickly that he had nothing new to report.[63] In doing so, the president neglected to give Congress information on intensified efforts to purchase Cuba. In April, Marcy had authorized Pierre Soulé, minister to Spain, to offer as much as $130 million. If the Spanish government refused to sell, Soulé's instructions asked him to aim at "the next most desirable object, which is to detach that Island from the Spanish dominion and from all dependence on any European power."[64]

Two weeks after Mason's resolution, Marcy requested that Soulé meet with John Y. Mason, minister to France, and James Buchanan, minister to Great Britain, to consult one another and adopt "measures for perfect concert of action."[65] In October, the three met at the Belgian town of Ostend. Their report reiterated the American desire to purchase Cuba (for no more than $120 million) and asserted that, if the offer were rejected and if the island endangered U.S. security, "we shall be justified in wresting it from Spain."[66]

The rest of what became known as the "Ostend Manifesto" contained similarly inflammatory language. The message arrived in Washington on November 4, and, with its substance already known by the press, the administration was criticized from numerous quarters both at home and abroad.[67] According to Pierce's private secretary, Sidney Webster, the document "filled the president and all the members of his cabinet with amazement."[68] Not expecting anything so blunt and undiplomatic, they repudiated any idea of "wresting" Cuba from Spanish hands.[69]

The entire fiasco left a bitter taste in many mouths. After 1854, sectional expansionism preempted national expansionism.[70] Marcy lamented that the crisis resulting from the Kansas-Nebraska Act had "sadly shattered our party in all the free states and deprived it of that strength which was needed and could have been much more profitably used for the acquisition of Cuba."[71] Heightened sensitivities in the North about any further aggrandizement of the South meant that, in the future, support for purchasing the island would come primarily from the slave states.

Over four years later, in January 1859, Louisiana's Sen. John Slidell, on behalf of Mason's Foreign Relations Committee, submitted to the Senate a bill of his own to appropriate $30 million for the purpose of negotiating a treaty according to which Spain would cede Cuba to the United States.[72] Mason rose immediately to voice his support for the bill, hyperbolically labeling the acquisition of Cuba the greatest question "that has been presented for more than one generation to the consideration of Congress." He claimed not to want the island merely for the sake of expansion; rather, he asserted that "there is a political necessity devolving on this country to become the owner of Cuba."[73]

Despite such supportive rhetoric, Mason was not among those who pushed hard for measures attempting to hasten that event. The Virginian used the occasion instead to resurrect the *Amistad* claims, asserting that the Senate should consider clearing up that issue before debating Slidell's bill. Otherwise, he reasoned, the twenty-year-old claims could be a stumbling block to any negotiations aimed at acquiring the island.[74]

The *Amistad* claims had an even slimmer chance of passing in 1859 than they had had when Mason mentioned them in earlier years.[75] But he did not worry about their incendiary nature increasing any hostility toward Slidell's bill. Still viewing the acquisition of Cuba as inevitable, Mason saw the measure as only a necessary device to aid President Buchanan's diplomatic efforts. As usual, when in doubt, he supported the president, "to whom belongs, by constitutional right, the conduct of our foreign intercourse."[76] With only lukewarm support from Mason and others in the Upper South and outright opposition from the North, Slidell's proposal faded into the background as other sectional crises arose.[77]

Latin American diplomacy did not always involve war and expansionism. In 1852, the Mexican government abruptly withdrew the rights under a grant held by an American company to build a railroad across the Isthmus of Tehuantepec. Mason, as we have seen, preferred this to other proposed transcontinental routes, and he believed that most Americans supported his view that Tehuantepec offered "the most certain means of constructing a railroad." With the enterprise facing new Mexican obstacles, on July 19, he presented a resolution asking President Millard Fillmore to provide the Senate with diplomatic correspondence on the subject.[78]

After receiving the documents, he remained unsatisfied. Throughout August, with his Foreign Relations Committee considering appropriate actions, Mason asked Secretary of State Daniel Webster for more information.[79] He met with both Webster[80] and the Mexican minister to discuss the situation.[81] On August 31, Mason reported committee resolutions warning that if, "within a reasonable time," the Mexican government did not reconsider its position regarding the grant, "it will then become the duty of this Government to review all existing relations with that Republic, and to adopt such measures as will preserve the honor of the country and the rights of its citizens."[82] With the end of the session on the horizon, the Senate printed the resolutions but did not consider them.

When Congress returned, once again Mason pushed for action. He began by complimenting the other unfortunately "weak and feeble" governments of Central America for not obstructing any U.S. efforts at improving communication with the Pacific Coast. Only Mexico had refused a right-of-way. He called the Mexican government's actions "an evil hour for the interests of the world." Mason looked upon it not necessarily "as an indignity intended towards this Government," instead viewing "it only as evidence of the unfortunate imbecility which renders them incapable of maintaining government, even from month to month." He argued that public law allowed the United States to "demand of Mexico a way across Tehuantepec; and Mexico cannot refuse it unless she becomes disloyal to the general compact of nations."[83]

The work of Mason and other senators succeeded when, later that year, the United States regained, in the Gadsden Treaty, freedom of transit across the isthmus.[84] Nonetheless, ambiguities remained, even though the Buchanan administration negotiated a new treaty in 1859. By then, however, the project had encountered many obstacles, including intensified sectional rivalries. The Senate never approved the new treaty, and the road never was built.[85]

If Mason became exasperated at the way Mexico conducted diplomatic affairs, other Latin American governments also tried his patience. In 1858, U.S. relations with Paraguay deteriorated when, as Mason described it, "a very gratuitous and gross insult was offered to one of our ships . . . which remains unatoned for."[86] A Paraguayan fort had fired upon the American steamer *Water Witch,* inflicting four casualties before the ship retreated. The vessel had been attempting to explore, for commercial purposes, the navigability of the Paraná River along the Argentine border "by the express invitation, of the Argentine Confederation."[87]

Mason reported a Foreign Relations Committee resolution urging President Buchanan "to adopt such measures and such force as in his judgment may be necessary and advisable, in the event of a refusal of just satisfaction by the Government of Paraguay."[88] Mason supported the resolution fervently, believing that it had been carefully worded to preclude any objections to it. He wanted to give the president wide latitude to settle the crisis and argued that, "if there be war, that war has been begun; it is not commenced by the passage of this resolution. There was hostility and bloodshed emanating from this Power with whom we were at peace."[89] Mason preferred negotiation but supported giving Buchanan the power to use force if all diplomatic efforts failed.

In particular, he wanted action that would contradict Latin American perceptions "that while other nations immediately redress wrongs that are committed against their Governments . . . from the character of our Government it is always tardy." As a result, other countries gained commercial advantages, while the United States gained only disrespect from "the semi-barbarians."[90] Mason warned sternly that "it would be humiliating again to approach that Government unless it was aware that our President had power to enforce the demand if it should be refused."[91]

Such bold talk toward Latin American governments was easy for Mason, given his opinions of both their leaders and their people. Contradicting those who labeled Paraguay's President Carlos Antonio López the "leading spirit" in South America, Mason pointed out that, instead, "his conduct has shown him to be the leading brigand of that whole region." Additionally, he used the occasion to denounce

Latin Americans in general, enunciating his fear that, because of "the unfortunate condition of their population, the character of their population, their ignorance, the character of the mixed races there, . . . the leading spirit among them always will be the leading brigand."[92]

Mason had no doubt that López would back down under a threat of force, believing that "all leading spirits of that sort cower and quail in a cowardly manner immediately, as soon as force is presented to enforce a demand."[93] On May 5, after opponents failed in their efforts to delete references to use of force, and with Mason again urging its approval, the Senate passed the resolution.[94] Diplomacy backed by the threat of force succeeded, as the Buchanan administration obtained from Paraguay both an apology and a $10,000 indemnity.[95]

When hemispheric diplomatic problems could be handled by direct dealings with a Latin American government, generally the United States prevailed. In the 1850s, however, more often than not, Latin American diplomatic affairs also involved European powers, particularly Great Britain. Supposedly, differences with Britain in that region had been settled by the Clayton-Bulwer Treaty of 1850. The treaty called for cooperation and joint control over any isthmian canal, and also prohibited either American or British colonization of Central America. Disagreements lay ahead, however, because the British did not interpret the treaty as being retroactive; they believed that their previously existing colonies at Belize and along the Mosquito Coast could remain.[96] That interpretation became clearer to the U.S. government as the decade wore on, particularly when, in 1852, the British declared that six islands off the coast of Honduras had become the "Colony of the Bay Islands."[97]

On January 26, 1853, referring to those islands, Mason asserted in the Senate that, "if it be true that the Government of Great Britain has established a colony at the place designated, whether it be or be not in contravention of the Clayton-Bulwer treaty, that colony must be discontinued."[98] Mason did not threaten war, because he saw Britain as "civilized and enlightened" and believed that, when it realized that the colony either "violated the treaty, or that it was dangerous to our peace and safety," good sense would lead to its removal.[99]

In March, he continued to insist that the British government live up to the American interpretation of the treaty. He refused to allow Britain to carve up the Western Hemisphere for empire, as it continued to do in the Eastern Hemisphere. Preferring a peaceful solution, Mason warned that any statesman "who would precipitate his country into a war carelessly, recklessly, or idly, upon the assertion of any abstract opinion, would go down, as he would deserve, to posterity with execration." But the statesman "who would jeopard the national honor or the national safety, from any fear of war, would go down with deeper execration still."[100] Despite such saber rattling, the United States relied upon diplomacy to deal with that disagreement.[101] But the process proved painstakingly slow, and in the meantime other crises arose to strain British-American relations further.

By 1854, the center of attention for European diplomats had become the Crimean War. Keeping intact its established policy of nonintervention in Europe's affairs, the United States remained neutral.[102] It did not interfere in that distant war, in stark contrast to what Mason described as a pattern of interference in Latin America by both Britain and France. He viewed the war as merely one instance of despotic European rulers defending a "balance of power" that in reality only amounted to the right of such men to govern, control, and divide as they please. Mason condemned the war as another example of "the great principle of the divine right to govern men."[103]

United States neutrality created an opening for even greater tension in British-American relations. The critical issue came to be British recruitment of Americans to fight in the war.[104] Mason labeled such conduct "a grave offense" and a violation of Britain's "duties toward this country under the international relations which subsist between nations, and . . . our domestic laws, made for the purpose of protecting our own peace and our national honor."[105] He claimed that restraint and conciliation had marked America's conduct, and he emphasized his "fixed and settled purpose to maintain the national honor at home, and to see that it is maintained in our foreign intercourse."[106]

British-American relations became extremely chilly, but the recruitment crisis faded away slowly by the summer of 1856. The war had ended. At the Pierce administration's request,[107] the British government recalled John F. Crampton, its minister to the United States, and three of its consuls, all of whom had been involved in the illegal recruiting.[108] In the Senate, Mason agreed with Pierce's demands but also expressed gratitude that Lord Clarendon, the British secretary for foreign affairs, had taken a conciliatory tone.[109] The United States had gained a diplomatic victory over a Great Britain preoccupied by concerns on the Continent.

Simultaneous with the raging Crimean conflict, negotiations regarding British colonies in Central America continued. In early 1856, Mason, in another expression of support for executive department control over foreign affairs, complimented President Pierce's diplomatic efforts. Continually he squelched Senate debate on the subject, to allow the administration's diplomacy to proceed.[110] Additionally, he sought to aid reconciliation efforts by introducing a joint resolution for the federal government to purchase and restore the British ship *Resolute*. The abandoned vessel lay stuck on an Arctic ice floe for two years, before being brought to the United States. Mason believed the honorable gesture of restoring the ship and returning it to the Royal Navy could only benefit diplomatic relations between the two countries. The measure passed unanimously.[111] Over a year later, he claimed, with perhaps a bit of exaggeration, that "the restoration . . . went more to fix national feeling in Great Britain towards this country than any event that had ever occurred."[112]

The negotiations culminated with the October 17 signing of the Dallas-Clarendon convention, designed to supplement the Clayton-Bulwer Treaty and settle British-American differences in Central America.[113] Despite the administration's apparent success, Marcy worried that the Senate would not approve the agreement. He believed that minor changes could satisfy Mason, but with other southerners firmly against it and without support from the president-elect, Buchanan, the treaty seemed doomed.[114] Surprisingly, it passed, but it was encumbered by amendments the British refused to accept.[115]

With the parties failing to achieve a diplomatic solution, the situation remained unresolved. Mason held no personal animosity toward Britain, believing that "she has done more than any other nation to foster and create, in the arts, in science, and in literature and to extend their influences." Nonetheless, he remained irritated by that government's use of "conquest, carnage and oppression" as methods to accomplish its goals.[116]

No tactic angered a southerner more than what the Senate called "British Aggressions" on the high seas. In 1858, Great Britain increased its efforts to stop the African slave trade. Vessels engaged in the trade had been known to raise the American flag to escape search and seizure, so, with the Crimean War over and France distracted by events in Italy, the British took the opportunity to begin firing at and searching American coastal vessels in the Caribbean.[117]

On May 28, on behalf of the Foreign Relations Committee, Mason presented resolutions to the Senate approving Buchanan's sending a naval squadron to the Gulf of Mexico to protect American shipping from British actions "in derogation of the sovereignty of the United States."[118] He defended the resolutions in a speech the next day, asserting that "international law denies absolutely any right of visitation upon the high seas in time of peace" and that "the time has arrived when this question must be settled, and settled forever."[119] He maintained that the committee had framed the resolutions with peaceful intentions, stating that "war is the resort of barbarism and ruffianism. Peace is the result of civilization and refinement. It is the great end that nations have attained in ages past; and . . . the honor of this great nation, which, I trust, it will pursue, is in its example, which it will set to the world, to look upon war as the greatest evil that can befall a country next to its degradation before a foreign Power."[120] Mason did not want war, but the proud Virginian wanted the honor of the United States upheld. He confidently expected success without war, writing that "it is not considered here I think, that we shall have serious trouble . . . given us by John Bull."[121]

President Buchanan considered the situation serious enough to require the Senate to stay past adjournment for a special session to approve the resolutions.[122] On June 16, these passed, by a vote of thirty-two to three.[123] Again Mason spearheaded the push for their approval, pointing out that, in the ensuing weeks, British violations had continued unabated, in total disregard of American rights.[124]

The crisis ended in a U.S. victory. The British press saw attempts to suppress the slave trade as extremely costly and yielding meager results. Criticism from that quarter, more than the American protests, propelled the British government in late June to order an end to the searches and seizures until arrangements could be made for joint patrols by the two countries, something that the Buchanan administration refused to agree to.[125] The slave trade crisis then dropped into the background, as sectionalism and domestic issues replaced foreign affairs at center stage.

Mason's strong support of the administration's desire for action did not go unnoticed. It led Buchanan to sound him out on whether he would be interested in succeeding George M. Dallas as minister to Great Britain. While flattered by the idea, Mason "had not thought of going abroad, and thus never considered the subject connected with such a change in position." He replied that "*under no circumstances*" could he consent to taking the job, because Mason thought that Dallas, a friend and a relative by marriage, had a "peculiar fitness" for that diplomatic position.[126] It was ironic that, in spite of his noted reputation in the Senate as a strict-constructionist lawyer and advocate of southern rights, foreign affairs evoked his only offer of promotion. Less than three years later, another chief executive asked Mason to undertake the same mission, and he did not turn down Confederate President Jefferson Davis.

Chapter 6

1847–1859

Home Life and Politics of a
Virginia Senator

During his first two years in the Senate, except for the premature death of his eldest son Ben, Mason's personal life did not interfere greatly with his duties. Some matters did keep him busy beyond his work in the Senate, however, as he regularly had to travel to Philadelphia on family business, and he still held his position as a visitor of the University of Virginia.[1] But the responsibilities of being a U.S. senator had become central to Mason's existence. The job proved an invigorating tonic, and with each passing year his power and confidence grew, so that, by 1860, even critics would comment that "Mason, of Virginia . . . appeared to own the Senate Chamber."[2]

He enjoyed being back at the center of politics, but the job kept him away from his beloved family. Missing Eliza and his children, James tried to spend time at Selma as often as possible; but during sessions he generally managed to spend only one weekend per month in Winchester.[3] Feeling most comfortable in family situations, he did his best to maintain some semblance of a home while in Washington. Upon joining the House of Representatives in 1837, Mason formed what he called "a mess," sharing accommodations with a number of colleagues, among them South Carolina's John C. Calhoun and Virginia's Robert M. T. Hunter. Each took monthly turns as housekeeper, a post that involved giving household orders and keeping account of expenses that then were divided equally.

Mason believed that the mess had provided a close approximation of family living, and that such close contact had fostered warm, lasting friendships among those involved.[4] Therefore, upon entering the Senate, Mason established a similar living arrangement. Mason and Hunter were joined by Sen. Andrew P. Butler of South Carolina, and in 1852 Missouri's David Rice Atchison completed the quartet.[5] The quarters were not always comfortable,[6] but, regardless of the amenities, a spirit of camaraderie developed among the four. Often his messmates would join Mason on his weekend visits to Selma, where politics could be discussed in a relaxed atmosphere far from the turmoil of the capital.[7] The mess became a bloc of southern power that needed to be reckoned with in any policy battle during the 1850s.[8]

In 1849, Mason gained an appointment as one of the regents of the Smithsonian Institution. He took an active interest in the position and held it until the end of his Senate career.[9] But adding that extra burden to his responsibilities as senator and his continued involvement with the University of Virginia[10] left less and less time for his private law practice. Unable to give proper attention to clients, he found it necessary to turn down prospective cases and recommend other lawyers for them.[11]

That same year, Mason's burdens increased even more with the death of his father.[12] The ensuing breakup of his paternal home meant that, for James and Eliza, there would be no more cheerful visits to Clermont. As James had handled many of his father's business affairs for years, his mother, brothers, and sisters all relied upon James to deal with John Mason's estate.[13] Struck by two emotional losses, he soldiered on as the responsibilities piled higher.

After a year or so, the hurt of losing his father and oldest son had subsided. He became the family patriarch and in 1851 wrote of having "*two* grand children, one of which is old enough to call me by that appalling title of *Grand Pa*."[14] Mason's daughter Virginia remembered the family waiting with great anticipation for each of his infrequent trips home to Selma. Even in periods of tribulation, they never knew him to be "gloomy or depressed" and viewed his cheerful presence "as the best tonic to encourage and strengthen the different members of the family."[15] The children honored their father, respecting Mason and his position so much that, in 1858, his eldest daughter Anna could not bring herself to ask her father to pull strings so her husband, John Ambler, could get an appointment to "some office in one of the Departments in Washington." She instead asked

Hunter and some of her father's other colleagues "to do for me the kindship which he, as my Father may not in honor bestow upon me."[16]

As Mason made few visits home or elsewhere, most of his extant letters and speeches in the 1850s come from Washington and involve Senate debates and other aspects of his political life. While most issues he dealt with related to foreign affairs, the Constitution, or slavery, some did not fit into those categories. Mason participated in discussions on subjects ranging from flogging in the U.S. Navy[17] to a resolution that called for the federal government to purchase houses in the capital for cabinet members.[18]

Like many Virginia congressmen through the years, he took an active interest in the affairs of the District of Columbia. Mason never talked of statehood, but he believed it to be the responsibility of the Congress to follow the wishes of the district's population, whenever possible, in legislating for them. In 1850, during debates on the re-chartering of the Potomac Insurance Company of Georgetown, Mason asserted that "the people of the District of Columbia are deprived by the supreme law of the power of legislating for themselves; and that power is vested in a body not responsible to them." District residents had given him a petition asking for the company's recharter. He called attention to the fact that "in a free government, . . . the people here are subject to the rule of others"; therefore "your action ought then to correspond to what you believe to be their will . . . if you can ascertain what it is."[19] Mason saw the situation as similar to that of any territory, and he decried the notion that congressional action in that case should contradict the principle of nonintervention, but his efforts proved fruitless.[20]

Mason even voiced support for federal government spending on internal improvements in the district, such as the building of a railroad along Pennsylvania Avenue.[21] In 1852, he supported a measure providing federal funds to repair a bridge across the Potomac to Virginia,[22] and in 1854, he introduced a bill to extend the Alexandria and Washington Railroad through the city to connect it with the Baltimore and Ohio Railroad.[23] That same year he fought against a proposal to stop putting federal money in a project that supplied water to Washington and Georgetown. He argued that city expenditures "are very largely increased, not by their own act, but by the act of the Government," noting that the city suffered from the fact that government property remained exempt from taxation.[24]

Mason believed that the uniqueness of a situation where people lived under two authorities demanded that Congress use discretion in ministering to the community's needs.[25] He thought it better not to legislate for them unless requested to do so by the people, so as to prevent "an act of civil injustice to the District of Columbia."[26] But Mason's rhetoric undoubtedly sprang from personal interests, including those of his home state. The water supply situation impacted him directly on a daily basis, as he lamented living "in a part of the city where the supply is much diminished."[27] And the railroad issues affected both his life in the district and the business interests of his constituents. He admitted to having the interests of Virginians in mind during a debate on regulating bank issues. In that same speech, however, Mason confessed to having "a feeling of sympathy and kindness in everything that affects the affairs of the people of this District," because of his years in residence there, dating back to his boyhood.[28] That experience served as the basis of passionate support for the people of the District of Columbia, such as rarely had been exhibited by a Virginia senator.

Nonetheless, Mason would not have supported the district's citizens if doing so meant sacrifices for his home state. Beyond the question of southern slavery, he sought to help his constituents whenever possible. He refused to support appropriating federal money for internal improvements in Virginia, since he believed that sort of spending to be unconstitutional. But he did push for such things as a post route from Winchester to Moorefield,[29] repeal of tariff duties on imported railroad iron (as instructed by the Virginia legislature),[30] and the payment of claims to the Orange and Alexandria Railroad.[31]

Mason also showed concern for the people of Harpers Ferry. In 1853, he supported the residents' desire to return the federal armory to civilian superintendency, which it had enjoyed before 1841. He claimed that "there is existing at Harper's Ferry . . . a great deal of disaffection, amounting almost to an odious feeling on the part of the citizens." Mason emphasized that work "by governmental routine" forces mechanics to be "mere operatives, made to do a certain class of work and a certain quantity of work in a certain manner, it dampens the inventive faculty and discourages everything like enterprise."[32]

Over a year later, he attempted to get federal money appropriated for improvements, repairs, and new machinery at the armory. Particularly, he wanted money to build a new arsenal because the current building storing the arms had been inundated by the Potomac River two or three years earlier.[33] In making both proposals, Mason stressed that his strong interest in the armory came in part from the proximity of Harpers Ferry to Winchester; he claimed, as a result, to have personal knowledge of the situation there.[34]

Fiercely proud of his native state, Mason defended it whenever he saw it attacked or ridiculed on the Senate floor. In 1852, he replied good-naturedly to a comment made by Senator Atchison that the Appomattox and James rivers were merely "little streams, which would not make good mill-streams in the West." Mason pointed out that the Appomattox "is an old and venerable river" and that the James "is one of the largest southern rivers," its entire length lying in Virginia. He then asked if Missouri "possesses a whole river within its borders?" He admitted that rivers passed through it, but asserted that the state could "not boast of a single river of its own." In spite of that, Atchison had the audacity "to contrast the rivers of the State of Virginia with those of the State of Missouri, when the latter State has no entire river of its own at all!" The Senate erupted in hearty laughter, a clear proclamation that Mason had won the argument.[35]

Unlike his grandfather, who found sessions of the Virginia House of Burgesses to be tedious settings for "pointless oratory . . . of irresponsibility and stupidity,"[36] James Murray Mason received great enjoyment from the legislative process itself, and especially Senate debates. Despite boasting that he took "up as little time in debate as any gentleman on this floor," Mason disagreed with the notion asserted by some of his colleagues that time spent debating was time wasted. He exclaimed that "ours is a Government of public opinion. It is not a Government of force. It is not a government of absolute will. It is a Government controlled and directed by the opinions and judgements of the people," and he saw those debates as necessary components of the legislative process that helped enable the people's will to be clearly expressed.[37]

Mason thrived on the daily political give-and-take of the U.S. Congress. But, in addition to the politics of the Senate floor, he reveled in politics in general. Elected, like his friend Hunter, as a champion of states' rights,[38] Mason's outspoken trumpeting of the southern cause made politics important far beyond getting himself reelected. He focused particularly on the deepening rift between North and South and saw the Democratic Party as the best hope to preserve the Union. After the Compromise of 1850, the Virginian believed that, although the clouds had passed, they had not gone forever. Mason wrote to Rives that he had "little faith in the present smooth aspect of our political sea." From "thirty years experience," he saw the North determined to destroy "large portions of our population as an element of political power." He hoped that "for all these forebodings God grant I may be found in error—But although yet certainly a young man, I am too old, to confuse hope with experience."[39]

He also followed presidential politics closely. As early as March

1851, Mason expressed certainty that General Winfield Scott would be the Whig Party candidate for president in 1852. He likened "little Stephen Douglass" to a David who could slay Goliath ahead of him, but Mason proclaimed himself "too politic" to venture an opinion on the Democratic side.[40] When New Hampshire's Franklin Pierce gained the Democratic nomination, Mason supported him without reservations, believing that "*our general*, I trust and believe will come nearer to the standard of old Virginia republicanism, as distinguished from wild northern democracy, than any man we have had since the days of Jefferson."[41]

Mason expressed no thoughts of disunion if Pierce lost and had only kind words for the Whig candidate, believing that, even in conquered Mexico, "the name of Scott will be treasured."[42] But when the South voted overwhelmingly Democratic, he rejoiced at what he labeled a massive "defection in the whig ranks."[43] When Pierce won, he took an active interest in the formation of a cabinet. He anticipated "his old friend" William L. Marcy's appointment as secretary of state[44] and urged a reluctant Jefferson Davis to accept an appointment as secretary of war because of its importance to "the state's rights party."[45]

By the time of the 1856 presidential election, the political scene had changed considerably. The Kansas-Nebraska Act of 1854 had led to the beginnings of a new two-party system in American politics. The Whig Party nationwide and the Democratic Party in the North splintered over the opening up of those territories to the possibility of slavery.[46] In northern states, those angered by the slavery issue coalesced slowly into a new party and began to call themselves Republicans.

The Republican Party took stands on all the usual issues from the Pacific railroad to the tariff, but its position on slavery drew all the attention.[47] The 1856 party platform labeled slavery a "relic of barbarism" and a blatant violation of Jefferson's words in the Declaration of Independence that "all men are created equal and have inalienable rights to life, liberty, and the pursuit of happiness."[48] The party denied that the federal government had any power to interfere with slavery in the slave states, but it sought to prevent any future expansion of the South's peculiar institution.[49]

For president, the Republicans nominated explorer John C. Frémont.[50] The Democrats rejected President Pierce and nominated Pennsylvania's James Buchanan. Having served most recently as minister to Great Britain, Buchanan had had the good fortune to be out of the country during the Kansas-Nebraska debates. That left him relatively untainted compared to other potential candidates.[51] With the South solidly in Democratic hands, Buchanan needed to carry only a few states in the North to win the election.

James Murray Mason and most other southerners saw a Buchanan victory as an absolute necessity if the Union were to be preserved. He could not stomach the thought of Virginians being ruled by a party that possessed attitudes directly hostile to the South. He prepared for the worst. At Selma in late September, he wrote to Secretary of War Davis that he believed "in the event of Frémont's election the South should not postpone but at once proceed to 'immediate, absolute, and eternal separation'." In addition, Mason urged Davis to agree to Gov. Henry A. Wise's request that the Virginia militia's outdated flint muskets be replaced by percussion arms, and offered to distribute the state's weapons throughout the South if necessary.[52]

That necessity never arose, as Buchanan carried the northern states of Illinois, Indiana, Pennsylvania, and New Jersey, to eke out a narrow victory.[53] In November, a committee on behalf of the Democrats of Richmond asked Mason to attend a dinner for Virginia's presidential electors. He declined the invitation because of prior engagements in Washington but pledged to be with them "in heart and sentiment." In a letter to the group, he delineated his deep feelings about their "noble Commonwealth."

Mason proclaimed grandly that "Virginia, the oldest of the States, and the pioneer to independence, has a great destiny to fulfill, and greatly has she realized that responsibility." At the same time, the Old Dominion remained "true to the Constitution, because always true to herself, the waves of faction at home, or of dark conspiracy abroad, break harmlessly at her feet." Mason believed that Virginia's "honor is in her own keeping" and that the "sacred trust, transmitted from sire to sire, and from generation to generation, shall vindicate her position as a free, sovereign, and independent Republic, submissive to her Federal obligations so long as they are respected by her associate Republics, but ready to assert and establish her separate existence when such submission is no longer consistent with honor."[54] Those proud words expressed the true sentiments of the statesman from Winchester. And the underlying message was that Virginia could only remain in the Union if the American people continued to deny the Republican Party control of the federal government.

Less than a year later, with the two sections enjoying a state of temporary truce, Mason received an invitation to go to Boston and participate in ceremonies surrounding the unveiling of a statue of Gen. Joseph Warren on Bunker Hill. He had never visited New En-

gland. And, despite having great differences with men such as
Massachusetts's Sen. Charles Sumner, Mason got along quite well
with a number of other "Yankees." He accepted.[55]

Mason spent an entire week in Boston, and on June 17, he spoke
at the dedication ceremonies. His words paid tribute to the fallen
heroes of the battle that took place there over eighty years earlier:
"Here upon Bunker Hill was laid the corner-stone of American independence and cemented with our blood." Mason pledged that, when
he returned to Virginia's "blessed hills," he would tell his people
"that I found the spirit of Massachusetts as buoyant, as patriotic, as
completely filled with the emanations that should govern patriotism
when I visited Bunker Hill, as it was when the battle was fought."[56]

Having dispensed with the nationalistic sentiments required for
the occasion, Mason finished his speech by taking the opportunity to
feed his states' rights line to the audience. The Virginian expressed an
earnest desire "to say to you people of Massachusetts that our Government is a government whose only sanction is in the honor and
good faith of the States; and to proclaim that so long as there are
honor and good faith in the States and in the people of the States, the
Union will be perpetuated." He went on to "invoke of you all that
you shall require of those who represent you that they administer the
Government as it was founded by our fathers under the Constitution, and not otherwise."[57] James Murray Mason had gone to New
England, in many ways the heart of abolitionism, and managed to
get in a few words in favor of strict constructionism!

After the ceremony, the festivities continued with a banquet, fire-
works, a band concert, and a grand ball that brought the day of won-
drous celebration to a close.[58] The *Boston Post* lauded the Virginia
senator, claiming that "no stranger who visited Boston to join the
ceremonies of the 17th has left a more agreeable impression upon
those with whom he came in contact, than the distinguished Senator
from the Old Dominion." The paper praised "his genial and affable
manners, his generous estimate of all he saw and heard, and his gratification at the frank and cordial civilities offered to him on all hands."
Complimenting both his speech and his charm, the paper asserted
that "he will leave many newly formed acquaintances in Boston who
will cherish the recollection of his visit as among the most pleasing
records of their memory; and we are sure, he will return to his home
with convictions in favor of men and facts here which will give additional ardor to his love of the Union, and increased strength to that
fraternal feeling which is the only link that can render our nationality
indissoluble."[59] Indeed, his 1857 trip did become one of Mason's

most cherished reminiscences, contrasting strongly with his return to Boston over four years later in a "visit" that received a much less friendly reception.

Fifteen years later, Gideon Welles, U.S. secretary of the navy during the Civil War, remembered Mason's reception at Bunker Hill as one of "sycophantic adulation," an occasion that "convinced him the Yankees were deficient in manly spirit and needed Virginians to govern and inculcate in them self-respect."[60] If Welles's summation was correct, that 1857 journey to Boston only reinforced negative opinions Mason previously had held toward New England and the North. Among other things, he saw the South as superior in terms of everything from education[61] and churches[62] to system of labor and economics.[63] Those beliefs grew even stronger with the Panic of 1857.

The panic originated as a simple recession, but a series of bank failures transformed it into a major crash.[64] Mason focused upon the railroads as the cause of the panic, because an expansion of credit to build them had led to rapid speculation and an unrealistic boom. He described the course of the panic in a letter to George M. Dallas, stating that "Philadelphia banks fell first—yielding to the first recoil of the first wave. The middle country south of New York went with it."[65]

Mason's appraisal had a high degree of accuracy. From 1850 to 1857, the number of banks in the United States nearly doubled. But the expanding economy more often indicated an increase in debt rather than an increase in returns.[66] In the Senate, Mason used the panic to reinforce his arguments against building a transcontinental railroad, asserting that many of the recent bankruptcies were due to construction of railroads in areas not yet prepared for them.[67] As a southerner, however, he came to a more important conclusion be-cause of the panic—that he and others were correct in their opinion that the South's economic system was superior to that of the North.

Mason emphasized to Dallas that "Virginia, in her old and long established banks," still paid specie.[68] Southerners did suffer from the panic, but not as deeply as northerners. In addition, recovery came sooner for them because of rising prices for cotton and other staple crops. They believed that recurring economic disasters came because of irresponsible northern bankers, merchants, and speculators. By 1858, the panic had given southerners even more evidence that an economy based upon agriculture and slavery had greater merit and stability than a commercial economy. This notion gave them one more reason to feel superior to northerners.[69]

The 1858 congressional elections moved the South even closer to breaking with the North once and for all. The Democratic Party suffered a net loss of eighteen seats, taking big losses in the key states of New York and Pennsylvania. That Republicans might win a future presidential election solely on the basis of northern votes had become a distinct possibility.[70]

Perhaps surprisingly, Mason spent more time in the Senate that year dealing with foreign affairs than any other set of issues. Even the simmering Kansas situation had reached an apparent stalemate. His influence continued to grow, even over his friend Hunter, who more and more frequently in letters to his wife remarked, "Mason says" this or that.[71] In addition, Mason remained involved with University of Virginia business, despite having given up his position as a visitor years earlier.[72]

The Thirty-fifth Congress came to a close in March 1859. Sectional issues did not dominate that session's final weeks. The nation's business could still go forward, despite hostile feelings between the North and the South. Mason criticized too much federal government spending as often as he criticized northern policies towards slavery. For the last time in his Senate career, foreign affairs took priority, particularly relations with Great Britain. Not always locked in bitter controversy, the two governments could be sociable. Sir Francis Napier, British minister to the United States, a man well thought of throughout the capital, retired from his position. On February 17, Mason attended the Washington social event of the season, a ball held in honor of the Napiers.[73]

The legislative session ended a few weeks later with a visit from Richard Cobden, a noted member of the British Parliament. Mason greeted him first, followed by Douglas and other colleagues.[74] For northern and southern legislators to spend February and March of 1859 courting foreign representatives must have seemed strange, given the tensions just below the surface. That picture becomes positively surreal if one realizes that, at that same time, in the mind of a fanatical abolitionist named John Brown, plans were being formulated that would make such harmonious behavior little more than a wistful memory.

Chapter 7

1859–1861

Mason and the Coming of the Civil War

In 1859, the sleepy village of Harpers Ferry, Virginia, became the focal point of a nation edging toward bifurcation. Located on the Potomac River in a picturesque mountain setting, the hamlet housed the federal government's armory and rifle works, where several hundred workers produced thousands of arms each year. Nearby stood the arsenal that contained military stores. Otherwise the town had the appearance of a quiet nineteenth-century river town. The Baltimore and Ohio Railroad crossed the river there, helping to keep the people in contact with the outside world, but the area still seemed isolated from the rest of civilization.[1]

Harpers Ferry was not isolated from one place, though; that was Winchester, the home of James Murray Mason. A branch of the railroad traveled the twenty miles between the towns, making them seem even closer to each other than they were. On the fateful Sunday night of October 16, 1859, with the first session of the Thirty-sixth Congress still seven weeks away, Mason was taking advantage of the break by spending time with his family. All of his children had reached adulthood by then,[2] but a few of them remained at home, and visits by grandchildren and friends warmed his heart and kept Selma a busy center of activity.

While Mason enjoyed the tranquil time at home with his family,

John Brown and a small band of abolitionist followers seized the armory, arsenal, and rifle works at Harpers Ferry, with the idea of fomenting a slave insurrection.[3] Although Brown's men had cut the telegraph wires, individuals traveling on horseback and by rail spread word of the situation to U.S. President James Buchanan and Virginia's Gov. Henry Wise. Late the next morning, private citizens heeded a call to arms and began to exchange fire with Brown and his men. Militia forces arrived late in the afternoon; before midnight, federal troops reached the scene, and Col. Robert E. Lee took command. The next morning, these troops stormed the fire engine house where Brown, his party, and his hostages had been trapped. Moments later, ten raiders—including two of Brown's sons—dead or dying, lay on the dew-soaked grass, and the old man himself had been captured.[4]

Not long after Brown's surrender, Senator Mason arrived at Harpers Ferry. He and others in Winchester had learned of the attack on Monday, when the alarm rang out through the surrounding countryside. Mason interrogated the wounded Brown in the company of Governor Wise, Colonel Lee, and others, including a reporter for the *New York Herald*.[5] That paper published the interview three days later, giving the world a glimpse into the mind of the leader of the abortive slave revolt.

More than anything else, Mason wanted to know who had provided the financial support for the invasion. But the grizzled abolitionist refused to implicate others, claiming that "no man sent me here; it was my own prompting, and that of my maker, or that of the devil, whichever you please to ascribe it to." Mason pressed him, asking, "How many are engaged with you in this movement?" Again, however, Brown would not give a satisfactory response. He gave solid answers only to questions regarding why he did what he did, stating, "We came to free the slaves, and only that." When Mason asked how he justified such actions as killing "some people who were passing along the streets quietly," Brown replied, "I think, my friend, you are guilty of a great wrong against God and humanity. . . . I think I did right, and that others will do right to interfere with you at any time and all times."[6]

Having formed a first-hand opinion of what happened and why, Mason returned to Selma. There he wrote a letter to the editor of the *Constitution,* so that "the material facts attending the late incendiary attack on the town of Harper's Ferry would be correctly understood." Mason emphasized that "there was no *insurrection,* in any form whatsoever, on the part of any of the inhabitants or residents of that town." Brown, "the leader of the armed miscreants," expected such an uprising but met disappointment. The Virginia senator exclaimed, "The fact is undoubted that *not a man, black or white, joined them* after they came into Virginia, or gave them aid or assistance in any form." As for "the negroes, it is certain that the only emotion evinced by them was of alarm and terror, and their only refuge sought at their masters' homes." He asserted that "abolition tracts, newspapers, and orators" had made an impression upon the invaders; Mason described the one thousand sharpened pikes they brought as being "a most effective arm for hands unskilled in military weapons—leaving no doubt for whom they were destined."[7]

It took no great imagination to visualize slaves armed with the pikes of northern abolitionists impaling innocent Virginia women and children.[8] Mason seized upon that image and tirelessly sought answers for his still unanswered questions. When the Senate opened on December 5, he rose to make the first order of business his resolution to appoint a committee "to inquire into the facts attending to the late invasion and seizure of the armory and arsenal of the United States at Harper's Ferry." Additionally, the committee was to investigate "whether any citizens of the United States, not present, were implicated therein, or accessory thereto by contributions of money, arms, munitions or otherwise."[9] He claimed to be "seeking to make no political capital of this" and stated that he wanted only "to get the facts before the people—nothing more." Nonetheless, the Virginian warned that, if the committee determined that Congress could not prevent a recurrence of the incident, not only the southern states but all the states would have "to provide measures for their own protection."[10]

Mason excoriated Brown and other abolitionists for believing "that the slaves are always ready for revolt." He pointed out that every one of the slaves whom Brown captured, as soon as he could escape, "ran home to his master's house." The Virginia senator went even further, proclaiming that Brown had failed because of the loyalty of Virginia's slaves. According to Mason, "The affection, the kindness, the love which they bear to their masters and to their masters' homes" prevented Brown from "raising a formidable insurrection."[11] Privately, Mason wrote that Harpers Ferry "served only to arouse, excite through the whole length and breadth of the old dominion—a feeling of State pride."[12]

Mason grasped the opportunity to become the spokesman for southern anger toward the North. He speculated broadly that the "funds and counsel" behind the invasion had come "chiefly from the New England States."[13] The Virginia senator attacked writings such as the antislavery propaganda book, *Impending Crisis,* by Hinton

Rowan Helper, which he labeled "the most, vile, false, truthless compendium of slander upon the South" he ever had read. He claimed that the author sought "to array man against man" in class warfare between southern slaveholders and nonslaveholders. But, since very few of those who rose to stop John Brown owned slaves, Mason could deny any distinction between the two groups and any chance for northerners to create one.[14]

The Virginian next turned his accusing finger toward the Republican Party, condemning it as an organization based solely upon abolitionism. He claimed that, without the slavery issue, the party would dissolve. Mason asked, "If you are not Abolitionists, why this constant war upon slavery?" Then he defended southern comments that electing a Republican president in 1860 would lead to a dissolution of the Union, declaring, "If I know anything of the condition of the southern States—a condition into which they have been brought by the conduct of your people, under your lead . . . the question will not be, shall the Union be dissolved?" Instead, he believed that "the question among patriots—honest-minded, thinking, responsible men there—will be: is there any mode on God's earth by which the Union can be preserved?"[15] In spite of such harsh partisan rhetoric, the Senate approved Mason's resolution unanimously later that day.[16]

Almost immediately, the Select Committee on the Invasion of Harpers Ferry began its six-month investigation,[17] with Mason chairing and doing most of the questioning.[18] He asked Governor Wise to send him relevant documents in the possession of the Virginia state government.[19] He wrote to prosecuting attorney Andrew Hunter, requesting information on the various witnesses to be called.[20] Seeking to leave no stone unturned, Mason even wrote to abolitionist Dr. Samuel Howe, requesting any correspondence he had had with Brown, Massachusetts Sen. Henry Wilson, and others.[21]

The committee examined thirty-two witnesses, including New York Sen. William H. Seward, Secretary of War John B. Floyd, and Colonel Lee.[22] The proceedings set a precedent for subpoenaing private citizens to testify,[23] but not all did so willingly.[24] Thus Mason spent a great deal of time doing all he could to force them to answer questions. "Contumacious witnesses" was the term the Senate used to describe such men as abolitionist Frank B. Sanborn, Brown lionizer James Redpath, and the invader's son, John Brown, Jr., who sought to avoid testifying.[25]

The latter two wrote mocking replies to the committee chairman[26] and never testified.[27] Efforts to secure testimony by Sanborn and New York abolitionist Thaddeus Hyatt, however, drew more publicity than any of the other cases. On April 3, U.S. deputy federal marshals arrested Sanborn in Concord, Massachusetts,[28] but soon thereafter he was rescued by what Mason termed "a tumultuous body of people, whom I call a mob."[29] A writ of habeas corpus for his release hastily followed and gained the approval of the Massachusetts Supreme Court. The situation led to a heated debate between Mason and his old nemesis, Massachusetts Sen. Charles Sumner, who denied that a mob had rescued Sanborn, claiming rather that the potential witness had been freed legally by the judicial process.[30] The debate evolved into one dealing with the broad question of the committee's authority, continuing off and on for almost a week.[31] Sanborn never testified.

Neither did Hyatt, even though the Senate, on February 21, approved a warrant for his arrest.[32] Officials took him into custody, and Mason continued to attempt to get answers from the abolitionist.[33] But Hyatt would reply only with what amounted to arguments about why he did not have to respond.[34] The entire affair left Mason flabbergasted. He believed it to be the patriotic duty of every citizen who had information needed by the Congress to "give it without hesitancy, without reserve, far more without denial." The committee chairman asserted angrily "that no man will be tolerated anywhere that will set up his conscience against the constituted authority of the country." He thundered, "If he has such a conscience, and it is really irritated, or vexed, or injured by the operation of the Government of his country and the laws of his country, let him leave it, and go elsewhere."[35] Mason's patience had run out. His legalistic mind could not countenance resistance to the committee, because he "could not doubt the power of the Senate to bring this witness here, and compel him to testify, unless I doubted the capacity of the American people for self-government."[36]

The committee wound up its business and submitted its reports to the Senate on June 15. Mason read the conclusions of the report he wrote on behalf of the majority. While not suggesting any specific measures that should be taken, he warned that, if the states "do not hold it incumbent on them, after the experience of the country, to guard in future by appropriate legislation against occurrences similar to the one here inquired into, the committee can find no guarantee elsewhere for the security of peace between the States of the Union."[37] As for backing Brown might have received for his deeds, the committee determined that he did not trust even those closest to him with his plans. But the report criticized all those who had given Brown financial support for being ignorant and irresponsible with funds that eventually came to be used for illegal purposes.[38]

After the months of vituperative debate, the report seemed anticlimactic. But the entire situation had heightened tensions as the federal government attempted to get on with the business of running the country. In the Senate, issues concerning slavery once again took center stage.[39] In January, Mason defended southern slavery as a vibrant, positive social system.[40] He asserted that "the experience of the southern States has shown that the condition of African bondage elevates both races."[41] The Virginian contrasted his beloved South with the North, stating that northern states should be labeled "servile states" rather than "free states." He argued that, "where, unhappily for them, they can have no slaves, they yet have a class of servants who are not as free as those whom they serve—whose will is subjected to that of another by contract." Therefore, he felt, the northern states were no freer than the southern states.[42]

In February, Mason's senate activities came to a halt when he rushed to Selma to be with Eliza, who was ill.[43] A week later, after assuring himself that his wife would recover and after conversing with people in Winchester, he returned to Washington, determined to make certain that the John Brown raid never would be repeated in his state. Earlier he had supported efforts to return the facilities at Harpers Ferry to civilian control,[44] but now Mason changed his mind and asserted that they needed to remain under military supervision. He wanted the federal government to station a military guard there permanently, because he had noticed that, at night, the public property's only protection consisted of a single "uneducated, illiterate man . . . who, for the little emolument that belongs to it, agreed to sit up all night, and was not of as much value, when the banditti came, as a good watchdog."[45]

Beyond the immediate defense of Harpers Ferry, Mason focused on the broader issue of protecting his home state as a whole. In the Senate, Mason announced regretfully that the deterioration of relations between states had caused the Virginia state legislature to appropriate money for the purchase of arms to defend the commonwealth. European arms were being considered, because "I should doubt very much whether you can trust private manufacturers as you can trust Government manufacture." He believed that "private interests, freed from public responsibility . . . will manufacture in the cheapest manner they can"; in something as important as arms for defense Virginia could not run such a risk.[46]

For a brief time in March and April, Mason's attention did shift away from slavery issues.[47] But discussions on topics such as Indian affairs[48] and railroad construction[49] could not keep the divisive issue away from the center of his attention for long. In April, a proposal to educate African Americans in the District of Columbia met vigorous opposition from Mason. Such a law would differ from laws in the surrounding states of Maryland and Virginia. Mason fought any attempts to pass different laws for the district, and he especially became agitated when the measure in question related to blacks and slavery. As to the education proposal, Mason pointed out that "the statute-books of the adjoining States, and of all the slave States, show that it is not considered expedient or wise in a State where there is negro slavery, to educate the negro race at all, bond or free." He again brought up the subject of how northerners treated free blacks and invited the freemen to return to bondage in Virginia if freedom proved too difficult.[50]

The reintroduction of homestead legislation also stirred up the slavery question. Mason viewed slavery as hopelessly entwined with any homestead proposal, because "the purpose is avowed by means of the gratuitous distribution of the public lands, to preoccupy the Territories by population from the free States, and thus incidentally, but of necessity, to exclude slavery."[51] The debates became quite contentious, as southerners, with the notable exception of Tennessee's Sen. Andrew Johnson,[52] presented a united front against the bill. Mason occupied the vanguard position, again lambasting Republicans as having abolitionism as their only "principle of cohesion." He quoted Seward to prove that they wanted "to destroy that condition of society which is mixed up with the very existence of the South" and claimed that homestead legislation would be the instrument used by them to gain control of the federal government and implement their antisouthern policies. This policy would give away public lands for partisan political ends, in "utter departure from the spirit, intent, and meaning of the Constitution which holds these States together."[53]

Mason used racial arguments, in addition to constitutional ones, against the bill's passage. Discussing free blacks as possible homesteaders, Mason stated that he could not "imagine a greater curse that can be inflicted on the white race anywhere, than to send them a parcel of negroes in any condition other than that of slavery." Similarly, he could not think of "a greater curse" for blacks than setting "them free to work out in freedom their own salvation. It would end . . . in their relapsing into utter and brutal barbarism." Canadians were trying to expel free blacks "as nuisances" who consume but do not labor; Haitians were "mere jobbers about the streets" who "pick up enough to answer the immediate necessities of the day, and then go to sleep. Thrift, providence, accumulation, are unknown to them." With freedom promising disaster for blacks, Mason wanted no more emancipation, preferring to leave blacks in bondage, "as the best condition" for them.[54]

Just weeks later, from April 23 to May 3, the Democratic Party met in Charleston, South Carolina, to adopt a platform and nominate a candidate for the 1860 presidential election. Northern delegates expected the convention to nominate Illinois Sen. Stephen A. Douglas, but southern delegates arrived in the Palmetto State determined to prevent such an outcome.[55] Douglas had stood in opposition to the South on Kansas, had expounded the "Freeport Doctrine" and, most recently, had fought resolutions, introduced by Mississippi Sen. Jefferson Davis, to protect slavery in the territories.[56]

The Davis resolutions denied the right of any territory's inhabitants to take measures that could discourage slavery, attacked northern personal liberty laws that hampered enforcement of Mason's Fugitive Slave Law, and demanded a federal slave code for the territories.[57] A bold final stand for southern rights, the proposal had no hope of passing, but it clearly delineated the South's position and dared northerners to disagree. President Buchanan gave his tacit approval, and the predominantly southern Senate Democratic Caucus concluded that Davis's resolutions embodied the correct interpretation of the Constitution.[58]

Southerners at the Charleston convention wanted Davis's resolutions put into the party platform. However, if Douglas supporters did not control the Senate, they did control the party's national organization, and they refused to adopt a platform plank that would prove detrimental to their election hopes in the North. The southern position lost by twenty-seven votes. With the announcement of the tally, fifty delegates from a cross-section of the slave states abruptly walked out.[59] The convention adjourned a few days later, having made plans to meet in Baltimore on June 18. Shattered by the dissension, the Democrats had proven themselves unable to agree upon a candidate.[60]

In the Senate, Mason and other southern Democrats were stunned. The crisis many of them had dared to provoke was unfolding before their eyes. Democratic disaster meant Republican success, which, beyond the implications of that for the South, would destroy their own power base as committee chairmen in Congress.[61] They appealed to those who had walked out to show up in Baltimore and delay a meeting at Richmond, which had been scheduled for June 11. Twenty congressmen signed the appeal, including Mason, Davis, Virginia's Robert M. T. Hunter, and Louisiana's Judah P. Benjamin and John Slidell. The group warned that acting prematurely in haste "would inevitably result in incurable division of our party, the sole conservative organization remaining in our country."[62]

While the crisis developed, Mason stubbornly continued to argue in favor of the Davis resolutions. He disagreed with Douglas's claims that Davis's ideas were mere abstractions, asserting that the questions raised needed to be settled once and for all. He then recounted a decade of southern disappointments, from the Wilmot Proviso to the Kansas-Nebraska Act. He discussed the Supreme Court's Dred Scott decision, in which "the power of Congress to prohibit slavery in the Territories was disaffirmed absolutely, unequivocally, without qualification." He asserted once more his conviction that the Constitution did not establish slavery but only "recognize[d] it as an existing condition." Mason attacked the notion of "popular sovereignty," claiming that sovereignty rested in the hands of the states,[63] which were "as completely independent of the Federal Government . . . as Great Britain or France."[64]

After cataloguing northern and southern differences of opinion, Mason added an incongruous call for unity. He declared that his "earnest anxiety" was "that the Government which has been transmitted to us by our forefathers shall be preserved." With great emotion, he claimed to be "attached to it, as you all are, doubtless, not only because it came as an inheritance from an honored line of ancestors, but because of its intrinsic merit, its excellence in itself. It seems almost to have been the work of an inspiration of the day." He asserted that preserving the Union was the duty "of all good men," a duty owed "to our race" and "to the world." Mason expressed certainty that, once it disappeared, it never could be reconstituted. Despite the numerous dark clouds surrounding it, he exclaimed that the Union could never be destroyed "if it is administered by the functionaries of the Government loyally, honestly, and honorably; in other words, if they and their constituents will keep the bargain which their fathers made."[65]

Two days before that speech, the Republicans nominated Abraham Lincoln of Illinois to carry their banner in the presidential contest.[66] In June, appeals from Mason and others came to naught, as the Democratic convention once more ended in an impasse, with southern delegations walking out. In the Baltimore convention, unlike the one in Charleston, however, Douglas held the upper hand and quickly emerged as the truncated Democratic party's candidate for president. Southern Democrats nominated their own candidate, Vice-President John C. Breckinridge of Kentucky, assuring that a divided party would enter the crucial electoral contest.[67]

Division also ruled in the Senate, where the emotionally charged issue of the slave trade reappeared in May. A bill had been introduced to strengthen U.S. efforts to enforce laws against the trade, as well as to authorize President Buchanan to make a treaty or contract by which the federal government would care for illegally seized Africans for twelve months after their return to their homeland. Mason rose to support an amendment offered by Jefferson Davis that would reduce the measure to one authorizing an appropriation for the execution of the existing law. The Virginian began by stressing that he "never could see any warrant in the Constitution by which the United States undertook to suppress the slave trade." He made that statement solely on the basis of constitutional law and admitted that, although the question should have been left with the states, the federal government could not overturn a now established policy.[68]

Mason sought to keep the United States from committing itself "to any general policy of philanthropy or humanity" when illegally shipped Africans were captured. He only wanted the letter of the law enforced, taking "care that no injury shall result." He did not want the federal government to assume the burden of "the maintenance and care" of those blacks after their return to Africa. He remarked that returning "them to the coast of Africa, we should take care after they get there, that they shall be put in some position where they will not starve. I do not see that we are called upon to go any further than that."[69]

Debates on the slave trade reached to the heart of the differences between northerners and southerners, revealing much about Mason's thinking regarding the South's relationship with the world around it. Over a year earlier, Mason had argued similarly, without success, against President Buchanan's sending illegally shipped blacks back to Africa. He asserted then that, if humanity had been consulted instead of the law, the Africans would have been allowed to stay in the United States and would have been put in bondage. Instead, they were "to return to savageism," where, despite supervision by the Colonization Society in Liberia, "one half, or two thirds, will escape like rabbits, and go in the bush to get away from the restraints of civilized life."[70] Mason wanted half-hearted enforcement of present laws rather than increased federal activity to stop the trade. He could not "imagine greater cruelty exercised upon any being of the human race than is now exercised on these Africans" by sending them back to Africa at tremendous cost to the government.[71]

In June, Mason broadened the issue into a diplomatic one. Making one of his last senatorial references to foreign affairs, he criticized France's and Great Britain's conduct regarding the slave trade. He reserved his harshest words for the British government, claiming that "all her professions of humanity, all her protestations against the alleged atrocity of that trade, are utterly hollow and insincere." He charged that Britain's protestation of leadership in suppressing the slave trade was "hypocritical, . . . false," and "disloyal to her race." Recent successes in stopping the trade had been American and not British, leading Mason to suggest canceling "all treaty obligations with Great Britain on this subject." That way, "whatever may remain to be done on our part shall be done separately; and then we can see where Great Britain really stands upon the subject of the African slave trade."[72]

Mason's efforts did little more than stir up passions. The issue faded as quickly as it had emerged, lost in a rising cacophony of voices from both North and South. All spoke very emotionally and refused to listen to any contrary opinions. Willingness to compromise vanished. Deliberation and debate were poisoned by extremism. Mason despaired that a dreaded democracy had overtaken his beloved American republic. He lamented that "we have known what was unknown forty years ago—citizens of the States canvassing the States, addressing the people in public assemblies for a seat in the Senate. . . . I say, sir, the Senate of the United States has changed its character in forty years. The Senate of the United States was intended by the Constitution to be a deliberative body; it was intended by the tenure of its office—a more extended tenure than is given to any office of the Federal Government, . . . to be placed beyond the reach of popular emotion. We have passed that stage. . . . The Government is undergoing a change." With that change, Mason saw disaster. "We are realizing Democratic proclivities. We are realizing that which the Constitution never intended. The Constitution has guaranteed a republican form of government, and that is as much an exclusion of a democracy as it is a monarchy."[73] The sixty-one-year-old patrician was trying to call back the world of his grandfather, but his words evoked only outdated echoes amid changing times.

The next day, Mason met with Virginia "fire-eater" Edmund Ruffin at the capitol. Ruffin entered in his diary that "Mr. Mason said we were approaching the end of the government."[74] In his final speech of the session, Mason warned that, if the government came "into the hands of an irresponsible numerical majority" in blatant disregard of the Constitution, "where it will end, Heaven knows. I presume it will vibrate for a time through anarchy, and terminate in despotism."[75]

Northerners and southerners irrevocably approached disaster as the election campaign unfolded. The Democratic Party, perhaps the last truly national organization to split over slavery, had left the door open for a Republican victory. Some Democrats attempted to reunite the party to prevent such an outcome, but those efforts proved futile.[76] Most party members, including Mason, merely braced themselves for the catastrophe instead of doing anything positive to ward it off. On November 6, Americans elected Abraham Lincoln the sixteenth president of the United States. While receiving less than 40 percent of the popular vote, the Illinois Republican swept the northern states to earn a clear majority in the electoral college.[77] A sectional party had won the White House, and the nation tensely waited to see what might ensue.

Mason knew that the situation was most volatile in South Carolina. Three days after the election, he wrote to South Carolina Rep. William Porcher Miles, urging the state's representatives to go to Washington until the state officially seceded.[78] In a letter to the editor of the *Richmond Enquirer*, he pointed out that everything that had "happened and much that is yet to come, was foreseen and predicted by those not claiming to be wise beyond their generation, as the legitimate and inevitable fruits of the ascendancy of the Abolition party in the North." He claimed that the Republican party's "open and avowed mission is to break up and destroy interests in property and in society in all the slaveholding States," which would "reduce their lands to deserts, and throw their people as outcasts upon the world." Southerners were to be subjected "against their will" to "a government to which they are not parties, and over which they hold not the slightest check."[79]

To Mason, that sort of government bore no resemblance to the constitutional republic of his ancestors. Whether the issue was fugitive slaves or condoning and canonizing John Brown[80] and others who sought "to foment divisions amongst our people, and to excite the servile class to insurrection and rapine," northerners refused to fulfill their obligations. He exclaimed, "The people of the North . . . have separated themselves from the people of the South, and the government they thus inaugurate will be to us the government of a foreign power."[81]

Mason supported a state convention to decide Virginia's fate[82] but had determined already what course he believed should be taken. In a letter to his sister-in-law, maintaining that northerners "really seem to be blind and deaf to the exigency which is upon us, and them," Mason proclaimed "the dissolution of the Union is a *fixed fact*." He predicted that, after South Carolina seceded, "her example will be followed by State after State as fast as they can assemble in convention, and by Virginia with like speed." The South had no choice "but to accept the 'irrepressible conflict' tendered us by the late election." Claiming that "a *social war*" had been "declared by the North, a war by one form of society against another distinct form of society," Mason concluded that the only question remaining was "whether it will be conducted in arms." He thought that "the North, which tenders the issue, will decide."[83] He told Virginians that "they must prepare."[84]

Mason, Davis, Hunter, and Slidell were asked by President Buchanan and southern members of the cabinet to come to Washington well in advance of the second session, so that they could help in drafting the outgoing administration's response to the crisis. But the resulting message pleased nobody.[85] The president claimed helplessness in preventing secession but angered southerners by condemning secession as unconstitutional. Northerners resented his criticism of abolitionist agitation as the primary cause of the crisis, as well as his support of southern demands for protecting slavery in the territories.[86]

The message did call for compromise, and Kentucky Democrat Lazarus W. Powell, in an attempt to save the Union, introduced a resolution to form a committee of thirteen to recommend ways to do so.[87] Mason voted for the proposal but did not wish to mislead his constituents into hoping or expecting "that it was within the reach of legislation here in some way to save the country from the dissolution that is imminently pending." Congress could do nothing "to reach the dangers with which we are threatened." Slave state conventions, including one in Virginia, would address the subject "as separate, sovereign communities" and "determine what is best for their safety." Their eyes did not turn to Congress "with any idea that it is competent to them to afford relief." He urged northern and western states also to go into convention, and he asked them to recognize that the "evil" to be addressed was their policy of "social war" against their southern brethren.[88]

The following day he returned to his favorite specific grievance—fugitive slaves. Once again he told the shopworn story of the Virginian whose slave escapes to Pennsylvania. Mason asserted that an owner would try to reclaim his property there "at the peril of his life, and at the peril of his liberty" because of that state's laws. He lamented, "We are humiliated and dishonored in our own eyes that we remain members of a common Government, when the covenant is not only not regarded, but when our people are imperiled if they go to enforce it." The southern gentleman asserted that the loss of property was painful enough but that "the loss of honor is felt still more."[89]

Even though he believed that northern obstruction of the fugitive slave law made that law "of no value to the South,"[90] Mason never had "the conviction that we in Virginia should break up this Union, or counsel others to break up this Union" solely for that reason. But he proclaimed this to be "only one of the list" of grievances. While reaffirming his "earnest desire to remain in the Confederation," he cautioned that Virginians wanted these concerns settled once and for all. Unless assured of "adequate and undoubted security" for southern property rights, "we are becoming satisfied that we cannot with honor remain under a common Government."[91]

South Carolina seceded on December 20.[92] Mason spent that day in the Senate discussing sovereignty and the Constitution. He claimed to "have never doubted the perfect and indefeasible right of one of the States of the Union to determine for herself whether her honor and her safety will admit of her continuing in this Confederacy." He criticized proposals for using force against South Carolina, stating that "the only effect of pressing such resolutions . . . to a vote will but increase and inflame bitterness, anger, and resentment."[93]

As the new year dawned, Mason's attention focused upon insuring that secession would be allowed to proceed peacefully. On January 5, he introduced a resolution requesting information on military plans involving U.S. forts and arsenals in the southern states.[94] He made a similar effort four days later, when he and Hunter unsuccessfully attempted to get President Buchanan's help on the subject.[95] In the Senate, Mason claimed pure intentions. He expressed a wish that the true state of affairs be laid before the people to dispel the "rumors and reports of the purposes of those in authority—the far greater proportion of them without any foundation in truth, and a great many of them with the truth perverted, whether designedly or ignorantly."[96]

His real motives were far less noble. Mason already had begun working behind the scenes for Virginia's secession,[97] and information on U.S. military preparations would be of immeasurable help to the South in planning for its uncertain future. Mason had become the equivalent of a spy behind enemy lines, fighting obstinately against any attempt to preserve the Union. In a letter to the secession manager of the

Virginia Legislature, Mason described a Senate speech by Seward as "fraudulent and tricky under cloak of seeming mildness," asserting that it contained "no offer of concession worth consideration."[98]

Additionally, Mason opposed a proposed constitutional amendment protecting slavery, on the grounds that it was to be voted upon by the people. He stressed that the national government "is a confederation of States; and when the people are spoken of in the Constitution, it means the people of each State *separatum,* as a separate independent political community, each State being sovereign." The founding fathers "never contemplated that the people of the United States, as a mass, a homogeneous mass, should be the parties to the Federal Government." George Mason's grandson would "never . . . agree to convert the form of government we now have, from a confederation of Republics into a consolidated Government."[99]

Responding to charges that he only wanted an excuse to leave the Union, Mason countered sarcastically that he needed an excuse "to remain in the Union . . . an excuse to get out of the Union is not necessary." Desiring secession to be peaceful, he admonished northerners that, if they decided to make war "upon us; we are to accept it, not to institute it. The whole responsibility will be with you, and you will have to answer to the generations which are to follow for all the consequences of that war."[100]

By the end of the month, the seven states of South Carolina, Georgia, Florida, Alabama, Mississippi, Louisiana, and Texas all had seceded from the Union.[101] Meanwhile, Mason and Hunter soldiered on, awaiting Virginia's action.[102] Both declined nominations to their state's secession convention because they wanted to remain in the Senate as long as possible, believing that peace would be preserved until Lincoln's inauguration. "After that," he wrote to his daughter Virginia, "we rely on having a Southern Confederacy organized and strong enough to defy assailants. All hope of adjustment is gone."[103]

Along with eight of the state's other congressmen, Mason and Hunter addressed a letter to the people of Virginia, informing them of the level of disunion in Washington. The letter blamed the Republicans, warned that no solutions would be forthcoming from the capital, and expressed "solemn conviction" that action by the Virginia convention "will afford the surest means, under the providence of God, of averting a civil war and preserving the hope of reconstructing a Union already dissolved."[104]

On January 28, Mason presented resolutions adopted by the Virginia State Legislature. The Old Dominion offered its services as a mediator between North and South, and called upon President

Buchanan "to refrain from any public act of which might bring into collision the public power of the United States with the public power of the States that have seceded." Once such a collision occurred, "it would be beyond the power of any mortal man to avert that greatest of all catastrophes to this country and to mankind—civil war between the States of this Union and the people of those States."[105]

Mason expressed Virginia's desire "to preserve the public peace" in case of a compromise but also to preserve it if "it should be decreed that the existing confederation is to be permanently dissolved." He warned that, when war began, negotiation would end; and he defended the seceded states' seizure of forts and military bases as only defensive precautions. He implored northerners to listen to Virginia, prevent civil war, and restore the people's "great path of prosperity and strength and honor from which they have been diverted."[106]

Mason declared, "If there be any man in this broad continent who valued that Union more than I did, I have yet to know who he is." Nonetheless, he said, "Let the Union go, with whatever regret, with whatever concern," but with "no remorse" if keeping it meant that the South had to sacrifice its safety, peace, self-respect, and "the very foundations" of its "social fabric."[107] The Virginian maintained that "the disintegration of this Union is going on by a power that cannot be arrested,"[108] and he took offense at talk of satisfying southern calls for "concessions." He maintained that the South never would make such a request but only wanted its constitutional "rights" secured.[109]

On January 31, Mason became particularly angry when he accused Seward of contributing nothing positive or helpful to the cause of unity. The New York senator had recommended that his constituents "employ themselves in the great work of restoring the breaches that have been made in the Government" by speaking for the Union, voting for the Union, giving money for the Union, and fighting for the Union. Mason claimed to understand the first two suggestions but expressed astonishment at the last two. He lambasted the Republican for requesting contributions of money from the great commercial center of Manhattan to "march the Army upon the South" with the aim of preserving a union that already had vanished, in order to reduce "them [the South] to colonies and dependencies."[110]

Subjugating southerners would not restore the Union. Mason believed that Seward had only one remedy for the nation's woes: "the argument of a tyrant—force, compulsion, power." He maintained that Seward's inflammatory words should end southern illusions of security within the Union. Sensing impending disaster, he again warned of the war "that must ensue when men's minds really are heated to madness, when passion usurps the throne of reason, and when negotiation and deliberation are ended." Even worse, it would be "that greatest of all calamities, a war between brother and brother; a war which could conquer a peace only in oceans of blood and countless millions of treasure."[111]

Despite such avowed fears, Mason continued to work for secession. He and Hunter traveled to and from Richmond in January and advised commissioners from the seceded states that Virginia would not secede if a radical such as Alabama's William L. Yancey were elected president of a southern confederacy. They suggested their friend and colleague, Jefferson Davis, as a conservative choice that would calm most Virginians' trepidation. Seeing Virginia as a necessary component of any successful southern government, the commissioners passed along the recommendation. On February 9, representatives of the seceded states meeting in Montgomery, Alabama, followed Mason and Hunter's advice and elected Davis president of the Confederate States of America.[112]

Three days later, Mason congratulated Davis and updated the new chief executive on Virginia's situation. Mason feared that "Virginia is still hanging back, on the delusive idea, that she can obtain adequate securities yet in the Union," but he expressed confidence that, once compromise talks broke down, the state "will go for separation at once." He also cautioned the new president that the United States would not recognize Confederate independence "until the strength and resources of this government have been tested in a struggle to subdue it." Mason predicted war, "first probably only by blockade, afterwards by more active measures—I trust before the war comes in earnest, the Old Dominion will haul along side." He pledged to leave nothing "undone on my part so to order."[113]

Nonetheless, he carried on in the Senate against increasingly long odds. He defended the withdrawal of representatives from the seven seceded states,[114] but that action depleted the southern ranks, leaving them with the ability merely to protest the agenda set by emboldened northern Republicans. One proposal called for an appropriation of over one million dollars for "seven steamers of small draught and heavy armament." Mason fought it, not only because of the dire state of the government's credit, but also on the grounds that no foreign affairs emergency called for such action.[115]

That reasoning ignored the domestic emergency. Mason in fact saw the measure as one designed to help the North make war upon the Confederacy. Pledging to fight any effort to increase the army or navy until a settlement had been reached, he criticized those who sought to keep the true purposes of such appropriations "darkly shadowed." Proclaiming Confederate independence a reality and deriding northern talk of "discontents in certain parts of the country," he compared plans to blockade southern ports with Great Britain's blockade of Boston over eighty years earlier.[116]

The new majorities also sought, over Mason's objections, to raise tariffs[117] and to appropriate federal money for the protection of emigrants to Oregon. He denounced the latter as unconstitutional, and, when criticized for being too strict, the Virginian responded, "Would to God, Mr. President, that the Constitution had been regarded, and then the country would have been in a very different condition today" than one in which states abandoned "a broken and violated Constitution."[118] But with his bitter enemy, Sumner of Massachusetts, having replaced him as chairman of the Senate Foreign Relations Committee, Mason's power in Washington had evaporated. One observer remarked that "Mason walks about like a caged tiger and is cross as a bear."[119] Congress refused to listen to him anymore.

He spent his last month in Washington trying to convince his northern colleagues that southern independence was an irreversible fact,[120] and he became particularly animated in debates regarding the southern senators who had left when their states seceded.[121] Discussions of compromise filled the air, and Mason kept in close contact with former President John Tyler,[122] chairman of a peace convention that was meeting in Washington at Virginia's suggestion. The convention's report reached the Senate on February 28. It called for extending the old Missouri Compromise line to the Pacific[123] and allowing slavery south of the line without congressional interference. The recommendation would be referred "to judicial cognizance in the Federal courts, according to the course of the common law."[124]

Mason the legalist opposed the proposal, wondering what its authors meant by "common law." He noted that "common law" in places as varied as Ohio and Great Britain prohibited slavery, and he argued that such tampering with the Constitution was unnecessary if northerners merely followed the southern strict interpretation. He foresaw a South at the mercy of the free states, controlled by federal authorities. Mason announced, "I deeply deplore, and I doubt not my State will deplore" that Virginia's mediation had proven unsuccessful.[125]

On March 2, although he opposed the peace proposal, Mason fought attempts by Douglas to give precedence to a House resolution to amend the Constitution to prohibit congressional interference with slavery in the states. The Illinois senator won the precedence vote, as well as a motion to open the doors of the ladies' galleries.

Mason protested and gave "up all hopes of preserving order in the Senate." As the women entered, he impotently demanded that "the order of the Senate be enforced" and asserted that "it is very manifest to me that the Senate is under the control of lawless power, that interferes with its deliberations."[126] Increasingly powerless, he could not win even a simple procedural vote.

Mason gave his last major speech later that day. He asserted that the House resolution amounted to an unacceptable embodiment of the Republican Party platform, because it guaranteed slavery only in the states, without addressing slavery in the territories. He ridiculed the proposal as a "placebo," declaring that he would "never venture back to my State, and say that I was induced to give you this bread pill." To "those States yet remaining in this Union which have this condition of African slavery among them," he issued a warning that, to "rely upon this security, you must of necessity abandon the institutions of your forefathers; you must abandon your form of society, and cast your lot among strangers, for it will give you none." Northerners refused to allow any compromise that would guarantee southern rights to take slavery into the territories; in three months of debate, Congress could produce only a "delusive amendment," while the South required genuine security.[127]

After trying again to obtain useful military information,[128] Mason made preparations to leave the capital. He spoke for the last time in the U.S. Senate on March 19, giving an inconsequential commentary on the postal service.[129] He departed for Selma on March 21, before the end of the special session of Congress called to consider peace proposals. He had greater interest in events in Richmond.[130] By the end of that month, James Murray Mason irreversibly had cast his lot with the Confederate States of America. His decision would become official when Virginia seceded from the Union.

In the months leading up to his departure from the Senate, Mason continued to exhibit the consistency of purpose that had marked his career. While many southern politicians may have seen slavery as the reason to secede, for Mason the North's increasing lack of regard for a strict enforcement of the Constitution proved sufficient. That disregard was coupled with his perception that northern attacks upon the hallowed document also cast aspersions upon southern honor and society. These two factors agitated the proud Virginia patrician as no specific grievance could have done. Only a series of significant insults and illegal actions could have brought the even-tempered Mason to call for secession. Mason always prefaced any speech regarding a southern grievance by recapping the wrongs that had come before. No individual grievance stood alone. Accumulating over years, their importance became magnified. Feeling cornered by those hostile to the South, and hearing an echo of the words *Pro Republica Semper,* Mason and other southern patriots found no choice but to leave the Union and set a course through uncharted, dangerous waters in an attempt to regain their independence.

Chapter 8

1861

Making of a Confederate Diplomat

After leaving Washington, James Murray Mason remained in Winchester for approximately three weeks. The time spent with friends and family gave him a respite from national problems. In a letter to Confederate President Jefferson Davis, he expressed his belief that Virginia eventually would join the Confederacy. He also wrote of having become discouraged by the "dreary and uninviting" affairs in the Senate during his final days there.[1] He needed the warmth and shelter of a pastoral vacation at home to renew his energies for the uncertain future ahead.

His spring break ended on April 15, when the outside world intruded in a way that changed the lives of Mason's family forever. Two days earlier, the U.S. garrison at Fort Sumter, in the harbor at Charleston, South Carolina, had surrendered after being bombarded by Confederate forces under Gen. Pierre G. T. Beauregard. After the firing of those first shots, President Abraham Lincoln issued a proclamation calling out seventy-five thousand militia from the various states of the Union.[2] The militia were to enforce federal authority in the seven seceded states by suppressing those who opposed that authority. The text of Lincoln's statement arrived at Selma on April 15. After reading it, Mason stated solemnly that "this ends the question; Virginia will at once secede."[3]

He left immediately for Richmond, arrived there the following evening, and met with leaders of the Virginia secession convention. Having promised to keep President Davis abreast of events, he wrote to the chief executive on April 17, "You may rely now that Virginia will secede, and promptly."[4] The convention voted for secession later that day.[5] The state joined the Confederacy a week later, pending popular approval of the secession ordinance. The vote on May 23 approved secession by more than four to one.[6] Mason also informed Davis that Robert E. Lee had resigned his commission in the U.S. Army and would be placed in command of Virginia's military forces. According to Mason, "The cannon of Fort Sumter, sundered the Union for Virginia." With the state's secession accomplished, Mason offered Davis his own personal help, declaring, "If in any thing I can serve you, or the great cause entrusted to your guidance[,] you have but to command."[7]

But Mason's first assignment came from Virginia Gov. John Letcher, who appointed Mason commissioner to the border state of Maryland, charged with ascertaining affairs and sentiments there.[8] Traveling throughout the central part of the state, he spoke with various Maryland representatives. He confidently reported from Baltimore that they were "so earnest and zealous in the cause of the South I feel sure they will take steps to place the authority of the state in hands ready and competent to act with Virginia."[9]

He spent ten days in Maryland, then went to Richmond to report his findings personally.[10] Mason told Edmund Ruffin that Maryland "would resist and effect what would be equivalent to secession" but could not formally do so, given "the weak, unarmed, and exposed condition of the people."[11] Returning to Winchester, Mason wrote to President Davis that he relied upon the Maryland legislature "to unite the State with the Southern Confederacy, as soon as it may be prudent for them to do so." But he warned that Maryland secessionists had great obstacles to overcome, particularly because "they have but little military organization, and are almost destitute of arms." To prevent Maryland's succumbing to the grasp of federal authority, Mason believed Virginia and the other Confederate states should furnish that state with arms to "redeem them to the South."[12]

After completing his "diplomatic" mission to Maryland, Mason's next task was to serve as one of Virginia's representatives in the Provisional Congress of the Confederate States of America. He did not go to the capital in Montgomery, Alabama, believing that he would have little time to accomplish anything before it was relocated to Virginia. Instead, he spent the next two months commuting between

Winchester and Richmond, in regular consultation with both civil and military authorities. Volunteers from across the South converged on Mason's home town, to be organized in the defense of the Confederacy. While the fledgling soldiers prepared, Gen. Joseph E. Johnston and other soon-to-be-famous military officers breakfasted at Selma daily while they commanded troops in the vicinity.[13]

Richmond then housed the Provisional Congress, and Mason took his seat there on July 24. On that day, his first speech paid tribute to those gallant soldiers who fell in battle three days earlier at Manassas.[14] While serving in Congress, Mason showed his greatest concern for Confederate sympathizers outside the new government's jurisdiction. He devoted a considerable amount of his time to resolutions providing aid for supporters in Maryland, Kentucky, Missouri, Delaware, and the District of Columbia.[15]

Of course, foreign affairs had been Mason's primary area of expertise during his Senate career, and numerous diplomatic issues needed to be considered by the new southern government. On July 20, President Davis proclaimed that the United States "recognizes the separate existence of these Confederate States, by the interdiction, embargo, and blockade" of its trade.[16] Great Britain recognized the Confederacy as a "belligerent" in May[17] but also declared British neutrality.[18] As the first summer of the war elapsed, the British government continued to observe the federal blockade and withhold full diplomatic recognition of the South. On August 13, in hopes of changing that position, the Confederate Congress passed a resolution whereby the Confederate States agreed to the terms of the 1856 Declaration of Paris.[19] It approved all the maritime provisions regarding neutral rights and blockades, with the notable exception of the one that prohibited privateering.[20]

Around that same time, Mason gained an impression of opinion in Great Britain from a letter written to him by William H. Gregory, a sympathetic member of the British Parliament. Even though Britain's upper classes had "the strongest feeling in your favor," Gregory wrote, "As far as recognition goes, I do not see any chance of it immediately," mainly because rumors of reconciliation prevented the ministry from taking steps toward intervention. He urged patience, asserting that, when the North became exhausted, the South would "be rejoiced at the joint action of England and France (for we go together) with a view toward mediation."[21]

To a large extent, Confederate foreign policy revolved around "King Cotton." Numerous books, pamphlets, and other statistical studies prior to the war had come to the identical conclusion that

Great Britain depended alarmingly on cotton from the southern states. Such information was translated by President Davis into unofficial government policy. The Confederacy never did *officially* embargo cotton, but nonetheless cotton was not being shipped. The government quietly discouraged its export, to make cotton a lever to induce Europe's greatest power to recognize Confederate independence.[22] Davis allowed debates on an embargo to continue as a not-so-subtle threat, while taking the rhetorical high road by calling for "the most unrestricted commerce with all nations."[23]

Mason's conviction that a legislator had the duty to support the president's prerogatives regarding foreign affairs remained intact when he joined the Confederacy. He gave strong backing to Jefferson Davis's diplomatic policies, including the "unofficial" embargo of cotton. On August 21, Mason introduced a resolution instructing the Committee on Foreign Affairs to "inquire whether tobacco or other produce of any of the Confederate States has been exported from any of the ports of those States by sea, since declaration of the blockade." If the committee reached an affirmative answer, Mason wanted recommendations as to "what legislation is necessary" to stop it.[24] He was rewarded for such loyalty to President Davis and his foreign policy three days later.

Mason's old friend Robert M. T. Hunter had become secretary of state, and, by late August, both Hunter and Davis were increasingly impatient with the lack of progress toward diplomatic recognition. A triumvirate of "Special Commissioners to Europe"—William L. Yancey, Pierre A. Rost, and A. Dudley Mann—had failed to produce any results.[25] With recognition proving more elusive than expected, Davis and Hunter concluded that permanent representatives at each European court would be preferable. Therefore, on August 24, Davis accepted Yancey's resignation, sent Mann to Belgium and Rost to Spain, and assigned Louisiana's John Slidell to France.[26] The key appointment as "special commissioner of the Confederate States to the United Kingdom of Great Britain and Ireland" went to James Murray Mason.[27] The president "invested him with full and all manner of power and authority for and in the name of the Confederate States, to meet and confer with any person or persons duly authorized by the British government, being furnished with like power and authority, and with him or them to agree, treat, consult, and negotiate concerning all matters and subjects interesting to both nations, and to conclude and sign a treaty or treaties, convention or conventions, touching the premises."[28] That same day, Davis wrote to Queen Victoria that, "animated by a sincere and earnest desire to establish and cultivate the most friendly relations," he had "selected the Hon. James M. Mason, one of our most intelligent, esteemed, and worthy citizens," to be "envoy extraordinary and minister plenipotentiary of the Confederate States, to reside near the court of your Majesty."[29]

Three years earlier, Mason had turned aside President James Buchanan's inquiries as to whether he would accept a diplomatic post in London,[30] but now Mason heeded the call of Jefferson Davis. He remained in Richmond as a member of the Provisional Congress through the end of the month,[31] then spent the first weeks of September preparing for his voyage. Leaving his family, Mason gave few instructions, relying upon Eliza's and his daughters' good sense, and the support of their friends in Winchester and Richmond, to guide them through any emergency. He refused to listen to suggestions that they go with him, leaving directions that, if the government needed it, the family silver should be given to the Treasury to be melted into coin. His final request was that the women "never allow themselves to be within the enemies' lines" and that they "make whatever sacrifices might be required to enable them to go, if necessary, from place to place until they reached the last village in the Confederacy."[32]

He returned to Richmond ready to sail, with no fears for his own safety and no doubt that the Confederacy would establish and maintain its independence.[33] Hunter relayed Davis's instructions that Mason "proceed to London with as little delay as possible, and place yourself, as soon as you may be able to do so, in communications with the Government." Defending secession and stressing cotton and the Declaration of Paris, he was "to explain the true position in which we appear before the world." He was to seek not favors but justly deserved recognition.[34]

In separate, more personal instructions, Hunter specified Mason's salary as twelve thousand dollars per year, half to be received up front and the rest to be drawn quarterly as needed. Knowing that Mason had never served overseas, Hunter also enlightened his friend on rules of protocol, deposition of papers, and other miscellaneous details related to the appointment. Among the most important overall duties of a Confederate diplomat, he wrote, "is that of transmitting to his own government accurate information concerning the policy and views of that to which he is accredited, in its important relations with other powers." He stressed that gaining such intelligence required "steady and impartial observation, a free though cautious correspondence with other agents of the Confederate States abroad, and friendly social relations with the members of the diplomatic body at the place of his residence."[35]

Mason met Slidell on September 24, and the pair proceeded to Charleston, South Carolina, where they were joined by Slidell's wife and three children, as well as the two secretaries of legation. Louisiana's George Eustis would go to Paris with Slidell, and Virginia's James E. MacFarland would accompany Mason to London.[36] In Charleston, they were disappointed to find their direct passage impeded by three U.S. steamers and a sloop of war that blockaded the harbor in plain sight of the shore.[37] The next day, the group sent a telegram to Hunter requesting permission to charter the steamer *Gordon,* a small, speedy riverboat, to follow the coastline and take the passengers to the West Indies. From there, they could continue the journey to Europe.[38] Hunter gave permission the next day, provided it be chartered as cheaply as possible.[39]

But the weather and the ever-watchful eye of the blockaders delayed their departure longer.[40] On October 9, Mason updated Hunter on the situation[41] and also began to write to Eliza, believing that he would set sail the next day. He assured her that there was "no risk of our being seen by the enemy as we go out," because of the precautions taken and the speed of the *Gordon.* He expected the trip to Havana to take seventy hours. Two days later, he still sat in Charleston and finished the letter. He reaffirmed his decision to leave Eliza and his daughters behind, even though there was "probably no real risk." Mason pronounced himself healthy, "in high hope and buoyant."[42]

On October 11, the two commissioners sent the charter for the *Gordon* to Richmond,[43] and Mason wrote to President Davis that they expected to sail around midnight "or as soon as the moon disappears."[44] On the last night that the southern diplomats spent in the Confederacy, the citizens of Charleston held a banquet for them. While entering the hall, Mason spoke with a soldier at the door. As both were away from home and family, he asked the young man to accompany him inside. But the youth, believing that a mere soldier would be unwelcome among the illustrious guests, declined. Mason insisted, however, and the youth remained by his side throughout the meal.[45] Hierarchy seemed less important at that moment. With his own family members fighting and dying for the Confederacy, a Virginia patrician could set aside his beliefs in class distinctions to honor and cheer a brave son of the South.

The journey began the next night, precisely at twelve. Heavy clouds added to the darkness, and, shortly after embarkation, it began to rain. The boat quietly left the harbor, keeping Fort Sumter between it and the enemy. In spite of what became a steady downpour, Mason and Slidell sat quietly on deck until the little steamer safely passed the federal ships. They clearly could discern the lights of the Yankee vessels, having come within a mile and a half of one of them.[46]

Mason cheerfully wrote to Eliza about being "on the deep blue sea, clear of all the Yankees," and recounted passing the federal blockaders. His mood was markedly upbeat, as he claimed that "the long heavy swell" had "made everybody on board sick" except himself. He wrote, "I have never had the slightest qualm, but had a good appetite and a clear head all the time." He confidently asserted that, "having run the blockade successfully[,] everything else is plain sailing, because under any foreign flag we are safe from molestation."[47]

The ship stopped at Nassau on October 14 and arrived in Cuba two days later. There Mason and Slidell learned that an English mail steamer had just departed.[48] Another one was supposed to leave on November 9, so they planned on making a full reconnaissance of the island during the interval. Again, Mason reported himself in good health, despite daily temperatures near 100° F.[49] He did not enjoy such warmth, however, as he turned down numerous invitations to balls, offering excuses to hide the fact that his real reason was the heat.[50]

The Virginian did enjoy the food, especially the fresh fruits which he termed "exquisite." Mason also exclaimed to Eliza that he and Slidell were received "with marked attention by the inhabitants, all of whose sympathies are with the Confederate States."[51] But news of their presence in Havana also reached the ears of some less friendly folk. Capt. Charles D. Wilkes of the U.S. Navy had landed the U.S.S. *San Jacinto* there on October 30. At an earlier stop in Jamaica, he had learned of Mason and Slidell's presence. Believing that they would continue their journey on a Confederate ship, he aimed to intercept the Confederate commissioners when they left.[52]

In Cuba, however, Captain Wilkes found it to be common knowledge that Mason and Slidell planned to cross the Atlantic on board the next departing British mail steamer.[53] On the morning of November 7, the *Trent* left Havana for Southampton, England, with the two Confederate commissioners and their entourage on board. The next day, around noon, British Capt. James Moir spotted a war steamer blocking his ship's path about five or six miles in the distance. He apprised Mason and Slidell of the situation, and the vessel continued forward cautiously. Suddenly the *San Jacinto* fired two shots across the bow of the *Trent*. As a boarding party approached, the Virginia diplomat knew that there could be trouble.[54]

Immediately, Mason called upon MacFarland to gather their papers and have the steamer's mail agent lock them in his mail room.[55] Returning to the deck, he saw Lt. Donald Fairfax of the U.S. Navy engaged in a heated conversation with Captain Moir. First Slidell and then Mason walked over to the pair, only to discover that the southerners were the topics of discussion.[56] Lieutenant Fairfax told Mason that his orders were to take both him and Slidell, as well as Eustis and MacFarland, into custody on the *San Jacinto*. Mason answered that he would not go "unless compelled by force greater than I can overcome. I know my rights—I am under the protection of a neutral flag and will be taken from that protection only by force." Twenty to thirty U.S. sailors soon boarded the *Trent* to apply that force. Lieutenant Fairfax ordered three or four of them to grab Mason and Slidell, compelling both to give up any idea of resisting. Other passengers protested, but, while expressing appreciation for the support, Mason urged that all concede the hopelessness of resistance. The Confederate representatives and their captors departed from the British vessel quietly, leaving behind the sounds of the passengers' angry protests and the anguished cries of Slidell's wife and three children.[57]

The situation calmed once they boarded the *San Jacinto*.[58] The ship made its way northward, proceeding slowly, hugging the Confederate coastline, and occasionally stopping amid federal blockaders. Captain Wilkes did what he could to make captivity bearable for the prisoners,[59] including passing a letter from Mason to Eliza through the lines to Richmond when the steamer anchored near Fort Monroe, Virginia. Informing her of their capture and predicting that "there will be all sorts of conjecture in the newspapers," Mason warned her not "to be affected by them, and draw no inference from my silence concerning them, except that I, of necessity, write under constraint." Mason reported himself in good health "and in no manner depressed, as I beg you will not be."[60]

The *San Jacinto* continued its journey to New York, which the prisoners had been told would be their ultimate destination. The vessel entered the harbor, but plans soon changed. While Mason and Slidell played a game of backgammon in their cabin, Captain Wilkes interrupted to inform them that, by orders of their old nemesis in the Senate, U.S. Secretary of State William H. Seward,[61] they were to be taken instead to Fort Warren in Boston harbor.[62] It made no difference to the pair where they would be imprisoned, but when, a couple of days later, the weather turned bad, they wished that their journey had ended in New York.[63]

The temperature plummeted as the steamer braced itself against a fierce northeastern storm. It landed briefly at Newport, Rhode Island, and the prisoners asked to be placed into custody there, so that they would not have to make the difficult winter journey by sea to Boston. They complained of "delicate health" and "tempestuous and disagreeable seas," promising not to try to escape or talk to anyone if their request were granted.[64] But Secretary of the Navy Gideon Welles refused, claiming that Newport had no place to confine them.

The ship reentered the Atlantic for the final leg of its journey and arrived at Fort Warren on November 24.[65] Reporting the landing of the prisoners, one Boston newspaper commented derisively that "Mr. Mason by great effort maintained his usual self-assurance and haughtiness; but Mr. Slidell's lips quivered, his knees trembled."[66] Charles Francis Adams, Jr., son of the U.S. minister to England, "looked at the low, distant walls of Fort Warren, surrounded by the steel blue sea, and reflected that . . . those amiable gentlemen [Mason and Slidell] were there, and there they would remain!" He wrote, "I remembered the last exhibition I saw Mason make of himself in the Senate Chamber, and I smacked my lips with joy."[67]

By that time, the world had awakened to the fact that a genuine diplomatic crisis was at hand. On November 18, Jefferson Davis addressed the Provisional Congress on various military and diplomatic matters, expressing personal outrage over the seizure of his diplomats. The chief executive called upon European governments to stop favoring the United States, a government that not only had violated "our rights under the law of nations at home," but also had "claimed a general jurisdiction over the high seas."[68] Such official protests masked an overall feeling of satisfaction within the Confederacy, rising from a belief that the United States had gone too far and that Great Britain would retaliate on their behalf.[69]

In the United States, feelings of satisfaction were not masked. With successes on the battlefield few and far between in 1861, northerners celebrated the seizure as a great victory. In the beginning, newspaper editors gave little thought to how the British would react. They sought to outdo each other in applauding Captain Wilkes's conduct; the *Boston Evening Transcript* went so far as to label the capture "one of those bold strokes by which the destinies of nations are determined."[70] Only when word came that Lincoln's government considered the matter a serious one did most of the strident journalism subside.[71]

On November 27, the day that Captain Moir's official report of the incident became public in England, Confederate commissioners Yancey, Rost, and Mann lodged an official protest with Lord John Russell, British secretary of state for foreign affairs, regarding the seizure. The trio hoped confidently "that Her Majesty's Government will cause those . . . illegally taken from the deck of a British vessel, to be restored to the position which they enjoyed under the protection of the British flag."[72] Russell instructed Lord Richard Lyons, Britain's minister in Washington, to protest the affront to British national honor and to demand redress in the form of the four captives' release "and a suitable apology for the aggression which has been committed."[73]

The ministry's actions had wide support among the British people. One American who had lived in London for a long time commented that "the people are frantic with rage, and were the country polled, I fear 999 men out of a thousand would declare for immediate war."[74] Another wrote from Liverpool that "this is considered a very high handed measure, the state of excitement here is such as we never before witnessed."[75] British newspapers expressed the country's indignation with varying levels of bellicosity. The *London Times* tended to be more conciliatory than others, but even it appealed "to the reasonable men of the Federal States . . . not to provoke war by such acts as these."[76]

While the politicians and newspapers debated courses of action, Mason and his fellow diplomats sat in Fort Warren. Their accommodations were surprisingly good. He wrote to Eliza that the four of them "have two rooms and a closet attached, good beds; and are allowed to get from Boston anything we want, and also have a good servant."[77] There were no restrictions on conversation; Mason was allowed to talk with other prisoners, who included Confederate military officers, secessionist members of the Maryland legislature, and other politicians from Baltimore.[78] He described them as "a most agreeable set of gentlemen" and expressed gratitude that, despite their confinement, all had "ample space for walking."[79]

Nonetheless, while admitting he had "nothing to complain of personally but the loss of liberty," he emphasized that "it is pretty hard, to be sure, to be seized and shut up."[80] In spite of the numerous privileges, Mason described prison life as "monotonous." He and Slidell did eat well, however, as friends in Baltimore sent them delicacies from the Chesapeake. They also received a large box of Christmas treats from the women of Hagerstown, Maryland. Mason expressed particular gratitude to a woman from Portland, Maine, who sent a package for Christmas dinner so large that he and Slidell shared it with prisoners of war from North Carolina.[81]

One significant privilege enjoyed by the southern diplomats was unrestricted access to newspapers from Boston, New York, Philadelphia, and England. Thus they were able to keep reasonably up to date on the diplomacy surrounding their capture. Mason never doubted that the British government would demand their release. Later he wrote that in discussions with his fellow prisoners, he continually asserted that, "however anxious England might be to avoid a quarrel, this must be made a fighting issue, and that no diplomatic delays would be allowed. It was an unmixed question of national honor." The southerners all agreed with him, but they could only speculate on what the Lincoln government would do in return. According to Mason, "All prayed earnestly that the Yankees would refuse to surrender us . . . knowing as we did that the war with England to follow such a refusal would speedily terminate the war with the South."[82]

Diplomatic maneuvers regarding the captured southerners unfolded throughout the month of December. Those maneuvers did not involve Confederate authorities, however, as the southern commissioners watched from the sidelines, expressing satisfaction that "unless the North has yielded at once war is certain." They predicted that France at first would be neutral and then, within a few months, would "come forward and command peace between the three belligerents."[83] British demands for the release of the captives coincided with an order for eight thousand troops to proceed to Canada, stepping up a reinforcement effort that had begun as early as June.[84] That show of force also included expanding the British fleet in the Atlantic, and the government placed an embargo upon sales of saltpeter to the United States.[85]

Simultaneously, the Lincoln administration faced two choices: war with England or national dishonor. The U.S. minister to England, Charles Francis Adams, stood in a delicate position. Adams wanted to alleviate tensions as best he could, but through much of December, poor communications between him and Washington left him in the dark as to the U.S. position.[86] Meanwhile, criticism of Secretary of State Seward and the Lincoln administration kept appearing in Lord Lyons's dispatches to Russell, in effect pouring kerosene on an already burning fire.[87]

Privately, Seward concluded that the administration had to find an honorable way to get out of the mess. The secretary of state recognized that peace with Britain was crucial to restoring the Union.[88]

Standing alone and facing pressure from both Britain and France,[89] Lincoln held a cabinet meeting on Christmas Day and another the day after, to map out a course of action. After painstaking discussion of the issues involved, the president decided to release the Confederate diplomats. Seward told Lord Lyons that the United States agreed to make reparations and would release the four prisoners.[90] But as the year ended, Britain, unaware of the concessions, continued its preparations for war, and the Confederate commissioners predicted that the British fleet would "sweep away the blockading squadrons from before our ports."[91]

Such dreams remained unrealized. The crisis dissipated even more quickly than it had begun. Neither Britain nor the United States wanted war, and both found ways to salvage their honor in the settlement.[92] That course was made easier by the fact that Confederate diplomatic efforts during the crisis were nonexistent. The South acted almost as a disinterested party. Jefferson Davis's foreign policy throughout the year could be characterized as passive, particularly during the *Trent* affair. The Confederate government quietly waited for events to work themselves out, instead of trying to make things happen.[93] It failed to gain any advantage from the incident. Diplomatic recognition would have been difficult to obtain, with Richmond's influence no match for Washington's, but authorities at least could have made their presence felt. The Confederacy could have stood up as the independent nation it claimed to be and tried to get something tangible out of the crisis, however small. Instead, satisfied that intervention had become imminent, its leaders exhibited only mild outrage and emerged empty-handed.

Pawns in the diplomatic posturing, Mason and Slidell awaited their release. On January 1, 1862, a special agent from the State Department arrived at Fort Warren to take the prisoners by tugboat to the H.M.S. *Rinaldo*, upon which the southerners would continue their original journey to Europe. Mason quickly scribbled a note to Eliza, "We are just going on board a steamer, to be placed, at sea, on board a British steamer for England. I am in perfect health and buoyant—will write by first chance—as you all must."[94]

High winds and waves crashing over the bow characterized the forty-mile tugboat ride,[95] and the trip aboard the *Rinaldo* was even worse, with snow and ice in addition to the turbulent seas.[96] During his first night on board, Mason awoke wet and cold. He noticed six to eight inches of water on the floor of his cabin, causing his clothes and boots to float around him, as more and more of the sea seeped in. Unable to walk without assistance on decks coated with two to three inches of ice and tormented by the constant roar of Neptune, the Virginian stayed below, seeking ways to keep warm and dry, however briefly. The situation improved when, after four days and nights of trying to fight nature on the way to Halifax, Nova Scotia, the ship changed course. It turned southward and headed for Bermuda. From there it continued to Saint Thomas, where, on January 14, the southern diplomats transferred to a British mail steamer, the *La Plata,* and headed for Southampton.[97]

That journey included more turbulent weather but no interference from the U.S. Navy. As the vessel carried Mason and Slidell to their destinations, the Confederate commissioners in Europe expressed great optimism. Mann wrote President Davis of his certainty "that we have seen the last of the darkest days" and that "bright skies are looming in the near distance."[98] He and Yancey wrote to Hunter that some type of intervention would "take place in a short time," with Britain and France probably demanding an armistice, with "differences of boundary between North and South" to "be settled by these powers."[99] It was not to be that simple. Upon reaching England, the Confederacy's diplomatic position, with its strengths and weaknesses, fell into the hands of James Murray Mason. His colleagues' optimistic rhetoric notwithstanding, the new diplomat had his work cut out for him.

♦♦♦ **Chapter 9** ♦♦♦

1862

Mason and the Confederate Quest for Diplomatic Intervention

After arriving in England on January 29, James Murray Mason spent much of his time receiving an array of visitors who were sympathetic to the Confederate cause and brought him "congratulations and other tokens of kindest welcome."[1] Such visits cheered him, and he optimistically wrote to Richmond that he would be "disappointed if Parliament does not insist on definite action by the ministry, inuring to the relief of their people as well as ours."[2] Such a conclusion appeared logical, because the new Confederate diplomat found himself deluged with wishes for success from the British gentry who dominated his social calendar.[3] Mary Chesnut, a critic of Mason, had written upon his appointment: "The English will like Mr. Mason; he is so manly, so straightforward, so truthful and bold."[4] Her words were prophetic; Mason's status and reputation impressed the British upper classes, while his geniality charmed them.[5]

Despite his busy social schedule and the large amount of correspondence he had to deal with,[6] Mason quickly set about his main task—to negotiate with and influence British policy makers to gain recognition of Confederate independence. Lord John Russell, secretary of state for foreign affairs, was the main target. On February 8, Mason was granted an unofficial interview with Russell, in which he planned to discuss the possibility of Great Britain's intervening, either by repudiating the federal blockade or by granting the diplomatic recognition the Richmond government believed it deserved. The meeting took place at Russell's house on Monday morning, February 10.[7]

Mason expected Russell to be "cold and repulsive," based on what he had heard, but that was not the impression he gained from this first encounter. According to the Virginian, Russell received him "in a civil and kind manner and expressed the hope that I had not suffered on the protracted voyage and its incidents." He then listened patiently while Mason detailed the foreign policy views of the Confederate government. The conversation was one-sided, as Russell interrupted only occasionally to ask a question or two. Mason emphasized that "in no possible contingency would the Confederate States come under a common Government with the North," stating that "none could really doubt we had ample resources of men and means to carry on the war so long as the enemy was in the field."[8] In their first meeting, Mason merely laid out the strengths of the Confederacy and did not press too strongly for recognition. It was really only a first opportunity for the southern diplomat and Lord Russell to gain personal impressions of each other.

Mason provided details of the meeting to the Confederate State Department, writing that Russell "seemed utterly disinclined to enter into conversation at all as to the policy of his Government" and that Russell's "personal sympathies were not with us, and his policy inaction."[9] On February 15, he wrote to Slidell in Paris that "the English mind seems averse to so strong a step as breaking the blockade,"[10] and several days later he labeled Russell's unofficial exposition of what was to be considered an effective blockade "little better than the old doctrine of paper blockade revived."[11] The British neutrality policy remained as steadfast as ever. The ministry continued to await further developments before it would take any new action regarding the war.

At that moment, what the Confederacy needed most was the breaking of the federal blockade. The blockade, according to Confederate authorities, was illegal; thus it was the duty of the European powers to ignore it.[12] The fourth provision of the Declaration of Paris (1856) stated that "blockades, in order to be binding, must be effective; that is to say, maintained by a force sufficient really to prevent access to the coast of the enemy."[13]

To prove that the federal blockade was merely a paper one, Mason forwarded to Lord Russell statistics concerning the number of ships leaving and entering Confederate ports. He emphasized that the Declaration of Paris was legally binding,[14] but Lord Russell had constructed a way of evading the technical requirements of the agreement. On February 15, Russell wrote to Lord Lyons that the blockade was effective not only as long as the number of ships guarding a Confederate port was "sufficient really to prevent access to it," as stated in the Declaration of Paris, but also when the number of ships was merely high enough "to create an evident danger of entering it or leaving it."[15] The latter part of that statement was an "amendment" to the treaty. A vague interpretation of danger was not an adequate reason to label a blockade effective, according to the Declaration of Paris.

In Richmond, the new Confederate secretary of state, Judah P. Benjamin, seized upon Russell's words to urge an increase in diplomatic criticism of the blockade.[16] Mason spent many of his later discussions with British authorities dealing with the question of the blockade's effectiveness and Britain's duty to intervene. Mason understood Britain's reluctance to do anything that would place itself on the brink of war with the United States,[17] but still he sought to bring about a change in British policy. In the legalistic minds of the architects of Confederate foreign policy, the statistics clearly proved that the federal blockade was ineffective,[18] rendering it illegal and undeserving of recognition.

Meanwhile, the issue of the blockade was being raised in both houses of Parliament throughout the month of February.[19] Those brief discussions served as mere preliminaries for major debates regarding the effectiveness of the blockade on March 7 in the House of Commons and on March 10 in the House of Lords. On March 7, Confederate sympathizer William H. Gregory moved that the British government declare the federal blockade ineffective. He pointed out explicitly that, with that motion, he was not talking about recognition of Confederate independence. His measure dealt only with the blockade. Gregory used the statistics that Mason had provided to Lord Russell on February 17, detailing vessels entering and clearing Confederate ports through October 1861.[20] He argued that Britain had an obligation to carry out the provisions of the Declaration of Paris regarding blockades, because the federal blockade was, in the almost unanimous opinion of the neutral powers, "ineffective and illegal."[21] The debate ebbed and flowed back and forth between each side's supporters until Gregory withdrew his motion, realizing that if the measure came to a vote it would be defeated. Confederate supporters believed it better for the outcome to be left in doubt than to run the risk of its being settled in defeat for the Richmond government.[22]

Three days later, Lord Campbell, another member of the Confederate lobby in Parliament, moved in the House of Lords "for copy of any correspondence on the subject of the blockade of the ports of the Confederate States of America," to provide a better explanation of the position taken by the British government.[23] That gave Lord Russell the opportunity to respond personally to those who questioned the ministry's position on the blockade. Russell stated that there existed no other hidden correspondence that would either prove or disprove his position that the blockade *was* effective and legal. He stressed caution, asking his colleagues to be patient and predicting that, "within three months—perhaps even sooner," the war would be over. Campbell's motion was withdrawn.[24] Mason quickly reported the results of the debates to Richmond, stating that those debates clearly showed that the British government intended to do nothing about the blockade.[25]

For the time being, Mason let it go at that. He did not refer to the cotton situation, as his predecessors had,[26] largely because there still was no word of the anticipated "cotton famine." Unfortunately for the Confederacy, the British had a sizable surplus of cotton to work with. The years before the war had been boom times for the southern staple. That, coupled with the fact that a particularly large harvest had been shipped out just before secession, meant that any "King Cotton" effects would not be seen until that supply was exhausted.[27] In a letter to Hunter on March 11, Mason wrote that those circumstances had caused the delay; but he also pointed out that the supply of cotton "was now very low" and that the long-awaited effects of "King Cotton" could be seen on the horizon. Only two-thirds of the cotton mills were operating, and those only at half time, while the working classes were being placated only "by sufficient alms, in aid of parish relief, to keep them from actual starvation."[28] Mason doubted that such a situation could continue very long.

When the initial rush after his arrival in London subsided, Mason's activities became a bit more routine.[29] Confederate authorities still viewed recognition as inevitable and sat back and awaited its arrival. On February 8, Hunter sent Mason contingency plans regarding a possible peace treaty that would result from the anticipated British recognition;[30] and on April 8, Benjamin wrote to Mason that "the President knows full well that it [recognition] must come at an early period as a concession to the stern logic of events."[31] Davis blamed the continuance of the war solely on the attitude taken by the European powers.[32] Diplomacy had become particularly crucial, and if Britain were determined to do nothing, there were other powers capable of intervention.

On April 16, Mason left London for Paris, accompanied by William S. Lindsay, a shipbuilder and a member of the British Parliament sympathetic to the South. Lindsay met with Napoleon III three times that month and provided Mason with more reasons for optimism. After discussing the situation with Slidell, Mason returned to London on April 21 and reported to Richmond that France would act alone as soon as there was "any decisive success" by Confederate armed forces, or merely "an absence of success and delays on the part of the enemy."[33] Napoleon III still desired to act jointly with the British but gave the Confederate commissioners the impression that he was willing to take the lead in forcing Britain's hand. That assessment proved to be erroneous, but for a time it contributed to Confederate high spirits.[34]

Besides his trip to Paris, Mason's schedule was filled with numerous social engagements at which American affairs were topics of discussion. Recognizing that a diplomat needed to see people and be seen in order to be effective, Mason met or dined with a virtual "Who's Who" of the British upper class and military. Using these occasions to gauge public opinion, he readily discussed just about any topic in American history, as well as the politics of the day. Simultaneously, he espoused the policies of the Confederate government and his firm belief that the Confederacy never could be conquered.[35] Mason clearly won social acceptance, despite the official cold shoulder he received from Lord Russell and the British ministry.

Those activities occupied much of Mason's time. He had no more interviews with Lord Russell in 1862, and even indirect contacts between the two were rare. Events affecting the South's diplomatic position unfolded beyond Mason's control, while his British advisors encouraged him to be patient. The Virginian went along with such a strategy. By that time, Mason was strongly under the influence of James M. Spence, whom Frank L. Owsley described as a "native propaganda agent" for the Confederacy.[36] Another author referred to Spence as an "*eminence gris* behind James Mason's official overtures."[37] In reality he was much more.

Born in Liverpool, Spence was a renowned British merchant, shipper, banker, and stockbroker, who dealt particularly with the iron trade and the Liverpool cotton exchange.[38] A staunch supporter of the South, in 1861 he wrote a book defending the right to secede,[39] as well as a series of anonymous letters to the *London Times* attempting to sway public opinion in favor of the Confederacy. When Mason arrived in Britain, he made Spence perhaps the most trusted of his British advisors. In the early months of 1862, Spence advised not to push too hard for recognition. He viewed the timing of any diplomatic pressure as critical, and he particularly wanted Mason to await the onset of the "cotton famine."[40] Mason kept Richmond informed of the dwindling British cotton supply[41] and wrote to President Davis that, in his opinion, "the higher and educated classes strongly sympathize with the South, and seem to deplore the coldness and inaction of the [British] Government."[42]

Since he was not being pushed by either Richmond or his British advisors, Mason's direct efforts toward gaining diplomatic recognition of the Confederacy faded into the background, and most of his time came to be devoted to social events of varying importance for the Confederate cause. Additionally, he became more involved with the day-to-day financial and purchasing problems that faced Confederate agents in Europe, and he served as a funnel for information from various southerners to and from Richmond.[43]

Mason also expressed a growing admiration for Spence. He went out of his way to point out the Britisher to the Richmond government, emphasizing Spence's book and describing the character of his propaganda work. In April and May, Mason penned scarcely a letter that did not contain praise for Spence's work.[44] His superlatives fell just short of Confederate propagandist Henry Hotze's dubious statement that Spence's book compared favorably with Alexis de Tocqueville's works on American democracy.[45] Mason even advised Benjamin to show President Davis the correspondence on Spence's suggestion that the Confederate States of America change its name to the "Southern Union." Spence contended that the name change would "cause the other party to be termed the 'Northern Union,'" and supposedly this would prevent the North from reaping benefits from the prestige associated with the name United States of America.[46] In 1862, Benjamin referred to Spence by name only once in a letter to Mason, and even then he mentioned Spence's book and his propaganda work only briefly, while brushing aside his additional "suggestions."[47] Such was Richmond's reaction to the Spence "proposal."

Mason remained in continual contact with various members of Parliament who had Confederate sympathies, but he did not press upon Lord Russell either the blockade issue or any real demands for recognition. By summer, there still was no noticeable movement by the British government toward intervention on behalf of the Confederacy. Except for his initial contacts with Russell shortly after his arrival in London, Mason had allowed the first months of 1862 to slip by unproductively. Certainly he had made many important acquaintances both inside and outside the government. With regard to the many factors that affected the Confederacy's diplomatic status in the first half of 1862, however, Mason's efforts to gain British intervention, being more passive than active, had not been a major determinant.

Mason's inactivity, encouraged by Spence and other British citizens, largely was due to the fact that the Confederacy and its supporters continued to cling to the "King Cotton" theory. Benjamin did use cotton aggressively in dealings with France, authorizing John Slidell to offer the French one hundred thousand bales of cotton, worth approximately $12.5 million, or 63 million francs. All the French had to do was come and get it.[48] But no simultaneous offer was made to the British. Because coming to get the cotton would have involved breaking the blockade, any such offer stood little chance of being accepted. Napoleon III would not be baited by the South's staple crop.

Meanwhile, by the middle of 1862, word of the long-expected "famine" of cotton reached Richmond. Hotze wrote, "The cotton famine, so long predicted and so unaccountably delayed, has at last overtaken the land, with all its train of destitution and ruin."[49] Mason still anticipated no action from the British government regarding the blockade, but he wrote to Pierre Rost in Spain that, if the famine truly had arrived, Lancashire cotton spinners would be "starving and dying."[50] Supporting the Confederacy's cotton policy vigorously, Mason believed that the King Cotton theory was about to be proved correct after all.

Over a month passed (after the numerous "Spence" letters) before he penned another official dispatch to the Confederate State Department. Then, on June 23, for the first time in weeks, he reported all the important occurrences. Mason wrote that Russell continued to state in Parliament that any intervention in the form of mediation "would be 'inopportune' at the present time." Britain appeared particularly resolute about not interfering with the federal blockade. The cotton situation, though, was Mason's primary focus. He reported that the "stock of cotton is almost exhausted, and it seems fully conceded that no approximation to a supply can be looked for in any quarter other than the Confederate States." When he wrote of the suffering in those areas that needed Confederate cotton, Mason used words such as "actual starvation" in the manufacturing districts, speaking of starved men, women, and children being "found dead in their houses."[51]

The timing could not have been better for the Confederacy. The summer of 1862 marked many of the greatest victories that southern arms would have. Gen. Robert E. Lee was finally in command of the Army of Northern Virginia. After a series of victories within the Confederacy, he prepared to invade Maryland in September, while Gen. Braxton Bragg simultaneously prepared to invade Kentucky. Confederate military successes peaked at the same moment when the cotton shortage hurt Britain the most.[52] By September, Britain's supply of cotton had plummeted to only half of what it was in 1861, and only one-third of what it had been in 1860.[53]

In late June, Mason continued to remain passive while the cotton shortage did the work for him. He still thought it "unwise" directly to ask the British ministry to recognize Confederate independence. Mason dreaded the possibility that such a suggestion might be rejected out of hand. Instead of taking bold action, he waited, refusing to undertake such a task "without the most grave and mature deliberation."[54] Mason needed to be pushed into action if Confederate diplomacy in England was to move forward, but the advice of his British friends only reinforced his hesitancy.[55]

The needed push came from President Davis and Secretary of State Benjamin. Unlike his predecessors, Benjamin never found his job dull and boring.[56] The new state department head reinvigorated both the president and Confederate foreign policy. Largely because of his great energy, the new secretary subtly began to move President Davis toward a more aggressive foreign policy stance.[57] In his first correspondences with Mason, Benjamin strongly emphasized Davis's diplomatic aims in no uncertain terms, as well as the president's belief that blame for the continuance of the war lay squarely on the shoulders of Europe.[58]

Unfortunately, communications were an everyday problem for diplomats in the 1860s. The normal delays associated with transatlantic communications were exacerbated by the war and the blockade.[59] For maximum effectiveness, diplomatic correspondence had to arrive at its destination with some degree of timeliness. Between London and Richmond, there often were long delays in the transmission of dispatches. Virtually all letters eventually reached the addressee, but the time lapses between arrivals often were unbearably long.[60] That meant that Mason frequently was left on his own, without guidance from the Confederate government across the sea.

There was just such a delay in the critical spring months of 1862, when Mason seemed to busy himself with more trivial details rather than with his prime responsibility of dealing directly with the British government regarding intervention. A critical dispatch from Benjamin, dated April 8, 1862, did not get to Mason until June 29. The time that elapsed between those dates marked the period when Mason was strongly influenced by Spence and others who urged him not to press hard for recognition. When it finally arrived, the letter pushed Mason to resume regular correspondence with Lord Russell. Benjamin specifically dealt with the porous nature of the blockade, detailing updated statistics on the number of ships that had entered or left Confederate ports in the first months of the year. He also addressed the question of why, if the blockade was so ineffective, so little cotton was reaching European shores. As an agricultural country, the Confederacy did not possess a commercial marine capable of transporting the cotton.[61] A large portion of the small number of merchant ships that existed in the South had been seized by the Confederate government for the use of its fledgling navy.[62] That left few ships available to transport Confederate cotton. Benjamin wrote, "The President trusts that you will lose no suitable opportunity of pressing these views on the consideration of the British Government."[63]

On July 7, Mason wrote to Lord Russell for the first time in three months, expressing Richmond's belief that the federal blockade was only a paper one and detailing vessels that had gotten through it in January and February. He also pointed out that there was "no policy in the Confederate States Government to prohibit or discourage the export of cotton," emphasizing that, if there was a shortage of cotton in Europe, it was because Europeans had not "thought it proper to send her ships to America" to get it.[64] The legalistic character of Confederate foreign policy, as originated by President Davis, was as strong as ever, because Mason explicitly referred to the Declaration of Paris and to Russell's earlier efforts to "amend" the wording in a way that was beneficial to the United States while being detrimental to the Confederacy.[65] The very nature of British "neutrality" finally was being questioned.

In Parliament, debates regarding American affairs grew more heated. Confederate supporters openly questioned the ministry about offering mediation to the warring parties. In the House of Commons, on June 30, one of them asked Prime Minister Palmerston, "Whether, considering the great and increasing distress in the country, . . . the Government intend to take any steps whatever . . . to endeavour to put an end to the Civil War in America?" Palmerston responded that there was no intention on the part of the British government to make such an offer, because it did not wish to irritate the belligerents.[66]

That response failed to prevent Lindsay from introducing a resolution on July 18 stating that "offering mediation, with the view of terminating hostilities between the contending parties, is worthy of the serious and immediate attention of Her Majesty's Government."[67] That night, in Palmerston's words, the House of Commons "had the American war waged here, in words, by champions on both sides."[68] The debate took a course similar to the discussions of March regarding the blockade.[69] Confederate sympathizers knew that they had insufficient support to pass the resolution, particularly with Palmerston clearly against any offer of mediation at that time.[70] The evening ended with Lindsay withdrawing his motion.

Mason's attitude during this flurry of activity is best illustrated in a letter written to his wife on July 20: "The Government here is tardy and supine . . . but the increasing distress for cotton, and the late apparent decided successes before Richmond, I think will move them." Word had just arrived in London of the Confederate victories in the Peninsular Campaign, and Mason was busy with numerous visits from interested members of Parliament. He looked "speedily for intervention in *some form*." Mason also wrote of more personal affairs, expressing his growing comfort with London society, which kept him "too much occupied in returning and acknowledging the visits of the immense number who call daily."[71] He was content overall with the way things were going, despite the British government's seeming intransigence.

Mason's optimism replicated that found in Richmond. President Davis wrote to his wife on July 6 that "the Yankees have gained from England and France as the last extension, this month, and expect foreign intervention if we hold them at bay on the first of August."[72] On July 19, Benjamin wrote to Mason that he believed the Confederacy's "series of triumphs will at last have satisfied the most skeptical of foreign cabinets that we are an independent nation, and have the right to be so considered and treated."[73] Countering to some extent Spence's continuing efforts to keep Mason from pushing too hard,[74] Benjamin urged him to "spare no effort to avail yourself of the favorable opportunity presented by our recent success in urging our right to recognition."[75]

That same month, Mason himself addressed the mediation question on behalf of the Confederate government. He wrote to Lord Russell that, while he of course could not speak for the United States, he knew that the Confederacy, although not inviting such an inter-position, saw "nothing in their position which could make either of-fensive or irritating a tender of such offices on the part of her Majesty's Government as might lead to a termination of the war."[76] Blame for continuance of the war was not going to be placed on President Davis's shoulders if the Virginia diplomat could prevent it.

Russell disagreed with Mason's assessment of the situation,[77] perhaps recognizing that the Confederate commissioner's state-ments could not have been dictated specifically from Richmond. Still, Mason kept up the pressure. Upon receiving the British minister's dismissal of any suggestion of mediation, Mason im-mediately requested an interview. He pointed out that five months had passed since their only face-to-face discussion and that, in that time, the Confederate States clearly had shown an ability to maintain their independence, regardless of what attempts at con-quest might be made by the United States.[78] To Mason, Davis, and Benjamin, Confederate independence was a given fact and deserved to be recognized by the states of Europe.

This optimism turned to disappointment when Russell, on July 31, politely but firmly turned down Mason's request for an inter-view.[79] The Confederate commissioner could not be put off so easily, however. He quickly responded to the British foreign minister in writing, detailing many of the views that he had intended to put for-ward in person. Mason angrily reiterated the strength of the Confed-eracy and its ability to maintain its independence. British neutrality and Russell's refusal to recognize "that the Southern States, now in a separate Confederacy, had established before the world, their compe-tency to maintain the Government of their adoption," only served to encourage "the continuance of a war, hopeless in its objects, ruinous alike to the parties engaged in it and to the prosperity and welfare of Europe."[80] Such language was as strong as any Mason had used up to that point, but still Russell refused to change his stance.[81]

Rebuffed by the ministry, Mason dropped back into the back-ground of the movement to gain British intervention. Nonetheless, with Russell and Palmerston working behind the scenes, in August and September, the British government came as close as it ever would come to granting the Confederacy diplomatic recognition. In all like-lihood, such a movement would have taken place even without Mason's presence in London,[82] primarily because the cotton supply continued to decrease and General Lee continued to pile up military victories. At no future date would the Confederacy's diplomatic posi-tion be as strong as it was late in the summer of 1862.[83]

The British government tried all summer to determine the northern public's state of mind, not wanting to offer mediation to a United States that believed itself certain of victory. As August gave way to September, Russell reviewed prospects for Britain's taking a more active role in the American conflict. News of Lee's victory at Second Manassas reached him during the second week of September. He concluded that the United States had been defeated and that, with the North's capital city in danger of being captured by Confederate forces, the time for some sort of intervention had come.[84] At last Russell believed that war-weariness had become strong enough in the northern states to allow British intervention to succeed.[85] He sought the cooperation of the other major European powers in mediating a settlement of the war on the basis of independence for the Confederacy. France and Russia supposedly would join Britain in the intervention, while Austria and Prussia were to be kept informed of developments.[86] Anticipation on both sides of the Atlantic heightened, as Confederate diplomatic fortunes clearly rode with the Army of Northern Virginia as it crossed the Potomac River into Maryland.

Mason knew that the British cabinet was closely divided on the subject of intervention, and he hoped that pressure from both Napoleon III and British public opinion might push the ministry in the desired direction.[87] Confederate diplomatic activity shifted to Paris. There Slidell pressed the French government, which he believed to be the real hope of the Confederacy since there was "no hope from England, because I am satisfied that she desires an indefinite prolongation of the war, until the North shall be entirely exhausted and broken down."[88] Napoleon III, however, never provided any tangible aid to the Confederate cause. He was all talk and no action, but at that stage, he remained a key prospect for the hopeful Richmond government.

Regardless of where the Confederacy's emphasis lay at any specific time, Britain remained the most important diplomatic arena. Russell became extremely active in pushing an offer of mediation.[89] If mediation were accepted, Russell's plan called for an armistice, with the blockade lifted. Then the separation of the states would be negotiated. If only the North refused, Britain would "acknowledge" Confederate independence.[90] But Palmerston hesitated, believing that it was crucial for Britain to act at precisely the right moment. He sensed that, with Lee's invasion of the North, that moment was near but not yet at hand. Despite his confidence in southern victory, Palmerston waited to bring the question before the full cabinet until word arrived of the expected battle on northern soil.[91]

Mason correctly anticipated that the critical discussions within the British cabinet would occur in October,[92] but the news that arrived from across the Atlantic on October 2 was not what had been expected. The battle at Sharpsburg, Maryland, was at best a draw and at worst a southern defeat. Lee's "invasion" had been repulsed. Baltimore and Washington were not captured. Instead, the United States appeared to be as strong as ever, and Palmerston believed that the Lincoln government would resist fiercely, with every available resource, any European interference.[93]

Lord Russell, however, continued to develop mediation proposals, and on October 13 he gave the other cabinet members a detailed memorandum on the subject. In that document, Russell recapped the military campaigns of the past months and also discussed Lincoln's Emancipation Proclamation.[94] He concluded that the great powers of Europe had to intervene in this war of indecisive battles between equally balanced armies, particularly because the situation had become "embittered by exciting the passions of the slave to aid the destructive progress of armies."[95]

Russell argued that the Confederacy had shown that it possessed the will and the ability to resist federal conquest. Believing that reconstruction sentiment in the South was minimal and fearing a slave insurrection as a result of the Emancipation Proclamation, he judged that conditions were indeed ripe for Europe to propose an armistice in order to focus both sides upon the benefits to be gained from peace.[96] But his arguments fell upon deaf ears, as, over the next week or so, Russell determined that only a few cabinet members, including Chancellor of the Exchequer William E. Gladstone, truly supported his proposition. By October 20, when he learned that, in all likelihood, Russia would refuse to join any mediation effort, the movement toward British intervention had slowed.[97]

James Murray Mason was not a part of those crucial developments. From late August through September 10, he made a "protracted visit to Scotland."[98] A great deal of business needing his attention piled up in his absence, but on the main question of recognition, Mason sat on the sidelines, ignored by the ministry during this critical period. But such relative idleness failed to dampen his spirits. In October, cheered by being "kindly and hospitably received by *society* in London, both Peers and Commons," Mason expressed his optimistic sentiments to his son George, writing that "England stands amazed at the courage, constancy, and self-sacrificing spirit of the South." He believed that "notwithstanding the supineness of the Government in refusing acknowledgment of our independence, the public judgment of the English mind is that independence is established."[99] Mason saw recognition by Britain and France as being just over the horizon. Uninformed about the maneuvering within the British ministry, he remained optimistic even after the news from Maryland arrived in London. His steadfast belief that Britain would act in favor of the Confederacy lasted virtually until the end of the year, as he continued to follow the progress of the "cotton famine."[100]

So far, cotton had played a minimal role in Confederate diplomacy. The British cabinet was sensitive to cotton developments, but that concern always was secondary to power politics. The prime concern of the Palmerston government was the likelihood that recognition of the Confederacy would be followed by a declaration of war by the United States. Such a war was undesirable militarily because of a number of factors, including the vulnerability of Canada. Additionally, war with the United States would have distracted Britain from European affairs. The British took northern military threats seriously, and those threats overshadowed any diplomatic power the Confederate States could derive from King Cotton.[101]

Northern diplomacy had proven to be more potent, in part because of the efforts of the U.S. minister to England, Charles Francis Adams. President Lincoln entrusted him with preventing England from recognizing the South's independence and convincing the British that selling arms to the "rebels" constituted a breach of neutrality. A grandson of John Adams and son of John Quincy Adams, the diplomat maintained the family tradition of being suspicious of John Bull's motives, but he tempered the often aggressive diplomacy of Secretary of State William Seward with the calm tact of a cultured Bostonian. Gradually he had earned the respect of Lord Russell.[102]

His potential for influencing British foreign policy dwarfed Mason's, because Adams had easy access to the British secretary of state for foreign affairs. The upshot of such meetings generally was that Russell assured Adams of the ministry's commitment to neutrality, regardless of what appeared in the press or was spoken in Parliament.[103] Those discussions also gave the New Englander a personal opportunity to emphasize northern determination, something his Virginia counterpart could not do.

On October 23, with rumors of intervention swirling around London, a concerned Adams sought an explanation from Russell. Adams stressed that the United States would reject any proposal for mediation and that his mission would be ended if Britain recognized the Confederacy.[104] Again the Englishman assured Adams that Britain would remain neutral for the present, but he refused to give promises beyond that. Each man believed that he understood the other, and Adams left the meeting satisfied that nothing would change in the foreseeable future.[105]

But Russell remained watchful regarding developments in the war, particularly noting how they affected U.S. politics and morale.[106] By the end of October, he and Palmerston privately agreed that spring of 1863 would be a better time to propose mediation. Yet, on November 11 and 12, at the first cabinet meetings held in over two months, Russell argued in favor of a French proposal for the two European powers to offer the Americans an armistice. He failed to win any converts. Cabinet opinion was decidedly against interfering in the war. Such sentiment was epitomized by Secretary for War George Cornewall Lewis, who, on November 7, had distributed to the cabinet a 15,000-word memorandum arguing against the premise that the Confederacy had earned recognition. He particularly stressed that any intervention would mean war with the United States, since only a military solution could decide which side was right in such a divisive conflict.[107]

Faced with such earnest opposition, Russell needed Palmerston's support to win the day, but any support from that quarter was meager at best.[108] Russell backed off, explaining in a letter to Earl Cowley that "it would be better to watch carefully the progress of opinion in America," since rejection of an armistice by the United States "would prevent any speedy renewal of the offer."[109] It remained Lord Palmerston's ministry, and the lack of vigorous support from the veteran statesman was the key to failure of the intervention movement in 1862.[110]

Mason spent October quietly, as he attempted to allow the natural course of events to affect the cabinet deliberations he knew to be taking place. Even the usually cautious Spence believed that the time for recognition was ripe, and he worked diligently writing "letters each week on Recognition, argument after argument, so as to keep it constantly before the public."[111] Mason busied himself with activities related to the purchasing of various war materials[112] and with Confederate finance.[113] Both those subjects fused with talk of diplomatic recognition and resulted in a surge of correspondence between Mason and the Confederate State Department through the end of the year. The dispatches reflected varying levels of optimism and pessimism, as Confederate fortunes ebbed and flowed.

On November 8, Mason wrote that "the Emperor of France has proposed to England and Russia that the three powers should unite in proposing to the belligerents of America an armistice for six months." The blockade would be "removed as part of the armistice, and it is confidently asserted that Russia has assented to it."[114] He further predicted that England would agree, stating that it was a definite fact even if other sources labeled it only a rumor. Slidell supported Mason's conclusion, writing from Paris that "England will join directly with Russia and France. . . . Should Russia and England withhold their assent, I now believe that France will act without them."[115] Neither commissioner was correct, but nonetheless the pair confidently reported developments throughout November.

Unfortunately for the Confederacy, there was very little real news to report. Behind the closed doors of the British cabinet, the recognition movement had failed. But the cotton famine seemed to become an important factor, as had been expected. In November, Mason informed Richmond that seven hundred thousand Englishmen were entirely dependent upon charity for subsistence, with the number increasing by ten to twenty thousand each week.[116] In December, he wrote to Benjamin that the famine "continues still to extend itself with apparently gigantic strides" and that only government aid would be able to prevent genuine starvation, despite the heroic efforts of private charity.[117]

Mason failed to comprehend that such matters were in many ways mere statistics to the British government and that importation of cotton from other areas, such as India and Russia, was on the verge of doing its part to end the suffering.[118] Some of the unemployment was absorbed by substitutes, such as wool and linen, whose levels of production increased in Great Britain for the first time in years.[119] Cotton was not the economic weapon of diplomacy that southerners had expected it to be.

Benjamin and Davis followed diplomatic events closely from Richmond, and in December they sent instructions to both Mason and Slidell, detailing how to handle things after recognition took place, since peace would be the result of such action.[120] Despite such positive rhetoric, the Confederate government in fact was discouraged as year's end approached. A series of military victories and the clear maintenance of independence for a second year notwithstanding, no British recognition had been forthcoming. As policy was formulated for 1863, Davis and Benjamin searched for someone to blame for Confederate diplomatic failures.

Their search took them to Lord Russell. Davis, Mason, and Benjamin heard only the public Russell, who espoused the firm line of British governmental policy. They knew nothing of Russell's efforts within the cabinet to gain support for mediation. Years later, Davis wrote that the British government did not care about the suffering of British cotton workers and that Russell, by failing to recognize Confederate independence, had stymied the "good intentions" of the British people.[121] On October 31, Benjamin wrote that all the recent events "force on the President the conviction that there exists a feeling on the part of the British ministry unfriendly to this Government." He instructed Mason to lodge a formal protest against the federal blockade.[122] The Confederates refused to beg for recognition but believed that legality was on their side, as the Richmond government continued to stress the porous nature of the blockade.

As usual, the dispatch was delayed, but finally, on January 3, 1863, Mason wrote to Lord Russell presenting "a formal protest on the part of the Government of the Confederate States against the apparent (if not executed) purpose of Her Majesty's Government to change or modify to the prejudice of the Confederacy the doctrine in relation to the blockade."[123] The language of the protest was diplomatic. Mason was still patient, perhaps because he was isolated from the sufferings on the battlefields and elsewhere within the Confederacy. He was out of touch with the realities confronting those who faced another year of war. He spent Christmas week at the estate of Confederate sympathizer Alexander Jones Beresford-Hope, some sixty miles from London, where he had the "favourable opportunity of witnessing the customs and partaking the hospitalities of English country life on the most extended scale." For Mason, the happy celebrations of the holiday brought back fond memories of his youth. He "found their Christmas usages" much like those at Clermont "in the better days of the Old Dominion." He described to Eliza his participation in the "abundant interchange of presents, church in the private chapel on Christmas eve and Christmas evening, a large dinner every day, at which the country neighbours were guests, and, of course, service in the village church on the day of Christmas."[124]

Such accommodations were far superior to those of most citizens of the Confederacy, including those of his own family. He regularly received news of increased privation in the South, but news of his wife and daughters, who abandoned Selma in March when northern troops prepared to capture Winchester, must have troubled the loving father and husband.[125] A young girl detailed the plight of the Mason women in her diary, writing, "We were grieved to hear what a terrible time the Masons have had, flying before the Yankees. They have suffered all kinds of hardships and discomforts. Anna and her five children went with them from Fauquier to Charlottesville in a wagon, for which with the horses Mrs. Mason paid one thousand dollars. And Mrs. Mason and the girls had to walk for miles through the rain."[126] That distressing tale should have increased Mason's determination to achieve quick action. Using his social calendar for 1862 as evidence, however, one can remain doubtful as to whether he felt the urgency that must have quickened the pulses of his own family members, Davis, and Benjamin.

Continually susceptible to the advice of men such as Spence, who counseled delay and dissuaded him from forcefully pressing the Confederate position upon the British ministry, Mason had become isolated from the realities of the South's situation. In 1862, more often than not, he observed diplomatic events rather than participating in them. Slidell seems to have made much more progress in gaining French intervention than Mason had in securing British help. The Virginian noticed the great differences between Slidell's mission and his own. On January 18, 1863, he wrote to Eliza, stating that the British government "remains impassive and impenetrable as ever." He lamented how the British ministry had treated him, compared with the treatment the French government had accorded Slidell, who "had interviews with the Emperor two or three times, and sees the different members of the ministry at his pleasure, and almost every day." In contrast, Mason had "seen none but Lord Russell, now nearly a year ago, and have never since had from any ministerial quarter, the least intimation of a desire to form acquaintance."[127] As the new year dawned, Mason wrote to Benjamin that he was "by no means hopeful."[128] After spending almost an entire year in England, the Virginia aristocrat had not moved the British government any closer to granting recognition to the Confederate States of America.

Harking back to the personal criticism of his enemies, it is easy to conclude that Mason must not have been "diplomatic" enough. If that were the case, however, it would be hard to explain the wide array of social and political acquaintances Mason made *outside* the British ministry. The answer does not lie in Mason's lack of the necessary social and diplomatic skills. He made friends with those who sympathized with the Confederacy. He met with men hostile to the Confederate cause at times, but he remained surrounded primarily by sympathetic individuals who were eager to listen and eager to give advice. Political considerations and their effects on decisions made behind the closed doors of the British ministry were much more important than any character flaws in the Confederate commissioner.

In 1863, one more clamor for recognition followed the successes of Lee's army, but never again would the British be as close to intervention as they were in the autumn of 1862. One reason Confederate foreign policy failed was its formulators' exclusive focus on "King Cotton." Such tunnel vision left its representatives inactive much of the year. Passivity in Richmond infected Mason in London and was reinforced by British advisors who urged him to sit quietly and await developments. That attitude could have been altered by Davis, Benjamin, or, across the sea, James Murray Mason.

Beyond the control of any Confederate leader, however, were the political considerations of the day. Great Britain did not want war with the United States, and that was precisely what the British ministry believed would follow any ill-timed intervention. Those shaping Confederate foreign policy needed to exhibit resourcefulness and ingenuity in combating that diplomatic fact of life, but they failed to do so. Since Mason could not prod Britain into recognizing Confederate independence in 1862, his day-to-day efforts thereafter increasingly focused on minor responsibilities beyond diplomatic intervention, while the odds for his beloved South grew longer and longer.

Chapter 10

1862–1865

Mason and Confederate Purchasing, Shipbuilding, and Finance

When the war began, one critical military element that the Confederacy lacked was a navy to send against the United States. President Davis lamented that, when the southern states seceded from the Union, southern naval officers turned over their vessels to federal authorities and then resigned their commissions. Reasoning that the U.S. Navy belonged to the individual states, Davis argued that, when the South seceded, naval property should have been divided, with the Confederacy gaining its appropriate share.[1] Since that had not occurred, ships needed to be built. Their construction required careful allocation of scarce credit and material resources. As the South lacked a strong tradition of shipbuilding, the Confederacy attempted to purchase the vast majority of vessels it needed in Europe, and particularly in Great Britain. Confederate authorities believed that international laws and practices permitted such action, and they expected European leaders to agree. The British government might refuse to intervene in the war directly by using the Royal Navy to break the federal blockade, but it appeared likely that the English would allow the Confederacy to purchase the ships it needed to do the job itself.

Efforts to arrange such a purchase began months before James Murray Mason arrived in London. James D. Bulloch and James H. North were the Confederacy's primary purchasing agents in Britain, but, from the beginning, they encountered problems. Lack of funds destroyed the spirit of naïve optimism that prevailed among all the agents in the war's early days. Bulloch related his first experiences, writing, "I soon learned that no contracts or purchases could be made without cash actually in hand, it being the invariable practice in England to pay a portion of the contract money at the time of agreement."[2] North similarly commented, "I am here without one dollar to carry out your orders, and the people of these parts are as keen after money as any people I ever saw in my life."[3]

Scarcity of funds linked the various parts of the southern war effort together.[4] The credit situation improved or worsened with the vicissitudes of the Confederate economy. Money was crucial to the success of everything from military actions to diplomacy. The lack of cash hampered not only Confederate purchasing agents, but also the armed forces and virtually every civil servant of the Richmond government. British policy makers watched to see if the Confederacy stood as a viable republic worthy of diplomatic recognition, and they believed that a government's financial condition was a measure of the soundness of the government itself.[5]

Appearances often led the British to a negative conclusion, particularly because there was no centralized coordination of Confederate financial activities in Europe until late in the war. The Davis government had no unified plan for buying materials and supplies overseas. Instructions conflicted, and jurisdictions overlapped. Rivalries and deep-seated jealousies abounded. Necessary items could not be purchased because one agent was short of funds, while others had a surplus.[6] Such confusion made the Confederacy easy prey for merchants and blockade runners seeking to make a quick profit.

By the fall of 1862, the financial status of the Confederacy had deteriorated to the point where letters of credit and bills of exchange no longer could be purchased by the traditional means of gold and silver coin. Possessing no alternative, the Confederates made cotton the unconventional replacement for purchasing efforts in Europe,[7] and Mason played a major role in crucial credit negotiations of marked delicacy. That plunged him deeper into the monetary side of the southern war effort.

As the highest-ranking Confederate official in Europe, Mason became the logical person to approach if a purchasing agent or someone else serving the Richmond government needed money. That caused him to devote a considerable amount of his time to such matters, particularly in 1863, when his primary task remained that of gaining diplomatic recognition from the British government. Instead, he spent a great many hours acting in an unofficial capacity as a "banker," disbursing what funds he had to agents all over Europe.[8]

His involvement with purchasing and finance began as soon as he reached London. In January 1862, Capt. Raphael Semmes, commander of the Confederate steamer *Sumter*, anchored at Gibraltar, desperately needed funds to have his vessel repaired and refueled. Over the next few weeks, Mason completed negotiations to place sixteen thousand dollars at Semmes's disposal with Fraser, Trenholm and Company.[9] That Liverpool company, with ties to both Charleston, South Carolina, and New York City, served as depository for Confederate funds in Europe and connected naval purchasing efforts with various European financial institutions.[10]

Through the spring and summer of 1862, matters of purchasing and finance remained no more than a secondary responsibility for Mason, but those activities were quite varied. He had continued dealings with Fraser, Trenholm and Company,[11] as well as with Captain Semmes,[12] both directly and through Bulloch.[13] Financial matters also crept into his letters that praised James Spence,[14] as Mason endorsed Spence's wish to be made a financial agent in addition to his propaganda activities.[15]

Except for a receipt for cotton bonds worth over two thousand dollars, there is no evidence that Mason was involved with southern cotton as a financial tool until the fall of 1862.[16] With recognition delayed indefinitely and its credit situation deteriorating daily, the Confederacy turned to its greatest staple crop. In September, Mason played a direct role in the first use of cotton certificates to finance the purchase of ships in Britain.[17] They financed the building of a ship contracted for by Lt. George T. Sinclair of the Confederate Navy through an arrangement with the banking firm of a sympathetic member of Parliament, William S. Lindsay. Mason urged Richmond to approve "the use of obligations for delivery of cotton by the Government on the terms and manner expressed." That delivery would "be made at any port in possession of the Confederate States when demanded by the holder of the bond, after reasonable (say thirty or more days) notice or within three months after a peace." He took full responsibility for fixing the price but asked Richmond to send instructions for the future.[18]

Although the bonds raised a relatively small amount (£62,000), the success of the venture gave those involved the idea that cotton bonds could work on a larger scale.[19] In Paris, John Slidell believed that he had the credit offer the Confederacy needed. He wrote Mason of being "quite surprised, at an uninvited suggestion on the part of a respectable banking house to open a credit to our Government of a considerable amount."[20] The proposal for a loan of £5 million came from European banker Émile Erlanger. Slidell believed that the loan would go far in meeting the financial needs of Confederate purchasing agents, but he also saw political benefits. He argued that a sound foreign loan would be equated by European governments with Confederate economic strength, increasing the likelihood of Richmond's gaining diplomatic recognition.[21]

Mason's reaction to the proposed Erlanger contract differed greatly from Slidell's.[22] Impressed with the Lindsay firm's handling of the Sinclair bonds, the conservative Virginian favored small loans administered by those experienced hands.[23] Lindsay believed that bonds worth up to £500,000 could be floated successfully by his company. That figure contrasted dramatically with the much larger Erlanger offer. Mason expressed a clear preference for Lindsay's proposal but admitted that Slidell probably knew more of the Erlanger offer's merits than he did. Wanting to give Richmond a choice, he presented the two options[24] and sat back to await Jefferson Davis's decision. In December, Mason wrote that he had "taken no further steps in regard to the plan proposed of raising money by means of obligations of delivery of cotton," beyond consulting with Confederate purchasing agents and his British advisors,[25] including James Spence.[26]

Spence and Mason both believed that accepting the initial Erlanger contract proposal would lead to a "frightful" loss of interest, "in addition to the heavy rate of commissions."[27] The harsh terms also stunned President Davis and Secretary of State Benjamin,[28] but Slidell's arguments that the political advantages outweighed the financial disadvantages prevailed.[29] Protracted negotiations resulted in the terms being made a bit more favorable to the Confederacy,[30] but by most standards they still appeared usurious. At the official exchange rate of the time, in Confederate money the loan amounted to approximately $14.5 million. The rate of interest was set at 7 percent. On every hundred-dollar bond sold, Erlanger received everything collected over a base of seventy-seven dollars, which went to the Confederacy, as well as a 5 percent commission.[31]

Slidell, not Mason, played the key role in the Erlanger negotiations;[32] but in London, the Virginian stood at the center of a circle of Confederate purchasing agents faced with a dwindling supply of funds. In January, he informed Slidell that "the time has arrived when the government must suffer with perhaps serious loss in meeting engagements unless money is supplied."[33] Continually asked by Bulloch when the Erlanger money was coming, he pleaded for patience.[34] Other agents also badgered Mason for money in the first weeks of 1863,[35] but he refused to interfere with the delicate negotiations.[36] On February 19, North wrote that he had run out of money and owed £18,000 immediately; two weeks later the increasingly desperate purchasing agent required £8,000 more.[37] Mason assured him both times that sufficient funds would be forthcoming in a few days.[38]

Not until March 18 could Mason finally tell North "with certainty" that he would receive the necessary funds.[39] The next day, the Erlanger bonds hit the market at a price of ninety. Erlanger determined that high figure, wanting the price to reflect confidence in the Confederacy but also wanting to earn his firm a handsome profit. Had the bonds been issued at a lower, more realistic price, financial advantages would have been gained, but at the expense of anticipated political advantages.[40] Mason believed confidently that the certificates would improve in value.[41] On the day of their issue, while informing Benjamin of his being "impressed by the judgement and good sense evinced by Erlanger," he reported "the decided and brilliant success of the Confederate loan."[42] By the end of March, he proclaimed with a great deal of satisfaction, "Cotton is king at last."[43] Slidell went even further, claiming "a financial recognition of our independence."[44] Such optimism reflected the bonds' initial rise in price, but before long the picture changed, and the price began to decline. Valiant attempts to prop up the price by intervening directly in the market[45] drove the price back above par value temporarily but were insufficient to maintain the bonds at what the financial markets clearly deemed an unrealistic price.[46]

Initially, Mason blamed the drop on U.S. operatives in Europe, who he said were "making concerted movements covertly to discredit the loan by large purchases at low rates."[47] But the price fall had a simpler cause. With the lingering cotton famine, investors initially jumped at the opportunity to purchase bonds backed by the southern staple crop. But their reaction was only a secondary factor affecting the market price of the certificates. The perceived viability of the Richmond government was the main determinant. The market price fluctuated widely with every rumor or fact about the strength of the Confederate military and economy. As the summer campaign season dawned, many in the British financial community believed that losing Port Hudson and Vicksburg would be fatal to the southern cause, for that would split the Confederacy into two parts at the Mississippi River.[48]

In July 1863, federal forces captured both sites. Those defeats, coupled with the results of the Gettysburg campaign, sent shock waves through the Confederacy's European creditors. The price of the bonds fell to sixty-five. The linkage between the battlefields and the money markets did not escape Mason, who in September wrote that the "late fluctuations" of the Erlanger bond prices "fully establish that its fortunes vary with the apparent varying fortunes of the war."[49] A few minor upturns occurred, but by the end of the year, when word arrived of the federal victory at Chattanooga, the price had fallen to thirty-seven.[50] It improved occasionally in 1864, but never again did the price reach par value.

It appeared that the bonds did not do well and that the loan had failed. Most early efforts at estimating the amount of funds the Confederacy gained from the Erlanger loan pointed to a financial failure. Historian Frank L. Owsley calculated the net cash proceeds as roughly $2.5 million.[51] For years, most other writers either took his figure at face value or used it as a starting point for their own calculations. A revisionist study of the Erlanger loan, however, recalculated the proceeds from scratch and came up with a figure of approximately $8.5 million.[52] The amount of the loan was only $15 million, so, using the revised figure, a failed loan can be seen as a success.[53]

With the increased availability of funds, however, problems due to the uncoordinated character of Confederate purchasing operations became magnified. The loan eased the monetary crisis for Confederate purchasing agents, but Mason had great difficulty finding time to meet with and satisfy all who sought pieces of the Erlanger pie. The Virginia diplomat faced repeated demands to distribute Confederate resources among them. Requests poured in from various agents, including Sinclair, Matthew F. Maury, and William G. Crenshaw.[54] In the first six months of 1863, finance and purchasing dominated Mason's correspondence. Discussions of diplomatic recognition surfaced only occasionally, as practical money matters took priority.

No purchasing agent contacted Mason as regularly as did James North. After receiving the £26,000 he asked for in February and March,[55] he reported that, with work "advancing rapidly," demands for money "increase in proportion." He then asked for £154,000 more so that the ship he contracted for could be completed.[56] North had tried unsuccessfully to get money from Bulloch and wrote to Mason, "I must have money to enable me to get on with my work."[57] On April 20, Mason promised that he would see Erlanger and attempt to alleviate North's difficulties.[58] But in May, little had changed, as North wrote, "My hands are tied and I can do nothing for the want of money."[59]

Mason did his best to satisfy the needs of the purchasing agents, trying in vain to achieve the needed coordination of Confederate financial activities[60] while other aspects of his job suffered. In May, he wrote to Eliza that the Confederacy "has necessarily many and large operations here, which, in the difficult and interrupted communication between the two countries, involve large responsibilities in the exercise of a discreet judgement." One way or another, burdens fell upon him that involved "constantly recurring and engrossing cares."[61] He anxiously awaited the arrival of Alabama's Colin J. McRae, whom Richmond had appointed special agent for the Erlanger loan. McRae landed in Europe on May 13,[62] only to learn that virtually all Confederate financial activities in Europe revolved around the Erlanger loan. That fact gave McRae great power. For the first time, the Confederacy had the opportunity to centralize its financial operations overseas.

On September 15, 1863, Benjamin notified the various department heads that President Davis had appointed Colin J. McRae chief purchasing agent.[63] McRae held the confidence of the other agents and brought about increased efficiency through the end of the war.[64] Additionally, while Mason still joined Slidell in exerting some supervision over the South's general financial status, the weight of day-to-day Confederate money matters was lifted from his shoulders, allowing him considerably more time for diplomacy.[65]

By that time, however, even diplomatic relations to a great extent revolved around finance and purchasing. Building Confederate ships in Britain produced a British neutrality policy that tended to favor the United States.[66] International law and practice, according to Great Britain, always had allowed a neutral to build ships for a belligerent as long as an armed ship was not sent directly from the neutral port to attack some friendly power.[67] But southern agents worried that the British government, pressured by the United States, would disregard legality, seize their new vessels, and never allow them to be put into service by the Confederate Navy.

In late 1862, despite its own long history of profiteering from other nations' wars, the government of the United States protested vehemently to the British ministry when two gunboats, the *Florida* and the *Alabama*, sailed from Liverpool and began raiding American shipping.[68] Those gunboats made handsome contributions to the southern war effort, but the Confederate government placed an even higher value upon ironclad ships and rams that could break the blockade. Richmond had concluded that unleashing even a small number of modern vessels upon the largely wooden U.S. blockading fleet would cause them to scatter.[69] Two ships under construction for that purpose became known as the "Laird rams."[70]

As early as December 1862, Richmond learned that a high level of diplomatic activity between Britain and the United States surrounded those vessels.[71] The ironclads were due to be completed by the middle of 1863, but mechanical difficulties and an increasingly hostile environment delayed the completion date considerably. Heightened concern for the vessels' security led to preparations for shifting Confederate shipbuilding efforts to France. Napoleon III himself, during an interview with Slidell in October 1862, first proposed that the Confederacy could construct vessels there.[72] Five months later, with suspicions concerning the rams growing, Slidell recalled the emperor's offer. Slidell noted, "We can not only build ships here but arm and equip them."[73] Benjamin instructed Mason to work with Slidell to transfer the ownership of the ironclads to France "if such a course should become necessary."[74]

Meanwhile, construction continued. But U.S. diplomatic pressure had claimed a victory. On April 5, 1863, British authorities seized the wooden steamer *Alexandra* at its Liverpool dock, confirming Mason and Slidell's worst fears. With Great Britain eager to remain neutral in the American conflict and Washington complaining loudly about southern shipbuilding in British ports, the legality of such construction, according to international law, might not be enough to protect Confederate property from being confiscated. Mason received only sketchy information about the seizure at first;[75] but, from a southern operative in New York City, he learned the sobering intelligence that U.S. Secretary of State William Seward reportedly claimed to have "sufficient legal evidence of the fact that fourteen (or more) vessels are now being constructed in England for the use of the Confederate States."[76]

Shortly thereafter, the Confederate commissioners began to arrange the transfer of the rams' ownership to a French company.[77] Mason spent the first week of June in Paris participating in those meetings.[78] Frenchman Adrien Bravay, supposedly as an agent for the Pasha of Egypt, became the nominal owner of the rams.[79] The southern commissioners hoped that the move would veil Confederate ownership from a British government determined to read the rules "in a manner not only injurious to the interests of the Confederate States, but so as to prohibit any further operations in their behalf within Her Majesty's dominions."[80]

That task proved impossible. The *Alabama*'s controversial construction and "escape" lingered in British minds,[81] so that even the untrained eye could deduce that the Laird rams were intended for use by the Confederate navy. Unleashing the rams on the U.S. blockading fleet could have changed the naval situation dramatically. Russell believed that, if those ironclad vessels forced the United States to end its close blockade of Confederate ports, the Lincoln government would switch to a "cruising squadron" blockade far from southern shores. The United States would need more ships for that type of blockade and might resort to privateers. British commerce would be disrupted, and the chances of war with the United States would increase.[82] He sought to prevent such an occurrence, regardless of law or precedent.

Diplomatic maneuvering regarding the ironclads involved primarily the United States and Great Britain. Beginning in July, tensions rose, as no issue between the two governments received nearly as much attention.[83] Confederate officials did little to interfere. Seeking to quiet suspicion and keep the ships' ownership wrapped in secrecy, they denied that the ships were intended for the Confederacy. That remained the policy through the end of the war. As late as February 1865, Mason, Slidell, and Mann responded to Russell's charges of "continued building by agents of the Confederate States within Her Majesty's dominions of ships of war" by asserting that they were entirely without foundation.[84] That mixed policy of believing in the legality of building ships in Britain while simultaneously denying Confederate ownership of the vessels under construction was doomed to fail. One side of the policy contradicted the other, and both sides failed to take into account the national interest that prompted the actions of the British ministry.[85]

On June 26, 1863, in the case regarding the *Alexandra* seizure, the jury ruled in favor of the Confederacy.[86] The decision confirmed southern opinion that British law allowed them to build ships in Britain, provided that they were armed elsewhere.[87] Confederate optimism revived briefly.[88] The decision, however, did not prevent British authorities, on orders from the Foreign Office, from formally seizing the Laird rams on October 9, 1863.[89] The power politics of the day had triumphed over legality as decreed by the British courts. Bulloch wrote, "No amount of discretion or management on my part can effect the release of the ships."[90]

Where was Mason at the crucial moment when the British government seized the rams? He had left England for Paris on September 30,[91] after receiving a letter from Benjamin. The secretary of state wrote that, because Britain had shown no intention of receiving Mason "as the accredited minister" of the Confederate Government,

President Davis had decided that his "continued residence in London is neither conducive to the interests nor consistent with the dignity of this Government."[92] Mason received the instructions to terminate his mission on September 14. He believed that Davis had made the "dignified and right" decision. He asked Slidell for his opinion,[93] and his colleague agreed with the president and urged that the withdrawal be publicized widely for maximum effect.[94]

The timing could not have been worse. Lack of diplomatic recognition had led to an executive temper tantrum that left the Confederacy without an official representative at precisely the moment when British authorities confiscated the rams. Pessimistically, Mason wrote to North in November, "I do not see the slightest possibility" that any Confederate vessels would be "allowed to go out, where the suspicion even of the Government is directed towards them."[95]

He did not return to London until February 1864, after his new appointment as "commissioner on the Continent" arrived. Little had changed with regard to British diplomatic recognition, and the Laird rams remained in British custody, but at least the Richmond government had acknowledged in some way the mistake of prematurely ending Mason's earlier mission. Benjamin wrote that Mason's "services are considered by your Government as too valuable and useful to be dispensed with."[96] The temper tantrum had passed.

Four months had passed as well. Mason's absence had left Bulloch alone to handle the Laird rams situation. The Confederate agent remained cautiously optimistic that Napoleon III would step forward and insist that the ships be delivered to their "legal" French owner.[97] But just weeks before the seizure, Bulloch had expressed more realistic concerns about the reliability of the French leader's promises.[98] Predictably, when the Confederacy called Napoleon's bluff, the emperor's assurances became less definite. The French leader failed to intervene, leaving the British government free to use every tactic available to prevent the Laird rams from leaving.[99]

Not only did Napoleon III fail to stop the British seizure of the rams, but on May 20, 1864, the French ministry took possession of six vessels under construction for the Confederacy in French ports. The French foreign minister, Edouard Drouyn de Lhuys, wanted France to maintain strict neutrality in the war, reasoning that such a policy increased the likelihood that the "Mexican adventure" would succeed.[100] French laws, similar to those of Britain, specified that no armed ships could sail from French ports directly to attack the United States or some other belligerent power. That made it particularly ironic when the six confiscated vessels were sold by the French government to Prussia and Denmark, who were at war with each other at the time. Clearly France, like Britain, based its actions upon policy considerations rather than upon legality; if selling those ships to the Confederacy for the purpose of fighting the United States was illegal, selling them to Prussia and Denmark also should have been illegal.[101] Bulloch summed up Confederate exasperation by contrasting Lord Russell, who had "always been an open enemy," with the French government, which "was warm in asseverations of friendship, and invited us to supply our necessities in France; but every pledge has been violated, and we have encountered nothing but deception and duplicity and are now their victim."[102] Napoleon III's pretense of friendship made France's actions more irritating to the Confederates than anything Britain had done.

But Russell and the British government joined France in making 1864 a dismal year for Confederate shipbuilding efforts. Regarding the rams, Lindsay wrote to Mason in January that he expected the sense of fair play of the British public to pressure the ministry into relenting.[103] Such an expectation was unrealistic. Bulloch read things more accurately in February, when he claimed that British and U.S. efforts had made it "settled beyond a doubt that no vessel constructed with a view to offensive warfare can be built and got out of England for the service of the Confederate States."[104]

Upon his return to England, Mason surveyed the situation and arrived at a similar conclusion. The Virginia diplomat informed Benjamin of "the total failure of our efforts to get ships either from France or England." He wrote, "The conviction has been forced upon us that there remains no chance or hope of getting ships out either from England or France and that, in consequence, those in prospect are to be disposed of in the best way that may be done." He added that it was "a painful disappointment, but I am satisfied that nothing was left undone to effect the object."[105] A day later, Mason penned a similar note to President Davis. He referred to "illusory" French assurances and stressed that the British government for almost a year had "shown itself more and more disposed to strain, or rather to disregard its own laws in order to avoid the possibility of any ships intended for war purposes getting to sea."[106] In Great Britain, international reality had triumphed over international law, to the detriment of the Confederate States of America.

That same month, with little or no hope of gaining release of the Laird rams and having no patience for the slow pace at which the British court system dealt with the ministry's appeals, Mason and Slidell decided that the time had come to sell the rams.[107] That way the Confederacy at least could get some of its investment back. The disheartening fiasco led an angry President Davis to write that "the plea of neutrality, which is used to sustain the sinister course of Her Majesty's present Government against the Government of the Confederate States, is so clearly contradicted by their actions, that [it] is regarded by the world, not even exempting the United States, as a mere cover for actual hostility."[108] In May, Bravay's company sold the two ironclads to the British government. That solved Lord Russell's diplomatic dilemma and prevented another embarrassing court case from winding its way through the British judiciary.[109] After that, Confederate efforts at building a navy in Europe came to an end.

Cotton bonds had proved to be a solid credit mechanism, providing the Confederacy with cash for the purchase of ships or other armaments and supplies, but by 1864 it had become difficult to put those funds to any productive use.[110] The environment surrounding Confederate purchasing had changed. Agents needed only money to acquire war materials in 1861, but by 1864, with the British government showing open hostility toward the Confederate cause, few European firms showed any interest in selling war supplies to southerners. Even when North or Bulloch found a businessman willing to offend the ministry, the latest war news, posing the likelihood that the Confederacy never would see the products even if they were bought and paid for, made sellers hesitate and then killed the prospective deal.[111]

Nonetheless, even after the U.S.S. *Kearsarge* sank the most successful raider in the southern navy, the *Alabama,* off the coast of France in June 1864,[112] Confederate vessels still plied the high seas.[113] But ironclad rams that could break the tightening stranglehold of the federal blockade never found their way into the southern navy. Visiting Liverpool in October, Mason looked upon one of the rams as it sat idly at its dock. In the gray melancholy air, he must have considered sadly what might have been.[114] The war had begun to edge toward its close, and now the Virginian's role in naval affairs was to sell ships rather than to buy them.[115]

In dangerous times, governments often are forced to ignore certain laws and ordinances for the sake of national security. Great Britain faced sizable national dangers. As the major commercial state of the world, Britain worried about how the American naval war might affect its economy and its trade.[116] With Confederate agents seeking supplies, influence, and recognition, the possibility of offending the United States and provoking actual hostilities was a real one. The British government understood it to be in the country's best interest to ignore legal precedents and prevent the Confederacy from using its ports to build ships intended to attack the United States. As a *London Times* editorial stated, the laws were "not in harmony with true neutrality."[117] Therefore, the ministry believed that its duty lay in ignoring the legality of Confederate shipbuilding, because it ran contrary to the national interest.

James Murray Mason did not subscribe to the theory that laws could be circumvented in times of national crisis. Even in wartime, Mason, like President Davis, took constitutional theories very seriously. That showed in their diplomacy. It clouded their vision as they tried to determine how the British government would act in a given situation. They expected international laws and practices to be followed with a high degree of precision. But that expectation betrayed a limited understanding of the complex international forces at work in the real world of the 1860s, particularly in 1863, when the Confederate States had their last real chance of diplomatic recognition.[118]

Chapter 11

1863

Disappointment, Disillusion, Defeat

James Murray Mason began 1863 by lodging the Confederacy's measured protest against the British government's conduct regarding the federal blockade.[1] That conduct, seen by Confederate officials as a blatant disregard for international law, led them to view British neutrality as being one that, out of fear, favored the United States.[2] Jefferson Davis never complained about Britain's being neutral *per se*, but he saw that neutrality as "delusive."[3] On January 12, the chief executive addressed the Confederate Congress, using the occasion to denounce the British government. He cited the "so-called" blockade as being the most perfect example of how neutrality could be "so shaped as to cause the greatest injury to the Confederacy and to confer signal advantages on the United States." With the cotton famine continuing to cause great suffering, Davis attempted to go over the heads of the British ministry by appealing directly to the British people. He wanted them to know that their own government's policies caused their pain.[4]

Ineffectual blockades were not supposed to be recognized, and the U.S. blockade can be labeled ineffectual. It existed primarily on paper, even more than earlier British ones had been. Historian Stephen R. Wise, in his definitive study of attempts to run the blockade, calculates that almost 77 percent of those tries succeeded.[5] Thus the

Confederacy acquired an impressive amount of goods by way of the fragile but quick blockade runners.[6] Despite such figures indicating the blockade's porous character, the barrier drawn by the Lincoln administration succeeded in preventing European governments from encouraging their citizens to cross it. That made the military situation decisive in determining the width and longevity of the tenuous Confederate lifeline.

Realistically, only Britain and France could have broken the blockade, and neither did. France, despite Napoleon III's boasting, played the role of a little brother seeking approval from big brother Britain for any actions regarding the war. The emperor had a greater interest in Mexican affairs than in assisting the Confederacy and could not afford to risk war with the United States at such a crucial time.[7]

That left Great Britain, which had a good reason not to interfere with the federal blockade. Given the strength and superiority of the Royal Navy, blockades were a mainstay of any British war effort. Previously Britain had used the blockade tactic regularly, and each time the United States had opposed it vehemently, championing neutral shipping rights. In the Civil War, the positions reversed. The United States set up the blockade, leaving Great Britain to speak for neutral rights. But the British generally refused to speak out for traditional neutral rights. They watched while the United States systematically contradicted all that it had argued for in the past. In the future, when Britain instituted a blockade, America would be unable to advocate neutral rights because of precedents it had established during the Civil War.[8] By year's end, even President Davis recognized that the British government had decided to grab the opportunity to establish "by the temporary sacrifice of their neutral rights, a precedent which will justify the future exercise of those extreme belligerent pretensions that their naval power renders so formidable."[9]

Mason faced that hidden agenda regarding the blockade again in 1863. In the first weeks, his diplomatic efforts proceeded much as before. He continued to stress to Lord Russell, in what had become repetitive and predictable terms, the illegality of the blockade.[10] Mason could do little more than reiterate, with updated statistics, the same old complaints, in an effort to prove how porous the blockade was. Russell refused to change his stance, insisting that the blockade was "practically effective" and that, as such, it would be respected by the British government.[11]

Nonetheless, the Virginian pressed on and awaited the opening of Parliament in February. He had been cheered by news of the military triumph at Fredericksburg, writing that the British had been shown "that the avowed object of the war on the part of the North is hopeless; whether that object be a restoration of the Union of the States or the subjugation of the South."[12] His active social life continued, highlighted by a dinner that he attended on February 11 at the invitation of the Lord Mayor of London. When toasts were made, the announcement of his name provoked a rousing applause from the guests, who urged the Virginian to say a few words. After joking that England had decided that his country "has not yet attained years of discretion, and is not capable of managing its own affairs" (which brought hearty laughter), Mason voiced "sincere thanks" for the kindness and welcome he had received. He went on to predict that soon the Confederacy and Britain would have a relationship "of close and intimate alliance."[13] Additionally, his social calendar included visits in the country with many in upper-class British society.[14]

Mason's "correspondence and the calls of business" also kept him quite busy. Mason complained to Eliza of being at times "oppressed by heavy responsibilities, in determining what is proper to be done to sustain the Government here, in absence of authority or instructions to meet unexpected events, etc." But he exclaimed with self-assurance, "So far I have gone right."[15]

In the first months of 1863, those heavy responsibilities included financial matters related to the Erlanger loan, as various purchasing agents pestered him for money.[16] Another situation proved even more distracting, however, as Mason stood in the middle of a heated controversy over his trusted advisor James Spence. Following Mason's recommendation, Richmond had made Spence financial agent in Great Britain for the first cotton certificates floated there.[17] When the Erlanger proposal arrived, however, Spence worried that it would intrude upon his territory. He believed that the entire loan should come within the scope of his own financial operations.[18] He did have permission to sell the bonds,[19] but, insecure about his own position, Spence expressed increasing distrust of the French banker.[20]

The negative comments cut both ways. Slidell, at the center of the Erlanger negotiations, complained bitterly about Spence's arrogance. He exclaimed to Mason, "I do not like the way in which Mr. Spence writes, he evidently considers his personal interests invaded by the arrangement made by Richmond and seems to think that it is to be submitted to his judgement."[21] The Virginia diplomat became caught in a crossfire of hostile assertions, as, a few days after reading Slidell's criticism, Mason received a letter from Spence stating that, after all the work he had done, "it will be mortifying to be treated with something like polite contempt in return and I am not the man to take it easily."[22] Mason straddled the fence between the two camps as best he could, but such bickering added to his burdens and served no productive purpose.

The war of words continued for months. Slidell wrote to Mason in April that he had "no great confidence" in Spence,[23] and in May he confessed, "I am getting heartily tired of his meddling. . . . Spence appears to consider that the powers of Secretary of Navy as well as of Treasury are vested in him."[24]

From the other side, Spence's complaints of mistreatment continued unabated. Richmond's appointment of Colin J. McRae as special agent for the Erlanger loan particularly injured his pride. He complained to Mason about "the pain I feel at the turn things have taken."[25] When the price of the bonds dropped, Spence jealously blamed Erlanger's mismanagement.[26] That summer, his criticisms spread to McRae's handling of Confederate finances as well.[27] The year ended with the Confederate Treasury Department finally revoking his appointment as financial agent, not for business reasons, but primarily because he had broadcast across Britain the idea that recognizing the Confederacy would be the surest way to end southern slavery.[28] He then wrote to Mason asking for money to compensate him for his services.[29]

Perhaps propagandist Henry Hotze, an early critic of Spence,[30] best summed up the entire affair. In reporting Spence's complaints of mistreatment to Secretary of State Benjamin, he wrote that the problem "was that he assumed to occupy at one and the same time two opposite and irreconcilable positions—that of a high official of our Government owing it allegiance and that of a disinterested alien friend."[31] Benjamin replied, "You have perceived with your usual acuteness the exact embarrassment under which we labor in dealing with this gentleman."[32]

Mason heard both sides throughout 1863 but refused to allow himself to be caught in the name calling. He kept Spence as both his friend and his advisor, in spite of the Englishman's problems relating to Confederate finances, while trying to stay focused on his primary objective, British diplomatic recognition of the Confederacy. Mason reported the opening of Parliament in February, writing, "While both the ministry and the opposition agree that the separation of the States is final, yet both equally agree, that in their judgement, the time has not yet arrived for recognition." He emphasized that "both parties are guided in this by a fixed English purpose to run no risk of a broil, even far less, a war with the United States." He then added, "For us it only remains to be silent and passive."[33]

That tendency for Mason to be "passive" in the face of opposition from the ministry kept recurring. Except for his official protests concerning the blockade, he did little to force the issue in the first months of the year, preferring to allow events to take their natural course while he focused on purchasing and finance. In Richmond, Benjamin and Davis, increasingly tired of British inaction, did not push the Virginia diplomat. Instead, Benjamin commented that perhaps "that haughty Government will find to its surprise that it needs a treaty of commerce with us, much more than we need it with Great Britain."[34]

That statement reflected continued faith in "King Cotton." Although the South relied upon cotton as a financial tool, Richmond discouraged its planting, not only to keep up the pressure on Europe engendered by a shortage, but also for a more practical reason. In a letter to Joseph E. Brown, governor of Georgia, President Davis expressed support for a new Georgia state law "prohibiting the cultivation of cotton in the State during the continuance of the war, and urging upon planters the necessity for increased attention to the production of provisions."[35] With the war going on and on, the South could not afford to use its land to grow cotton anymore. The necessity of growing food had become more crucial.

The Richmond government could not know that the cotton famine had reached its peak in late 1862. Its hope of gaining European recognition in 1863 still relied upon preaching the rightness of the southern cause and applying pressure based on a shortage of cotton. Support remained strong for the King Cotton policy. John Milton, governor of Florida, wrote to the president, "Foreign nations cannot exist without the cotton produced by slave labor in the Southern states."[36] In the meantime, the effects of the shortage lingered, and Hotze noted in March that "the patience of the sufferers is diminishing."[37]

Parliament discussed the distress in the cotton manufacturing districts in February and April, seeking to determine some way to secure a permanent supply of the staple. Beyond giving the politicians a chance to voice sympathy for the unemployed workers' plight, the debates accomplished little, however.[38] Mason, still a firm believer in the diplomatic power of the South's most important crop, observed the debates quietly from the sidelines. He thought that it should have been obvious to British leaders that recognizing the Confederate States would be the easiest way for their country to gain a secure flow of cotton. But once more he followed the advice of those who urged against pushing the issue at that time.[39] On March 18, William H. Gregory warned him that, in the House of Commons, "any motion on the subject will be received with disfavour, consequently the way in which it will be treated will only make the North more elated, and will irritate the South."[40]

In the House of Lords, however, Lord Campbell insisted on introducing a motion for recognition. Mason and others convinced him to postpone the idea a few weeks,[41] but on March 23, he went ahead with his plans. He debated the issue head-to-head with Lord Russell, who, while refusing to predict future actions, thought it best for the two sections to sort out their differences without interference. Faced with a hostile reception, Campbell withdrew the motion before it could be voted on.[42] Besides, the European continent now posed a concern more pressing for the British government than the war in America.

Ever since Russia, Prussia, and Austria had partitioned and abolished the state of Poland in the eighteenth century, the Poles periodically had banded together to demand increased autonomy. Most of those uprisings were aimed at the Russians. In 1861, Polish nationalism again surfaced, giving rise to a plan for a major uprising in the spring of 1863. Learning of the plan, the Russians countered by conscripting the most likely rebels into the army. In response, the Poles formed guerrilla bands and began an all-out revolt.[43]

The Polish revolt flamed as a minor brush fire on the prairie of European politics, but British government officials recognized the potential for a more widespread conflagration. Public opinion in France supported the Poles, and Napoleon III determined that he could gain popular favor there to offset criticism of his Mexican policies.[44] In February, when Prussia signed an agreement to aid the Russians, Napoleon saw an opportunity to revise the Franco-Prussian frontier, if he acted in strong support of the Polish insurgents.[45]

British public opinion also favored the Poles but did not want to go to war for them. The government tried to be a moderating force in restraining Napoleon III from acting rashly. Over the next few months, Britain, France, and Austria all sent communications to Alexander II protesting Russian conduct and calling for constitutional reforms for the Poles. Russia rejected such interference with its internal affairs, which served to keep the tension level in Europe high throughout 1863.[46]

Those events could not have taken place at a time more inopportune for the Confederacy. In March, Slidell wrote to Mason that, "until the Polish imbroglio is settled," he had no hope that France would take action regarding southern independence.[47] He communicated to Benjamin that, in Paris, the subject of Poland "engrosses the attention of the Government, the press, and the public to the exclusion of every other."[48] From London, both Mason[49] and Hotze reported that "what attention could be bestowed elsewhere has been given to Poland."[50] Another Confederate official characterized Lord Palmerston as "far more deeply engrossed with the conferences, jealousies, and rivalries between the leading powers of Europe than with the fate of constitutional government in America."[51] The Confederate commissioners had lost control of their diplomatic situation. Only a stunning military victory might have turned European eyes back toward North America.

Lord Russell feared that, if Britain mishandled the Polish problem, the United States and Russia would come to an agreement leading to a new balance of power.[52] British concerns about Canada, and French concerns about Mexico were genuine. Emotions ran high in the United States because of Confederate shipbuilding in British ports. In a general European war, the British ministry foresaw that the federal navy might support Russia by attacking English shipping.[53] With war fever high in the European capitals, no action could be taken that would alienate the United States. Thus, support for the Confederacy was out of the question.

As the Polish crisis unfolded, Mason maintained his passive, quiet, patient posture. Although Lord Russell would not change his position on the federal blockade, the Virginian maintained that the two had "amiable relations."[54] In April, he wrote confidently that British public opinion had become increasingly "incensed at the arrogant and exacting tone of expression found in the public speeches and the press in the Northern States." While still not predicting any tangible movement, he reported that the House of Commons realized that the war "to restore the Union, is hopeless; and the sympathies of four-fifths of its members are with the South."[55]

A June exchange with Virginia abolitionist Moncure D. Conway exemplified Mason's confident determination that southern independence would be maintained, regardless of British action or inaction. Conway, claiming to have authority from the "leading anti-slavery men in America," asserted that, if the Confederacy emancipated its black slaves, northern abolitionists would oppose any further prosecution of the war. He expected that action to end the conflict, because antislavery forces held the balance of political power in the North.[56] At first Mason asked for proof of Conway's authorization.[57] But a week later, he abruptly terminated the correspondence, promising to have it published so that northerners could see what Conway had done. The Confederate commissioner exclaimed defiantly to the abolitionist "that the Northern States will never be in relation to put this question to the South, nor will the Southern States ever be in a position requiring them to give an answer."[58]

Reports from Richmond bolstered Mason's confidence. Benjamin reported that public opinion within the Confederacy was "bright and confident—almost too much so." The secretary of state said that he had nothing further to say about the war that Mason could not read in a northern newspaper, since the northerners "paint their own condition in colors so dark that we can scarcely desire to add anything to the gloomy picture."[59] Even in March, when federal forces closed in on Vicksburg and Port Hudson on the Mississippi River, Benjamin remained upbeat in writing Mason.[60] Another southerner wrote Mason that, in spite of the food shortage, the "greatest confidence and hopefulness prevails."[61]

One piece of news from Virginia did not cheer him. Few towns changed hands as often as Mason's beloved Winchester. As he had instructed, however, Eliza and his daughters stayed behind southern lines at all times, spending most of their time in Richmond. That left Selma open for depredation, however; after Union troops occupied Mason's home in March 1862,[62] they demolished it little by little over the next ten months. The federal soldiers began by chipping off pieces of it to send north as souvenirs.[63] Then, on January 20, 1863, the Mason family's next-door neighbor, Mrs. Cornelia McDonald, recorded in her diary, "Today the walls of Mr. Mason's house were pulled down; they fell with a crash; the roof had gone long ago. The house has disappeared now . . . every outbuilding is gone . . . nothing is left of them but heaps of logs which the Yankees carry away for firewood. . . . They have taken the stones of Mr. Mason's house as well as many of our stone fences to build their fortifications."[64] One account related that, "because Senator Mason was in London as special commissioner for the Confederacy, the Yankees razed his home to the ground, stone by stone."[65] But while federal soldiers may have taken special satisfaction in tearing down Selma, the house was not alone in its fate. Other unoccupied houses around Winchester, as well as barns, stables, and even churches met destruction at the hands of the northern troops.[66]

Mason wrote to Eliza about receiving a letter from his sister Anna Maria that contained a "graphic account . . . of deep and melancholy interest," describing "the utter ruin and destruction" of their "bright and happy home." He mourned the loss but, keeping a sense of perspective, labeled it "nothing, compared with what has been sustained by others in conducting the resistance to the war waged against us—and is light in the balance compared with what those have suffered who remained at home and have borne, without change of front, the contumely and cruelties of the brutes of the Yankee army. I feel a debt, almost of personal obligation, when I call to mind what those valued friends have endured, and are yet enduring, in the face of a vindictive enemy, without blenching or giving in."[67] After Confederate troops reclaimed the northern end of the Shenandoah Valley, Mason's daughters paid a brief visit to Selma to collect some of the debris left behind by the predators; then they helped their mother set up a new household.[68] Their father pledged never to return to Winchester.

The Masons made the best of the situation, doing all they could to put their losses behind them. James had it easiest, because he could plunge into his work,[69] knowing that anything he accomplished would in some way avenge the rampage of the northern soldiers. He spent the first two weeks of May in Ireland, where the clean air cleared his mind, leaving him "very much refreshed." But the exchange of bad news within his family caused him to miss them more than ever. He wrote to Eliza that, even if it did not sound patriotic, his "first wish . . . as to the fruits of recognition" was that it would "bring you and the girls to England." From "the hard teachings of experience," however, he believed that the South had "nothing to look to from the European powers." He suggested that perhaps it was best that southerners "work out their own salvation," because they could "then stand beside them as a peer, without obligation, and with as much right to dictate as they."[70]

When Mason returned to London, he received word of a problem that Richmond expected him to address as quickly as possible. Benjamin asked for information on federal recruiting in Ireland.[71] Evidence had become more and more irrefutable that the federal armies were being bolstered by recruitment of aliens willing to immigrate to the United States and fight for the Union. An estimated half-million men, primarily Irish and German Catholics, ultimately left Europe and replaced captured or killed federal troops.[72] Thus federal casualties had proportionately less impact than Confederate ones did.

Mason knew of the problem and promised to do what he could.[73] He asked Robert Dowling, Confederate commercial agent in Ireland, to collect evidence on the situation.[74] Benjamin promised to send a few Irish citizens of the Confederacy to communicate "directly with the people" and to spread "among them such information and intelligence as may be best adapted to persuade them of the folly and wickedness of volunteering their aid in the savage warfare waged against us."[75] But Mason doubted that such a propaganda campaign would succeed, arguing that "such seems the ignorant and destitute condition of most . . . that the temptation of a little ready money and promise of good wages would lead them to go anywhere."[76] The Virginian saw no point in wasting further efforts on the problem. Davis and Benjamin shifted their focus to getting Pope Pius IX to intervene. After publication of correspondence between the president and the pontiff,[77] European recruiting numbers did level off. But they did not decline, as the old country continued to provide fresh blood for the federal army through the end of the war.[78]

While Mason addressed the federal recruiting problem, supporters of the Confederacy in Parliament prepared to make one more major attempt to get their government to recognize southern independence.[79] That effort coincided with the dawn of the summer campaign season. The Army of Northern Virginia was again on the march after winning a great victory against heavy odds at Chancellorsville.[80] Lee and Davis gambled once more on invading the North. In late June, the Army of Northern Virginia entered Pennsylvania, taking the war's bloodshed as far onto Union soil as it ever would be carried. European eyes watched anxiously for news of the southern incursion.

Mason's British advisors believed that Lee's military victory had established a favorable environment for movement in the diplomatic arena. But the Virginia diplomat needed to be convinced. Passive waiting for events to unfold had become his norm. On May 16, he wrote to Benjamin that the time for applying pressure on the ministry had not yet arrived.[81] But the next day, Lord Clanricarde informed Mason that he would be opening a discussion of the federal blockade in the House of Lords.[82] Before the end of the month, William S. Lindsay called fellow Confederate sympathizer John A. Roebuck and Mason to his country estate "to talk over the expediency of again bringing the subject of recognition before the House of Commons." Both Roebuck and Lindsay urged doing so, but only after consulting "with some of the leaders of the opposition." Mason did not believe that a change in British policy lay on the horizon. Nonetheless, he gave his approval and then left for France to meet with Slidell and other Confederate officials in Paris.[83]

Mason, who always wanted to coordinate any diplomatic efforts in England with those being made in France, spent the first part of June there, discussing a wide range of Confederate activities with Slidell.[84] Slidell doubted that the British cabinet would change its mind but expressed a willingness to approach Napoleon III to make the Confederate pressure double-pronged. He asked for an interview with the emperor[85] and spoke with the French leader on June 18. Slidell informed Mason that Napoleon III "was very cordial" but again stressed that he could recognize the Confederacy only in concert with Great Britain.[86] Nonetheless, the emperor agreed to discuss the matter with his cabinet, which decided that the British government should be notified that France stood ready at any time to join in intervention.[87]

Roebuck planned to introduce the recognition motion on June 30,[88] and, along with Lindsay, he traveled to Paris to speak with Napoleon III. On June 22, the pair used the conversation to recapitulate the case for recognizing southern independence. The emperor assured them that he had instructed Baron Gros, the French minister to England, to sound out the British government on granting the Confederacy diplomatic recognition.[89] The Englishmen sailed back to London confident that they had France's support.

Shortly after their return, however, the entire plan began to unravel. On June 26, in the House of Lords, Clanricarde asked Russell whether or not he had received a proposal from France to recognize Confederate independence. Russell replied firmly "that no such communication has been received."[90] Upon hearing such a clear denial, a flabbergasted Mason proceeded to question the "veracity" of the emperor.[91] But Slidell reassured him that Napoleon III planned to grant diplomatic recognition no matter what, writing, "It renders me comparatively indifferent what England may do or omit doing."[92]

On June 30, Russell again denied any notion that he had received a proposal from the French government. He stated that, when he saw Napoleon III's minister just an hour earlier, Gros confessed knowledge of the rumors but asserted that Paris had given him no orders to make such a suggestion.[93] That evening, with Mason in the audience, Roebuck introduced his resolution, and the House of Commons once again discussed recognizing the Confederacy. The debate was an unmitigated disaster. Roebuck's remarks referring to French overtures about granting recognition were countered easily by opponents who needed only to quote Russell's denials.[94] Roebuck made matters worse by taking a strident, condescending tone in relaying his conversation with Napoleon III. To most observers Roebuck appeared either a liar or a fool who had been taken advantage of by the French emperor.[95]

The debate continued into July,[96] but the outcome was a foregone conclusion. Mason blamed the entire fiasco on Napoleon III for sending different signals to different people.[97] Disgusted, he wrote to Slidell that "unless the Emperor will show his hand *on paper*, we shall never know what he really means, or derive any benefit from his private and individual revelations." Mason added that "it would be uncivil to say that I have no confidence in the Emperor but certainly what has come from him so far can only invite distrust."[98] But Slidell continued to defend Napoleon III, expressing satisfaction that the emperor had kept his promise. He argued instead that either the instructions were not carried out or Russell had lied.[99]

Spence predicted that, if put to a vote, the motion would be defeated overwhelmingly, and he urged Mason to have it withdrawn, using the excuse of waiting for news of Lee's invasion to justify the postponement.[100] Grasping for something positive, Mason latched onto Lord Palmerston's statement "that England was now ready to interchange views with France on the American question," calling it "a great step gained." With further action postponed, he looked forward to hearing that General Lee had captured Washington and Baltimore. He predicted that recognition then would come quickly.[101]

But neither city was captured. Lee's second invasion of the North ended just as the first had. Unlike the battle at Sharpsburg ten months earlier, however, the battle at Gettysburg in the first three days of July was a clear U.S. victory.[102] The July 4 fall of Vicksburg to the army of Gen. Ulysses S. Grant dealt the Confederacy a second devastating blow. From these two defeats its military, financial, and diplomatic prospects would never recover. Spence wrote to Mason that the news had made him "ill all the week."[103] The shattering importance of those battles in Pennsylvania and Mississippi, however, became evident to most observers only with the benefit of hindsight.[104]

But in Parliament the importance of the events was clear immediately. The British government would not recognize Confederate independence. Meanwhile, the blockade tightened each day, strangling the Confederacy slowly but surely. Among the southern people there grew a widespread, bitter resentment against Great Britain. British consuls became targets of that anger.

The consuls had been allowed to remain at their posts after secession, even though their credentials had been presented to the United States rather than to the Confederate States. Southern officials ignored that diplomatic slight for two years, but they nonetheless found the special status of the British consuls irritating. George Moore, the British consul at Richmond, particularly irritated the Confederates by attempting to interfere with southern efforts to draft each and every able-bodied man, including aliens, into the armed forces.[105] In February, Benjamin reported to Mason his fiery dialogue with the Englishman;[106] in June, he informed the commissioner of

Moore's expulsion.[107] As instructed, Mason passed along copies of the relevant dispatches to Lord Russell.[108] The British minister replied that he hoped the Confederacy would allow the consuls to function normally, as in the past.[109] But Mason defended Benjamin's actions, while encouraging a continuation of dialogue on the subject.[110]

Hostility increased throughout the summer, until Benjamin expelled the remaining British consuls on October 8.[111] But when news of that action reached Europe, Mason did not present the situation to Lord Russell. He had left England after learning that President Davis wanted him to end his mission. The decision resulted from the chief executive's "perusal of the recent debates in the British Parliament" regarding the Roebuck motion.[112] Davis and Benjamin had become convinced that Britain would never recognize Confederate independence, at least not as long as the United States remained a military threat.[113] Benjamin assured Mason that "the President is entirely satisfied with your own conduct of the delicate mission confided to you, and that it is in no want of proper effort on your part that necessity for your recall has originated."[114]

The Confederacy's diplomatic situation in Britain remained "delicate," as perpetual problems involving recognition and the blockade were augmented by the seizure of the Laird rams. A pleased but puzzled Henry Adams, secretary for his father Charles Francis Adams, wrote to his brother, "I am at a loss to understand why this step has been taken . . . but as I look at it, this . . . is a blunder." He added, "Mr. Mason's mere presence at this place has been a source of annoyance both to us and to the British Government. His departure will tend greatly to allay the dangers of our foreign affairs."[115] The U.S. minister himself recognized that President Davis's surprising termination of Mason's mission benefited the United States. The New Englander wrote, "We get on pretty quietly now," noting that the rams had been "detained, and Mr. Mason has been very solemnly withdrawn from here on the ground that Lord Russell treats him with hauteur. If I could have any confidence in the duration of this time of lull, I should not ask anything better."[116] He had cut through to the real reason behind the Confederate move—southern pride and sense of honor. True, diplomatic recognition did not appear imminent, but an emotional Davis had taken a pointless, drastic step. The ill-conceived, ill-timed withdrawal of Mason served only to make the North's diplomacy easier and the South's more difficult.

The Virginia aristocrat too suffered from wounded pride and honor, much as his president did. Therefore, encouraged by Slidell,[117] Mason notified Benjamin that he agreed with Davis's angry decision[118] and left for Paris on September 30.[119] Nine days earlier, he took the time to inform Lord Russell of his mission's termination.[120] The British minister responded that the situation regarding recognition had not changed but that he regretted "that circumstances have prevented my cultivating your personal acquaintance, which, in a different state of affairs, I should have done with much pleasure and satisfaction."[121] Mason then left behind his books and papers for safekeeping in the trusted hands of his personal London bankers and Henry Hotze.[122] Upon reaching Paris, he informed President Davis that he would remain on the European continent until he received instructions to proceed elsewhere. He wanted to remain close to Britain in case some drastic change in the Confederate position occurred.[123]

Mason returned to England for a few weeks in November but avoided going to London. Optimistically thinking that his withdrawal would cause the British people "to reflect . . . on the sullen and perverse course of Earl Russell," he observed British "public sentiment setting even more strongly with us than before, with a strong disposition to organize and agitate against the Ministry, for recognition."[124] Such feelings could prove critical, because, regardless of the cordiality Lord Russell showed in his September letters, Mason believed that were the minister replaced, "the policy of England in regard to our country would undergo great modification."[125]

By the end of the year, however, disillusion resulting from repeated disappointment at last infected those involved with Confederate diplomacy in Britain. For example, Spence, who in August had written that the Polish situation and other circumstances argued against pushing for recognition,[126] noted in December that "the war news is gloomy—very, and I really do not see how the war is to be worked out to success without the action of Europe."[127] His conclusion that "unless we get Europe to move—or some improbable convulsions occur in the North—the end will be a sad one," led him to reverse his earlier stance and contend that no effort "to move our government" could be "too strenuous."[128]

But that time had passed. The Union victory at Chattanooga capped a year in which the few southern triumphs were transient and usually followed by more significant defeat.[129] The Confederacy remained a formidable opponent for the United States, but in December 1863 the South was significantly weaker than at any previous time. Bisected at the Mississippi River with the fall of Vicksburg and Port Hudson, and facing an ever-tightening federal blockade, the cards the Confederacy had to play were decreasing in number.

Even "King Cotton" was no longer available as a policy. After

Mason's withdrawal, Confederate officials rarely mentioned cotton except when referring to its purchasing power. The cotton famine had peaked and, despite continued suffering among British workers, would never be important in diplomacy after 1863. Importation of the staple from India and Russia actually enabled Britain to export cotton and cotton products to the European continent, particularly to France.[130] In economic terms, the Confederates believed that the British demand for southern cotton was inelastic, when in reality it was quite elastic. Britain's manufacture of cloth using cotton from other countries, as well as alternative fibers, meant that southerners were well off the mark in determining how much of a diplomatic weapon "King Cotton" could be.[131]

Additionally, King Cotton's effectiveness had been hurt by the size of the harvests immediately before the war. Even so, Richmond expected King Cotton to work once the surplus had been used up. But that surplus of raw cotton also led to a surplus of finished products. Rather than place all their finished goods on the market, which would have caused prices to drop, British manufacturers held a large amount of their production off the market. That kept prices at a desirable level and allowed them to stretch what they had during the time when the drop in available Confederate cotton was greatest.[132] Britain might not have had that kind of surplus to rely on if secession had been timed differently.

Hearing only of defeats, anger, and despair from Davis, Benjamin, Spence, and others made James Murray Mason dispirited, too. Sitting in France relatively inactive, as the war pressed inexorably through another year, proved extremely disheartening for the Virginian. Christmas 1863, spent in France without his family, depressed Mason much more than Christmas in England the year before had. Lindsay recognized his friend's misery and tried to improve Mason's mood by starting the new year with an "earnest wish that by another New Year you may be with your family and equally enjoy your home, for this New Year must be a dull and lonely one for you."[133]

Shortly thereafter, Mason mustered enough optimism to make an effort to cheer Eliza by writing, "What a bright day it will be, when we are all once more reunited, and I feel the assurance of certainty that that day will yet come." But in the same letter he bemoaned his lonely life in Paris, exclaiming, "I am plodding on in this Babel, but with little in it to interest me, except a large circle of Confederates, embracing some very agreeable families, who intermingle very sociably." He lamented, "I have seen nothing in Paris, except the streets, have not been to the theater or opera, or anywhere except once, to the corps Legislatif (the Chamber of Deputies) to hear their most celebrated orator." Sounding like a defeated man, Mason confessed that he no longer had "the heart or spirit to gaze after new things, or else I am getting too old for new excitements."[134]

Over two years of disappointment, disillusion, and defeat had taken a noticeable toll on the Virginia diplomat. At age sixty-five, he found himself alone, away from family and friends, sitting idle, while his home and homeland went up in flames. He needed somehow to be reinvigorated so that he could contribute his energy and talents to keeping the sinking Confederate ship of state afloat. With or without Mason's help, though, the South faced a daunting task.

♦♦♦ Chapter 12 ♦♦♦

1864

Hopes, Fears, and Defiant Determination

The necessary reinvigoration occurred when Mason received a new commission. Richmond's recognition that his earlier mission had ended prematurely included flattering words from Secretary of State Benjamin regarding Mason's value to the Confederacy.[1] Believing that European affairs were in a "disturbed condition," Davis and Benjamin wanted Mason to have an official commission. Then he would be in a position to return to London or deal with any European power on the Continent if a situation arose that could benefit the Confederacy diplomatically.[2] Cheered immeasurably, Mason looked forward to a fresh start as "commissioner on the continent." He even began numbering his correspondence with the secretary of state at number one again, to symbolize beginning anew. On January 25, 1864, he wrote Richmond that he would return to London within two weeks, for the next meeting of Parliament. He asserted that, in Parliament, the Confederacy had "a body of earnest and sincere friends, some of whom have told me it would be very desirable to have an opportunity of occasional conference with me for information."[3]

But Mason's good cheer did not mean that he had high hopes for a change in the policies of the British ministry. The attention of European policy makers once more had become diverted from American affairs.[4] While some tension lingered because of Poland,[5] a new

crisis appeared in central Europe. A dispute between Prussia and
Denmark over the principalities of Schleswig and Holstein would result in Prussia and Austria attacking Denmark in February.[6] That
roused British sympathies for the Danes, much as Russia's attack on
the Poles had done in 1863. Before the war began, Mason warned
that "peace and repose in Europe are just now of great importance to
us, waiting for European recognition."[7] But the first of Otto von
Bismarck's three wars for German unification disrupted that peace,
relegating the American Civil War to the back burner.[8]

The Danish situation dominated debates in the British Parliament
from February to June.[9] Mason updated Richmond on the crisis, writing that British public opinion remained focused upon Schleswig-Holstein[10] and opining that, until peace reigned there, "it will be utterly
impracticable, in my judgement, to fix the attention of European powers upon what it may become them to do in regard to relations with
us."[11] But Mason hoped that the Confederacy could benefit indirectly
from the hostilities in Europe's center. He wrote to President Davis, "It
is very certain that the Danes were led to believe, that England would
not witness the present invasion without coming to their aid." The
Virginian believed that Bismarck had called Lord Palmerston's bluff
and that the repercussions could lead to the overthrow of his ministry.
If that happened, "any new cabinet would be compelled, in obedience
to general sentiment, materially to modify its policy in regard to us—I
should hope even to the extent of recognition."[12]

Otherwise, Mason could not foresee "any prospect of an early
movement anywhere advantageous to us unless it arise from agita-
tions before the people."[13] Upon returning to London, he wrote
Eliza of having nothing hopeful to report because "England will do
nothing that might by possibility offend the Yankees." But he expressed excitement regarding British public opinion, exclaiming that,
"with all classes in England which have an opinion, their entire sympathy is with us." The Virginian added that "societies are forming all
through the kingdom, headed by noblemen and eminent public men,
whose object is by public addresses, publications, etc., and by petitions to Parliament, to bring about a recognition of our independence."[14] With British advisors again cautioning him against pushing
for recognition formally,[15] Mason waited for public opinion to work
the magic that "King Cotton" could not.

The Confederacy had been attempting to sway British public
opinion for almost three years. Henry Hotze's journal, the *Index,*
had been spouting southern propaganda in the guise of a British newspaper since May 1862. Seeking quietly to persuade, it avoided the

use of shrill language that could have offended proper English gentlemen, particularly Lord Russell and other members of the ministry. In 1863, with Richmond's approval and encouragement, Hotze widened his activities to include printing circulars and placards, as well as subsidizing the circulation of pro-southern books and pamphlets.[16] His arguments followed the legalistic, constitutional thinking of Davis and Mason, and they failed to sway the British into active intervention on behalf of a government that cherished chattel slavery.[17]

As his assignments broadened, Hotze worked more and more with James Spence and other British subjects who sympathized with the Confederate cause, to establish pro-southern societies. British supporters of the South particularly used the cotton famine as a tool for organizing such clubs, as well as mass meetings, in the industrial regions of the country. But such agitation tended to follow the peaks and valleys of the Confederacy's military fortunes.[18] Periods of quiet occurred at the same time Spence and others advised Mason to sit still and do nothing, and periods of fervor occurred when they wanted the Virginia diplomat to push hard for diplomatic intervention.

Confederate propaganda efforts continued in 1864, but Mason erred in expecting public opinion to work magic for the Confederacy at that late date. He failed to recognize that, as the cotton famine had peaked and faded, the main tool for gaining the support of the British masses had disappeared. Without a tangible, pressing reason to intervene, the British government would remain content to sympathize quietly on the sidelines. The Virginian had noted correctly the *efforts* toward getting Parliament to move on recognition.[19] But by the time Mason returned to London, there had been no changes in the likelihood of their succeeding. He was deluding himself if he thought otherwise.

Technically, Mason was not even supposed to be in Great Britain. Davis had designed his new commission to be "very wide . . . to embrace unforeseen events which may render necessary prompt action by an accredited diplomatic agent." Embittered toward the British government, the Confederate president did not want Mason to visit that country even in a private capacity "unless some urgent necessity should compel your presence there" or a move toward recognizing southern independence appeared to be imminent.[20] The day after receiving those instructions, Mason wrote to assure Davis and Benjamin that only "a few private friends" knew he was in England and that he would return to Paris shortly.[21]

Mason arrived in Paris on April 2,[22] immediately after Slidell admitted the failure of his diplomatic maneuvers regarding France and

Mexico. For months, Confederate officials had encouraged Napoleon III to go ahead with his plans for Mexico. As early as July 1862, Slidell had notified the French government that the French military expedition to Mexico was "regarded with no unfriendly eye by the Confederate States."[23] In 1863, Mason, expecting relations between the United States and France to deteriorate over the situation, expressed hope that complications would compel Napoleon III to take diplomatic action to help the Confederacy.[24] Those complications increased over the winter months, as Archduke Maximilian of the House of Hapsburg prepared to ascend a French-sponsored throne in Mexico.[25] Designed to provide France with an economic foothold in the Western Hemisphere and increase Napoleon III's prestige,[26] that sponsorship defied the Monroe Doctrine.[27] But with the North and South at war, the United States could do nothing to prevent the French action.[28]

Throughout the winter, Mason had been kept up to date on the situation through regular letters from propagandist James Williams. Williams spoke with Maximilian often and labeled him "one of the most enlightened Princes of Europe."[29] Mason drew encouragement from what he heard and asserted confidently that the Lincoln government would not interfere with the French move.[30] Confederate officials in Richmond reached a similar conclusion, seeing Maximilian as a new source of leverage in their quest for French diplomatic recognition.[31] Jefferson Davis told the Confederate Congress that "if the Mexican people prefer a monarchy to a republic, it is our plain duty cheerfully to acquiesce in their decision."[32]

But all parties concerned realized that if federal forces crushed the Confederacy, Maximilian's days as an emperor likely would be numbered. In December 1863, Slidell wrote that Maximilian considered the Confederate cause to be "identical with that of the new Mexican Empire, in fact so inseparable that an acknowledgment of the Confederate States of America by the Governments of England and France should take place" before he accepted the throne.[33] On January 22, Williams emphasized to Mason similarly that "Maximilian believes truly that the Mexican Empire *cannot be securely established except through a friendly alliance with the Confederacy*."[34]

With one eye on Britain and the other on the United States, Napoleon III could not allow Maximilian to follow such an independent course. In March, Slidell requested a meeting with the archduke, but it never took place. He concluded that the French emperor prevented it.[35] A. Dudley Mann supported that assessment of the situation. He reported to Richmond that not only did the French emperor forbid the archduke to meet Slidell, but he also "enjoined upon Maximilian to hold no official relations with our Commissioner to Mexico,"[36] Gen. William Preston.[37] Williams informed Mason that the United States and France were negotiating away their differences so that both governments could pursue their respective policies in North America without interference from the other.[38] By then, the Virginian understood the reality of the archduke's position. He exclaimed that Maximilian "will be as little disposed to enter into diplomatic relations with us as is the controlling power on the Continent under whose auspices he is to be placed upon the throne."[39] A disgusted Slidell summarized Confederate feelings by writing, "I find it very difficult to keep my temper amidst all this double dealing. . . . This is a rascally world and it is most hard to say who can be trusted."[40]

Despite all this turmoil in Paris, Mason found that he had a greater amount of free time there than he had had in London, enabling him to think more of Eliza and the situation at home. Pleased that she remained "in comparative comfort" in Richmond, he commented on "the noble and courageous bearing of our friends in Winchester."[41] Beyond battle news, Mason took greatest interest in words about the sacrifices and trials of Virginians and their southern compatriots. Those reports made him more defiant as hopes for diplomatic intervention dimmed. Having been wrong so many times before, he stopped trying to analyze European actions, particularly those of France. Mason remarked that "the policy of the Emperor here, always mysterious, has had certainly that feature in regard to our affairs; whatever the motive, the result remains the same." Looking "for no movement of any kind," he asserted that, "thanks to the spirit of our people and the gallantry of our troops, under whatever loss and suffering, we can yet unaided work out our own salvation."[42]

Jefferson Davis agreed. In a speech to the Confederate Congress on May 2, he defiantly made the prediction that the Confederacy would preserve its independence without European help. He stressed that, "when our independence by the valor and fortitude of our people shall have been won against all the hostile influences combined against us, and can no longer be ignored by open foes or professed neutrals, this war will have left with its proud memories a record of many wrongs. . . . in the meantime it is enough for us to know that every avenue of negotiation is closed against us."[43] Benjamin relayed the president's proud defiance to Mason, advising him not to appear too eager to jump at any chance for an interview with European government officials.[44]

Instead of worrying about diplomatic recognition, Mason gave attention to matters peripheral to foreign relations, such as a statue of Stonewall Jackson that a group of British citizens wished to give to the State of Virginia.[45] He also spent time on the Great Seal of the Confederacy. On May 20, 1863, Benjamin had written to Mason about a law passed by the Confederate Congress to commission a great seal. He instructed the Virginian to "give your best attention to this" by finding an artist and engraver for it.[46] Mason monitored the effort closely, as the seal took months to finish.[47] Benjamin sent shipping instructions in April,[48] and, after numerous delays, Mason reported on July 6 that the seal had been completed.[49] It arrived in Richmond on September 4,[50] with the ambitious mission of putting the official stamp of prestige upon an unrecognized government.

What could not be accomplished with cotton, arms, and diplomacy could not be done with a small piece of engraved silver. In 1864, more than ever before, Confederate fortunes rested with the southern armies. In June, as another summer campaign dawned, Mason voiced optimism once again.[51] But in Ulysses S. Grant the federal forces had found a commanding general who refused to allow the Confederate armies a moment's rest. Rather than retreating after every engagement to regroup, Grant sought to bleed the Confederacy dry on the battlefield, constantly pressuring Lee until the South's men and resources ran out.[52] President Davis had no stomach for such a war of attrition. He later wrote that, "to those who can approve the policy of attrition without reference to the number of lives it might cost, this may be justifiable, but it can hardly be regarded as generalship."[53]

By the time Generals Lee and Grant locked horns on the fields of the battered Old Dominion, Mason had returned to London. In April, Benjamin and others had succeeded in getting Davis to change his mind about Mason's mission, allowing the commissioner to use his own discretion in deciding where he should be at any given moment.[54] But Mason had arrived in London on June 5, three days before receiving the new instructions.[55] He had returned because Confederate supporters in Parliament were preparing for another attempt at gaining British diplomatic intervention.

Lord Clanricarde believed that "if God grants one [a victory] to Gen. Lee's Army I think peace may finally come before winter."[56] Lindsay continued to stress in Parliament that continuation of the war ran against British interests. Sensing weariness in the United States, he wondered if "mediation on the basis of separation" might be accepted. Wishing to introduce such a resolution, he asked for Mason's approval, while asserting that "the question is quite ripe *for fresh agitation* and from experience I find that agitation must be started by a debate in Parliament."[57]

Lindsay provided the immediate impetus for Mason's return to London. After a meeting with Lord Palmerston, Lindsay told his friend that the prime minister was most gracious and was willing to see Mason, although no formal invitation would be made.[58] Lindsay argued that *"much good will follow your meeting Lord Palmerston. It will lead to other meetings,* and besides in other matters I think if you come here you might *at present* prove of much service to the cause of the South."[59]

Mason declined to meet with Palmerston but approved the plan to introduce a motion for mediation on the basis of independence for the Confederacy. He insisted on following Davis's instructions by not engaging in such an interview without "some intimation from that Government of its disposition to enter into official relations with my own." But he supported the idea of mediation, believing that "the intelligent and responsible mind of the Northern people I know is at last fully satisfied that any conquest of the South is hopeless." As to the military situation, Mason wrote that President Lincoln dared not admit defeat in Virginia; therefore Grant "may continue to force his troops to be slaughtered until they mutiny, but you may receive it as a fact accomplished that he will never get to Richmond."[60]

Lord Palmerston, in an interview with Lindsay, similarly had "expressed the decided opinion that the North could never overcome the South and his belief that the people of the North were getting to be alive to the fact." Lindsay entreated Mason "to come here,"[61] as did James Spence.[62] Thus, after reporting to Richmond his reasons for turning down the Palmerston interview,[63] Mason reluctantly left for England. In a letter to Eliza, he commented that he had "yielded to the opinions and wishes of those whose opinions on the matter I am not at liberty to disregard."[64]

Lindsay postponed his motion, while all concerned parties waited for further news from the battlefields.[65] While publicly he voiced confidence, in private Mason sounded less certain about the military situation. He wrote to Eliza about suffering through the "painful suspense" of not knowing until weeks later what had happened on the bloodstained soil of Virginia. When he did hear news, Mason told her that he felt "more than ever, the earnest desire to be in your midst."[66] He also expressed increased concern for his sons who were serving in the Confederate armies, although he admitted that "one can hardly engage in personal anxieties amidst the terrible carnage occasioned by those battles."[67]

When the news arrived, it raised the hopes of Mason and his advisors. On July 8, Mason wrote to Benjamin about receiving "the cheerful accounts of our great successes against Grant in Virginia, and as far as we can determine through the imperfect and disjointed intelligence from the North, of like successes against Sherman in Georgia." The Virginian did "not doubt the result in either quarter" and added that, "should they prove so decisive as finally to dispose of both armies of invasion, I entertain a strong hope, let the ministerial issue [be] as it may, that public opinion in England will compel the Government to move in some manner advantageous to us."[68] That same day, Lord Palmerston narrowly escaped Parliament's censure because of his policies regarding the Danish war.[69] That event, combined with the war news, led Mason to change his mind and agree to see the prime minister.

On July 14, Mason left Lindsay's home in Middlesex, where he had been staying, for the interview. The southern diplomat did most of the talking. Palmerston asked about the military situation and about the fall presidential election in the United States. Mason replied that the South could not be conquered and that the North would acknowledge that fact by rejecting the Lincoln administration at the polls. He asserted that if Grant, Sherman, and then Lincoln were defeated, the North would be grateful for European intervention to stop the bloodletting.[70] In reporting the interview to Slidell, Mason wrote that, while "the Ministry fears to move under the menaces of the North," Palmerston "is as well satisfied as I am, that the separation of the States is final and the independence of the South an accomplished fact."[71]

Always easily flattered, Mason left the interview optimistic. But Slidell had become realistic almost to the point of being cynical. He responded to his colleague that the conversation went "very much as I had anticipated excepting that his Lordship appears to have said even less than I had supposed he would." Similarly disgusted with Napoleon III, Slidell added that "the time has now arrived when it is comparatively of very little importance what Queen or Emperor may say or think about us. A plague, I say, on both your Houses."[72]

Slidell's assessment proved to be more accurate. As happened with previous efforts to intervene in the American conflict, Parliament adjourned without the Lindsay motion coming to a vote.[73] Spence looked upon Mason's meeting with Palmerston as a consolation prize,[74] but the main goal of diplomatic recognition remained as elusive as ever. The tide for intervention on behalf of the South had risen once again, only to peak and recede in the face of ministerial opposition.

With "the political world generally being in recess for the summer" and "there being nothing special calling me to the Continent," Mason decided to remain in Britain for the immediate future. He informed Benjamin that he would "visit different points in England and Ireland, not to return to London unless specially called."[75] John R. Thompson, an editor of the *Index,* kept a journal that recorded Mason's movements from August 4 through November 4. Thompson accompanied the commissioner to places such as Belfast, Glasgow, and Liverpool. Mason kept up his correspondence, but otherwise his life had become rather casual and commonplace. Besides his usual busy calendar of dinners with friends and advisors, Mason engaged in activities as varied as playing cards, trout fishing, long walks in the countryside, mushroom picking, and playing croquet with the children of Lord Donoughmore.[76]

None of those activities had anything to do with Confederate foreign relations. As Grant besieged Lee's army in the trenches of Petersburg and Sherman marched through Georgia, the Confederacy's increasingly precarious military situation took precedence in diplomacy. Southern hopes had been reduced to holding on long enough for the North to tire of the war and vote Lincoln out of office. In September, Mason wrote that Gen. George B. McClellan's nomination by northern Democrats "upon a platform of which 'the immediate cessation of hostilities' is the great basis—it is believed generally here, must result in a peace, should he be elected." He asserted confidently, "From accumulating evidences at the North it is manifest that the people there have no further stomach for the fight—and under whatever stimulant, whether money or patriotism, can no longer be got to the field." Coupling that with "their immense debt, and the hopeless condition of their finances," Mason believed "that an armistice once entered upon, there is little to fear they will enter upon the worn-out experiment of war."[77] That summer, informal talks concerning peace took place in Canada[78] and in Richmond, but Davis and Benjamin rejected northern proposals of reunion and the abolition of southern slavery as nothing more than surrender terms.[79]

Meanwhile, the killing continued unabated. England and France refused to intervene, and Mason had become resigned to that fact. Convincing himself that Europe's conduct did not matter and that the Confederacy would triumph on its own, the Virginian enjoyed his social activities more than ever. In September, he wrote to Eliza of being "fortunate in England, in attaching many agreeable and hospitable friends, as well within, as without the circles of the statesmen and public men." He always had an "abundance of invitations to visit them at their charming country homes, of which I avail myself as far as consistent with other duties."[80]

Thompson received immense enjoyment from the experience of joining Mason in his social activities. He remarked that Mason particularly liked to talk with the ladies and asserted, "I need not say to you that all my consideration and honors were due to the accident of my being the companion of Mr. Mason, who is everywhere treated, as he deserves, with great hospitality and distinction."[81] But amid the compliments and gaiety, the reality of war stayed close at hand, as in October, when their travels took them to Liverpool for a fair "for the benefit of the sick and wounded Confederates, and for the relief of our men, prisoners at the North."[82]

Virginia remained prominent in Mason's thoughts. While he kept focused upon "a termination of the war, through the dissensions and disorganization manifest in the North," Mason mourned the suffering in his home state. He lamented to his son George that "the accounts I get from home, of the devastation and ruin of that part of our dear old State, where the enemy is in possession, or their armies have passed, are truly distressing; the populations in those districts, chiefly women and children, and old or infirm men, reduced to absolute starvation, yet they give not the slightest evidence of submission, but are content to die rather than return to the brutal Government we have shaken off, Virginia has indeed shown herself worthy her ancient renown."[83] In Richmond that devastation had become more of a reality than any hopes of northern exhaustion. Benjamin wrote to Mason that he wished the Virginian had stressed harder in his interview with Lord Palmerston that the war would continue unless Europe recognized the Confederacy. Otherwise, "although the war may gradually lose its intensity," the secretary of state feared "that it may long continue a lingering existence if European powers persist in the encouragement which is afforded the North by their obstinate refusal to recognize us."[84]

In October, after weeks of relative inactivity, the Confederate commissioners prepared to attack that obstinacy by making another push for recognition. On June 14, the Confederate Congress had issued a manifesto regarding secession and southern independence. It bluntly demanded recognition as a right but primarily rehashed the legality of the southern cause. The manifesto asserted that the Confederacy desired only "immunity from interference with their internal peace and prosperity." If the United States stopped "aggressions upon us," the war would end. The Richmond government wanted the document laid before European governments, committing "our cause to the enlightened judgement of the world, to the sober reflections of our adversaries themselves, and to the solemn and righteous arbitrament of Heaven."[85]

Mason convinced Slidell and Mann that the three should communicate the manifesto by joint note.[86] It took longer than usual for the document to reach Europe, but, by November, the trio was ready to present the demand for recognition.[87] Mason labeled the manifesto "a most able and impressive paper." Confidence had increased to the point at which even "King Cotton" made one last appearance, as the Virginian wrote to Benjamin that "distress in the manufacturing districts is again exhibiting itself to an extent causing much alarm." He hoped that it would produce positive results for the Confederacy when Parliament returned in February.[88]

Confederate officials had become gluttons for punishment. In 1864, most developments in the war had been negative. It was too late to move the British with such a demand. The diplomatic triumvirate's note of November 11 produced the predictable response from Lord Russell: Britain had maintained an impartial neutrality and would continue to do so.[89] While some of his advisors focused on the note's "relaxation in tone," Mason saw nothing in it.[90] The affair proved to be an utter waste of time for all Confederates involved, as, besides England, only France, Sweden, and the Papal States bothered to reply.[91]

Rebuffed by all the governments that could have helped, the Confederacy was left to rely upon its own resources and upon its armies in the field. On November 7, 1864, an indignant President Davis declared before the Confederate Congress that history would "be unable to absolve the neutral nations of Europe from a share in the moral responsibility for the myriads of human lives that have been unnecessarily sacrificed."[92] By year's end, even Benjamin's perpetual optimism had faded, as he bitterly lashed out at Britain and France for siding with the United States while the Confederacy fought their battles for them.[93]

Nearing the end of the game, Davis and Benjamin began to explore playing their last card, hoping it would be a trump. With Lee's army being stretched ever closer to the breaking point in the trenches of Petersburg, Davis believed, despite public pronouncements to the contrary, that recognition from Europe was the Confederacy's last hope. And by late 1864, Confederate officials in Richmond faced up

to the possibility that, all along, the institution of slavery had prevented European recognition. If the Confederate government offered
to free the slaves, perhaps Europe finally would step in to guarantee
southern independence and put an end to the suffering.[94]

Davis instructed Mason and Slidell to determine if Britain and
France had failed to tell them of specific objections that raised obstacles to diplomatic recognition. That the barrier could be southern
slavery, Benjamin implied only vaguely. Concern that the United States
could learn about Confederate consideration of emancipation led all
correspondence on the subject to be cryptic. Therefore, before approaching British and French officials, the commissioners were to
meet with Louisiana Rep. Duncan Kenner, who had been appointed
as a special envoy to transmit specific information on the subject
orally.[95] Then, if Britain and France insisted on abolition in exchange
for recognition, the Confederacy would know of that condition before another year of war destroyed more lives and property.

The instructions, as usual, took weeks to arrive. In the meantime, Mason heard rumors "from the South of a purpose to increase
our military force by arming a large body of slaves," but he discounted
them.[96] He spent the last weeks of 1864 traveling all over Europe,
from London to Paris to Frankfurt to Brussels. At each stop he surveyed opinions and related his unwavering confidence in the resil-
ience of the southern people. Labeling President Davis's November
7 speech a "calm and truthful review of events in the late Campaign,"
the Virginian believed that those words "must convince all, not willingly blind, that the idea of reunion or subjugation is hopeless."[97]

But the British ministry would not be moved by such rhetoric.
Lincoln's November reelection meant that the United States would
prosecute the war to its inexorable conclusion. As the new year began, Mason found nothing new. He remained popular within pro-
Confederate circles, reporting to Richmond that he saw "public men
from time to time, and have been kindly received at their homes in
the country." But their sympathy and politeness did not translate
into government action. He remarked that those same Englishmen
expressed "the same interest as ever in our success in the war; but I
am not aware that there is any increased disposition, either with liber-
als or conservatives, to overrule the policy of the administration."[98]

In Mason's view, that administration would not be moved by the
Confederacy's abolishing slavery in its territory. But the conservative
defender of the peculiar institution soon would have to address that
possibility. In late December, far from London, in what remained of
the Confederacy, the diplomat's son, James Murray Mason, Jr., on

furlough from the army, wrote a letter to his father. In ominous tones, he reported "a gloomy day in our Revolution." He confessed that he did "not see much ground for hope." While "a bright future may await the Confederacy . . . before we reach the goal, this generation will be so travel worn and wearied as to be unfit to enjoy the result of their labor."[99]

Battle-hardened at the tender age of twenty-five, the younger Mason wrote of dissension, despair, and "the want of men for the ranks." Convinced that "the government is utterly at a loss what to do" and believing "that the country will be overrun next summer," he predicted disaster unless his father gained something from Europe. He lamented that "the darkest hours of the war are yet before us," even though "now and then a bright gleam of sunshine may gladden for a brief interval, the universal gloom." The young Virginian concluded that, "if the North continues her present energy, the long night of ruin, misery and agony will surely come unless indeed, you in Europe, do something for our aid." Even though the rank-and-file soldiers opposed it, Mason's son believed that the time had come to arm the slaves. He pledged to volunteer to lead a company of them, believing that "with proper discipline they will fight as well as any mercenaries."[100]

That letter must have stunned the elder Mason. His own son spoke, in chillingly depressing words, of imminent Confederate defeat. Additionally, he learned that his son supported the very action that Mason believed would undermine the fabric of southern society. Exchanging slavery for diplomatic recognition amounted to the last diplomatic option the Confederacy had. And Davis and Benjamin, as well as his own son, had chosen James Murray Mason to suggest it. Despite finding the thought repellent, the Virginia diplomat had no alternative.

◆◆◆   **Chapter 13**   ◆◆◆

1865–1866

From Diplomat to Exile

On January 21, 1865, Mason discussed the emancipation rumors in a letter to Secretary of State Benjamin. He had tried to ignore them, but "many enquiries have been made of me by our well-wishers whether I thought it would be done." Mason responded to them that, while the matter would be considered as only a matter of expediency, "our people would have no fear of bringing our slaves into the field to fight an enemy common alike to them and their masters." Mason believed that "slaves would make better soldiers" in southern armies "than in those of the North," but he had serious objections that he believed would prevent such a policy from being enacted.[1]

In the short term, he argued, "It would diminish our agricultural labor." But looking toward the future, Mason warned that "to offer freedom" to those slaves who took up arms for the Confederacy would be disastrous for southern society because "great mischief and inconvenience would result from any increase in the number of free blacks amongst us."[2] Years had passed and circumstances had changed, but Mason remained steadfast in his view of the proper place for African Americans. Given the blessings of instruction and guidance from Confederate officers, blacks would be able to fight. But that did not alter Mason's conviction that giving them freedom would be a disruptive action. Images of poor freemen in Haiti and in northern cities lingered in his mind even then. Unsupervised blacks could not be allowed a place in Confederate society.

Shortly after writing that letter to Benjamin, Mason's attention became diverted by a U.S. Sanitary Commission pamphlet he received from Boston. It discussed mistreatment of northern prisoners of war in the South. It came with a note from the sender, who believed that Mason had not been "aware of this state of things" and could work "indirectly to ameliorate this appalling suffering."[3] Mason replied that he knew nothing about prisoners of war on either side except for what he read in the "public prints; but I am fully aware that the conditions of prisoners of war, wherever they may be, must of necessity be attended with privation and suffering."[4]

That taken as an assumption, the commissioner proceeded to defend the Confederate States and attack the United States on all issues concerning prisoners of war. Receiving regular reports of death and destruction throughout the South, Mason linked the treatment of captive northern soldiers with general arguments against the aggressive war forced upon the South by the North. At great length, he defended the South as doing what it could for prisoners, given "the atrocious manner in which the war is waged by those who conduct your armies in my country." He blamed the Lincoln government for the suffering and countered with charges of northern mistreatment of southern soldiers in captivity. Angrily denouncing the Sanitary Commission pamphlet as "a political work, and of the lowest type, intended to excite and inflame the popular mind at the North by false and exaggerated pictures," Mason gave the correspondence to the London press.[5]

In February, as Parliament prepared to open a new session, no talk arose about pushing for recognition. Instead, Mason and his advisors worried about the Confederate military situation. But they remained "cheered and elevated here by the defiant tone of the South, with the renewed declaration of Congress that the war will be prosecuted to independence, at whatever cost or hazard."[6] Slidell seconded that determination, writing, "I cannot permit myself for a moment to suppose that President Davis would listen to any terms of which independence was not the indispensable preliminary condition."[7]

A few days later, the still feisty commissioners particularly became agitated when they received a letter from Lord Russell. On February 13, the British Foreign Minister addressed a note to Mason, Slidell, and Mann to complain that the Confederacy was taking advantage of Great Britain's neutrality. Specifically, he charged the trio with "undue and reprehensible attempts . . . to involve her Majesty in a war in which her Majesty had declared her intention not to take part." He wanted their assurances that the illegal activities would cease.[8] Slidell suggested to Mason that the letter "requires something more than a formal answer," arguing that Russell had provided "an opportunity to expose the pretended neutrality" of the British government.[9]

Agreeing with his compatriot, Mason went to Paris to meet Slidell so they could coordinate a vigorous Confederate response. Those discussions were soon interrupted, however, by the arrival of Duncan Kenner with Richmond's instructions regarding southern slavery and emancipation.[10] Learning about the drastic new diplomatic move with which they were being entrusted, the commissioners decided to temper their reply to Russell's note. Mason believed "that it would be more prudent to avoid raising new issues . . . immediately in advance of such a communication."[11] Instead, they asserted that Russell's charges of "continued building by agents of the Confederate States within Her Majesty's dominions of ships of war" were entirely without foundation, and they pledged to refer his complaints to Richmond.[12]

That issue being disposed of, Mason had to face the topic of emancipating southern slaves. The Virginian returned to London to meet Lord Palmerston and broach the subject in conversation. But on March 5, before Mason talked with the British prime minister, Slidell spoke with Napoleon III. The emperor reiterated that he was "willing and anxious to act with England" but also stated that he would "not move without her" and saw no point in his proposing any intervention. His earlier overtures having been rejected by the British, Napoleon "could not suppose that they would now be listened to with more favor." Toward the end of the conversation, Slidell raised the slavery issue directly. The French leader replied that "he had never taken that into consideration; that it had not, and could not have, any influence on his action, but that it had probably been differently considered in England."[13]

On March 13, Mason requested an interview with Palmerston. The meeting took place at the prime minister's residence the following day. Mason knew that Napoleon III had told Slidell that slavery had not been an issue. That bolstered his confidence that the British would answer the inquiry similarly. Still viewing southern slavery as a positive, humane condition, Mason wanted such a negative response. The Virginia patrician could not even bring himself to state the question directly, as Slidell had done, or even to hint at emancipating southern slaves. To Mann he remarked proudly, "I went over the whole matter contained in the despatches with such form of allusion to the *concession* we held in reserve, as would make him necessarily comprehend it: but I did not mention it *by name*."[14] Mason claimed that, out of fear that word of the discussion would leak to the United States, he only alluded to the subject. If the offer became public and then were declined, it would cause unnecessary but "incalculable" harm. Despite his use of ambiguous language to describe the "concession" he referred to, Mason felt certain that Palmerston understood that he meant slavery.[15]

The prime minister assured him that "there was nothing '*underlying*,' and not stated" that prevented Britain from recognizing Confederate independence. Mason concluded that diplomatic recognition had been prevented because of "the fear of war with the U.S., and secondly, a tacit conviction in the English mind that the longer the war lasted in America the better for them, because of the consequent exhaustion of both parties."[16] On March 26, Mason spoke with his friend and advisor, Lord Donoughmore, who basically confirmed that conclusion. Donoughmore opposed slavery personally, however, and, unlike Mason, he thought it had played a significant role in preventing recognition when Confederate fortunes ran high earlier in the war. But in March 1865, even if Richmond offered to "insure abolition in a fair and reasonable time," Britain would not grant recognition. That "time had gone by, now especially that our fortunes seemed more adverse than ever."[17]

Grant and Lee still confronted each other across the trenches at Petersburg, Virginia. But southern ranks had become thinner over the months of the siege. Meanwhile, Gen. William Tecumseh Sherman, after cutting a wide swath through Georgia, had turned northward into the Carolinas. Mason, however, remained satisfied that "whenever a battle is fought with Sherman . . . his defeat will be a rout."[18] While Richmond hoped that diplomatic recognition would rescue a Confederacy facing military disaster, its commissioner in Great Britain, far from the battlefield, looked for military victories over Grant and Sherman to produce recognition.[19] Southerners on both sides of the Atlantic, ignorant of reality, grasped at increasingly frail straws.

There would be no last-minute diplomatic success to save the Confederacy. Mason despaired of his inability to produce any results through his diplomacy. In private conversations, the Virginia diplomat had taken to expressing "great regret" that the United States had released him and Slidell to end the *Trent* affair peacefully. He lamented "that surrender so flattered and satisfied the national vanity of England, that her people were disposed to receive more complacently than they otherwise would have done, the subsequent insults and demands of the Northern Government."[20] He could do nothing to change that.

With the war news becoming ever gloomier, Mason worried about home. He maintained an "unabated confidence in those who hold the helm, and above all, in our gallant armies." But he wanted his family to be prepared to evacuate Richmond if necessary, even though he termed it "an event I don't contemplate." He wrote to Eliza of being "sometimes sorely tried in my exile. Were I with you, I could at least, share your privations and to that extent seem to diminish them." He discussed providing for their financial needs. Nervously he awaited events.[21]

On Sunday, April 2, 1865, Jefferson Davis received word from General Lee that Richmond had to be evacuated. Quickly the president prepared for the removal of his executive papers and the government.[22] Accompanied by Benjamin and other cabinet members, Davis traveled southward, hoping that the fall of Richmond did not mean the end of the Confederate cause. If the worst came to pass, he planned to reach the Trans-Mississippi Department of the Confederacy to carry on the fight until reunion could be accomplished on more favorable terms. Davis did not even rule out the possibility of rallying the fortunes of the Confederacy and the spirit of the southern people to preserve independence.[23] Gen. Wade Hampton, part of the presidential escort in the Carolinas, wrote to Davis that the Confederacy had "not less than 40 to 50 thousand men in arms on *this* side of the Mississippi. On the other there are as many more . . . if we disband we give up at once and forever all hope of foreign intervention. Europe will say . . . 'why should we interfere if you choose to re-enter the Union?' But if we keep any organization, however small, in the field we give Europe the opportunity of aiding us."[24] But that flight from reality ended when federal cavalry captured Jefferson Davis on May 10, 1865, near Irwinsville, Georgia.[25] For all practical purposes, the heart of the Confederacy then ceased to beat.

To the end, Confederate officials believed that European intervention could solve their problems. But thoughts of Britain's or France's intervening to save the Confederacy at the last moment were extremely far-fetched. Davis had written on March 22, "It cannot be doubted that the obstacle to the recognition of the Confederacy had been an unwillingness to be embroiled in a quarrel with the United States."[26] One month later, that obstacle remained, and, with the Confederate government on the run, it had become questionable whether anything existed to recognize.

James Murray Mason, however, continued to wear rose-colored glasses. On April 23, he wrote to Mann that news of the evacuation of Richmond and General Lee's surrender "has cast gloom over our friends here, but in which I do not participate. I am hopeful certainly though I will not say confident." Mason affirmed, without any reference to reality, that Lee had to have given in at Davis's express instructions, because "*I know* that no terms of peace would be accepted, that did not embrace independence." The surrender must have been in "immediate expectation of a cessation of hostilities, and a peace to follow."[27]

Mason addressed a similar letter to Slidell,[28] but the Louisiana native replied, "I cannot share your hopefulness." In bitter, mournful, pained words, Slidell wrote to his colleague, "We have seen the beginning of the end. I, for my part, am prepared for the worst. With Lee's surrender there will soon be an end to our regular organized armies and I can see no possible good to result from a protracted guerrilla warfare." He lamented that the South had been "crushed and must submit to the yoke, our children must bide their time for vengeance, but you and I will never revisit our homes under our glorious flag." He then vowed never to set "foot on a soil from which flaunts the hated Stars and Stripes. I am sick, sick at heart."[29] For Slidell, the struggle had ended. In Paris, far from the front lines of his native land, the white-haired diplomat admitted southern defeat.

Mason obstinately refused to go along with him. He wanted to publish, along with Slidell and Mann, a letter that would counter talk of defeat. After receiving Slidell's funereal letter, he wrote back that, while certainly he felt "depressed and disturbed at the manifestations of weakness which compelled Lee after the evacuation of Richmond, to surrender his army—but I have never doubted, and do not now doubt, but that the war will go on to final success." He predicted a war of partisan resistance that the South would win. He remained confident "in the spirit of our people—they have before them but success, or bondage a thousandfold worse than Egyptian . . . and against such they must and will struggle on to the death."[30]

Mason believed that the likelihood that a defeated South would suffer such a horrible fate had become "more certain than ever, by the accession of Johnson."[31] On the evening of April 14, President Abraham Lincoln had been shot in the head by John Wilkes Booth, a famous actor and fanatical supporter of the South. Lincoln died early the next morning, leaving the presidency, and the delicate task of reconstructing the Union, to Andrew Johnson of Tennessee.[32] With Washington, D.C., in turmoil, northerners looked beyond

Booth, attempting to find a wider conspiracy. Their search aimed at Richmond.[33]

American charges of Confederate culpability reached England very quickly. A telegram from Secretary of War Edwin M. Stanton to Charles Francis Adams appeared in the London papers on April 27. It spoke "of a conspiracy deliberately planned and set on foot by rebels under the pretence of avenging the South and aiding the rebel cause."[34] Mason termed such accusations "calumnious" and sought to refute the charges in a letter to the editor of the *Index*. He defended the South, while simultaneously attacking the North. Mason wrote, "As to the crime which has been committed, none will view it with more abhorrence than the people of the South; but they will know, as will equally all well-balanced minds, that it is the necessary offspring of those scenes of bloodshed and murder in every form of unbridled license which have signalized the invasion of the South by the Northern armies, unrebuked certainly, and therefore instigated by their leaders, and those over them."[35] The Confederate commissioner granted that Stanton probably had composed the letter in "hurried excitement." But Mason denounced the secretary for unscrupulously using the murder "for base political effect."[36]

The next day, Mason elaborated upon his thinking in a letter to his friend Lord Shaftesbury. He reiterated the South's revulsion toward such action, asserting that "assassination for any cause has never been a vice of my countrymen." In addition, however, Mason explained "that considering the numberless . . . crimes that have been perpetrated upon defenseless . . . men and women in my country at the instigation and under the license of the assassin's victim," he did not believe "that any expression was due from me" until he read Stanton's "slanderous" accusations.[37]

Three days later, on May 1, Mason wrote what proved to be his final official letter to Benjamin. He mourned that "the evacuation of Richmond and surrender of Lee have produced the confident belief here, and throughout Europe generally, that further resistance is hopeless and that the war is at an end." Observers believed that the South would then submit passively to its fate. But Mason kept his lone candle of hope flickering, stressing that "I entertain no such impression and endeavor as far as I can to disabuse the public mind." He pledged that "in the uncertainty of the future, or of what may be the views of the Government relative to the continuance of commissioners or other agencies abroad, I can only remain where I am and await its orders."[38] Along with the fleeing Jefferson Davis, Mason remained a last believer.

Mason expressed fears for the president's safety in a May letter to Mann. He also exhibited thinking similar to that of the chief executive in discussing the possibility that Davis might reach Texas and continue the war from the Trans-Mississippi Department.[39] But all such ephemeral hopes ended with Davis's capture. The news slapped Mason in the face, awakening him to the reality of southern defeat. He suffered the news of the disaster alone, as his British friends and advisors stayed away from him, being afraid to ask the Virginian how bad things really were. One of them wrote belatedly, "The collapse is, to me, unintelligibly sudden, being so complete."[40]

The diplomatic front, too, had collapsed. In close coordination, France and Britain withdrew the belligerent rights of the Confederacy, marking the official end of the diplomatic activities of the Confederate States of America.[41] That action had been delayed throughout the month of May,[42] but with the federal capture of Jefferson Davis, there remained no reason to believe that southern resistance would continue. On June 2, Lord Russell instructed the British Admiralty that the American war had ended. But two Confederate cruisers remained at sea, raiding northern shipping. This meant that, to the United States, the war had not officially ended.[43]

For James Murray Mason, however, the war indeed was over. When the British government rang the death knell for Confederate diplomatic hopes, he did not protest. He had been relaxing in the "quiet inland town" of Leamington for two or three weeks "to get away from the crowd and distractions of London." Mason's concern had shifted toward his family. He had learned that Eliza and his daughters had arrived in Baltimore on May 22, intending to continue their journey all the way to Quebec. Mason wrote his wife, "I can not tell you how much I am relieved by the intelligence that you and our dear girls are at last beyond the domain of the brutal Yankees who have made our land a desert." Feeling more isolated than ever, he begged her to write him frequently to provide him whatever information she could. He sent "his best love and welcome to the English flag."[44]

Mason yearned to initiate his plans to join them in Canada, despite James Spence's warnings that Canada was too cold.[45] But from "a sense of duty," the Virginian pledged to stay at his post until Texas surrendered. If it kept up the fight, Mason "felt it due to remain until I see whether that State looks to my services in Europe."[46] That possibility vanished quickly, making Mason's last official duty his participation in efforts to inform the commerce raider *Shenandoah* that the war had ended.

In the northern Pacific Ocean, that vessel continued to sink U.S. shipping vessels weeks after hostilities had ceased on land. As soon as word of Davis's capture reached England, James Bulloch approached Mason about trying to stop such actions. But Mason thought it impracticable to do so.[47] By June 13, he had changed his mind and promised to transmit to Lord Russell any letter Bulloch wrote to the ship's captain.[48] Bulloch wrote that letter to explain the surrender and to instruct the *Shenandoah* to end its war, too.[49] He sent the letter to Mason,[50] who passed the correspondence along to Lord Russell, with the request that British authorities find the rampaging vessel and deliver the surrender news.[51] On August 2, the British succeeded in delivering the message, ending the war on the high seas[52] and also ending Mason's diplomatic service for the Confederacy.

According to Jefferson Davis, European states had insured the downfall of the Confederacy, particularly by honoring and refusing to challenge the federal blockade. He wrote, "Every prescription of maritime law and every right of neutral nations to trade with a belligerent under the sanction of principles heretofore universally respected were systematically and persistently violated by the United States,"[53] and Europe allowed that violation to go on unmolested. Some blame must be assigned to Confederate policy makers, including Mason, for pursuing a wait-and-react foreign policy most of the time. Primarily, however, European inaction was a function of the political realities of the time.

In the real world of European balance-of-power politics, the American Civil War did not merit primary concern. Even for Great Britain, European matters occupied center stage. From 1861 to 1865, foreign policy concerns in Europe included lingering problems related to the recent unification of Italy, an insurrection in Poland, and a war that pitted Denmark against Prussia and Austria. For France, Napoleon III's "Mexican adventure" complicated matters further. Keeping the general peace was the main goal, and relatively minor problems could not be allowed to explode into a major war. The overriding desire for stability made it easy for the topic of Confederate recognition to be placed on the diplomatic back burner, for Great Britain as well as the other countries of Europe.[54]

European balance-of-power politics injured Confederate diplomatic efforts, but so did transatlantic politics, involving the major European powers and the United States. Each of the major states of Europe was concerned that a U.S. declaration of war would follow any recognition of the Confederacy. A war with the United States was undesirable militarily, but, beyond that, it would have distracted the power involved from active participation in European affairs. Austria, in particular, did not want Britain distracted from European affairs. Russia and Prussia both had been friendly with the United States, if for no other reason than the balancing effect that U.S. sea power had on British power at that time.[55] Continental Europe refused to risk a war with the United States and hoped that Britain would do the same. For four years, Europeans watched and waited, most believing that the South would win. When the Confederacy lost, they were able to proceed with life as usual, having been affected only minimally. From Europe's standpoint, war's end meant that it had dodged the American bullet.

Despite the end of the shooting, Mason's work in England was not quite over. From across the Atlantic, the Virginian took responsibility for arranging the defense of the imprisoned Jefferson Davis. Desiring either a speedy trial or the Confederate leader's release rather than an unnecessary prolongation of a national tragedy, Charles O'Conor of New York City had offered to serve as Davis's counsel. Mason accepted the offer on his friend's behalf[56] and suggested that financial agent Colin McRae set up an account to pay for the New Yorker's services.[57] Mason wrote to O'Conor that "we in Europe can now confidently reply that whatever can be done will be done for his defense."[58] But O'Conor refused any money, having volunteered for the good of his country.[59]

In July, in a rambling memorandum composed while staying with William S. Lindsay, Mason reflected on the condition of the South. Thinking of both past and future, he commented that, because of the war, "the whole South is now prostrate and powerless—that war was for independence—an independence believed to be from political considerations indispensable to the safety and welfare of the people." The Virginian believed that "its value may be estimated by the price paid in the attempt to obtain it. . . . proud and spirited people have been made to feel the bitterness of subjugation." He pointed out that the North had lost as well, because the United States was "no longer a republic. It is no longer a government of limited power. It is no longer a federation of States." The government had become "centralized and consolidated, and its power is measured only by the will of the Congress and the President, as they are adapted from time to time to the shifting expedients of ignorance or fraud."[60] Mason's lifelong devotion to the words *Pro Republica Semper* had proved fruitless. The republic of his grandfather was gone.

Southerners, according to Mason, would have to sit back and await events. Pride might say, "Flee to a foreign land." But "reason and manhood" made it the smart choice to stay. Southerners should bide their time until "the people of the South will be in fair competition with the people of the North for the dominion." Then, when the South had gained its ultimate independence, "the sufferings, privations, and even humiliations through which it was attained will only the more enoble it."[61] He continued to dream that, even though he could not live in an independent South, at least his children and grandchildren would do so.

While he hoped that southerners would not run from their native land, Mason had no immediate plans to cross the Atlantic. As long as Jefferson Davis remained in prison, his own arrest remained a distinct possibility.[62] He continued with preparations to join his family in Canada. He wrote to Eliza on August 9, "My passage is engaged in the 'Peruvian,' to leave for Quebec on the 24 instant, which I trust will put me once more with you and our dear daughters at an early day in September."[63] A week later, however, he had changed his mind. Mason had learned that Judah Benjamin had evaded capture and would arrive in England from Havana on August 28.[64] He did not want to depart for Canada without conferring with Benjamin first.[65] Therefore, he postponed his planned departure until the end of the month.[66]

The delay soon became indefinite. On August 23, Mason asked his family to come to Britain instead. He wrote to Eliza of "remonstrances from friends here, both Confederate and English, resting chiefly on political considerations," that he not leave yet. He had not suggested such a plan earlier, "from a general apprehension that you and the girls might be disinclined to the sea voyage." He tried hard to assure them that, if they sailed in the tranquil month of October, they would have a pleasant voyage. He argued that, "on the score of comfort and peace, we shall be far better off than when near the Yankee frontier."[67]

After Benjamin arrived, he and McRae added their voices to those recommending that Mason stay in England. They warned their Virginia friend of personal risk in Canada, but political reasons predominated. Unfortunately for Mason, his family declined to join him in his British exile. Eliza cited personal reasons for not crossing the Atlantic. While both sides claimed to understand why the other would not be sailing, neither could hide disappointment.[68] Mason expressed an "earnest desire to be once more united to you all," particularly because, "in the condition of things around me here, Europe presents but little interest."[69] To his daughters, he asserted "that not only your excellent mother and all of you, but that *I* too, considering all that you have undergone in the last four years, '*deserve*' that we should be united, and to remain united once more."[70]

While he remained in Britain, Mason busied himself with the loose ends of the late Confederate States of America. Bulloch and other southern agents continued to require help in money matters.[71] With virtually all former Confederate officials faced with belt-tightening in the wake of Richmond's defeat, Mason joined Benjamin and McRae in distributing the remnants of the Confederacy's funds in Europe.[72] Additionally, through the end of the year, he continued to receive letters from O'Conor. Besides discussing Jefferson Davis's legal situation, these also described U.S. politics.[73]

The more Mason learned about President Johnson's disagreements with the radical members of the Republican Party over reconstruction policies,[74] the more he came to think that it might yet "be possible, that things may be so arranged that we may be enabled to go back where we came from . . . in the course of next year." While he had expected little from Johnson, Mason remarked that he had "certainly shown, in his policy so far, a fixed purpose to disappoint that party who reveled in the ruin of the South."[75]

Despite hints that reconstruction would be milder than he had feared, Mason recognized that the situation that kept him in exile would not change overnight. In November, he wrote to his daughters that "Canada may be our residence for some time to come—we can only make the best of it." Despite the reversal of his opinion on Johnson, he mourned that the South "yet lies prostrate, and powerless under a despot's foot. It can never be what it was, and unless, in a hope that I could render some possible service to my countrymen who are compelled to remain there, I can have no wish to return." Mason had become satisfied that he "could render no service now unless I were to aid in adjusting the yoke that is upon them, an office for which I have no inclination."[76] Spence tried to cheer him by writing that, because of its rich soil and cotton, the South would bounce back sooner than expected.[77] But that thought gave little solace to a proud Virginian, away from his loved ones for four years, who found himself without a country to call his own.

That status presented Mason with legal difficulties. For business related to Eliza's family inheritance, he needed to make an affidavit at the U.S. consulate in London. The vice-consul asked Mason if he was a U.S. citizen. Mason said no. When asked "of what country are you a citizen," he replied, "I am at present, and have been for some time, resident in England." Befuddled, the vice-consul said, "But . . . you must belong to some country." Mason responded that he had been a

U.S. citizen but, "after the rupture there, became a citizen of the Confederate States . . . when the Government of the latter had been *unfortunately* overthrown, I was in Europe, where I remained since and without any purpose of returning to the United States." Hesitating, the vice-consul uttered, "I suppose you may still be considered a citizen of the United States." But Mason exclaimed, "*You* may consider it, if you please, but it will be your act, not mine."[78]

Mason's family kept busy, moving from St. Catherine's to Montreal for the winter.[79] In Britain, James, although spending time with friends as often as possible, found himself with less and less to do. He read as many newspapers as possible, particularly to follow the debates in Congress, but he complained of his overall idleness and wrote to Eliza of having "nothing to tell you of myself except that time drags on at a slow and heavy pace." He kept up his "usual habit of exercise, walking one, two, or three miles every day," but he stated that his "great want is the lack of *active* mental occupation."[80] He had remarked that the past had become "ever present, and will engross all my thought,"[81] but that struck him as serving no real purpose beyond mere enjoyment of reflection.

His business in Europe completed, Mason resolved to sail for Canada in the spring. He spent some of his time engaged in charity work, feeling "really gratified in having it thus in my power to do something, even at this distance," by accepting voluntary contributions amounting to £300 for the "relief of our suffering countrymen in the South."[82] He wanted to do anything he could, particularly after hearing more news about conditions in Winchester. That information caused Mason's bitter disdain for the North to erupt into full hatred.

The picture of Winchester drawn for him included "the depraved and vagabond condition of the negroes, and of the usurpations in society there, by the Yankees, male and female."[83] He believed it would be "painful" to go back there "and witness the melancholy ruins of that once peaceful and exemplary society." Mason combed his memory for recollections of the various people he had encountered in his sixty-seven years. Some he disliked, some he held "in contempt, as unworthy," and some he believed "were essentially *bad*." But he could not remember that his "feelings toward any such amounted to acrimony, or *insuperable hate*. Now it is otherwise." He confessed "that toward every man or thing North, there has arisen within me a feeling of detestation that I can not express or qualify, if I would." Mason castigated northerners as being "demons" in war and "fiends" in victory. Ever the Virginia cavalier, he labeled their actions of the last five years "a disgrace to manhood."[84]

While his hatred for everything northern blossomed, Mason's
love for everything southern grew even stronger. He cherished reports "that the people of our noble South remain unsubdued in spirit."
Though his countrymen had suffered terribly, he took heart "from
the condition of the enemy." Except for France during the French
Revolution, Mason concluded that "no country was ever environed
with greater perils, or was in more incompetent hands, than that represented by the Government at Washington." If the North did not
find a Napoleon to rescue it from chaos, the South could benefit
from the convulsions. If it did find one, then the South could use the
ensuing wars to rise like a phoenix from the ashes.[85]

Such musings reflected an idle mind long since removed from
the scene in question. Mason went back and forth between rambling
predictions of eventual southern triumph and despondent portraits
of a South whose "sources of wealth are dried up, and her social
structure destroyed forever," one that had to colonize Australia and
other British colonies to avoid living under the rule of Yankee task-
masters. The aging diplomat was "getting very tired and lonesome."[86]
The time had come to sail.

Mason arranged to leave England aboard the *Moravian* on May
3, 1866.[87] He spent those last days "busily engaged in packing up the
material that has accumulated around me in the last four and a half
years, to take with me," and saying good-bye to his British friends.
He arrived in Liverpool on April 30 and stayed with Spence until the
steamer set out to sea.[88] Much had changed since he landed at
Southampton in January 1862. The Confederate States of America
no longer existed. The United States held a tormented Jefferson Davis
prisoner. Thousands of young Americans from the North and South
had been killed and mutilated on the bloodstained fields of Gettysburg,
Chickamauga, Cold Harbor, and other famous and unknown grave-
yards. Abraham Lincoln was numbered among the casualties.

James Murray Mason's beloved home had been razed by occupying northern troops. He had lost a daughter, Anna, to illness and
the ravages of war. He had spent four of his golden years fighting on
the foreign relations battleground, with little to show for his efforts
save the memories of good friends and acquaintances in a distant
land. Mason pledged to "ever cherish grateful recollections of my
residence in England, and of the many valued friendships contracted
here, whatever the harshness of its Government toward us."[89] He
took those feelings across the Atlantic to Canada, one step closer to
home.

Chapter 14

1866–1871

Virginia Homecoming

The long-awaited Mason family reunion took place in May 1866, in Montreal. The Masons spent several weeks there, enjoying a quiet respite from five troubled years.[1] Canada had become the chosen refuge of a number of Confederate exiles, including James Buchanan's vice-president, John C. Breckinridge, who had served the Richmond government as secretary of war and as a general in the field. After General Lee's surrender, Breckinridge had escaped to England, where he spent a great deal of time with Mason. In August 1865, the two had planned to sail to Canada together,[2] until Mason changed his mind about leaving Great Britain.

In Canada, Breckinridge settled with his family in the small town of Niagara. His description of the quiet, secluded village induced the Masons to leave Montreal in July. They spent the rest of the summer along the Niagara River with various Confederate refugees.[3] There they shared an ability to look across the majestic falls to glimpse their former home, the United States. True, they could see only Yankee New York State, but the land seemed to beckon them nonetheless.

The exiles remained deeply interested in American politics, particularly as these related to their beloved South. From newspapers, Mason followed the ongoing debates over reconstruction policy, but he did not like what he read. He saw little prospect for any eventual return to the United States and wrote to Colin McRae that "things look gloomy for the South." Those words reflected Mason's reaction to the proposed Fourteenth Amendment to the Constitution. He believed that its passage would "leave the Southern States deprived of all self-authority for years and under the uncontrolled domination of the North—God help them for He only can."[4]

In addition to following U.S. politics, the Confederates in exile monitored the continued imprisonment of Jefferson Davis. The harsh treatment Davis received at the hands of his northern jailers had made the southern leader a living martyr of the Lost Cause.[5] In late 1866, as Davis entered his second winter in captivity, Judah Benjamin wrote to Mason "about our unfortunate friend." He wondered "if an additional rigorous season passed in confinement should prove fatal." Benjamin thought that President Andrew Johnson would have released Davis if he had not been "cowed by the overbearing violence of the Radicals." Benjamin exclaimed that he had "ceased to hope for anything that justice or humanity demands from the men who seem now to have uncontrolled power over public affairs in the United States."[6]

For the winter months, the Masons moved to Toronto. Despite his unsettled life, Mason had found a bit of contentment. Just having his wife and daughters by his side led him to assert, "We have once more something like a home, though in exile."[7] The pace of his life had slowed, but still he relished rare moments of celebrity, as when the Ladies of the Hollywood Memorial Association in Richmond asked for an autograph. Mason hoped that they found his handwriting legible and complimented the women on their "honored devotion to the memories of our gallant dead so eminently becoming the matrons and maids of Virginia." As "an Exile in a foreign land," he could only add his "earnest wishes, for the success" of their "noble enterprise."[8]

While in Toronto, Mason began severing his last tie with the United States by filing legal documents disposing of the ruins of Selma and settling various claims for debts against his Winchester property.[9] On July 3, 1867, a notice appeared in the *Winchester Times,* announcing a special auction to be held on July 25. Special Commissioner John J. Williams would sell "to the highest bidder, that valuable property known as 'SELMA,' formerly the residence of Hon. James M. Mason, lying on the suburbs of Winchester, . . . comprising TEN ACRES, more or less." The announcement admitted that "the buildings are all destroyed" but labeled the land "very valuable for building or other purposes."[10] The property finally passed out of Mason's hands on October 10, 1867, making it easier for him to keep his pledge never to return to Winchester.[11]

When spring arrived, the Masons held a family council and decided to return to Niagara and await further developments in Washington. James rented a small house there and adapted to a simple routine of gardening and raising poultry. He gathered the eggs himself, "taking infinite pride and pleasure in his success when he brought in a basket of eggs or reported another brood of little chickens."[12] Mason long had dreamed of retiring to the quiet life of a farmer, and, "fortunately," he had "some remnant of my wife's property beyond the reach of the enemy," to provide his family "the means at present of living without want."[13] He went for walks or rides in the countryside, read newspapers and history books, and kept up his correspondence with friends back in England as well as in the United States.[14] The time passed slowly.

In May, the picture brightened, as news arrived that Jefferson Davis had been released from captivity. Mason wrote to congratulate him on being "at last at liberty" and invited him to join the other Confederates in Canada, where the southern leader could "be and remain in a country, freed from the tyranny and brutality now dominant, at our once happy homes." He expressed "little prospect at present" of returning to Virginia, but he longed to be with Davis once more, "to talk over what may be the future of our unhappy country."[15]

Davis already had left the United States for Montreal. He followed Mason back to Niagara, where they spent several days sharing the simple pleasures of conversation and freedom. From across the Niagara River, they looked upon Fort Niagara and the U.S. flag that flew proudly overhead. Davis remarked, "Look there, Mason, there is the gridiron we have been fried on."[16] After the visit ended, the Virginian repeatedly urged his friend to come back for a calm, cool, quiet summer of fishing and sunshine.[17] But Davis did not return.

The term of Mason's exile remained open-ended. In August he wrote, "Our plans for the future still unsettled—though we have pretty well determined, when we camp for the winter, to make it a tenantcy of two years at least." He hoped "that in that time, which covers the next election of President, the Yankees will realize the general smash up, which is impending, and when honest men, and gentle-men, may get back to their own."[18] Back in England, Judah Benjamin understood Mason's predicament, knowing that "no one could expect you to ask for '*pardon*.'" Nonetheless, he believed that, with Davis freed, "if the Southern States are restored to their rights of representation, you will find it consistent with self-respect to return to Virginia."[19]

As the calendar changed to 1868, however, Mason and his family remained in Niagara. Their accommodations had improved; they had moved into a larger house located twelve miles north of the falls. James labeled it "the most attractive Summer residence I have known, after the Mountains of Virginia."[20] He again asked Jefferson Davis to join them for the summer, trying to tempt his friend with the house's "ample grounds," including "a room always convenient at your command—and . . . quite a large and attractive Confederate circle."[21]

But that circle had begun to dwindle in size, as, one by one, the Confederate exiles returned home. On July 4, 1868, President Johnson proclaimed a general amnesty for all Confederates except those indicted for treason or some other felony. That allowed virtually all the exiles to return home without fear of punishment.[22] Increasingly spending his time alone, Mason yearned more and more for visits from old friends. To W. W. Corcoran he wrote, "You will understand what a treat it is to me, though seldom enjoyed, to have Southern people to talk to."[23]

Mason paid closer and closer attention to news from the United States but still found little to his liking. In March, he exclaimed that "the distressed and unhappy South" had only "one hope—that the Government at Washington will pass from its present anarchy to dissolution—which I think, and hope, impends, and which may God speed."[24] In June, he expressed the lone southern hope as being "that bondage will become too vile at the North, for even the vile to bear, and an internecine war there may follow—then we may come to our own."[25] Nearing the age of seventy with but a few friends in close proximity, Mason's bitterness had returned with a vengeance.

The novelty of being in Canada waned when fewer Confederate exiles stopped to see him. By October 1868, only the Breckinridge family remained, and even they were planning to return home shortly. He wrote that, when that happened, "I shall be alone indeed."[26] But his daughter Virginia remembered that her father continued to remark that he could not "endure life in Virginia under existing circumstances." He likened it to "death by slow degrees of torture; I should feel as though I was bound hand and foot and forced to be a silent witness while the graves of my parents were desecrated by savages."[27] He followed the 1868 presidential campaign but did not believe that the results would affect "his movements." In a letter to Corcoran, he asserted, "I can never return to dear old Virginia and be there under any dominion but her own." Instead, he thought about returning to England, believing it "better to drag out what remains to me of life, an alien in a foreign land than voluntarily to subject myself to such degradation."[28]

But the winter of 1869 saw some softening in Mason's position. Perhaps his seventieth birthday warned him that his days were growing short. As early as May 1868, he had taken great pains to draw up a last will and testament,[29] but he kept any concerns about his health concealed from his family until after the new year began. Then, suddenly, he asserted repeatedly, "I can not be much longer with you, and I am not willing to leave you so far from home and in a foreign land. I feel that I ought to take you back to your own people."[30] The time had arrived for the return to Virginia.

He crossed the border on May 3, 1869, and wound his way slowly toward the place to which he had pledged never to return. Even with Selma destroyed and his land sold, memories of happier days in Winchester tugged at his heart. Although the town had been ravaged by the war, Mason was determined to start his house hunting there. He planned to go from there "to other parts of Virginia to visit my brothers and sisters—and on a tour of reconnaissance to see if the waters have subsided, and whether I can find a dry spot, where I may live once again amongst my own people."[31] First he stopped in Pennsylvania to visit his sister-in-law Anne Chew, and then he spent a few days with friends and relatives in Baltimore. He enjoyed those visits immensely but felt differently when he at last reached Winchester.

People he remembered had gone. Places he remembered had vanished. The changes he saw saddened and literally sickened him.[32] Mason claimed that he could not find a "house to suit us at Winchester," but returning there pained him so much that he probably did not want to find one. Leaving the valley, he proceeded eastward "through the Piedmont country, and afterwards a reconnaissance in Fairfax, the quarter whence I sprung."[33] There, in the vicinity where he spent his youth, Mason found Clarens.

At that time, Clarens was located three miles west of Alexandria, in a neighborhood named "Seminary Hill" after the Episcopal Theological Seminary found only a short walk away.[34] The estate covered some twenty-six acres[35] and previously had been a boys' school. A variety of fruit trees surrounded the house, a section of which dated back to 1783. The gardens would provide Mason with ample opportunities to practice the simple rural life he had come to enjoy in Canada. Additionally, the property lay next to the home of his brother-in-law, Gen. Samuel Cooper, organizer of the Confederate War Department, who had served in Richmond as the South's highest-ranking military officer. The chance to pass the hours in quiet conversation with an old friend made Clarens Mason's choice as the "dry spot" he needed to return to his people.[36]

When Mason arrived back in Niagara after his grueling trip, his appearance shocked his family. Being with him on a daily basis, they had not noticed the onset of any infirmities due to old age. But after not seeing him for several weeks, he appeared as an old man after his long, emotionally taxing journey. While Mason expressed obvious happiness at finding a perfect "resting-place," his daughter Virginia wrote that her father's "step was slow and heavy, its elasticity was all gone."[37] Even if his health had deteriorated, though, that did not prevent him from spending the summer of 1869 wrapping up his affairs in Canada and packing the family to go home.

On September 24, the Masons moved into Clarens.[38] James wrote to his old friend, Robert M. T. Hunter, who at the time was in Great Britain, to announce that, "after a long and wearying exile of more than eight years, I have at last got back to the Old Dominion . . . and have turned farmer and gardener." In his leisure time, he reflected on the past even more than before and wanted Hunter to join him in an effort to preserve Confederate history. He exclaimed, "I think when we put our heads together, looking back at the past, and viewing the material before us we might project something, not without its value to those who are to come after us." He wanted to hear Hunter's "history of the *latter* days and perhaps I would impart something of my experience, that might interest you." Mason yearned for his old Senate colleague, or anybody else, to visit him, and wrote that he would "be at home all the time—having no place to go, and no dis-position to go any place if I had."[39]

Hunter could not visit Mason just then, but in responding to earlier entreaties, he lamented, "I wish I could see you, for of all the persons in the world I had rather talk to you just now." Despondent over the Confederacy's defeat, Hunter expressed concerns for the future of the South that made Mason's outlook appear downright cheerful. But he agreed with his friend about the desirability of the two of them comparing views and stories. He wanted to hear from Mason about "our Confederate experiences abroad, in return for which I might possibly give you some of them at home of which perhaps you have something still to learn."[40]

Despite being somewhat dependent for entertainment upon corre-spondence and visits from those afar, Mason enjoyed his first months back in Virginia. He spent countless hours with General Cooper, usu-ally engaged in domestic activities related to their gardens and orchards, leading the life of a retired country farmer. Mason's daughter particularly remembered a November afternoon when the two sat side by side shucking corn, until her father's hands blistered.[41] Those simple pleasures brought him much enjoyment. But, according to the former chairmen of the Senate Foreign Relations Committee, Clarens had one drawback. He complained that "the dome of the Capital is in prominent view from the front postace."[42] Therefore, whenever he sat in quiet reflection on his porch, he never looked toward Washington, but instead always faced his chair toward Richmond.[43]

As the days and weeks passed, ever so gradually Mason's health deteriorated. He attended to his chores as best he could, but by the spring of 1870, it had become clear that his body was failing him. He continued to request that friends come to visit him,[44] but when others asked him to do the traveling, he declined. Gen. Robert E. Lee, himself in poor health, asked Mason to come see him at Lexington, Virginia, in March;[45] and in June, Jefferson Davis wanted his old friend to join him on a trip to Europe. Davis planned to spend two months abroad and asserted to Mason, "Your friends would be rejoiced to see you and I would endeavor to be as little disagreeable on the way as is possible for me."[46]

But Mason could not go.[47] He replied to Davis's invitation, "Another visit to Europe, even to accompany you, is forbidden me." He described his maladies as a "general derangement of the digestive organs, liver, stomach, etc., perhaps the wearing out of the machine." He found particularly troublesome the fact that his vision had "become so much impaired[,] probably in sympathy with deranged viscera," that he could "no longer read even with glasses." No longer able to read or write, he passed "most of the time out of doors, supervising and interested in whatever is doing there."[48]

His mind, however, retained its usual sharpness. Davis had written him of the South's "deep undercurrent of patriotism" and "manifest detestation of the Yankees, their tricks and their manners."[49] Mason responded that southerners could "only wait events, with what ever patience we may, preserve the traditions of our Fathers and preserve our faith, not without hope." He added that, "if there be anything in the experience of human affairs, in the management of human affairs, there are events yet in store for us, when to transpire, I will not undertake to foretell, which will restore us to our inheritance of self government with independence." Mason also predicted that "the Yankee government must fall to pieces of its own rottenness—the North and West sluff off, and the result a disintegration of the States and afterwards, new forms of connection." The

Virginian remained unreconstructed. To Davis he commented upon living so close to Washington, claiming to "never go there of course, nor have I seen, so far as I know, any man from north of Mason and Dixon, since I returned to Virginia—except once the rascally Yankee tax-gatherer."[50]

He kept up his correspondence by dictating letters to Eliza. Striving to stay as active as possible, Mason refused to sit idly by and wait for his condition to worsen. He tried various medicinal suggestions. In July, one of his daughters took him "to try the waters of the White Sulphur Springs," where he hoped to play backgammon with his friend Corcoran.[51] In the fall, he made a number of trips to see a doctor in Baltimore, but the visit did nothing to improve his vision. His daughter Virginia wrote to Corcoran, "Father's blindness, I regret to say increases rather than improves."[52]

While he felt better otherwise, Mason received little encouragement from the visits. In a letter of his own to Corcoran, he stressed, "I never had much faith in the Doctors. My doubt is they can't help me, but it is not professional to say so." He lamented that "two old codgers have little left to interest us (certainly as to one of us) but to inquire about each other."[53] In January 1871, he wrote to Hunter, "I have been pretty much confined at home, all this dreary winter. My health very indifferent, and my sight so much impaired, that I cannot write or read a line with the aid of any glasses."[54] From Europe, Benjamin sent his "best wishes for your speedy restoration of health,"[55] while another friend hoped "that with the return of Spring and more good weather you will get better."[56] But Mason himself exhibited no such optimism and wrote to Hunter that, even though "it is impossible for me to get to you . . . we ought to meet again, before the scene closes on us."[57]

With the aid of Eliza and his daughters, Mason kept up with his mail. His interest in history and current affairs refused to wane even as his strength did. He exchanged information on topics that ranged from Confederate affairs to the Franco-Prussian War.[58] Hunter still focused on the idea of discussing matters personally, for the sake of Confederate history.[59] Mason's old colleague used words reminiscent of their days in the U.S. Senate, when "Mason says this" and "Mason says that" had riddled letters to his wife. Hunter wrote that there were "many things" he wanted "to say which cannot be written and our political lives have been so mingled in the past that I wish to have your retrospect and compare it with my own." Confused and fighting an overwhelming cynicism in defeat, he wanted Mason's "views too in regard this new world in which we are living. I confess it puzzles me. You can explain to me much that is dark, in the course of Foreign Nations towards us."[60]

But by the time Mason received that letter, his general condition had worsened. Family members gathered, noticing that his "increased infirmities . . . made him more dependent than ever before." He had become "so feeble," with his "sight so much impaired," that he could "no longer give or receive any pleasure by visiting his friends." Seeming to become frailer each day, the old Virginian passed the hours sitting or lying "languid . . . sadly depressed by his blindness."[61] Even so, he had the calm assurance of knowing that he had done all he could to arrange his affairs and prepare his family for a life without him.[62]

On April 14, Mason asked to see Bishop Johns[63] and wanted to go to church so that he could "confess Christ before men" and "give my testimony for the benefit of those who come after me."[64] But, being bedridden by then, he could not fulfill that wish. On Sunday night, April 23, "he had a slight attack of apoplexy which left him speechless."[65] His family drew comfort from the fact that, though his voice was muted, "he would answer by pressure of the hand to any question, and always answered that he was comfortable and free from pain."[66]

At ten o'clock on the evening of April 28, 1871, at the age of seventy-two, James Murray Mason died. His granddaughter Lucy wrote that he died "so peacefully that none of us knew he had ceased to breathe till some time after he had passed away."[67] His daughter Ida commented that he had remained "at times perfectly conscious to his very last hour" and that he had "died as he lived, calm and serene." Through her eyes, she could not "imagine any thing more grand and majestic, than his appearance in death—so noble, it seemed as tho' his peculiar dignity and strength left its impress on the destroyer—death could not rob him of it."[68]

The family took his passing well, having "seen him so sad and worn for so long a time that they could not repine at his going to rest."[69] On the afternoon of April 30, his funeral took place at Christ Church in Alexandria. Mourners filled not only the pews, but also the aisles. After singing "Nearer, My God, to Thee," the pallbearers, who included General Cooper, Mason's son George, and two members of the Lee family, took the body to the cemetery.[70] Ida recalled that her father had often said that, in buying Clarens, "he was coming home, to place his remains by the side of his Father and Mother." Therefore they "laid him to rest in the Clermont lot."[71] Eliza died less than three years later, and the two lay beneath an obelisk inscribed "To the Memory of James

M. Mason and Eliza M. Chew." The stone says nothing about his career but reads simply: "James Murray Mason, of Selma, near Winchester, Va. Born November 3, 1798, Died at Clarens, Fairfax Co., Va.,
April 28, 1871."[72]

For the *Richmond Enquirer,* former Virginia Gov. Henry A. Wise
wrote "A Tribute to This Exalted Patriot," James Murray Mason.
Wise wanted all Virginians to mourn the state's loss, and he traced
Mason's life and career from Analostan Island to Philadelphia, from
William and Mary to Winchester, from Richmond to Washington,
and across the ocean to London. He labeled Mason "an honest man,
a highly cultivated gentleman, a well trained and practised lawyer, a
sound statesman, and a pure patriot." In the end, however, "the disasters to the Confederacy and the South, the wounds to his pride,
the aching agony of seeing all his hopes of liberty and self-government and the State Rights blasted, and the desecration of sacred things,
and the devastation and demoralization he witnessed on coming home,
were too much tension on the nerves of an aged man of delicate
sensibilities and proud sense of honor."[73] While doctors may dismiss
such factors as unlikely to cause death, in Mason's case, Wise accurately described what led his friend's system to fail. Having nothing
left to give and having seen all that he had worked for and believed in
destroyed by the Confederacy's defeat, Mason died of a broken heart.

Had the Confederacy won its independence, much would have
been different, including Mason's role in history. His accomplishments on behalf of the South in the Senate and in Europe would
have left more than a transient shadow. Unfortunately for the conservative Virginian, however, both he and the Richmond government
belonged to a different era. However determined their futile efforts
were, they sought to preserve their version of the status quo in an
ever-changing world.

Belief in the incontrovertible sovereignty of his beloved state of
Virginia formed the core of Mason's political convictions, and Mason fought throughout his career to live up to the motto *Pro
Republica Semper* and maintain the republic of his grandfather. But
the United States had moved toward becoming a democracy. James
fought to maintain a strict interpretation of the U.S. Constitution.
But that cherished document needed to be interpreted loosely to
adapt to the requirements of the growing nation. He fought throughout his entire career to maintain chattel slavery, believing it to be the
crucial element that held southern society together by uplifting all
parties involved. But such a vision bore little relationship to the evil
that southern slavery truly embodied. In passionately devoting his

life to fighting the inexorable forces of consolidated government, democracy, and freedom for all races, Mason became an anachronism. His failure to prevent the powerful political and social shifts of the mid-nineteenth century rendered him little more than a pathetic remnant of the patrician fantasy world known as the "Old South." By 1871, the end had arrived for both that illusion and its defender from Virginia, James Murray Mason.

♦♦♦ Notes ♦♦♦

Abbreviations

ALUV	Manuscripts, Alderman Library, University of Virginia, Charlottesville, Virginia
GHL	Gunston Hall Library, Lorton, Virginia
HLWV	Handley Library, Winchester, Virginia
JMM	James Murray Mason
LC	Manuscripts Division, Library of Congress, Washington, D.C.
NA	National Archives, Washington, D.C.
ORUCN	*Official Records of the Union and Confederate Navies in the War of the Rebellion*, 31 vols. (Washington, D.C.: U.S. Government Printing Office, 1894–1927)
VHS	Manuscripts, Virginia Historical Society, Richmond, Virginia
VMPL	Virginia Mason, *The Public Life and Diplomatic Correspondence of James M. Mason, with Some Personal History by Virginia Mason (His Daughter)* (New York: Neale Publishing Company, 1906)
VSL	Archives and Records Division Virginia State Library and Archives, Richmond, Virginia
WROR	*The War of the Rebellion: A Compilation of the Official Records of the Union and Confederate Armies*, 128 vols. (Washington, D.C.: U.S. Government Printing Office, 1880–1901)

Introduction

1.   Mary Boykin Chesnut, *A Diary from Dixie, as Written by Mary Boykin Chesnut, . . .*, ed. Isabella D. Martin and Myrta Lockett Avary (New York: Appleton, 1905), 92 and 124.

2.   One writer referred to James Murray Mason (JMM) as "a hero of the advanced school of Southern rights, and at the same time . . . in Northern circles almost the most odious figure in American public life." Burton J. Hendrick, *Statesmen of the Lost Cause: Jefferson Davis and His Cabinet* (New York: Literary Guild of America, 1939), 237.

3.   For physical descriptions of JMM, see Hendrick, *Statesmen of the Lost Cause*, 242; and Norman B. Ferris, *The 'Trent' Affair: A Diplomatic Crisis* (Knoxville: Univ. of Tennessee Press, 1977), 3.

4.   During the Civil War, in addition to Mrs. Chesnut, Charles Francis Adams, Jr., son of the U.S. minister to Great Britain, and Benjamin Moran, assistant secretary of the U.S. legation in London, noted sarcastically what Mason wore and what he chewed. See Chesnut, *Diary from Dixie*, 123–24; Charles Francis Adams, Jr., *1835–1915: An Autobiography* (Boston, Mass.: Houghton Mifflin, 1916), 47; and Benjamin Moran, *The Journal of Benjamin Moran, 1857–1865*, ed. Sarah A. Wallace and Frances E. Gillespie (Chicago: Univ. of Chicago Press, 1949), vol. 2:1040–41.

5.   Hendrick, *Statesmen of the Lost Cause*, 235–36 and 240–41.

6.   William R. Taylor, *Cavalier and Yankee: The Old South and American National Character* (New York: George Braziller, 1961). The best of the more recent studies of southern character are: Bertram Wyatt-Brown, *Southern Honor: Ethics and Behavior in the Old South* (Oxford, England: Oxford Univ. Press, 1982); and Bertram Wyatt-Brown, *Yankee Saints and Southern Sinners* (Baton Rouge: Louisiana State Univ. Press, 1985).

7.   Hendrick, *Statesmen of the Lost Cause*, 235–36.

8.   Henry A. Wise, "James Murray Mason," *Southern Historical Society Papers* 25 (1897): 189.

9.   JMM's next-door neighbor, Cornelia McDonald, wrote in her diary, "The soldiers, who I suppose having heard of the Trent affair, and the Commissioners Mason and Slidell, always connect the two. As that was Mr. Mason's house, they fancy this is Mr. Slidell's." See Cornelia McDonald, *A Diary with Reminiscences of the War and Refugee Life in the Shenandoah Valley, 1860–1865*, annotated and supplemented by Hunter McDonald (Nashville, Tenn.: Cullom and Ghertner Co., 1934), 73.

10.   For example, Virginians had much greater concern for the fugitive slave issue due to their proximity to the free states of the North. The cotton states of the Deep South had less to fear from northern personal liberty laws.

11.   Robert W. Young, "Jefferson Davis and Confederate Foreign Policy" (M.A. thesis, Univ. of Maryland, 1987), 109–17.

12.   Charles A. Beard and Mary R. Beard, *The Rise of American Civilization* (New York: Macmillan, 1927), vol. 2:52–121.

13.   The most recent of many books that have attacked and modified the Beardses' contentions is James M. McPherson, *Abraham Lincoln and the Second American Revolution* (Oxford, England: Oxford Univ. Press, 1991), 37–38.

14.   The conservative Confederate revolution is discussed in Emory Thomas, *The Confederacy as a Revolutionary Experience* (Englewood Cliffs, N.J.: Prentice-Hall, 1971; rpt. Columbia: Univ. of South Carolina Press, 1991).

15.   On the political dimension of 18th-century Virginia, see Charles S. Sydnor,

American Revolutionaries in the Making: Political Practices in Washington's Virginia (New York: Free Press, 1965).

16. JMM, remarks in the U.S. Senate, July 28, 1856, *Congressional Globe,* 34th Cong., 1st sess., pt. 3, p. 1805.

17. JMM to William Cabell Rives, July 9, 1852, in Rives Papers, container 83, LC.

18. JMM, comments in the U.S. Senate, May 28, 1856, *Congressional Globe,* 34th Cong., 1st sess., pt. 2, p. 1324.

19. JMM, remarks in the U.S. Senate, Mar. 3, 1849, *Congressional Globe,* 30th Cong., 2d sess., p. 672.

20. William A. Crozier, ed., *Virginia Heraldica, Being a Registry of Virginia Gentry Entitled to Coat Armor with Genealogical Notes of the Families* (New York: Virginia County Record Series, 1908; rpt. Baltimore, Md.: Genealogical Publishing Company, 1965), 42.

21. JMM, comments in the U.S. Senate, Aug. 23, 1852, *Congressional Globe,* 32d Cong., 1st sess., appendix, p. 1073.

22. JMM to J. H. Clifford, July 30, 1857, in Clifford Papers, Massachusetts Historical Society, Boston.

23. Edmund S. Morgan, *American Slavery, American Freedom: The Ordeal of Colonial Virginia* (New York: Norton, 1975).

24. *Richmond Enquirer,* May 10, 1871, rpt. in Henry A. Wise, "James Murray Mason," 188.

25. Clifford Dowdey, *The Land They Fought For: The Story of the South as the Confederacy, 1832–1865* (Garden City, N.Y.: Doubleday, 1955), 145–46.

Chapter 1. 1798–1832: Heritage, Family, and Education

1. Hendrick, *Statesmen of the Lost Cause,* 241.

2. JMM to Rives, Dec. 28, 1857, in Rives Papers, container 89, LC. The ancestry story is told in somewhat greater detail in VMPL, 1–9.

3. He was the first of five generations of George Masons. Their story is told in Pamela C. Copeland and Richard K. MacMaster, *The Five George Masons: Patriots and Planters of Virginia and Maryland* (Charlottesville: Published for the Board of Regents of Gunston Hall by the Univ. Press of Virginia, 1975).

4. JMM to Rives, Dec. 28, 1857, in Rives Papers, container 89, LC.

5. VMPL, 1–2.

6. JMM to Rives, Dec. 28, 1857, in Rives Papers, container 89, LC.

7. Robert Rutland, *George Mason: Reluctant Statesman* (Charlottesville: Univ. Press of Virginia, 1961), 3–4.

8. VMPL, 4.

9. Sydnor, *American Revolutionaries,* 14, 84, and 98.

10. This George Mason's accomplishments are summarized in Rutland, *George Mason,* ix–xvi.

11. The relevant Mason family trees are in Copeland and MacMaster, *Five George Masons,* tables 14 and 15, pp. 281–82.

12. Mollie Somerville, "General John Mason of Analostan Island," *Iron Worker* 26, no. 2 (Spring 1962): 3.

13. Letter of Mrs. Benjamin Stoddard, written in 1796, qtd. in Anne Hollingworth Wharton, *Social Life in the Early Republic, with Numerous Reproductions of Portraits, Miniatures and Residences* (Philadelphia: J. B. Lippincott, 1902), 87.

14. VMPL, 8–9.

15. Somerville, "General John Mason," 4.

16. Accounts differ on whether JMM was born in Georgetown or on Analostan Island, but, given the patterns of residence for this family, it is much more likely that Georgetown was his birthplace.

17. Hendrick, *Statesmen of the Lost Cause,* 237.

18. VMPL, 9–10.

19. Mollie Somerville, "The Confederacy's Special Commissioner to Great Britain," *Virginia Record* 90 (Sept. 1968): 25.

20. From JMM's obituary in the *Washington Herald,* Apr. 28, 1871.

21. See VMPL, 8; Somerville, "General John Mason," 9–10.

22. An example: according to his older brother, at the age of twelve, JMM spent much of his summer reading Virgil and the Greek Testament. John Mason, Jr., to Dr. James Murray (their maternal grandfather), June 7, 1811, qtd. in Somerville, "General John Mason," 9.

23. VMPL, 10.

24. Ibid., 11–13; Eliza Chew Mason's ancestry also is charted in W. G. Stanard, "Abstracts of Virginia Land Patents," *Virginia Magazine of History and Biography* 1 (1893): 87–88.

25. Cliveden was occupied by British troops for ten months during the American Revolution, and in 1777 it was damaged by cannons of the Continental Army in the Battle of Germantown. It stands today in what has become part of the city of Philadelphia.

26. VMPL, 13.

27. VMPL, 10.

28. Anne Chew to JMM, Mar. 6, 1819, in Custis-Lee-Mason Papers, Acc. #20975, Items 54–63, VSL.

29. VMPL, 13; Copeland and MacMaster, *Five George Masons,* 263.

30. Somerville, "Confederacy's Special Commissioner," 25.

31. VMPL, 13–14.

32. JMM to "My dear Father," May 20, 1821, in John Mason Papers, 5036, ALUV.

33. Ibid.

34. The amounts involved ran as high as $200. JMM to "My dear Father," Apr. 17, 1823, in John Mason Papers, 5036, ALUV.

35. JMM to John Mason, Jr., Sept. 1, 1823, in John Mason Papers, 5036, ALUV.

36. VMPL, 15.

37. Benjamin Chew to JMM , July 9, 1822, Custis-Lee-Mason Papers, Acc. #20975, Items 54–63, VSL.

38. Eliza Chew Mason to Anne Chew, 1822, qtd. in VMPL, 17.

39. Eliza Chew Mason to her mother, 1824, qtd. in VMPL, 17.

40. Eliza Chew Mason to Anne Chew, 1822, qtd. in VMPL, 16.

41. Eliza Chew Mason to her mother, 1824, qtd. in VMPL, 17.

42. "Practise together" refers to JMM's playing the flute while his wife played the piano. Eliza Chew Mason to Anne Chew, 1824, qtd. in VMPL, 19.

43. She was the first of eight children—four daughters and four sons. See Mason family tree in Copeland and MacMaster, *Five George Masons,* table 15, p. 282.

44. An example of this is seen in JMM to Joseph Nourse and Daniel Bussard, Mar. 11, 1823, in JMM Papers, Ch.D.6.7A, Manuscripts, Boston Public Library, Boston, Mass. The letter discusses business involving lands owned by the Bank of Columbia in Virginia and Maryland. JMM's father was president of that bank. Also see Eliza Chew Mason to Anne Chew, 1824, qtd. in VMPL, 19; Eliza writes that her father-in-law had

called JMM away to Fredericksburg to handle business that might take two weeks to complete.

45. Hendrick, *Statesmen of the Lost Cause*, 240.

46. *Richmond Enquirer*, Apr. 11, 1826. In a three-way race, JMM received over 40% of the vote.

47. *Richmond Enquirer*, July 18, 1826.

48. *Richmond Enquirer*, July 28, 1826.

49. Leonard D. White, *The Jeffersonians: A Study in Administrative History, 1801–1829* (New York: Free Press, 1951), 491–92.

50. Leonard I. Richards, *The Life and Times of Congressman John Quincy Adams* (Oxford, England: Oxford Univ. Press, 1986), 11–12.

51. Giles had a long career in politics, representing Virginia in the U.S. House of Representatives in 1790–98 and 1801–3 and in the U.S. Senate in 1803–15, as well as serving four terms in the Virginia House of Delegates.

52. For the entire text of these resolutions, see William Branch Giles, comp., *Political Miscellanies* (Richmond, Va., 1829), 155–63.

53. *Richmond Enquirer*, Feb. 3, 1827.

54. For examples specifically involving internal improvements, see *Richmond Enquirer*, Dec. 12, 19, 21, 1826, and Mar. 1, 1827.

55. See *Richmond Enquirer*, Apr. 10, 1827; for part of the speech, see VMPL, 22–26.

56. James L. Bugg, Jr., "The Political Career of James Murray Mason: The Legislative Phase" (Ph.D. diss., Univ. of Virginia, 1950), 89.

57. *Richmond Enquirer*, Apr. 10, 1827; and VMPL, 22–26.

58. Eliza Chew Mason to Anne Chew, July 1827, qtd. in Wharton, *Social Life in the Early Republic*, 225–27.

59. Hendrick, *Statesmen of the Lost Cause*, 242.

60. *Richmond Enquirer*, Jan. 19, 1828.

61. *Richmond Enquirer*, Mar. 7, 1828.

62. JMM received over 28% of the vote; see Bugg, "Political Career of James Murray Mason," 93.

63. Randolph to JMM, Apr. 12, 1828, in VMPL, 26.

64. *Richmond Enquirer*, Apr. 17, 1829.

65. *Richmond Enquirer*, Mar. 24, 1829.

66. *Richmond Enquirer*, May 12, 1829.

67. *Proceedings and Debates of the Virginia State Convention of 1829–30: To Which Are Subjoined, the New Constitution and the Votes of the People* (Richmond, Va.: Printed by S. Shepherd and Co. for Ritchie & Cook, 1830; rpt. New York: Da Capo Press, 1971), vol. 2:631–33.

68. Merrill D. Peterson, ed., *Democracy, Liberty, and Property: The State Constitutional Conventions of the 1820s* (New York: Bobbs-Merrill Co., 1966), 271–85.

69. *Proceedings and Debates of the Virginia State Convention of 1829–30* 2:635–36.

70. For the entire speech, see ibid., 2:686–89.

71. JMM, speech in the Virginia House of Delegates, Jan. 3, 1829, qtd. in VMPL, 27.

72. *Proceedings and Debates of the Virginia State Convention of 1829–30* 1:53.

73. JMM, speech in the Virginia House of Delegates, Jan. 15, 1829, qtd. in Bugg, "Political Career of James Murray Mason," 107–10.

74. *Proceedings and Debates of the Virginia State Convention of 1829–30* 2:688.

75. Ibid., 2:882.

76. The vote for approval grew higher as one moved from west to east across the state. The results, by county, are given in ibid., 2:903.

77. Built in 1813, Selma stood as one of Winchester's grand but simple houses until northern soldiers destroyed it during the Civil War. Today, on the same site, at 514 Amherst Street in Winchester, stands a Victorian home bearing the same name. See Garland R. Quarles, *Some Worthy Lives: Mini-Biographies of Winchester and Frederick County* (Winchester, Va.: Winchester–Frederick County Historical Society, 1988), 172–73.

78. VMPL, 29–30.

79. VMPL, 32–33.

80. Eliza Chew Mason to Anne Chew, Nov. 1829, qtd. in VMPL, 31.

81. VMPL, 33.

82. For the dates of the legislative sessions JMM participated in, as well as the membership roster of each, see Cynthia Miller Leonard, comp., *The General Assembly of Virginia, July 30, 1619, to Jan. 11, 1978: A Bicentennial Register of Members* (Richmond, Va.: Published for the General Assembly of Virginia by the Virginia State Library, 1978).

83. VMPL, 34 and 40. The latter page quotes a memorandum by JMM about his career in the 1830s.

84. See Eliza Chew Mason to Anne Chew, Apr. 1831, qtd. in VMPL, 34–35.

85. "Appointment of Presidential and Vice-Presidential Electors for Andrew Jackson," 1832, Virginia Governor, 1830–1834 (John Floyd) Papers, Mss4 V8194 F6693b, VHS.

86. A full treatment of the nullification crisis, including the role played by the slavery issue, is found in William W. Freehling, *Prelude to Civil War: The Nullification Controversy in South Carolina, 1816–1836* (New York: Harper and Row, 1965).

87. *Richmond Enquirer,* Jan. 8, 1833. In the report detailing the Winchester meeting, JMM was referred to as "Colonel" Mason, because he held that rank in the Virginia militia.

88. Ibid.

89. Ibid.; also in VMPL, 36.

90. For a study of Virginia's reaction to the insurrection, see Alison Goodyear Freehling, *Drift Toward Dissolution: The Virginia Slavery Debate of 1831–1832* (Baton Rouge: Louisiana State Univ. Press, 1982).

91. *Richmond Enquirer,* Apr. 10, 1827; VMPL 22–26.

Chapter 2. 1832–1847: Steps toward the Grand Arena

1. JMM to Eilbeck Mason, Nov. 3, 1833, in Mason Family Papers, GHL.

2. JMM to Samuel H. Smith, Sept. 12, 1835, in Norcross Papers, Massachusetts Historical Society, Boston.

3. JMM to Anne Chew, late 1830s, qtd. in VMPL, 36.

4. Hendrick, *Statesmen of the Lost Cause,* 239–40.

5. VMPL, 36.

6. VMPL, 36–37.

7. VMPL, 37–38.

8. There he was involved particularly in the hiring of teachers, as can be seen in JMM to John Townsend, Oct. 31, 1837, in Personal Papers, Acc. #22175, VSL.

9. JMM to Wyndham Robertson, Lt. Gov. of Virginia, July 1, 1833, in *Calendar of Virginia State Papers and Other Manuscripts Preserved in the Capitol at Richmond, Ar-*

ranged, Edited, and Printed under the Authority and Direction of H. W. Flournoy, Secretary of the Commonwealth and State Librarian (Richmond, Va., 1892), vol. 10:586.

10.   VMPL, 38.

11.   The two served together on the Committee of Finance. See Minutes of Meeting of Board of Visitors of the Univ. of Virginia, June 1846, Papers of R. M. T. Hunter, Hunter-Garnett Collection, Box 25, ALUV.

12.   See, e.g., JMM to Rives, June 22, 1844, and June 28, 1848, in Rives Papers, containers 70 and 78, LC; also JMM to Joseph C. Cabell, Nov. 23, 1846, in Autographs, Miscellaneous Americans, Pierpont Morgan Library, New York.

13.   Two letters dealing with chair vacancies are JMM to Rives, Sept. 26, 1839, and June 28, 1847, in Rives Papers, containers 60 and 77, LC.

14.   Rives was among the supporters. See Rives to George Tucker, Mar. 23, 1835, in Socrates Maupin Papers, 2769, ALUV.

15.   JMM to George Tucker, Mar. 29, 1835, in Maupin Papers, 2769, ALUV.

16.   Ibid.

17.   Richard P. McCormick, *The Second American Party System: Party Formation in the Jacksonian Era* (New York: W. W. Norton, 1966), 178–81.

18.   JMM to Col. Braxton Davenport, Feb. 18, 1837, in *Richmond Enquirer,* Mar. 11, 1837.

19.   Ibid.

20.   Ibid. Most biographical works on Andrew Jackson contain some discussion of the Bank of the United States, but the classic works specifically dealing with the issue remain Bray Hammond, *Banks and Politics in America from the Revolution to the Civil War* (Princeton, N.J.: Princeton Univ. Press, 1957), and Peter Temin, *The Jacksonian Economy* (New York: W. W. Norton, 1969).

21.   JMM to "Gentlemen," Feb. 25, 1837, *Richmond Enquirer,* Mar. 11, 1837.

22.   JMM to Rives, Mar. 3, 1837, in Rives Papers, container 55, LC.

23.   *Richmond Enquirer,* May 5, 1837.

24.   JMM to Rives, May 18, 1837, in Rives Papers, container 55, LC.

25.   William J. Cooper, Jr., *The South and the Politics of Slavery, 1828–1856* (Baton Rouge: Louisiana State Univ. Press, 1978), 86–88.

26.   An old but still useful book on the subject is Reginald Charles McGrane, *The Panic of 1837: Some Financial Problems of the Jacksonian Era* (Chicago: Univ. of Chicago Press, 1924).

27.   For a discussion of that period and the reasons behind the suspension, see Temin, *Jacksonian Economy,* 113–17.

28.   McGrane, *Panic of 1837,* 209–13.

29.   JMM, speech in the U.S. House of Representatives, Oct. 11, 1837, *Congressional Globe,* 25th Cong., 1st sess., appendix, p. 214.

30.   Ibid., 216.

31.   Ibid., 217–18.

32.   JMM to Rives, Nov. 7, 1837, in Rives Papers, container 56, LC.

33.   JMM believed that postal routes were the one internal improvement sanctioned by the Constitution, and he introduced resolutions on that subject in the House on Feb. 19, 1838, and Jan. 14, 1839. See *Congressional Globe,* 25th Cong., 2d sess., p. 190, and ibid., 3rd sess., p. 123.

34.   JMM introduced a joint resolution for land grants to the Winchester & Potomac Railroad on Mar. 19, 1838. See *Congressional Globe,* 25th Cong., 2d sess., p. 242.

35.   JMM, speech in the U.S. House of Representatives, May 12, 1838, *Congressional Globe,* 25th Cong., 2d sess., 599–600.

36.   The recovery resulted primarily from a restored flow of capital from Britain and an increase in government spending. See Temin, *Jacksonian Economy*, 148–52.

37.   JMM, remarks in the U.S. House of Representatives, May 12, 1838, *Congressional Globe*, 25th Cong., 2d sess., p. 601.

38.   Cooper, *South and Politics of Slavery*, 144–45.

39.   JMM to Rives, Oct. 2, 1838, in Rives Papers, container 58, LC.

40.   JMM to Anne Chew, Jan. 1, 1839, in VMPL, 44–47.

41.   JMM, speech in the U.S. House of Representatives, Jan. 30, 1839, *Congressional Globe*, 25th Cong., 3rd sess., p. 159.

42.   JMM, memorandum on his career, in VMPL, 41.

43.   *Winchester Virginian*, Mar. 13, Mar. 27, and Apr. 3, 1839.

44.   For a discussion of the disruptive changes involved in creating a two-party system in Virginia in the 1830s, see McCormick, *Second American Party*, 191–99.

45.   Providing leadership in Virginia to conservative critics of the administration, Rives drifted more and more toward the Whig camp, and he changed parties officially in 1840. Cooper, *South and Politics of Slavery*, 102.

46.   JMM to Anne Chew, May 24, 1838, in VMPL, 43–44.

47.   JMM to Anne Chew, Jan. 1, 1839, in VMPL, 44–47.

48.   JMM, memorandum on his career, in VMPL, 41.

49.   JMM to Rives, Mar. 29, 1840, in Rives Papers, container 60, LC.

50.   Bugg, "Political Career of James Murray Mason," 242–43.

51.   See the relevant Mason family tree in Copeland and MacMaster, *Five George Masons*, 282.

52.   Benjamin Chew to JMM, July 24, 1841, Custis-Lee-Mason Papers, Acc. #20975, Items 54–63, VSL.

53.   This letter does not state the year, but, based on its contents, probably dates from her 1841 visit. Eliza Chew Mason to JMM, Oct. 2, [1841], Custis-Lee-Mason Papers, Acc. #20975, Items 54–63, VSL.

54.   Virginia Mason discusses the winters of the late 1830s in VMPL, 42.

55.   JMM to Judge Tucker, Dec. 5, 1842, in John M. Mason Papers, Ch.D.6.7, Boston Public Library.

56.   VMPL, 48.

57.   Numerous letters discuss the Chew estate. JMM to Rives, June 22, 1844, in Rives Papers, container 70, LC. Also Daniel Agnew to JMM, May 1, 1845; William Chew to Eliza Chew Mason, Oct. 1, 1845; William Chew to JMM, Oct. 25, 1846; and William Chew to JMM, Oct. 31, 1846, all in Custis-Lee-Mason Papers, Acc. #20975, Items 54–63, VSL.

58.   JMM to "My dear Father," Dec. 24, 1845, in Miscellaneous Manuscripts, Manuscripts Department, New-York Historical Society, New York City.

59.   JMM, memorandum on his career, in VMPL, 50.

60.   JMM always referred to those living arrangements as his "mess," a place where, despite its distance from home, he still could have some semblance of a "family" life with other political leaders.

61.   JMM to Anne Chew, Jan. 1, 1839, in VMPL, 44–47.

62.   Ibid.

63.   JMM to Rives, July 23, 1842, in Rives Papers, container 66, LC.

64.   JMM to Rives, Aug. 11, 1842, in Rives Papers, container 66, LC.

65.   JMM to Rives, Nov. 26, 1842, in Rives Papers, container 66, LC.

66.   Ibid.

67.   VMPL, 48–49.

68. JMM to "My dear Father," Dec. 24, 1845, in Miscellaneous Manuscripts, Manuscripts Department, New-York Historical Society.

69. JMM to Rives, Feb. 1, 1847, in Rives Papers, container 76, LC.

70. VMPL, 48.

71. JMM to W. W. Corcoran, Dec. 12, 1846, in Corcoran Papers, vol. 6, LC.

72. JMM left Richmond, even though the case that had taken him there had not yet been decided. See JMM, memorandum on his career, in VMPL, 50–51.

73. *Winchester Virginian,* Jan. 21, 1847.

74. JMM received almost 70% of the vote. *Richmond Enquirer,* Jan. 22, 1847.

75. Hendrick, *Statesmen of the Lost Cause,* 241.

76. VMPL, 51.

77. *Congressional Globe,* 29th Cong., 2d sess., p. 245.

78. JMM to Rives, Feb. 1, 1847, in Rives Papers, container 76, LC.

79. JMM dealt particularly with his father's financial situation, as discussed in JMM to "My dear Father," May 2 and 20, and Sept. 9, 1847, in John Mason Papers, 5036, ALUV.

80. JMM, memorandum on his career, in VMPL, 50.

Chapter 3. 1847–1859: Defender of the Constitution

1. JMM, speech in the U.S. Senate, Feb. 13, 1847, *Congressional Globe,* 29th Cong., 2d sess., pp. 410–11.

2. JMM, open letter to "Freeholders of Frederick County," *Richmond Enquirer,* Apr. 10, 1827; excerpted in VMPL, 22–26.

3. *Richmond Enquirer,* Jan. 8, 1833.

4. See JMM, speech in the House of Representatives, May 12, 1838, *Congressional Globe,* 25th Cong., 2d sess., appendix, pp. 599–601.

5. The federal convention debates can be found in Max Farrand, ed., *The Records of the Federal Convention of 1787,* 4 vols. (rpt. New Haven, Conn.: Yale Univ. Press, 1966). Excerpts of George Mason's speeches in the Virginia convention against ratification are in John P. Kaminski and Richard Leffler, *Federalists and Anti-Federalists: The Debate Over the Ratification of the Constitution* (Madison, Wisc.: Madison House, 1989), 42–44, 92–95, and 100–102.

6. JMM, remarks in the U.S. Senate, Mar. 3, 1849, *Congressional Globe,* 30th Cong., 2d sess., pp. 672, 675–77, and 679–80. Excerpts are in VMPL, 68–70.

7. JMM, speech in the U.S. Senate, Jan. 4, 1859, *Congressional Globe,* 35th Cong., 2d sess., pt. 1, pp. 210–11.

8. JMM, speech in the U.S. Senate, May 28, 1856, *Congressional Globe,* 34th Cong., 1st sess., pt. 2, pp. 1320–24.

9. JMM, comments in the U.S. Senate, Mar. 3, 1851, *Congressional Globe,* 31st Cong., 2d sess., appendix, p. 358.

10. Ibid., 363.

11. JMM, comments in the U.S. Senate, Aug. 16, 1852, *Congressional Globe,* 32d Cong., 1st sess., appendix, p. 947.

12. JMM, remarks in the U.S. Senate, Aug. 18, 1852, *Congressional Globe,* 32d Cong., 1st sess., appendix, p. 986.

13. JMM, speech in the U.S. Senate, Aug. 19, 1852, *Congressional Globe,* 32d Cong., 1st sess., appendix, p. 1004.

14. JMM, comments in the U.S. Senate, Aug. 20, 1852, *Congressional Globe,* 32d Cong., 1st sess., appendix, p. 1009.

15. JMM, remarks in the U.S. Senate, Aug. 23, 1852, *Congressional Globe,* 32d Cong., 1st sess., appendix, p. 1150.

16. JMM, comments in the U.S. Senate, July 29, 1854, *Congressional Globe,* 33rd Cong., 1st sess., appendix, pp. 1170–71.

17. JMM, speech in the U.S. Senate, May 28, 1856, *Congressional Globe,* 34th Cong., 1st sess., pt. 2, pp. 1320–24.

18. Ibid., 1324.

19. The vote is recorded in July 7, 1856, *Congressional Globe,* 34th Cong., 1st sess., pt. 2, p. 1544.

20. JMM, comments in the U.S. Senate, Feb. 20, 1856, *Congressional Globe,* 34th Cong., 1st sess., pt. 1, p. 465.

21. JMM, remarks in the U.S. Senate, July 28, 1856, *Congressional Globe,* 34th Cong., 1st sess., pt. 3, pp. 1810–11.

22. JMM, comments in the U.S. Senate, July 29, 1856, *Congressional Globe,* 34th Cong., 1st sess., pt. 3, p. 1833.

23. *Richmond Enquirer,* Dec. 12, 1856. Excerpts rpt. in VMPL, 122.

24. *Richmond Enquirer,* Dec. 10, 1850, and Dec. 18, 1855.

25. JMM, remarks in the U.S. Senate, Feb. 24, 1853, *Congressional Globe,* 32d Cong., 2d sess., pp. 817–18.

26. JMM, speech in the U.S. Senate, Feb. 18, 1853, *Congressional Globe,* 32d Cong., 2d sess., pp. 676–79.

27. Ibid., 678.

28. JMM, speech in the U.S. Senate, Feb. 1, 1853, *Congressional Globe,* 32d Cong., 2d sess., appendix, pp. 134–38.

29. JMM, remarks in the U.S. Senate, Feb. 19, 1855, *Congressional Globe,* 33rd Cong., 2d sess., pp. 809–10.

30. JMM, comments in the U.S. Senate, Jan. 24, 1859, *Congressional Globe,* 35th Cong., 2d sess., pt. 1, pp. 380–81.

31. JMM, remarks in the U.S. Senate, Jan. 27, 1859, *Congressional Globe,* 35th Cong., 2d sess., pt. 1, p. 631.

32. JMM, speech in the U.S. Senate, Apr. 15, 1858, *Congressional Globe,* 35th Cong., 1st sess., pt. 2, pp. 1600–1603.

33. Ibid., 1602.

34. Ibid., 1603.

35. JMM, comments in the U.S. Senate, Mar. 2, 1853, *Congressional Globe,* 32d Cong., 2d sess., p. 1018. One year later, he still opposed it; see June 29, 1854, *Congressional Globe,* 33rd Cong., 1st sess., pt. 2, p. 1568.

36. The vote is recorded in July 5, 1854, *Congressional Globe,* 34th Cong., 1st sess., pt. 3, p. 1601.

37. JMM, speech in the U.S. Senate, Mar. 2, 1859, *Congressional Globe,* 35th Cong., 2d sess., pt. 2, pp. 1587–89.

38. Ibid., 1589.

39. Jefferson Davis, remarks in the U.S. Senate, Mar. 2, 1859, *Congressional Globe,* 35th Cong., 2d sess., pt. 2, 1588.

40. JMM, remarks in the U.S. Senate, Mar. 2, 1859, *Congressional Globe,* 35th Cong., 2d sess., pt. 2, pp. 1589.

41. His amendment lost, 25 to 16; see *Congressional Globe,* 35th Cong., 2d sess., pt. 2, p. 1590.

42. The vote is recorded in Mar. 3, 1859, *Congressional Globe,* 35th Cong., 2d sess., pt. 2, p. 1612.

43. JMM, comments in the U.S. Senate, Aug. 15, 1856, *Congressional Globe*, 34th Cong., 1st sess., pt. 3, p. 2148.

44. JMM, speech in the U.S. Senate, Mar. 1, 1855, *Congressional Globe*, 33rd Cong., 2d sess., pp. 1056–59.

45. The Senate passed a substitute measure, sponsored by Robert M. T. Hunter of Virginia, that called for 25¢ an acre being payable after 5 years, but the House refused to discuss such a bill. See Allan Nevins, *Ordeal of the Union* (New York: Charles Scribner's Sons, 1947), vol. 2:334–35.

46. JMM, remarks in the U.S. Senate, July 19, 1854, *Congressional Globe*, 33rd Cong., 1st sess., pt. 3, pp. 1817–18.

47. Ibid., 1814.

48. JMM's rhetoric of the second day is in July 20, 1854, *Congressional Globe*, 33rd Cong., 1st sess., appendix, pp. 1097–99, while the vote is recorded on p. 1103.

49. JMM, speech in the U.S. Senate, Feb. 1, 1859, *Congressional Globe*, 35th Cong., 2d sess., pt. 1, pp. 718–19.

50. JMM, remarks in the U.S. Senate, Mar. 7, 1854, *Congressional Globe*, 33rd Cong., 1st sess., pt. 1, p. 554.

51. JMM, comments in the U.S. Senate, July 19, 1854, *Congressional Globe*, 33rd Cong., 1st sess., pt. 3, pp. 1817–18.

52. Ibid., 1817.

53. For a thorough discussion of education in America before the Civil War, see Carl F. Kaestle, *Pillars of the Republic: Common Schools and American Society, 1780–1860* (New York: Hill and Wang, 1983).

54. JMM, speech in the U.S. Senate, Feb. 1, 1859, *Congressional Globe*, 35th Cong., 2d sess., pt. 1, pp. 718–19.

55. JMM, comments in the U.S. Senate, July 6, 1848, *Congressional Globe*, 30th Cong., 1st sess., appendix, pp. 883–84.

56. Ibid., 885.

57. The best monograph on those debates remains Holman Hamilton, *Prologue to Conflict: The Crisis and Compromise of 1850* (Lexington: Univ. of Kentucky Press, 1964).

58. Discounting cases of not voting, only 4 senators voted yes to all parts of the compromise: Augustus C. Dodge, Iowa Democrat; Daniel Sturgeon, Pennsylvania Democrat; Sam Houston, Texas Democrat; and John Wales, Delaware Whig. The congressional votes for each measure are given in Hamilton, *Prologue to Conflict*, 191–200.

59. For the text of Clay's resolutions as well as his initial defense of them, see Jan. 29, 1850, *Congressional Globe*, 31st Cong., 1st sess., pt. 1, pp. 244–47.

60. David M. Potter, *The Impending Crisis, 1848–1861*, ed. Don E. Fehrenbacher (New York: Harper and Row, 1976).

61. See *Congressional Globe*, 31st Cong., 1st sess., pt. 1, pp. 99 and 103, and appendix, p. 79. An excellent discussion of the Fugitive Slave Law of 1850 is found in Stanley W. Campbell, *The Slave Catchers: Enforcement of the Fugitive Slave Law, 1850–1860* (Chapel Hill: Univ. of North Carolina Press, 1968).

62. JMM, speech in the U.S. Senate, Jan. 28, 1850, *Congressional Globe*, 31st Cong., 1st sess., pt. 1, pp. 233–36.

63. The key points are summarized in Frank H. Hodder, "The Authorship of the Compromise of 1850," *Mississippi Valley Historical Review* 22, no. 3 (Fall 1936): 526–27.

64. JMM, comments in the U.S. Senate, Jan. 29, 1850, *Congressional Globe*, 31st Cong., 1st sess., pt. 1, p. 248.

65.   They included Lewis Cass of Michigan and Stephen Douglas of Illinois. JMM to Robert Hubard, Feb. 3, 1850, in Hubard Family Papers, ALUV.

66.   Ibid.

67.   JMM to Rives, Feb. 4, 1850, in Rives Papers, container 81, LC.

68.   JMM to Beverly Tucker, Mar. 1, 1850, qtd. in Henry T. Shanks, *The Secession Movement in Virginia, 1847–1861* (Richmond, Va.: Garrett and Massie Publishers, 1934), 32.

69.   The most detailed biography of Calhoun, including a discussion of his final days, remains Charles Maurice Wiltse, *John C. Calhoun,* 3 vols. (Indianapolis, Ind.: Bobbs–Merrill, 1944–51).

70.   Merrill D. Peterson, *The Great Triumvirate: Webster, Clay, and Calhoun* (Oxford, England: Oxford Univ. Press, 1987), 460.

71.   Accounts of JMM's reading include ibid., 460–61; Hamilton, *Prologue to Conflict,* 71–74; and VMPL, 72.

72.   Calhoun speech, as read in the U.S. Senate by JMM, Mar. 4, 1850, *Congressional Globe,* 31st Cong., 1st sess., pt. 1, pp. 451–55.

73.   JMM, memorandum, qtd. in VMPL, 72–73.

74.   JMM, resolution and remarks in the U.S. Senate, Apr. 3, 1850, *Congressional Globe,* 31st Cong., 1st sess., pt. 1, p. 631.

75.   R. M. T. Hunter to his wife, Apr. 20 and 28, 1850, in Papers of R. M. T. Hunter, Hunter-Garnett Collection, Box 25, ALUV.

76.   Proposed by Mississippi Sen. Henry S. Foote, the committee included JMM among its members. It gained Senate approval on Apr. 18. See Hamilton, *Prologue to Conflict,* 92–94.

77.   Clay, speech in the U.S. Senate, May 8, 1850, *Congressional Globe,* 31st Cong., 1st sess., pt. 1, pp. 944–48.

78.   JMM's votes are summarized in Hamilton, *Prologue to Conflict,* 192.

79.   For an account of the debates on JMM's bill, see Campbell, *Slave Catchers,* 3–23.

80.   JMM, speech in the U.S. Senate, Aug. 21, 1850, *Congressional Globe,* 31st Cong., 1st sess., appendix, pt. 2, pp. 1604–5.

81.   JMM, remarks in the U.S. Senate, Aug. 19, 21, 22, and 23, 1850, *Congressional Globe,* 31st Cong., 1st sess., appendix, pt. 2, pp. 1581–84, 1586, 1589–90, 1600, 1604–5, 1607, 1610–13, 1619, and 1624–25.

82.   JMM, speech in the U.S. Senate, Aug. 22, 1850, *Congressional Globe,* 31st Cong., 1st sess., appendix, pt. 2, pp. 1610–13.

83.   The measure passed the House on Sept. 12. See Hamilton, *Prologue to Conflict,* 141, 191–92, and 195–200.

84.   They voted 30 to 20 to approve it, while the bill passed in the House on Sept. 6 by only 11 votes. See Hamilton, *Prologue to Conflict,* 191–92 and 195–200.

85.   JMM, remarks in the U.S. Senate, June 7, 1850, *Congressional Globe,* 31st Cong., 1st sess., pt. 2, pp. 1164–65.

86.   The votes took place on July 25 and 30, 1850, and are reported in *Congressional Globe,* 31st Cong., 1st sess., appendix, pt. 2, p. 1435, and 31st Cong., 1st sess., pt. 2, pp. 1456–57.

87.   JMM, comments in the U.S. Senate, Aug. 9, 1850, *Congressional Globe,* 31st Cong., 1st sess., appendix, pt. 2, pp. 1570–71.

88.   JMM, speech in the U.S. Senate, Sept. 10, 1850, *Congressional Globe,* 31st Cong., 1st sess., appendix, pt. 2, pp. 1637–38.

89. It passed in the House the next day. See Hamilton, *Prologue to Conflict*, 141–42, 191–92, and 195–200.

90. JMM, comments in the U.S. Senate, Apr. 5, 1850, *Congressional Globe*, 31st Cong., 1st sess., pt. 1, pp. 650–51.

91. JMM, remarks in the U.S. Senate, Aug. 1, 1850, *Congressional Globe*, 31st Cong., 1st sess., appendix, pt. 2, p. 1489.

92. JMM, speech in the U.S. Senate, May 27, 1850, *Congressional Globe*, 31st Cong., 1st sess., appendix, pt. 1, pp. 649–55. Later he even offered the more southern line of 35°30′ as a more natural boundary. JMM, comments in the U.S. Senate, Aug. 1, 1850, *Congressional Globe*, 31st Cong., 1st sess., appendix, pt. 2, p. 1488.

93. JMM to David Hedrick and others, July 23, 1850, in VMPL, 76–77.

94. JMM, memorandum, Aug. 9, 1851, excerpted in VMPL, 84–85.

95. "Protest Against the Passage of the Bill Admitting California as a State," Aug. 2, 1850, in VMPL, 78–81.

96. "Statement on the Admission of California," Aug. 2, 1850, in *The Papers of Jefferson Davis*, ed. Haskell M. Monroe, Jr.; James T. McIntosh; Lynda Lasswell Crist, Mary Seaton Dix; and Kenneth H. Williams (8 vols. to date; Baton Rouge: Louisiana State Univ. Press, 1971–), vol. 4:124.

97. The House approved it on Sept. 7. See Hamilton, *Prologue to Conflict*, 191–92 and 195–200.

98. JMM, speech in the U.S. Senate, May 27, 1850, *Congressional Globe*, 31st Cong., 1st sess., appendix, pt. 1, pp. 649–55.

99. In contrast, the southern Democratic newspaper in Richmond supported the compromise as beneficial to the South. See *Richmond Enquirer*, Sept. 17, 1850.

100. R. H. Foote, Wm. Brent, and Wm. Payne to Paulus Powell, Sept. 23, 1850, in Paulus Powell Papers, Mss1 P8717a 1–58, VHS.

101. *Richmond Enquirer*, Nov. 12, 1850. Excerpts from the speech appear in Shanks, *Secession Movement*, 38.

102. R. M. T. Hunter to his wife, Dec. 10, 1850, in Papers of R. M. T. Hunter, Hunter-Garnett Collection, Box 25, ALUV.

103. JMM, memorandum, Aug. 9, 1851, excerpted in VMPL, 84–85.

104. JMM, speech in the U.S. Senate, Mar. 24, 1858, *Congressional Globe*, 35th Cong., 1st sess., pt. 2, pp. 1300–1302.

105. JMM, comments in the U.S. Senate, Mar. 25, 1858, *Congressional Globe*, 35th Cong., 1st sess., pt. 2, pp. 1326–27.

106. Ibid.

107. The upheavals in Kansas are best described in James A. Rawley, *Race and Politics: "Bleeding Kansas" and the Coming of the Civil War* (Philadelphia: J. B. Lippincott, 1969).

108. JMM, speech in the U.S. Senate, Feb. 1, 1858, *Congressional Globe*, 35th Cong., 1st sess., pt. 1, pp. 498–500.

109. JMM to editor of *The South*, July 22, 1857, in VMPL, 127–28.

110. JMM, remarks in the U.S. Senate, Apr. 7, 1858, *Congressional Globe*, 35th Cong., 1st sess., pt. 2, p. 1512.

111. JMM, speech in the U.S. Senate, Mar. 31, 1858, *Congressional Globe*, 35th Cong., 1st sess., pt. 2, pp. 1419–20.

112. JMM, comments in the U.S. Senate, Apr. 7, 1858, *Congressional Globe*, 35th Cong., 1st sess., pt. 2, p. 1512.

113. Ibid., 1420.

114. The authoritative study of the decision is Don E. Fehrenbacher, *The Dred Scott*

Case: Its Significance in American Law and Politics (Oxford, England: Oxford Univ. Press, 1978).

115.   From Chief Justice Taney's opinion, as qtd. in Kenneth M. Stampp, *America in 1857: A Nation on the Brink* (Oxford, England: Oxford Univ. Press, 1990), 93.

116.   Ibid., 95–96.

117.   JMM to George Bancroft, July 28, 1857, in Bancroft Papers, Massachusetts Historical Society, Boston.

118.   Ibid.

119.   Examples are JMM to Rives, Dec. 20 and 28, 1857, in Rives Papers, container 89, LC.

120.   For instance, he provided information regarding his grandfather, in JMM to Hugh B. Grigsby, Aug. 13, 1858, in Pamela C. Copeland, Mason Family Research File, Main Research File, GHL. JMM to George Bancroft, Feb. 17, 1858, in Bancroft Papers, Massachusetts Historical Society, deals with James Madison and religious freedom.

121.   VMPL, 4–7.

122.   George Mason, speech at the Constitutional Convention, Aug. 22, 1787, in Farrand, *Records of the Federal Convention of 1787* 2:370.

123.   For a discussion of George Mason's opposition to slavery in both Virginia and national politics, see Rutland, *George Mason,* 53–54, 57, and 86–88.

124.   JMM, speech in the U.S. Senate, Jan. 8, 1850, *Congressional Globe,* 31st Cong., 1st sess., pt. 1, pp. 121–22.

Chapter 4. 1847–1859: Senator Mason and Slavery

1.   JMM to Col. Braxton Davenport, Feb. 18, 1837, printed in *Richmond Enquirer,* Mar. 11, 1837.

2.   JMM to Anne Chew, Jan. 1, 1839, in VMPL, 44–47.

3.   JMM owned nine during the crisis of 1850 and seven in 1860, on the eve of the Civil War. See Frederick County Personal Property Books, 1827–1850, and U.S. Census, Slave Schedules, Frederick County, Sept. 3, 1860, both in Archives Room, HLWV.

4.   VMPL, 39–40.

5.   In that same letter, she wrote of their dining-room servant getting drunk. As punishment James sent him to his room and ordered him "not to dare to show himself until he had made atonement." The man apologized, and JMM forgave him. Eliza Chew Mason to her mother, ca. 1830, qtd. in ibid., 18.

6.   For a discussion of "Sambo" as well as other slave personality types, see John W. Blassingame, *The Slave Community: Plantation Life in the Antebellum South* (Oxford, England: Oxford Univ. Press, 1972).

7.   VMPL, 39.

8.   For a discussion of slavery's role in southern politics, see Cooper, *South and Politics of Slavery.*

9.   The undated memorandum referred to is three pages long. At the bottom is a penciled note saying that it was "taken from the dwelling of the Rebel Senator Mason." The file dates the manuscript "ca. 1829," with a question mark. The handwriting of the memorandum is definitely that of JMM, but, after examining the references made in the manuscripts, I believe that the pages were written around 30 years later, after the Harpers Ferry raid. JMM, undated memorandum, "Emancipation," ca. late 1859, in Mason Family Papers, GHL.

10.   JMM, speech in the U.S. Senate, Jan. 23, 1860, *Congressional Globe*, 36th Cong., 1st sess., pt. 1, p. 557.

11.   JMM, comments in the U.S. Senate, July 6, 1848, *Congressional Globe*, 30th Cong., 1st sess., appendix, p. 886.

12.   JMM, remarks in the U.S. Senate, Mar. 2, 1858, *Congressional Globe*, 35th Cong., 1st sess., pt. 1, p. 925.

13.   JMM, comments in the U.S. Senate, Mar. 15, 1858, *Congressional Globe*, 35th Cong., 1st sess., appendix, p. 85.

14.   JMM to J. H. Clifford, July 30, 1857, in Clifford Papers, Massachusetts Historical Society, Boston.

15.   JMM, speech in the U.S. Senate, July 6, 1848, *Congressional Globe*, 30th Cong., 1st sess., appendix, pp. 886–87.

16.   JMM, remarks in the U.S. Senate, Mar. 15, 1858, *Congressional Globe*, 35th Cong., 1st sess., appendix, pp. 79–81.

17.   JMM, speech in the U.S. Senate, May 5, 1858, *Congressional Globe*, 35th Cong., 1st sess., pt. 2, pp. 1967–68.

18.   Ibid., 1968.

19.   JMM, comments in the U.S. Senate, Mar. 15, 1858, *Congressional Globe*, 35th Cong., 1st sess., appendix, pp. 81–82.

20.   JMM, undated memorandum, "Emancipation," ca. late 1859, in Mason Family Papers, GHL.

21.   Ibid.

22.   JMM, remarks in the U.S. Senate, Jan. 10, 1849, *Congressional Globe*, 30th Cong., 2d sess., p. 209.

23.   JMM, comments in the U.S. Senate, Aug. 23, 1850, *Congressional Globe*, 31st Cong., 1st sess., appendix, pt. 2, p. 1619.

24.   JMM to Rives, Feb. 4, 1850, in Rives Papers, container 81, LC.

25.   JMM, remarks in the U.S. Senate, Aug. 1, 1850, *Congressional Globe*, 31st Cong., 1st sess., appendix, pt. 2, p. 1488.

26.   The Virginia resolutions of Jan. 20, 1849, are specifically referred to by JMM in speeches in the U.S. Senate: Feb. 28, 1849, *Congressional Globe*, 30th Cong., 2d sess., appendix, p. 309; and May 27, 1850, 31st Cong., 1st sess., appendix, pt. 1, pp. 649–55.

27.   JMM, comments in the U.S. Senate, Jan. 22, 1849, *Congressional Globe*, 30th Cong., 2d sess., p. 311.

28.   Ibid., 311–12.

29.   JMM, speech in the U.S. Senate, Jan. 8, 1850, *Congressional Globe*, 31st Cong., 1st sess., pt. 1, p. 121.

30.   JMM, comments in the U.S. Senate, Aug. 19, 1850, *Congressional Globe*, 31st Cong., 1st sess., appendix, pt. 2, p. 1583.

31.   JMM, remarks in the U.S. Senate, Jan. 28, 1850, *Congressional Globe*, 31st Cong., 1st sess., pt. 1, p. 234.

32.   JMM, speech in the U.S. Senate, Aug. 22, 1850, *Congressional Globe*, 31st Cong., 1st sess., appendix, pt. 2, pp. 1610–13.

33.   JMM, comments in the U.S. Senate, Sept. 14, 1850, *Congressional Globe*, 31st Cong., 1st sess., appendix, pt. 2, p. 1667.

34.   JMM, speech in the U.S. Senate, Jan. 28, 1850, *Congressional Globe*, 31st Cong., 1st sess., pt. 1, pp. 233–36.

35.   JMM, remarks in the U.S. Senate, Jan. 21, 1851, *Congressional Globe*, 31st Cong., 2d sess., appendix, p. 294.

36. Ibid., 294–95.

37. The cases and their results are summarized in Campbell, *Slave Catchers*, 199–207.

38. William W. Freehling, *The Road to Disunion: Secessionists at Bay, 1776–1854* (London: Oxford Univ. Press, 1990), 536–37.

39. JMM, memorandum, Aug. 9, 1851, excerpted in VMPL, 84–85.

40. Ibid., 85.

41. JMM, speech in the U.S. Senate, Dec. 17, 1851, *Congressional Globe*, 32d Cong., 1st sess., pt. 1, pp. 112–15.

42. Ibid., 115.

43. For Senator Sumner's role in debates of the 1850s, see David Herbert Donald, *Charles Sumner and the Coming of the Civil War* (New York: Alfred A. Knopf, 1960).

44. JMM, remarks in the U.S. Senate, July 28, 1852, *Congressional Globe*, 32d Cong., 1st sess., pt. 3, pp. 1950–51.

45. Roy Franklin Nichols, *The Democratic Machine, 1850–1854* (rpt. New York: AMS Press, 1967), 30–32.

46. JMM, comments in the U.S. Senate, Aug. 23, 1852, *Congressional Globe*, 32d Cong., 1st sess., appendix, p. 1073.

47. The most thorough treatment of the Kansas-Nebraska question is Gerald W. Wolff, *The Kansas-Nebraska Bill: Party, Section, and the Coming of the Civil War* (New York: Revisionist Press, 1977).

48. Michael F. Holt, *The Political Crisis of the 1850s* (New York: John Wiley & Sons, 1978), 144–46.

49. Roy Franklin Nichols, *Franklin Pierce: Young Hickory of the Granite Hills*, rev. ed. (Philadelphia: Univ. of Pennsylvania Press, 1958), 321–22; and Jefferson Davis, *The Rise and Fall of the Confederate Government* (New York: Belford Co., 1890), vol. 1:27–28.

50. William W. Freehling, *Road to Disunion*, 550–51 and 555–56.

51. Cooper, *South and Politics of Slavery*, 346–48.

52. See Potter, *Impending Crisis*, 161; and Nichols, *Franklin Pierce*, 322–23.

53. Qtd. in William E. Parrish, *David Rice Atchison of Missouri: Border Politician* (Columbia: Univ. of Missouri Press, 1961), 148.

54. See Ivor Debenham Spencer, *The Victor and the Spoils: A Life of William L. Marcy* (Providence, R.I.: Brown Univ. Press, 1959), 278–80; Nichols, *Franklin Pierce*, 323; and Potter, *Impending Crisis*, 161–62.

55. An excellent short discussion of those debates is found in Robert Royal Russel, "The Issues in the Congressional Struggle Over the Kansas-Nebraska Bill, 1854," *Journal of Southern History* 29, no. 2 (1963): 187–210.

56. JMM, comments in the U.S. Senate, Mar. 2, 1854, *Congressional Globe*, 33rd Cong., 1st sess., appendix, pp. 298–99.

57. Ibid., 299.

58. Some texts state the vote totals as 41 for and 17 against. Those figures are based on the totals given by historian Robert R. Russel, which include the absent senators who later declared how they would have voted. See Russel, "Issues in Kansas-Nebraska Bill," 208–9.

59. For an analysis of the Senate vote, see Gerald W. Wolff, "Party and Section: The Senate and the Kansas-Nebraska Bill," *Civil War History* 18, no. 4 (1972): 332–50.

60. Potter, *Impending Crisis*, 165–67.

61. JMM, comments in the U.S. Senate, Mar. 14, 1854, *Congressional Globe*, 33rd Cong., 1st sess., pt. 1, pp. 618–19.

62. Ibid., 618.

63. JMM, remarks in the U.S. Senate, May 25, 1854, *Congressional Globe*, 33rd Cong., 1st sess., appendix, pp. 785–86.

64. JMM, comments in the U.S. Senate, June 26, 1854, *Congressional Globe*, 33rd Cong., 1st sess., pt. 2, p. 1517.

65. For a thorough discussion, see Rawley, *Race and Politics.*

66. JMM, remarks in the U.S. Senate, Apr. 9, 1856, *Congressional Globe*, 34th Cong., 1st sess., pt. 2, p. 840.

67. JMM, comments in the U.S. Senate, Apr. 10, 1856, *Congressional Globe*, 34th Cong., 1st sess., pt. 2, p. 864.

68. For the entire speech, see Sumner, speech in the U.S. Senate, May 20, 1856, *Congressional Globe*. 34th Cong., 1st sess., appendix, pp. 529–44.

69. Ibid., 544.

70. JMM, speech in the U.S. Senate, May 20, 1856, *Congressional Globe*, 34th Cong., 1st sess., appendix, pp. 546–47.

71. Ibid., 546.

72. Ibid.

73. Ibid., 546–47.

74. Sumner, comments in the U.S. Senate, May 20, 1856, *Congressional Globe*, 34th Cong., 1st sess., appendix, p. 547.

75. The most recent treatment of the incident is William E. Gienapp, "The Crime Against Sumner: The Caning of Charles Sumner and the Rise of the Republican Party," *Civil War History* 25, no. 3 (1979): 218–45. Other discussions of Sumner's speech and the Brooks attack include: Potter, *Impending Crisis,* 209–11; Donald, *Charles Sumner,* 278–311; and Nevins, *Ordeal of the Union* 2:437–48.

76. Holt, *Political Crisis of the 1850s,* 194–95.

77. JMM, remarks in the U.S. Senate, June 10 and 11, 1856, *Congressional Globe*, 34th Cong., 1st sess., pt. 2, pp. 1382 and 1391–93.

78. JMM, comments in the U.S. Senate, Aug. 26, 1856, *Congressional Globe*, 34th Cong., 2d sess., pp. 30–32.

79. Ibid., 30.

80. JMM, remarks in the U.S. Senate, Dec. 2, 1856, *Congressional Globe*, 34th Cong., 3rd sess., pp. 12–13.

81. Stampp, *America in 1857,* 6–7.

82. JMM, comments in the U.S. Senate, Dec. 2, 1856, *Congressional Globe*, 34th Cong., 3rd sess., p. 13.

83. Buchanan to Congress, Dec. 8, 1857, in James D. Richardson, ed., *A Compilation of the Messages and Papers of the Presidents, 1789–1908* (New York: Bureau of National Literature and Art, 1896–1910), vol. 5:449–54.

84. JMM, remarks in the U.S. Senate, Dec. 8, 1857, *Congressional Globe*, 35th Cong., 1st sess., pt. 1, p. 7.

85. JMM to editor of *The South,* July 22, 1857, in VMPL, 127–28.

86. Douglas, speech in the U.S. Senate, Dec. 9, 1857, *Congressional Globe*, 35th Cong., 1st sess., pt. 1, pp. 14–18.

87. JMM, speech in the U.S. Senate, Dec. 9, 1857, *Congressional Globe*, 35th Cong., 1st sess., pt. 1, pp. 18–19.

88. Ibid., 19–20.

89.   JMM, comments in the U.S. Senate, Mar. 8, 1858, *Congressional Globe*, 35th Cong., 1st sess., pt. 1, pp. 988–89.

90.   JMM, remarks in the U.S. Senate, Mar. 25, 1858, *Congressional Globe*, 35th Cong., 1st sess., pt. 2, pp. 1321–22.

91.   JMM, speech in the U.S. Senate, Mar. 15, 1858, *Congressional Globe*, 35th Cong., 1st sess., appendix, pp. 75–82.

92.   JMM to J. H. Clifford, July 30, 1857, in Clifford Papers, Massachusetts Historical Society, Boston.

93.   For an analysis of the Lincoln-Douglas debates, see Harry V. Jaffa, *Crisis of the House Divided: An Interpretation of the Issues in the Lincoln-Douglas Debates* (Chicago: Univ. of Chicago Press, 1959).

94.   JMM, remarks in the U.S. Senate, Feb. 23, 1859, *Congressional Globe*, 35th Cong., 2d sess., pt. 2, pp. 1248–49.

95.   Ibid., 1249.

96.   Ibid.

97.   JMM, remarks in the U.S. Senate, Jan. 3, 1860, *Congressional Globe*, 36th Cong., 1st sess., pt. 1, pp. 301–2.

98.   For a discussion of the proslavery response to abolitionism, see Wyatt-Brown, *Yankee Saints*, 155–82.

Chapter 5. 1847–1859: Mason and United States Foreign Relations

1.   JMM, remarks in the U.S. Senate, Mar. 3, 1849, *Congressional Globe*, 30th Cong., 2d sess., 672.

2.   VMPL, 87.

3.   See Magne B. Olson, "The Evolution of a Senate Institution: The Committee on Foreign Relations to 1861" (Ph.D. diss., Univ. of Minnesota, 1971).

4.   Such "Makers of American Foreign Policy" are listed in Richard Dean Burns, ed., *Guide to American Foreign Relations since 1700* (Santa Barbara, Calif.: ABC-Clio, for the Society for Historians of American Foreign Relations, 1983), 1215–17.

5.   For examples, see JMM, speech in the U.S. Senate, Feb. 1, 1853, *Congressional Globe*, 32d Cong., 2d sess., appendix, pp. 134–38; and JMM to William L. Marcy, Nov. 1, 1853, in William L. Marcy Papers, vol. 44, LC.

6.   JMM, comments in the U.S. Senate, Apr. 6, 1852, *Congressional Globe*, 32d Cong., 1st sess., appendix, p. 407.

7.   JMM, remarks in the U.S. Senate, Dec. 16, 1858, *Congressional Globe*, 35th Cong., 2d sess., pt. 1, p. 105.

8.   JMM, comments in the U.S. Senate, Jan. 19, 1853, *Congressional Globe*, 32d Cong., 2d sess., appendix, pp. 100–101.

9.   JMM, speech in the U.S. Senate, Apr. 6, 1852, *Congressional Globe*, 32d Cong., 1st sess., appendix, pp. 401–7.

10.   An American in Britain wrote to JMM that, while few cared about the doctrine originally, as U.S. power grows, "it begins to wear a somewhat different aspect before Europe." R. R. to JMM, Apr. 3, 1853, in Personal Papers, Acc. #13776, VSL.

11.   JMM, speech in the U.S. Senate, Jan. 19, 1853, *Congressional Globe*, 32d Cong., 2d sess., appendix, pp. 100–101.

12.   JMM, comments in the U.S. Senate, Mar. 26, 1860, *Congressional Globe*, 36th Cong., 1st sess., pt. 2, p. 1349.

13. JMM wrote dozens of letters to the various secretaries of state relating to claims for compensation; they are in Miscellaneous Letters of the Department of State, 1789–1906, Microfilm Series, M-179, NA.

14. See JMM, speech in the U.S. Senate, Aug. 25, 1852, *Congressional Globe,* 32d Cong., 1st sess., pt. 3, p. 2341; and JMM to Daniel Webster, June 18 and 19, 1852, in Miscellaneous Letters of the Department of State, 1789–1906, Microfilm Series, M-179, Roll 131, NA.

15. JMM to William L. Marcy, Jan. 9, 1855, Miscellaneous Letters of the Department of State, 1789–1906, Microfilm Series, M-179, Roll 143, NA.

16. Examples of JMM's correspondence about War of 1812 claims are JMM to Daniel Webster, Feb. 25, 1852; and JMM to William L. Marcy, June 23, 1854; both in Miscellaneous Letters of the Department of State, 1789–1906, Microfilm Series, M-179, Rolls 129 and 141, NA.

17. The definitive study of the *Amistad* case is Howard Jones, *Mutiny on the 'Amistad': The Saga of a Slave Revolt and Its Impact on American Abolition, Law, and Diplomacy* (Oxford, England: Oxford Univ. Press, 1987).

18. JMM wanted the Senate to approve the compensation as recommended by President James K. Polk in 1847. See JMM, remarks in the U.S. Senate, Feb. 4, 1851, *Congressional Globe,* 31st Cong., 2d sess., p. 402.

19. JMM, resolution in the U.S. Senate, Feb. 1, 1851, *Congressional Globe,* 31st Cong., 2d sess., p. 385.

20. JMM, resolution in the U.S. Senate, Mar. 9, 1852, *Congressional Globe,* 32d Cong., 1st sess., pt. 1, p. 702.

21. JMM to William L. Marcy, Nov. 1, 1853, in Marcy Papers, vol. 44, LC.

22. JMM, remarks in the U.S. Senate, Feb. 26, 1853, *Congressional Globe,* 32d Cong., 2d sess., p. 877.

23. JMM, speech in the U.S. Senate, Feb. 16, 1858, *Congressional Globe,* 35th Cong., 1st sess., pt. 1, pp. 718–20.

24. JMM, remarks in the U.S. Senate, Feb. 11, 1858, *Congressional Globe,* 35th Cong., 1st sess., pt. 1, p. 664.

25. JMM, comments in the U.S. Senate, Feb. 28, 1857, *Congressional Globe,* 34th Cong., 3rd sess., pt. 1, pp. 1017–19.

26. JMM, speech in the U.S. Senate, Mar. 26, 1860, *Congressional Globe,* 36th Cong., 1st sess., pt. 2, pp. 1347–49.

27. JMM, remarks in the U.S. Senate, Mar. 2, 1855, *Congressional Globe,* 33rd Cong., 2d sess., pp. 1093–94; and JMM to William L. Marcy, Feb. 6, 1855, in Miscellaneous Letters of the Department of State, 1789–1906, Microfilm Series, M-179, Roll 144, NA.

28. JMM, speech in the U.S. Senate, Aug. 27, 1852, *Congressional Globe,* 32d Cong., 1st sess., pt. 3, pp. 2402–5.

29. JMM, comments in the U.S. Senate, Aug. 5, 1856, *Congressional Globe,* 34th Cong., 1st sess., pt. 3, p. 1930.

30. See Samuel Flagg Bemis, *John Quincy Adams and the Foundations of American Foreign Policy* (New York: Alfred A. Knopf, 1949), 196, 234–35, and 499–509.

31. See Ivor Debenham Spencer, *Victor and Spoils: Marcy,* 240–42.

32. JMM, remarks in the U.S. Senate, July 23, 1852, *Congressional Globe,* 32d Cong., 1st sess., pt. 3, p. 1890.

33. Ibid., 1893.

34. JMM, comments in the U.S. Senate, Aug. 12, 1852, *Congressional Globe,* 32d Cong., 1st sess., appendix, p. 911.

35.   Charles Levi Woodbury to JMM, Feb. 25, 1852, in VMPL, 92–93.

36.   Samuel Flagg Bemis, ed., *The American Secretaries of State and Their Diplomacy* (New York: Alfred A. Knopf, 1928), vol. 6:276; and Ivor Debenham Spencer, *Victor and Spoils: Marcy,* 241.

37.   Ivor Debenham Spencer, *Victor and Spoils: Marcy,* 300–308.

38.   See ibid.; and JMM to William L. Marcy, July 12, 1854, in Miscellaneous Letters of the Department of State, 1789–1906, Microfilm Series, M-179, Roll 141, NA.

39.   JMM, speech in the U.S. Senate, Feb. 24, 1855, *Congressional Globe,* 33rd Cong., 2d sess., pp. 916–18. JMM entertained strong doubts only about the provision to keep foreigners out of the service; almost two years later, he tried unsuccessfully to repeal that provision. See JMM, comments in the U.S. Senate, Jan. 19, 1857, *Congressional Globe,* 34th Cong., 3rd sess., pp. 365, 370, and 373.

40.   JMM to William L. Marcy, Feb. 13, 1855, in Miscellaneous Letters of the Department of State, 1789–1906, Microfilm Series, M-179, Roll 144, NA.

41.   JMM, remarks in the U.S. Senate, Feb. 24, 1855, *Congressional Globe,* 33rd Cong., 2d sess., pp. 916–18.

42.   JMM, speech in the U.S. Senate, Apr. 1, 1856, *Congressional Globe,* 34th Cong., 1st sess., pt. 1, pp. 786–87.

43.   JMM, comments in the U.S. Senate, July 28, 1856, *Congressional Globe,* 34th Cong., 1st sess., pt. 3, pp. 1797–98.

44.   The two best treatments of Mexican War diplomacy are David M. Pletcher, *The Diplomacy of Annexation: Texas, Oregon, and the Mexican War* (Columbia: Univ. of Missouri Press, 1973); and Norman A. Graebner, *Empire on the Pacific: A Study in American Continental Expansion* (New York: Ronald Press, 1955; rpt. Santa Barbara, Calif.: ABC-Clio, 1983).

45.   For a discussion of the war with greater emphasis on the military aspects, see Seymour V. Connor and Odie B. Faulk, *North America Divided: The Mexican War, 1846–1848* (New York: Oxford Univ. Press, 1971).

46.   Pletcher, *Diplomacy of Annexation,* 499–563, Graebner, *Empire on the Pacific,* 192–214.

47.   JMM, comments in the U.S. Senate, Apr. 12, 1848, *Congressional Globe,* 30th Cong., 1st sess., p. 623.

48.   JMM, remarks in the U.S. Senate, Mar. 15, 1848, *Congressional Globe,* 30th Cong., 1st sess., p. 467.

49.   JMM, speech in the U.S. Senate, Feb. 1, 1853, *Congressional Globe,* 32d Cong., 2d sess., appendix, pp. 134–38.

50.   JMM, comments in the U.S. Senate, Feb. 17, 1858, *Congressional Globe,* 35th Cong., 1st sess., pt. 1, pp. 735–37.

51.   Three excellent discussions of "manifest destiny" are Albert K. Weinberg, *Manifest Destiny: A Study of National Expansionism in American History* (Baltimore, Md.: Johns Hopkins Univ. Press, 1935); Frederick Merk, *Manifest Destiny and Mission in American History* (New York: Random House, 1963); and Reginald Horsman, *Race and Manifest Destiny: The Origins of American Racial Anglo-Saxonism* (Cambridge, Mass.: Harvard Univ. Press, 1981).

52.   For a monograph on southern expansionism, see Robert E. May, *The Southern Dream of a Caribbean Empire, 1854–1861* (Baton Rouge: Louisiana State Univ. Press, 1973).

53.   Nichols, *Franklin Pierce,* 266–67.

54.   Nevins, *Ordeal of the Union* 2:348–49.

55.   Pierce to the House of Representatives, Mar. 15, 1854, in Richardson, *Compilation of the Messages and Papers of the Presidents* 5:234–35.

56. JMM, comments in the U.S. Senate, Dec. 23, 1852, *Congressional Globe,* 32d Cong., 2d sess., p. 139.

57. Ibid., 139–40.

58. JMM did support recognizing William Walker's government in Nicaragua. JMM wanted *de facto* recognition of a simple change in government in a manner no different from that accorded the rise of Louis Napoleon in France. But when, after his ousting, Walker attempted to return to power in 1858, unlike most southern senators, JMM supported his arrest to preserve peace and enforce U.S. neutrality laws. See JMM, remarks in the U.S. Senate, May 15, 1856, *Congressional Globe,* 34th Cong., 1st sess., pt. 2, pp. 1227–28; and JMM, speech in the U.S. Senate, Jan. 7, 1858, *Congressional Globe,* 35th Cong., 1st sess., pt. 1, pp. 216–18.

59. JMM, remarks in the U.S. Senate, Jan. 23, 1854, *Congressional Globe,* 33rd Cong., 1st sess., pt. 1, p. 209.

60. Franklin Pierce, "Proclamation by the President of the U.S.," May 31, 1854, in Richardson, *Compilation of the Messages and Papers of the Presidents* 5:272–73.

61. William L. Marcy to Pierre Soulé, Mar. 15, 1854, in William R. Manning, ed., *The Diplomatic Correspondence of the United States: Inter-American Affairs, 1831–1860* (Washington, D.C.: Carnegie Endowment for International Peace, 1932–39), vol. 11:174–75.

62. JMM, resolution in the U.S. Senate, Aug. 1, 1854, *Congressional Globe,* 33rd Cong., 1st sess., pt. 3, p. 2040.

63. Franklin Pierce to the U.S. Senate, Aug. 1, 1854, *Congressional Globe,* 33rd Cong., 1st sess., pt. 3, p. 2040.

64. Marcy to Soulé, Apr. 3, 1854, in Manning, *Diplomatic Correspondence of the United States* 11:175–78.

65. Some historians have confused the minister to France and JMM; while both were Virginians, they were not related. William L. Marcy to John Y. Mason, Aug. 16, 1854, in Manning, *Diplomatic Correspondence of the United States* 6:482.

66. James Buchanan, JMM, and Pierre Soulé to William L. Marcy, Oct. 18, 1854, in John B. Moore, ed., *The Works of James Buchanan, Comprising His Speeches, State Papers, and Private Correspondence* (rpt. New York: Antiquarian Press, 1960), vol. 9:260–65.

67. Nevins, *Ordeal of the Union* 2:362.

68. Sidney Webster, "Mr. Marcy, the Cuban Question, and the Ostend Manifesto," *Political Science Quarterly* 8, no. 1 (1893): 23.

69. William L. Marcy to Pierre Soulé, Nov. 13, 1854, in Manning, *Diplomatic Correspondence of the United States* 11:196–201.

70. May, *Southern Dream of a Caribbean Empire,* 56–76.

71. William L. Marcy to John Y. Mason, July 23, 1854, in Marcy Papers, vol. 51, LC.

72. Slidell, speech in the U.S. Senate, Jan. 24, 1859, *Congressional Globe,* 35th Cong., 2d sess., appendix, pp. 90–94.

73. JMM, comments in the U.S. Senate, Jan. 24, 1859, *Congressional Globe,* 35th Cong., 2d sess., pt. 1, p. 538.

74. JMM, remarks in the U.S. Senate, Feb. 9, 1859, *Congressional Globe,* 35th Cong., 2d sess., pt. 1, pp. 904–5.

75. For all JMM's efforts, the claims never were paid, and all talk of them disappeared with secession and civil war. See Howard Jones, *Mutiny on the Amistad,* 216–18.

76. JMM, comments in the U.S. Senate, Jan. 24, 1859, *Congressional Globe,* 35th Cong., 2d sess., pt. 1, p. 538.

77.   May, *Southern Dream of a Caribbean Empire,* 175–86.

78.   JMM, speech in the U.S. Senate, July 19, 1852, *Congressional Globe,* 32d Cong., 1st sess., pp. 1833–34.

79.   JMM to Daniel Webster, July 31, 1852, in Miscellaneous Letters of the Department of State, 1789–1906, Microfilm Series, M-179, Roll 132, NA.

80.   JMM to Daniel Webster, Aug. 12, 1852, in Miscellaneous Letters of the Department of State, 1789–1906, Microfilm Series, M-179, Roll 132, NA.

81.   JMM to Webster, Aug. 28, 1852, in Miscellaneous Letters of the Department of State, 1789–1906, Microfilm Series, M-179, Roll 132, NA.

82.   The resolutions are printed in Aug. 31, 1852, *Congressional Globe,* 32d Cong., 1st sess., pt. 3, p. 2465.

83.   JMM, speech in the U.S. Senate, Feb. 1, 1853, *Congressional Globe,* 32d Cong., 2d sess., appendix, pp. 134–38.

84.   Bemis, *American Secretaries of State* 6:274–75.

85.   Ibid., 6:327–31, 335–39, and 347.

86.   JMM, remarks in the U.S. Senate, Apr. 21, 1858, *Congressional Globe,* 35th Cong., 1st sess., pt. 2, p. 1704.

87.   Ibid., 1704–5.

88.   The resolution is in ibid., 1704.

89.   JMM, comments in the U.S. Senate, Apr. 22, 1858, *Congressional Globe,* 35th Cong., 1st sess., pt. 2, pp. 1727–28.

90.   Ibid., 1728.

91.   JMM, remarks in the U.S. Senate, Apr. 26, 1858, *Congressional Globe,* 35th Cong., 1st sess., pt. 2, pp. 1784–85.

92.   Ibid., 1785.

93.   Ibid.

94.   JMM, comments in the U.S. Senate, May 5, 1858, *Congressional Globe,* 35th Cong., 1st sess., pt. 2, p. 1963.

95.   Bemis, *American Secretaries of State* 6:380.

96.   Nevins, *Ordeal of the Union* 1:550–52.

97.   May, *Southern Dream of a Caribbean Empire,* 87–88.

98.   JMM, comments in the U.S. Senate, Jan. 26, 1853, *Congressional Globe,* 32d Cong., 2d sess., appendix, p. 132.

99.   JMM, remarks in the U.S. Senate, Jan. 27, 1853, *Congressional Globe,* 32d Cong., 2d sess., p. 416.

100.   JMM, speech in the U.S. Senate, Mar. 14, 1853, *Congressional Globe,* 32d Cong., special sess., appendix, pp. 263–66.

101.   Bemis, *American Secretaries of State* 6:217–24.

102.   The definitive book on U.S. foreign policy during the Crimean War is Alan Dowty, *The Limits of American Isolation: The United States and the Crimean War* (New York: New York Univ. Press, 1971).

103.   JMM, remarks in the U.S. Senate, Feb. 20, 1855, *Congressional Globe,* 33rd Cong., 2d sess., pp. 832–34.

104.   American public opinion—particularly in the South, which exhibited noticeable pro-Russian tendencies—rose against such practices. See Horace Perry Jones, "Southern Opinion on the Crimean War," *Journal of Mississippi History* 29, no. 2 (1967): 95–117.

105.   JMM, comments in the U.S. Senate, Feb. 29, 1856, *Congressional Globe,* 34th Cong., 1st sess., pt. 1, p. 541.

106.   JMM, remarks in the U.S. Senate, Feb. 29, 1856, *Congressional Globe,* 34th Cong., 1st sess., pt. 1, pp. 493–94.

107. William L. Marcy to George M. Dallas, May 27, 1856, in Kenneth Bourne and D. Cameron Watt, eds., *British Documents on Foreign Affairs: Reports and Papers from the Foreign Office Confidential Print, Part I: From the Mid-19th Century to the First World War,* Series C, North America, 1837–1914 (Bethesda, Md.: University Publications of America, 1986), vol. 4:443–51. Upon receipt, Dallas, U.S. minister to Great Britain, presented the letter to Lord Clarendon. It detailed American reasons for insisting on the recalls.

108. Dowty, *Limits of American Isolation,* 208–24.

109. JMM, speech in the U.S. Senate, May 29, 1856, *Congressional Globe,* 34th Cong., 1st sess., pt. 2, pp. 1339–41.

110. JMM, comments in the U.S. Senate, Jan. 24 and Feb. 12, 1856, *Congressional Globe,* 34th Cong., 1st sess., pt. 1, pp. 285 and 394–95.

111. Joint resolution introduced by JMM in the U.S. Senate, June 24, 1856, *Congressional Globe,* 34th Cong., 1st sess., pt. 2, p. 1462.

112. JMM, remarks in the U.S. Senate, Feb. 16, 1858, *Congressional Globe,* 35th Cong., 1st sess., pt. 1, p. 718.

113. Bemis, *American Secretaries of State* 6:230–33.

114. Ivor Debenham Spencer, *Victor and Spoils: Marcy,* 378–80.

115. Bemis, *American Secretaries of State* 6:233–36.

116. JMM to George M. Dallas, Oct. 15, 1857, in Mason Family Papers, GHL.

117. See Harral E. Landry, "Slavery and the Slave Trade in Atlantic Diplomacy, 1850–1861," *Journal of Southern History* 27, no. 2 (1961): 184–207.

118. The resolutions are printed in May 28, 1858, *Congressional Globe,* 35th Cong., 1st sess., pt. 3, p. 2452.

119. JMM, remarks in the U.S. Senate, May 29, 1858, *Congressional Globe,* 35th Cong., 1st sess., pt. 3, pp. 2492–93.

120. JMM, speech in the U.S. Senate, June 7, 1858, *Congressional Globe,* 35th Cong., 1st sess., pt. 3, pp. 2743–44.

121. JMM to Robert C. Winthrop, June 8, 1858, in Winthrop Papers, Massachusetts Historical Society, Boston.

122. James Buchanan, proclamation, June 14, 1858, in *Congressional Globe,* 35th Cong., special sess., p. 3051.

123. The vote is in June 16, 1858, *Congressional Globe,* 35th Cong., special sess., p. 3061.

124. JMM, remarks in the U.S. Senate, June 14, 1858, *Congressional Globe,* 35th Cong., special sess., pp. 3051–52.

125. Landry, "Slavery and the Slave Trade," 201–3.

126. JMM to James Buchanan, Nov. 2, 1858, in VMPL, 48–49.

Chapter 6. 1847–1859: Home Life and Politics of a Virginia Senator

1. JMM to "My dear Father," May 2 and Sept. 9, 1847, in John Mason Papers, 5036, ALUV; and JMM to Rives, June 28, 1847, in Rives Papers, container 77, LC.

2. Charles Francis Adams, Jr., *1835–1915,* 47.

3. VMPL, 52.

4. JMM and R. M. T. Hunter became particularly close and shared a house in the capital throughout JMM's congressional career. See ibid., 41–42 and 52.

5. Parrish, *David Rice Atchison,* 115–16.

6. See Hunter to his wife, Dec. 12, 1857, and Jan. 6, 1858, Papers of R. M. T. Hunter, Hunter-Garnett Collection, Boxes 28 and 29, ALUV.

7. On his visits to Selma, Senator Butler commented, "I have lived for years in the same house with Mason . . . but I find I never fully appreciated the man until I saw him in his own house among his neighbors, his children, grandchildren, and servants." Qtd. in VMPL, 52.

8. William W. Freehling, *Road to Disunion*, 550; and Holt, *Political Crisis of the 1850s*, 142.

9. JMM attended his last meeting on Feb. 19, 1861. See VMPL, 53.

10. JMM to Rives, July 26, 1849, in Rives Papers, container 80, LC.

11. JMM to C. Neale, Jan. 7, 1849, in Autographs, Miscellaneous Americans, Pierpont Morgan Library, New York.

12. JMM's mother lived another eight years, dying in 1857. Both parents are buried in the family plot at Christ Church Episcopal Cemetery, Alexandria, Va.

13. E.g., in one letter, he asked for "one thousand dollars to provide for some demands upon the estate of my Father." JMM to Corcoran, Apr. 17, 1849, in Corcoran Papers, vol. 7, LC. See also VMPL, 48–49.

14. JMM to Rives, Mar. 31, 1851, in Rives Papers, container 82, LC.

15. VMPL, 49.

16. Anna Mason Ambler to Hunter, Oct. 4, 1858, in Papers of R. M. T. Hunter, Hunter-Garnett Collection, Box 29, ALUV.

17. JMM opposed its abolition, believing that "it would be utterly impracticable to have an efficient navy without this mode of punishment." See JMM, remarks in the U.S. Senate, Sept. 28, 1850, *Congressional Globe*, 31st Cong., 1st sess., pt. 2, p. 2057.

18. JMM supported it, thinking it proper that, "when gentlemen are called from their residences, remote from the capital, . . . for four years only, that . . . they should have an establishment prepared for them." The proposal lost by one vote. See JMM, speech in the U.S. Senate, Feb. 28, 1853, *Congressional Globe*, 32d Cong., 2d sess., pp. 898–99.

19. JMM, comments in the U.S. Senate, Dec. 16, 1850, *Congressional Globe*, 31st Cong., 2d sess., p. 63.

20. Ibid., 58–59 and 62–63.

21. JMM, comments in the U.S. Senate, Feb. 7, 1859, *Congressional Globe*, 35th Cong., 2d sess., pt. 1, pp. 858–59.

22. JMM, remarks in the U.S. Senate, Aug. 23, 1852, *Congressional Globe*, 32d Cong., 1st sess., pt. 3, p. 2294.

23. JMM, speech in the U.S. Senate, June 22, 1854, *Congressional Globe*, 33rd Cong., 1st sess., pt. 2, pp. 1472–75.

24. JMM, remarks in the U.S. Senate, July 24, 1854, *Congressional Globe*, 33rd Cong., 1st sess., pt. 3, pp. 1879–80.

25. JMM, speech in the U.S. Senate, Apr. 25, 1856, *Congressional Globe*, 34th Cong., 1st sess., pt. 2, pp. 1025–26.

26. JMM, comments in the U.S. Senate, Feb. 16, 1860, *Congressional Globe*, 36th Cong., 1st sess., pt. 1, p. 803.

27. JMM, remarks in the U.S. Senate, July 24, 1854, *Congressional Globe*, 33rd Cong., 1st sess., pt. 3, p. 1879.

28. JMM, comments in the U.S. Senate, Feb. 16, 1860, *Congressional Globe*, 36th Cong., 1st sess., pt. 1, pp. 802–3.

29. JMM resolution in the U.S. Senate, Feb. 24, 1851, *Congressional Globe*, 31st Cong., 2d sess., p. 671.

30. JMM, speech in the U.S. Senate, Feb. 28, 1853, *Congressional Globe*, 32d Cong., 2d sess., p. 906.

31.   JMM, remarks in the U.S. Senate, Aug. 27, 1850, *Congressional Globe,* 31st Cong., 1st sess., pt. 2, pp. 1673–74 and 1676.

32.   JMM, comments in the U.S. Senate, Feb. 23, 1853, *Congressional Globe,* 32d Cong., 2d sess., p. 792.

33.   The Senate rejected his amendment by a vote of 25 to 21. See JMM, remarks in the U.S. Senate, Aug. 3, 1854, *Congressional Globe,* 33rd Cong., 1st sess., pt. 3, p. 2188.

34.   JMM also proposed the building of a National Foundry either there or at nearby Shepherdstown. See JMM, resolution in the U.S. Senate, Aug. 8, 1858, *Congressional Globe,* 35th Cong., 1st sess., pt. 2, p. 1531.

35.   JMM, comments in the U.S. Senate, Aug. 20, 1852, *Congressional Globe,* 32d Cong., 1st sess., appendix, pp. 1011–12.

36.   Qtd. in Rutland, *George Mason,* 25.

37.   JMM, remarks in the U.S. Senate, June 24, 1852, *Congressional Globe,* 32d Cong., 1st sess., pt. 2, p. 1609.

38.   Their victories came in spite of opposition from the Jacksonian "Richmond junto," but that opposition remained strong enough to squelch a movement among Virginia Democrats to push JMM as a vice-presidential candidate in 1848. See Shanks, *Secession Movement,* 15.

39.   JMM to Rives, Mar. 31, 1851, in Rives Papers, container 82, LC.

40.   Ibid.

41.   JMM to Rives, July 9, 1852, in Rives Papers, container 83, LC. After Pierce left office, JMM promised to "advise him occasionally of what may occur in Washington." See JMM to Pierce, Nov. 16, 1857, Franklin Pierce Papers, series 2, LC.

42.   JMM, remarks in the U.S. Senate, Dec. 22, 1853, *Congressional Globe,* 33rd Cong., 1st sess., pt. 1, pp. 82–83.

43.   JMM to Rives, Nov. 23, 1852, in Rives Papers, container 83, LC. JMM's comment was not completely accurate, however, as many southern Whigs actually decided to stay at home rather than vote for a Democrat. See Cooper, *South and Politics of Slavery,* 340–41.

44.   JMM to Rives, Feb. 24, 1853, in Rives Papers, container 83, LC.

45.   Jefferson Davis to Stephen Cocke, Dec. 19, 1853, in Dunbar Rowland, ed., *Jefferson Davis, Constitutionalist: His Letters, Papers and Speeches* (Jackson: Printed for the Mississippi Department of Archives and History, 1923), vol. 2:334–37.

46.   Holt, *Political Crisis of the 1850s,* 148–50.

47.   For a discussion of the positions taken by the Republican Party, see Eric Foner, *Free Soil, Free Labor, Free Men: The Ideology of the Republican Party before the Civil War* (Oxford, England: Oxford Univ. Press, 1970).

48.   Qtd. in Holt, *Political Crisis of the 1850s,* 187–88.

49.   Foner, *Free Soil, Free Labor, Free Men,* 130.

50.   Nevins, *Ordeal of the Union* 2:460–69.

51.   Potter, *Impending Crisis,* 259–60.

52.   JMM to Jefferson Davis, Sept. 30, 1856, in *Papers of Jefferson Davis,* ed. Monroe, McIntosh, Crist, Dix, and Williams, vol. 6:504; and VMPL, 117–18. Davis replied to Governor Wise that no provision existed for the exchange of militia arms, but that they could be altered at federal arsenals. Jefferson Davis to Wise, Oct. 6, 1856, in Rowland, *Jefferson Davis, Constitutionalist* 3:62–64.

53.   Holt, *Political Crisis of the 1850s,* 198.

54.   JMM to W. A. Patterson et al., Dec. 2, 1856, in VMPL, 118–19.

55.   Ibid., 123.

56.   JMM, speech at Bunker Hill, June 17, 1857, in VMPL, 124–25. It was also in the *Boston Post,* June 18, 1857.

57.   JMM, speech at Bunker Hill, June 17, 1857, in VMPL, 124–26, and in *Boston Post,* June 18, 1857.

58.   Bugg, "Political Career of James Murray Mason," 622.

59.   *Boston Post,* June 18, 1857; also in VMPL, 123–24.

60.   Welles's comments from Welles, *Galaxy* 15 (1873); rpt. in VMPL, 126.

61.   JMM, speech in the U.S. Senate, Feb. 1, 1859, *Congressional Globe,* 35th Cong., 2d sess., pt. 1, pp. 718–19.

62.   JMM, remarks in the U.S. Senate, May 25, 1854, *Congressional Globe,* 33rd Cong., 1st sess., appendix, pp. 785–86.

63.   JMM, comments in the U.S. Senate, May 20, 1856, *Congressional Globe,* 34th Cong., 1st sess., appendix, pp. 546–47.

64.   The most recent study of the panic is James L. Huston, *The Panic of 1857 and the Coming of the Civil War* (Baton Rouge: Louisiana State Univ. Press, 1987).

65.   JMM to George M. Dallas, Oct. 15, 1857, in Mason Family Papers, GHL.

66.   Stampp, *America in 1857,* 213–21.

67.   JMM, speech in the U.S. Senate, Apr. 15, 1858, *Congressional Globe,* 35th Cong., 1st sess., pt. 2, pp. 1600–1603.

68.   JMM to George M. Dallas, Oct. 15, 1857, in Mason Family Papers, GHL.

69.   Stampp, *America in 1857,* 230–31.

70.   Holt, *Political Crisis of the 1850s,* 213.

71.   Hunter repeated JMM's opinions on political as well as household matters. E.g., see Hunter to his wife, Feb. 28, 1858, in Papers of R. M. T. Hunter, Hunter-Garnett Collection, Box 29, ALUV.

72.   Hunter to his wife, Mar. 13, 1858, in Papers of R. M. T. Hunter, Hunter-Garnett Collection, Box 29, ALUV.

73.   Nevins, *Ordeal of the Union* 2:431. JMM had dined with a number of British statesmen, including Lord Napier, earlier in the month and had gotten along extremely well with them. See Hunter to his wife, Feb. 12, 1859, in Papers of R. M. T. Hunter, Hunter-Garnett Collection, Box 30, ALUV.

74.   Nevins, *Ordeal of the Union* 2:432–33.

Chapter 7. 1859–1861: Mason and the Coming of the Civil War

1.   Allan Nevins, *The Emergence of Lincoln* (New York: Charles Scribner's Sons, 1950), vol. 2:70–72.

2.   The eldest, Anna, was 34; while the youngest, John, was 18. See Copeland and MacMaster, *Five George Masons,* 282.

3.   There are many biographies of John Brown, but one of the best recent studies is Stephen B. Oates, *To Purge the Land with Blood: A Biography of John Brown* (New York: Harper and Row, 1970).

4.   One Marine died in the assault, and during the entire 36-hour period, Brown's men killed 4 and wounded 9. Nevins, *Emergence of Lincoln* 2:78–84; and Potter, *Impending Crisis,* 369–71.

5.   Bugg, "Political Career of James Murray Mason," 689.

6.   JMM, interview with John Brown, Oct. 18, 1859, *New York Herald,* Oct. 21, 1859.

7.   JMM, letter to editor of the *Constitution,* Oct. 21, 1859, rpt. in the *Richmond Enquirer,* Oct. 28, 1859, and excerpted in VMPL, 147–48.

8.   That picture particularly haunted Eliza and other southern women. Shortly after the raid, Mrs. Mason, using her middle name "Margaretta," aired her views in a heated exchange of letters with Massachusetts abolitionist Lydia Maria Child. See Wendy Hamand Venet, "'Cry Aloud and Spare Not'": Northern Antislavery Women and John Brown's Raid," in Paul Finkelman, ed., *His Soul Goes Marching On: Responses to John Brown and the Harpers Ferry Raid* (Charlottesville: Univ. Press of Virginia, 1995), 106–11.

9.   JMM, resolution in the U.S. Senate, Dec. 5, 1859, *Congressional Globe,* 36th Cong., 1st sess., pt. 1, p. 1.

10.   JMM, remarks in the U.S. Senate, Dec. 6, 1859, *Congressional Globe,* 36th Cong., 1st sess., pt. 1, p. 6.

11.   Ibid., 13–14.

12.   JMM, undated memorandum, "Emancipation," ca. late 1859, in Mason Family Papers, GHL.

13.   JMM, comments in the U.S. Senate, Dec. 14, 1859, *Congressional Globe,* 36th Cong., 1st sess., pt. 1, p. 141.

14.   Ibid., 148.

15.   Ibid., 149.

16.   Ibid., 152.

17.   The committee met for the first time on Dec. 16, 1859, and submitted its report on June 14, 1860. See U.S. Congress, Senate, Select Committee on the Harpers Ferry Invasion, *Mass Violence in America: Invasion at Harpers Ferry* (rpt. New York: Arno Press and the *New York Times,* 1969), 27–28.

18.   Mississippi's Jefferson Davis served on the committee but was preoccupied with other matters, and Indiana Democrat Graham N. Fitch followed JMM's leadership. The Republicans, Wisconsin's James R. Doolittle and Vermont's Jacob Collamer, had little impact on the investigation, because they were consistently outvoted three to two. See Keith A. Sutherland, "The Senate Investigates Harpers Ferry," *Prologue* 8 (Winter 1976): 192–207.

19.   JMM to Wise, Dec. 15, 1859, in *Calendar of Virginia State Papers* 10:93.

20.   JMM to Andrew Hunter, Esq., Dec. 20, 1859, in Miscellaneous Papers, Massachusetts Historical Society, Boston.

21.   JMM to Dr. Samuel Howe, Feb. 3, 1860, in Howe Papers, Massachusetts Historical Society, Boston.

22.   U.S. Congress, Senate, Select Committee on the Harpers Ferry Invasion, *Mass Violence in America,* 27–43.

23.   Sutherland, "Senate Investigates Harpers Ferry," 195.

24.   One private citizen who did testify willingly was wealthy Boston merchant George Luther Stearns, who had been a financial supporter of Brown since the days of "Bleeding Kansas." Alone with JMM in the committee room after finishing his testimony, the pair had an interesting informal chat. JMM said, "I think when you go to that lower place, the old fellow will question you pretty hard about this matter, and you will have to take it." But Stearns replied, "Before that time comes[,] I think he will have two hundred years of slavery to investigate, and before he gets through with that will say 'we have had enough of this business, better let the rest go.'" JMM roared his hearty laugh and left the room. Stearns to Dr. Samuel Howe, Feb. 27, 1860, in Howe Papers, Massachusetts Historical Society, Boston, qtd. in Edward J. Renehan, Jr., *The*

Secret Six: The True Tale of the Men Who Conspired with John Brown (New York: Crown Publishers, 1995), 250–51.

25. The Senate approved warrants to take the three into custody in February. See JMM, resolution in the U.S. Senate, Feb. 15, 1860, *Congressional Globe,* 36th Cong., 1st sess., pt. 1, p. 778.

26. Redpath to JMM, Jan. 26 and Feb. 1, 1860, and John Brown, Jr., to JMM, Jan. 25, 1860, all in *Records of the Senate Committee That Investigated John Brown's Raid at Harpers Ferry, Virginia, in 1859,* Microfilm Series, M-1196, NA.

27. Sutherland, "Senate Investigates Harpers Ferry," 195–97.

28. Ibid., 201.

29. JMM, remarks in the U.S. Senate, Apr. 10, 1860, *Congressional Globe,* 36th Cong., 1st sess., pt. 2, p. 1627.

30. Sumner, comments in the U.S. Senate, *Congressional Globe,* 36th Cong., 1st sess., pt. 2, pp. 1626–27.

31. See JMM, speeches in the U.S. Senate, Apr. 13 and 16, 1860, *Congressional Globe,* 36th Cong., 1st sess., pt. 2, pp. 1699 and 1722–24.

32. JMM, resolution and remarks in the U.S. Senate, Feb. 21, 1860, *Congressional Globe,* 36th Cong., 1st sess., pt. 1, pp. 848–50.

33. JMM, comments in the U.S. Senate, Mar. 5, 1860, *Congressional Globe,* 36th Cong., 1st sess., pt. 2, pp. 999–1000.

34. JMM, speech in the U.S. Senate, Mar. 9, 1860, *Congressional Globe,* 36th Cong., 1st sess., pt. 2, pp. 1077–86.

35. JMM, remarks in the U.S. Senate, Mar. 12, 1860, *Congressional Globe,* 36th Cong., 1st sess., pt. 2, pp. 1108–9.

36. Ibid., 1108.

37. Conclusions of the Harpers Ferry Committee, read by JMM in the U.S. Senate, June 15, 1860, *Congressional Globe,* 36th Cong., 1st sess., pt. 4, p. 3006.

38. U.S. Congress, Senate, Select Committee on the Harpers Ferry Invasion, *Mass Violence in America,* 1–19.

39. JMM commented on the general paralysis of the legislative branch, in JMM to Philip Clayton Pendleton, Jan. 26, 1860, in JMM Papers, Special Collections Department, William R. Perkins Library, Duke Univ., Durham, N.C.

40. JMM, remarks in the U.S. Senate, Jan. 3, 23, and 26, 1860, *Congressional Globe,* 36th Cong., 1st sess., pt. 1, pp. 302, 557, and 596.

41. JMM, speech in the U.S. Senate, Jan. 26, 1860, *Congressional Globe,* 36th Cong., 1st sess., pt. 1, p. 596.

42. JMM, comments in the U.S. Senate, Jan. 4, 1860, *Congressional Globe,* 36th Cong., 1st sess., pt. 1, p. 324.

43. Robert M. T. Hunter to his wife, Feb. 8, 1860, in Papers of R. M. T. Hunter, Hunter-Garnett Collection, Box 31, ALUV.

44. JMM, comments in the U.S. Senate, Feb. 23, 1853, *Congressional Globe,* 32d Cong., 2d sess., p. 792.

45. JMM, speech in the U.S. Senate, Feb. 23, 1860, *Congressional Globe,* 36th Cong., 1st sess., pt. 1, pp. 863–64.

46. JMM, remarks in the U.S. Senate, Mar. 1, 1860, *Congressional Globe,* 36th Cong., 1st sess., pt. 2, pp. 949–50.

47. The respite even enabled him to take a short trip home to Selma. See Hunter to his wife, Apr. 9, 1860, Papers of R. M. T. Hunter, Hunter-Garnett Collection, Box 31, ALUV.

48. On Mar. 20, regarding negotiations with Indian tribes, JMM expressed his

conclusion that U.S. policy should be "fixed and settled" as one of "acquiring no further land from the Indian tribes, if it can be avoided." His decision came not from empathy for the plight of American Indians but rather from concern that securing more Indian territory "enlarges the public domain, encumbers the Government, demoralizes it, and leads to the spectacle which we witness here from session to session, of an attempt to bribe the popular mind by largesses of the public lands." He favored using force to restrain the Indians, even at the prospect of more Indian wars. To JMM, such a course would be preferable to passing bills that took away Indian land and then further corrupted the U.S. Treasury. JMM, comments in the U.S. Senate, Mar. 20, 1860, *Congressional Globe*, 36th Cong., 1st sess., pt. 2, p. 1246–49.

49.   JMM argued in favor of building a railroad in the District of Columbia along Pennsylvania Avenue to connect Georgetown with Washington. JMM, remarks in the U.S. Senate, Apr. 7, 1860, *Congressional Globe*, 36th Cong., 1st sess., pt. 2, p. 1592.

50.   JMM, speech in the U.S. Senate, Apr. 13, 1860, *Congressional Globe*, 36th Cong., 1st sess., pt. 2, pp. 1680–81.

51.   JMM, comments in the U.S. Senate, Apr. 10, 1860, *Congressional Globe*, 36th Cong., 1st sess., pt. 2, p. 1634.

52.   A strong supporter of homestead legislation, Johnson attacked JMM and his arguments on Apr. 11. That led the Virginian to respond that he only had tried to show that the Tennessean stood on the wrong side of the issue as the South saw it. He felt he did not deserve to "have poured upon me the extraordinary violence of wrath in which the honorable Senator has indulged today." JMM, speech in the U.S. Senate, Apr. 11, 1860, *Congressional Globe*, 36th Cong., 1st sess., pt. 2, pp. 1655–56.

53.   JMM, comments in the U.S. Senate, Apr. 7, 1860, *Congressional Globe*, 36th Cong., 1st sess., pt. 2, p. 1636.

54.   Ibid., 1636–37.

55.   For short discussions of the convention, see Nevins, *Emergence of Lincoln* 2:200–228; and Roy Franklin Nichols, *The Disruption of American Democracy* (New York: Free Press, 1948), 288–320.

56.   Holt, *Political Crisis of the 1850s*, 205–6.

57.   Jefferson Davis, resolutions in the U.S. Senate, Feb. 2, 1860, *Congressional Globe*, 36th Cong., 1st sess., pt. 1, p. 658.

58.   Nevins, *Emergence of Lincoln* 2:179–80.

59.   Potter, *Impending Crisis*, 403–10.

60.   Nichols, *Disruption of American Democracy*, 305–7.

61.   Ibid., 309–10.

62.   Jefferson Davis, "Address to the National Democracy," May 7, 1860, in *Papers of Jefferson Davis*, ed. Monroe, McIntosh, Crist, Dix, and Williams, vol. 6:289–93.

63.   JMM, speech in the U.S. Senate, May 18, 1860, *Congressional Globe*, 36th Cong., 1st sess., appendix, pp. 317–21, excerpted in VMPL, 152–54.

64.   JMM, comments in the U.S. Senate, Apr. 19, 1860, *Congressional Globe*, 36th Cong., 1st sess., pt. 2, p. 1792.

65.   JMM, comments in the U.S. Senate, May 18, 1860, *Congressional Globe*, 36th Cong., 1st sess., appendix, p. 321; rpt. in VMPL, 153.

66.   For a short discussion of the Republican convention, see Nevins, *Emergence of Lincoln* 2:229–60.

67.   Nichols, *Disruption of American Democracy*, 312–18.

68.   JMM, speech in the U.S. Senate, May 24, 1860, *Congressional Globe*, 36th Cong., 1st sess., pt. 3, pp. 2306–8. Less than a year later, Cornelia McDonald of Winchester recorded in her diary a conversation between her husband and friends. She

quoted JMM as "declaring that it was the restrictions on the trade which had caused the sufferings on slave vessels." Therefore, after "Virginia took her proper stand with the Confederacy he intended to use his influence (which he expected to be considerable) toward reviving the trade in its most unrestricted form." Diary of Mrs. Angus McDonald, early Feb. 1861, qtd. in Julia Davis, *The Shenandoah* (New York: Farrar and Rinehart, 1945), 153.

69.   JMM, remarks in the U.S. Senate, May 24, 1860, *Congressional Globe,* 36th Cong., 1st sess., pt. 3, p. 2307. The Davis amendment was defeated 38 to 17, and the bill passed 41 to 14. The votes are recorded in *Congressional Globe,* 36th Cong., 1st sess., pt. 3, p. 2308–9.

70.   JMM, comments in the U.S. Senate, Feb. 16, 1859, *Congressional Globe,* 35th Cong., 2d sess., pt. 2, p. 1055.

71.   JMM, speech in the U.S. Senate, June 16, 1860, *Congressional Globe,* 36th Cong., 1st sess., pt. 4, pp. 3069–70.

72.   JMM, comments in the U.S. Senate, June 18, 1860, *Congressional Globe,* 36th Cong., 1st sess., pt. 4, pp. 3098–99.

73.   JMM, remarks in the U.S. Senate, June 12, 1860, *Congressional Globe,* 36th Cong., 1st sess., pt. 4, p. 2884.

74.   William Kauffman Scarborough, ed., *The Diary of Edmund Ruffin* (Baton Rouge: Louisiana State Univ. Press, 1972), vol. 1:429.

75.   JMM, comments in the U.S. Senate, June 22, 1860, *Congressional Globe,* 36th Cong., 1st sess., pt. 4, pp. 3244–45.

76.   Jefferson Davis made one such attempt, as he convinced both Breckinridge and Constitutional Union candidate John Bell of Tennessee to withdraw in favor of a compromise candidate. Stephen Douglas, however, refused. See Jefferson Davis, *Rise and Fall* 1:52.

77.   For accounts of Lincoln's victory, see Nevins, *Emergence of Lincoln* 2:261–317; and Potter, *Impending Crisis,* 430–47.

78.   JMM to Miles, Nov. 11, 1860, in William Porcher Miles Papers, Southern Historical Collection, Univ. of North Carolina, Chapel Hill. See Nichols, *Disruption of American Democracy,* 371.

79.   JMM to Nathaniel Tyler, editor, Nov. 23, 1860, in *Richmond Enquirer,* Nov. 30, 1860; also in VMPL, 155–60.

80.   For the most recent discussion of how abolitionists turned John Brown into a martyr for their cause, see Paul Finkelman, "Manufacturing Martyrdom: The Antislavery Response to John Brown's Raid," in Finkelman, *His Soul Goes Marching On,* 41–66.

81.   JMM to Nathaniel Tyler, editor, Nov. 23, 1860, printed in *Richmond Enquirer,* Nov. 30, 1860; also in VMPL, 155–60.

82.   Ibid.

83.   JMM to Anne Chew, Nov. 29, 1860, in VMPL, 160–61.

84.   Hunter to his wife, Dec. 6, 1860, in Papers of R. M. T. Hunter, Hunter-Garnett Collection, Box 31, ALUV.

85.   Nevins, *Emergence of Lincoln* 2:350–54; and Nichols, *Disruption of American Democracy,* 382–87.

86.   Buchanan to Congress, Dec. 3, 1860, in *Congressional Globe,* 36th Cong., 2d sess., appendix, pp. 1–7.

87.   Powell, resolution in the U.S. Senate, Dec. 6, 1860, in *Congressional Globe,* 36th Cong., 2d sess., pt. 1, p. 19.

88. JMM, comments in the U.S. Senate, Dec. 10, 1860, *Congressional Globe*, 36th Cong., 2d sess., pt. 1, p. 35.

89. JMM, remarks in the U.S. Senate, Dec. 11, 1860, *Congressional Globe*, 36th Cong., 2d sess., pt. 1, pp. 55–57.

90. JMM, speech in the U.S. Senate, Jan. 10, 1861, *Congressional Globe*, 36th Cong., 2d sess., pt. 1, pp. 315–16.

91. JMM, comments in the U.S. Senate, Dec. 11, 1860, *Congressional Globe*, 36th Cong., 2d sess., pt. 1, pp. 56–57.

92. Nichols, *Disruption of American Democracy*, 407–9; and Dwight Lowell Dumond, *The Secession Movement, 1860–1861* (New York: Century Press, 1931), 138–41.

93. JMM, remarks in the U.S. Senate, Dec. 20, 1860, *Congressional Globe*, 36th Cong., 2d sess., pt. 1, pp. 155–56.

94. JMM, resolution in the U.S. Senate, Jan. 5, 1861, in *Congressional Globe*, 36th Cong., 2d sess., pt. 1, p. 249.

95. JMM and Hunter to Buchanan, Jan. 9, 1861, and Buchanan to JMM and Hunter, Jan. 10, 1861, both in John B. Moore, ed., *Works of James Buchanan: Comprising His Speeches, State Papers, and Private Correspondences* (1908–10; rpt. New York: Antiquarian Press Ltd., 1960), vol. 11:102–4.

96. JMM, comments in the U.S. Senate, Jan. 15, 1861, *Congressional Globe*, 36th Cong., 2d sess., pt. 1, p. 353.

97. The day after he called for laying the real truth before the people, he wrote to South Carolina Gov. Francis W. Pickens to inform him that "Virginia, I think, will go out by 20th of February." See JMM to Hon. F. W. Pickens, Jan. 16, 1861, in WROR, ser. 1, vol. 51, pt. 2, p. 6.

98. JMM to Lewis E. Harvie, Jan. 13, 1861, in WROR, ser. 1, vol. 51, pt. 2, p. 5.

99. JMM, speech in the U.S. Senate, Jan. 16, 1861, *Congressional Globe*, 36th Cong., 2d sess., pt. 1, pp. 403–5.

100. JMM, remarks in the U.S. Senate, Jan. 21, 1861, *Congressional Globe*, 36th Cong., 2d sess., pt. 1, pp. 494–96.

101. Dumond, *Secession Movement*, 189–210.

102. They coordinated their efforts as much as possible during the crisis. See Hunter to his wife, Jan. 22 and 25, 1861, in Papers of R. M. T. Hunter, Hunter-Garnett Collection, Box 32, ALUV.

103. JMM to his daughter Virginia Mason, Jan. 27, 1861, in VMPL, 176.

104. JMM et al. to the people of Virginia, Jan. 26, 1861, in VMPL, 176–78.

105. JMM, speech in the U.S. Senate, Jan. 28, 1861, *Congressional Globe*, 36th Cong., 1st sess., pt. 1, pp. 590–91, excerpted in VMPL, 179–82.

106. JMM, remarks in the U.S. Senate, Jan. 28, 1861, *Congressional Globe*, 36th Cong., 1st sess., pt. 1, p. 590, excerpted in VMPL, 180–81.

107. JMM, comments in the U.S. Senate, Jan. 21, 1861, *Congressional Globe*, 36th Cong., 1st sess., pt. 1, pp. 494–96.

108. JMM, speech in the U.S. Senate, Jan. 22, 1861, *Congressional Globe*, 36th Cong., 1st sess., pt. 1, pp. 506–8.

109. JMM, remarks in the U.S. Senate, Jan. 30, 1861, *Congressional Globe*, 36th Cong., 1st sess., pt. 1, p. 635.

110. JMM, comments in the U.S. Senate, Jan. 31, 1861, *Congressional Globe*, 36th Cong., 1st sess., pt. 1, pp. 657–62.

111. Ibid., 659.

112.   Nichols, *Disruption of American Democracy,* 460–62; and Dumond, *Secession Movement,* 210–12.

113.   JMM to Jefferson Davis, Feb. 12, 1861, in *Papers of Jefferson Davis,* ed. Monroe, McIntosh, Crist, Dix, and Williams, vol. 7:39.

114.   JMM, speech in the U.S. Senate, Jan. 22, 1861, *Congressional Globe,* 36th Cong., 1st sess., pt. 1, p. 503.

115.   JMM, comments in the U.S. Senate, Feb. 11, 1861, *Congressional Globe,* 36th Cong., 1st sess., pt. 1, pp. 850–51.

116.   Ibid., 851–53.

117.   JMM particularly argued in favor of cheap tobacco and wine, and stressed the foreign relations implications of increasing tariff rates to protectionist levels. See JMM, speeches in the U.S. Senate, Feb. 16 and 19, 1861, *Congressional Globe,* 36th Cong., 1st sess., pt. 2, pp. 949, 956–57, and 1022–23.

118.   JMM, remarks in the U.S. Senate, Feb. 26, 1861, *Congressional Globe,* 36th Cong., 1st sess., pt. 2, pp. 1219–20.

119.   D. Weston to Mrs. M. W. Chapman, Mar. 20, 1861, in JMM Papers, Ms.A.9.2, vol. 30, no. 58, Boston Public Library.

120.   JMM, comments in the U.S. Senate, Feb. 20, 1861, *Congressional Globe,* 36th Cong., 2d sess., pt. 2, pp. 1045–46.

121.   JMM fought those who wanted to keep the seats vacant until new elections and punish those who left. To JMM, who saw contradictions in northern arguments, the seats were not vacant. The states were gone, so the seats no longer existed. JMM, comments in the U.S. Senate, Mar. 11 and 14, 1861, *Congressional Globe,* 36th Cong., special sess., pp. 1449–50 and 1454–56.

122.   JMM to John Tyler, Mar. 2, 1861, John Tyler Papers, series 2, LC.

123.   For an account of the peace convention, see L. E. Chittenden, ed., *Report of the Debates and Proceedings of the Peace Convention Held at Washington D.C., February 1861* (rpt. New York: Da Capo Press, 1971).

124.   JMM, speech in the U.S. Senate, Mar. 1, 1861, *Congressional Globe,* 36th Cong., 2d sess., pt. 2, pp. 1311–13.

125. Ibid.

126.   JMM, remarks in the U.S. Senate, Mar. 2, 1861, *Congressional Globe,* 36th Cong., 2d sess., pt. 2, pp. 1362–66.

127.   JMM, speech in the U.S. Senate, Mar. 2, 1861, *Congressional Globe,* 36th Cong., 2d sess., pt. 2, pp. 1387–91.

128.   His resolution inquiring into the number of troops in the District of Columbia went nowhere. See JMM, resolution in the U.S. Senate, Mar. 15, 1861, *Congressional Globe,* 36th Cong., special sess., p. 1457.

129.   JMM, comments in the U.S. Senate, Mar. 19, 1861, *Congressional Globe,* 36th Cong., special sess., p. 1476.

130.   JMM to Jefferson Davis, Mar. 25, 1861, in *Papers of Jefferson Davis,* ed. Monroe, McIntosh, Crist, Dix, and Williams, vol. 7:81.

Chapter 8. 1861: Making of a Confederate Diplomat

1.   JMM to Jefferson Davis, Mar. 25, 1861, in *Papers of Jefferson Davis,* ed. Monroe, McIntosh, Crist, Dix, and Williams, vol. 7:81.

2.   James M. McPherson, *Battle Cry of Freedom: The Civil War Era* (New York: Ballantine Books, 1988), 264–74. Accounts of the shelling of the fort include Robert Hendrickson, *Sumter: The First Day of the Civil War* (Chelsea, Mich.: Scarborough

House/Publishers, 1990); and W. A. Swanberg, *First Blood: The Story of Fort Sumter* (New York: Charles Scribner's Sons, 1957).

3. VMPL, 191.

4. JMM to Jefferson Davis, Apr. 17, 1861, in WROR, ser. 1, vol. 51, pt. 2, p. 14.

5. For the proceedings of the Virginia convention, see George H. Reese, ed., *Journals and Papers of the Virginia State Convention of 1861,* 4 vols. (Richmond, Va.: Virginia State Library, 1965).

6. James M. McPherson, *Battle Cry of Freedom,* 278–80. In a letter to the editor, *Winchester Virginian,* May 16, 1861, JMM urged his fellow Virginians to approve the ordinance. The letter is in Edward McPherson, ed., *The Political History of the United States of America During the Great Rebellion, 1860–1865* (1865; rpt. New York: Da Capo Press, 1972), 7.

7. JMM to Jefferson Davis, Apr. 21, 1861, in *Papers of Jefferson Davis,* ed. Monroe, McIntosh, Crist, Dix, and Williams, vol. 7:113–14.

8. VMPL, 196.

9. JMM to Letcher, Apr. 25, 1861, Executive Branch, Governor's Office, Letters Received, VSL.

10. He also spent two days at Col. Thomas J. Jackson's headquarters in Harpers Ferry. Jackson, soon to be known to the world as "Stonewall," discussed the military situation in northern Virginia with JMM, who commented upon the political considerations involved in defending the border with Maryland. JMM made suggestions about both in: JMM to Gen. Robert E. Lee, May 15, 1861, in WROR, ser. 1, vol. 2:848–50.

11. Scarborough, *Diary of Edmund Ruffin* 2:15–17.

12. JMM to Jefferson Davis, May 6, 1861, in *Papers of Jefferson Davis,* ed. Monroe, McIntosh, Crist, Dix, and Williams, vol. 7:148–51. In the Virginia Legislature, a resolution to appoint a committee of public safety to effect JMM's suggestion failed, never coming to a vote. See ibid., 7:152.

13. Johnston was a close friend of James's youngest brother, Joel Barlow Mason, who arrived at Selma with plans to volunteer for the army. The 48-year-old Joel became a member of Johnston's staff and was mortally wounded at Manassas on July 21, 1861. See VMPL, 196–97.

14. Ibid., 197–98.

15. Confederate States of America, Congress, *Journal of the Congress of the Confederate States of America, 1861–1865* (Washington, D.C.: U.S. Government Printing Office, 1904), vol. 1:288, 302, 313, 323, and 383–84.

16. Jefferson Davis, speech to the Provisional Congress, July 20, 1861, in Rowland, *Jefferson Davis, Constitutionalist* 5:111–18.

17. Ephraim Douglass Adams, *Great Britain and the American Civil War* (New York: Longmans, Green and Co., 1925), vol. 1:86–94.

18. "Proclamation by Queen Victoria," May 13, 1861, in Bourne and Watt, *British Documents on Foreign Affairs* 5:203–5.

19. Resolution in the Provisional Congress, Aug. 13, 1861, *Journal of the Congress of the Confederate States of America* 1:341.

20. Four months earlier, President Davis had called for privateers by offering letters of marque and reprisal to any interested parties. See "Proclamation by the President of the Confederate States," Apr. 17, 1861, in James D. Richardson, ed. *The Messages and Papers of Jefferson Davis and the Confederacy, Including Diplomatic Correspondence, 1861–1865* (1905; rpt. New York: Chelsea House–Robert Hector Publishers, 1966), vol. 1:60–62.

21. William H. Gregory to JMM, July 27, 1861, in JMM Papers, vol. 1, LC.

22. Frank L. Owsley, *King Cotton Diplomacy: Foreign Relations of the Confederate States of America* (Chicago: Univ. of Chicago Press, 1931; rev. Harriet C. Owsley, 1959), 2–10 and 30–32.

23. Jefferson Davis, *Rise and Fall* 1:244–45.

24. JMM, resolution in the Provisional Congress, Aug. 21, 1861, *Journal of the Congress of the Confederate States of America* 1:377–78.

25. Official Confederate demands for British recognition were rejected by the ministry. See Yancey, Rost, and Mann to Lord John Russell, Aug. 14, 1861, and Russell to Yancey, Rost, and Mann, Aug. 24, 1861, in ORUCN, ser. 2, vol. 3:238–48.

26. Frank L. Owsley, *King Cotton Diplomacy,* 76–77.

27. Through the years, historians have criticized Jefferson Davis's choice of James M. Mason. They follow the lead of the contemporary southern belle, Mary Chesnut, who wrote, "My wildest imagination will not picture Mr. Mason as a diplomat." See Chesnut, *Diary from Dixie,* 123–24. Unflattering caricatures based upon his tobacco chewing and how he dressed often include even harsher commentaries on his intelligence. See, e.g., Allan Nevins's introduction to Richardson, *Messages and Papers of Jefferson Davis,* 1:xxxviii; Clement Eaton, *A History of the Southern Confederacy* (New York: Free Press, 1954), 71; and Frank J. Merli, *Great Britain and the Confederate Navy* (Bloomington: Indiana Univ. Press, 1970), 31. For more generous opinions, see Frank L. Owsley, *King Cotton Diplomacy,* 203–4, and Emory M. Thomas, *The Confederate Nation: 1861–1865* (New York: Harper and Row, 1979), 173.

28. Jefferson Davis to "all to whom these presents shall come," Aug. 24, 1861, in JMM Papers, Mss2 M238133b, VHS; also in ORUCN, ser. 2, vol. 3:110.

29. Jefferson Davis to Queen Victoria, Aug. 24, 1861, in ORUCN, ser. 2, vol. 3:111–12.

30. JMM to Buchanan, Nov. 2, 1858, in VMPL, 148–49.

31. JMM voted in Congress for the last time on Aug. 30, 1861. That vote is in *Journal of the Congress of the Confederate States of America* 1:455–56.

32. VMPL, 198.

33. Ibid., 199.

34. The handwritten instructions were 28 pages long. See Hunter to JMM, Sept. 23, 1861, in JMM Papers, vol. 1, LC; also in ORUCN, ser. 2, vol. 3:257–64.

35. Hunter to JMM, Sept. 23, 1861, in JMM Papers, vol. 1, LC.

36. JMM, memorandum on his voyage to England, in VMPL, 209–46.

37. Ibid., 209–10; Slidell and JMM to Hunter, Oct. 3, 1861, Confederate States of America, Department of State Papers (often referred to as "Pickett Papers"), vol. 53, LC; also in ORUCN, ser. 2, vol. 3:275.

38. Before running the blockade, to further befuddle any pursuers, the vessel's name was changed from the *Gordon* to the *Theodora.* Both names are used in the various accounts of the voyage. JMM, memorandum on his voyage to England, in VMPL, 210; Slidell and JMM to Hunter, Oct. 4, 1861, Confederate States of America, Department of State Papers, vol. 53, LC; also in ORUCN, ser. 2, vol. 3:276.

39. Hunter to Slidell and JMM, Oct. 5, 1861, Confederate States of America, Department of State Papers, vol. 53, LC; also in ORUCN, ser. 2, vol. 3:276.

40. JMM to Hunter, Oct. 5, 1861, Confederate States of America, Department of State Papers, vol. 53, LC; also in ORUCN, ser. 2, vol. 3:276–78.

41. JMM to Hunter, Oct. 9, 1861, Confederate States of America, Department of State Papers, vol. 53, LC; also in ORUCN, ser. 2, vol. 3:280–81.

42. JMM to Eliza Chew Mason, Oct. 9, 1861, in VMPL, 199–200.

43. Slidell and JMM to Hunter, Oct. 11, 1861, Confederate States of America, Department of State Papers, vol. 53, LC; also in ORUCN, ser. 2, vol. 3:281.

44. JMM to Jefferson Davis, Oct. 11, 1861, in *Papers of Jefferson Davis,* ed. Monroe, McIntosh, Crist, Dix, and Williams, vol. 7:356.

45. Bugg, "Political Career of James Murray Mason," 846–47.

46. JMM, memorandum on his voyage to England, in VMPL, 210–11.

47. JMM to Eliza Chew Mason, Oct. 14, 1861, in VMPL, 200–201.

48. JMM to Eliza Chew Mason, Oct. 16, 1861, in VMPL, 201; and JMM, memorandum on his voyage to England, in VMPL, 211.

49. JMM to Eliza Chew Mason, Oct. 18, 1861, in VMPL, 201–2. JMM to Hunter, Oct. 18, 1861, Confederate States of America, Department of State Papers, vol. 53, LC; also in ORUCN, ser. 2, vol. 3:282–83.

50. JMM to Eliza Chew Mason, Oct. 29, 1861, in VMPL, 202–4.

51. Ibid., 203.

52. Ferris, *Trent Affair,* 18–19.

53. Two of Captain Wilkes's officers had conversations with JMM, but the Virginian claimed that he provided nothing beyond that basic information. See JMM, memorandum on his voyage to England, in VMPL, 215.

54. Ibid., 215–16.

55. This action succeeded, as JMM found the papers unmolested and waiting for him when he arrived in England almost three months later.

56. JMM had to be particularly galled at the sight of Lieutenant Fairfax, a Virginian, whose family for years had been "at odds with the Mason clan." Qtd. in Glyndon G. Van Deusen, *William Henry Seward* (New York: Oxford Univ. Press, 1967), 308.

57. See JMM, memorandum on his voyage to England, in VMPL, 216–20. Other accounts of the capture tell virtually the same story. See Ferris, *Trent Affair,* 19–25 and 208–10.

58. That same day, the diplomats recorded the events of their capture in a letter to Wilkes that, at their request, he forwarded to Washington. See Slidell, JMM, Eustis, and MacFarland to Wilkes, Nov. 8, 1861, and Wilkes to Slidell, JMM, Eustis, and MacFarland, Nov. 13, 1861, in JMM Papers, vol. 1, LC. The letter to Wilkes is also in ORUCN, ser. 1, vol. 1:139.

59. Ten days afterwards, the prisoners wrote Wilkes to state "that since we have been on board . . . we have been treated by you with uniform courtesy and attention." Slidell, JMM, Eustis, and MacFarland to Wilkes, Nov. 18, 1861, in JMM Papers, vol. 1, LC. Mason later wrote that, "from the time of our capture, the deportment of Captain Wilkes toward us, was of marked attention and courtesy." JMM, memorandum on his voyage to England, in VMPL, 221–24.

60. JMM to Eliza Chew Mason, Nov. 15, 1861, in ORUCN, ser. 2, vol. 3:296.

61. In describing his voyage to England, JMM repeatedly lambasted Seward, saying that his name "would go with infamy to posterity, were it not rescued from such elevation by contempt." JMM, memorandum on his voyage to England, in VMPL, 232.

62. Ironically, the fort was named after the same Gen. Joseph Warren whom JMM had honored at Bunker Hill over four years earlier.

63. JMM, memorandum on his voyage to England, in VMPL, 224–25.

64. Slidell, JMM, MacFarland, and Eustis to Wilkes, Nov. 20, 1861, in WROR, ser. 2, vol. 2:1096.

65. JMM, memorandum on his voyage to England, in VMPL, 225–27.

66. *Boston Evening Transcript,* Nov. 25, 1861.

67.   Charles Francis Adams, Jr., *1835–1915,* 127–28.

68.   Jefferson Davis, speech to the Provisional Congress, Nov. 18, 1861, in *Papers of Jefferson Davis,* ed. Monroe, McIntosh, Crist, Dix, and Williams, vol. 7:412–19.

69.   For a summary of Confederate editorials and opinions, see Ferris, *Trent Affair,* 117–19; and Gordon H. Warren, *Fountain of Discontent: The Trent Affair and Freedom of the Seas* (Boston: Northeastern Univ. Press, 1981), 43. Historians Lynn M. Case and Warren F. Spencer utilize reports of Confederate glee over the seizure and other pieces of circumstantial evidence to construct an interpretation that stands in stark contrast to all other studies. They conclude that the Richmond government deliberately planned and provoked the incident to gain British intervention. Lynn M. Case and Warren F. Spencer, *The United States and France: Civil War Diplomacy* (Philadelphia: Univ. of Pennsylvania Press, 1970), 190–94.

70.   Using particularly inflammatory language, that paper recalled JMM's 1857 visit to Boston in highly derogatory terms, often using the word *traitor.* See *Boston Evening Transcript,* Nov. 18 and 19, 1861.

71.   Ferris, *Trent Affair,* 32–36; Warren, *Fountain of Discontent,* 38–43.

72.   Yancey, Rost, and Mann to Lord John Russell, Nov. 27, 1861, in Bourne and Watt, *British Documents on Foreign Affairs* 5:352–53.

73.   Russell to Lyons, Nov. 30, 1861, in Bourne and Watt, *British Documents on Foreign Affairs* 5:348–49.

74.   Qtd. in Ephraim Douglass Adams, *Great Britain* 1:217.

75.   Brown Shipley & Co. to Brown Brothers & Co., Nov. 27, 1861, in Pamela C. Copeland, Mason Family Research File, Main Research File, GHL. The file contains 8 letters written in Liverpool by American businessman James Brown. Covering approximately 7 weeks ending on Jan. 17, 1862, all have the *Trent* affair as their primary focus.

76.   *London Times,* Nov. 28, 1861, p. 9. For other British editorial opinions, see Ferris, *Trent Affair,* 47–48; Merli, *Great Britain and the Confederate Navy,* 79–80; Warren, *Fountain of Discontent,* 106–8; and Ephraim Douglass Adams, *Great Britain* 1:216–18.

77.   JMM to Eliza Chew Mason, Nov. 29, 1861, in VMPL, 205–6.

78.   JMM to Eliza Chew Mason, Dec. 3, 1861, in VMPL, 206–7.

79.   JMM to Eliza Chew Mason, Dec. 12, 1861, in VMPL 207–8.

80.   JMM to Eliza Chew Mason, Nov. 29 and Dec. 3, 1861, in VMPL, 205–7.

81.   JMM, memorandum on his voyage to England, in VMPL, 228–31.

82.   Ibid., 232–34.

83.   Rost to Jefferson Davis, Dec. 24, 1861, Confederate States of America, Department of State Papers, vol. 61, LC; also in ORUCN, ser. 2, vol. 3:311–12.

84.   Philip Van Doren Stern, *When the Guns Roared: World Aspects of the American Civil War* (Garden City, N.Y.: Doubleday, 1965), 19–20.

85.   Howard Jones, *Union in Peril: The Crisis over British Intervention in the Civil War* (Chapel Hill: Univ. of North Carolina Press, 1992), 84–85.

86.   Ibid., 88–89.

87.   As early as Nov. 19, Lyons stressed that the secretary of state had a marked tendency to insult the British. Lyons to Russell, Nov. 19, 1861, in Bourne and Watt, *British Documents on Foreign Affairs* 5:361–62.

88.   Van Deusen, *William Henry Seward,* 312–13.

89.   For a detailed account of French actions during the crisis, see Case and Spencer, *United States and France,* 190–249.

90.   Seward to Lyons, Dec. 26, 1861, in Bourne and Watt, *British Documents on Foreign Affairs* 6:9–16.

91.   Yancey to Jefferson Davis, Dec. 30, 1861, in *Papers of Jefferson Davis,* ed. Monroe, McIntosh, Crist, Dix, and Williams, vol. 7:449–50.

92.   Ferris, *Trent Affair,* 192–203.

93.   Young, "Jefferson Davis," 26–27.

94.   JMM to Eliza Chew Mason, Jan. 1, 1862, in VMPL, 208.

95.   JMM, memorandum on his voyage to England, in VMPL, 237.

96.   Extracts from the logbook of the H.M.S. *Rinaldo,* Jan. 1–14, 1862, in JMM Papers, vol. 1, LC.

97.   JMM, memorandum on his voyage to England, in VMPL, 238–45.

98.   Mann to Jefferson Davis, Jan. 18, 1862, Confederate States of America, Department of State Papers, vol. 61, LC; also in ORUCN, ser. 2, vol. 3:318–19.

99.   Yancey and Mann to Hunter #14, Jan. 27, 1862, in ORUCN, ser. 2, vol. 3:319–21.

Chapter 9. 1862: Mason and the Confederate Quest for Diplomatic Intervention

1.   JMM to Hunter #1 and #2, Feb. 2 and 7, 1862, in JMM Papers, Dispatch Book, LC; also in ORUCN, ser. 2, vol. 3:326–28, 330–32.

2.   JMM to Hunter, Jan. 30, 1862, Confederate States of America, Department of State Papers, vol. 53, LC; also in ORUCN, ser. 2, vol. 3:323.

3.   Frank L. Owsley, *King Cotton Diplomacy,* 203.

4.   Chesnut, *Diary from Dixie,* 124.

5.   Frank L. Owsley, *King Cotton Diplomacy,* 203–4.

6.   The array of letters JMM took the time to write in his first weeks in England included one to the first lord of the admiralty, expressing gratitude for "the kindships and hospitality received from the Naval authorities of Great Britain everywhere, on our late protracted voyage"; and one reporting the good health of a prisoner at Fort Warren to the man's son. JMM to the Duke of Somerset, Feb. 13, 1862, JMM Papers, vol. 2, LC; and JMM to Charles Green, Mar. 1, 1862, Mason Family Papers, GHL.

7.   Behind-the-scenes arrangements for the interview were done by a member of Parliament, William H. Gregory. See Gregory to JMM, Feb. 7, 1862; JMM to Russell, Feb. 8, 1862; and Russell to JMM, Feb. 8, 1862, all in JMM Papers, vol. 1, LC; also in ORUCN, ser. 2, vol. 3:332–33, 345, and 346.

8.   JMM to Hunter #4, Feb. 22, 1862, JMM Papers, Dispatch Book, LC; also in ORUCN, ser. 2, vol. 3:343–45.

9.   Ibid.

10.   JMM to Slidell, Feb. 15, 1862, in JMM Papers, vol. 2, LC.

11.   JMM to Slidell, Feb. 27, 1862, in JMM Papers, vol. 2, LC.

12.   Young, "Jefferson Davis," 43–47.

13.   Ephraim Douglass Adams, *Great Britain* 1:140.

14.   JMM to Russell, Feb. 17 and Apr. 1, 1862, in JMM Papers, vol. 2, LC; also in ORUCN, ser. 2, vol. 3:342–43, 373.

15.   Russell to Lyons, Feb. 15, 1862, in Bourne and Watt, *British Documents on Foreign Affairs* 6:42–43.

16.   Benjamin to JMM #2, Apr. 8, 1862, in JMM Papers, vol. 2, LC; also in ORUCN, ser. 2, vol. 3:379–84.

17. JMM to Hunter #5, Feb. 28, 1862, in JMM Papers, Dispatch Book, LC; also in ORUCN, ser. 2, vol. 3:354–55.

18. The most recent and most thorough study of the numerous ships that sailed in and out of Confederate ports during the war is Stephen R. Wise, *Lifeline of the Confederacy: Blockade Running During the Civil War* (Columbia: Univ. of South Carolina Press, 1988).

19. Great Britain, Parliament, *Hansard's Parliamentary Debates*, 3d ser., vol. 165:92–97 (Feb. 7, 1862); 113–15 (Feb. 10, 1862); 526–32 (Feb. 20, 1862); 846–47 (Feb. 28, 1862).

20. JMM to Russell, Feb. 17, 1862, in JMM Papers, vol. 2, LC; also in ORUCN, ser. 2, vol. 3:342–43.

21. Great Britain, Parliament, *Hansard's Parliamentary Debates*, 3d ser., vol. 165:1169 (Mar. 7, 1862).

22. The entire debate is in ibid., vol. 165:1158–1231 (Mar. 7, 1862).

23. Ibid., vol. 165:1236 (Mar. 10, 1862).

24. Ibid., vol. 165:1243 (Mar. 10, 1862).

25. JMM to Hunter #6, Mar. 11, 1862, in JMM Papers, Dispatch Book, LC; also in ORUCN, ser. 2, vol. 3:358–60.

26. William L. Yancey, Pierre A. Rost, and A. Dudley Mann to Russell, Aug. 14, 1861, in ORUCN, ser. 2, vol. 3:238–46.

27. Frank L. Owsley, *King Cotton Diplomacy*, 2–10.

28. JMM to Hunter #6, Mar. 11, 1862, in JMM Papers, Dispatch Book, LC; in ORUCN, ser. 2, vol. 3:358–60.

29. JMM's miscellaneous expense records through Nov. 16, 1863, are in JMM Papers, vol. 2, LC.

30. Hunter to JMM #4, Feb. 8, 1862, in JMM Papers, vol. 1, LC; also in ORUCN, ser. 2, vol. 3:333–36.

31. Benjamin to JMM #2, Apr. 8, 1862, in JMM Papers, vol. 2, LC; also in ORUCN, ser. 2, vol. 3:379–84.

32. Benjamin to JMM #3, Apr. 12, 1862, in JMM Papers, vol. 2, LC; also in ORUCN, ser. 2, vol. 3:384–86.

33. JMM to Benjamin #8, Apr. 21, 1862, in JMM Papers, Dispatch Book, LC; also in ORUCN, ser. 2, vol. 3:397–99.

34. For a full discussion of French foreign policy with regard to the American Civil War, see Case and Spencer, *United States and France*.

35. Details of JMM's social calendar from January through July 1862 are provided in VMPL, 340–42.

36. Frank L. Owsley, *King Cotton Diplomacy*, 610.

37. Mary Ellison, *Support for Secession: Lancashire and the American Civil War* (Chicago: Univ. of Chicago Press, 1972), 110.

38. A biographical note on James Spence appears in appendix 12 of Richard I. Lester, *Confederate Finance and Purchasing in Great Britain* (Charlottesville: Univ. Press of Virginia, 1975), 241–42. Also see Frank L. Owsley, *King Cotton Diplomacy*, 365; and Ephraim Douglass Adams, *Great Britain* 1:266.

39. James Spence, *The American Union: Its Effect on National Character and Policy, with an Inquiry into Secession as a Constitutional Right, and the Causes of Disruption* (London: Richard Bentley, New Burlington Street, Publisher in Ordinary to Her Majesty, 1862).

40. Spence to JMM, Mar. 18, 1862, in JMM Papers, vol. 2, LC.

41.   JMM to Benjamin #8, Apr. 21, 1862, in JMM Papers, Dispatch Book, LC; also in ORUCN, ser. 2, vol. 3:397–99.

42.   JMM to Jefferson Davis, May 16, 1862, in JMM Papers, Dispatch Book, LC; also in ORUCN, ser. 2, vol. 3:425–26.

43.   This was usually done by way of "enclosures," so that Richmond received copies of JMM's correspondence with others regarding financial matters.

44.   JMM to Benjamin #9, #10, #11, May 2, 15, and 16, 1862, in JMM Papers, Dispatch Book, LC; also in ORUCN, ser. 2, vol. 3:401–2, 420–22, 424–25.

45.   Hotze to Hunter, Feb. 28, 1862, in Confederate State Department Papers, vol. 54, LC; also in ORUCN, ser. 2, vol. 3:352–54.

46.   Spence to JMM, Apr. 28, 1862, in JMM Papers, vol. 2, LC; also in ORUCN, ser. 2, vol. 3:402–5, enclosed with JMM to Benjamin #9, May 2, 1862, in JMM Papers, Dispatch Book, LC; also in ORUCN, ser. 2, vol. 3:401–2.

47.   Benjamin to JMM #6, July 19, 1862, in JMM Papers, vol. 2, LC; VMPL, 295–303.

48.   Benjamin to Slidell #3, Apr. 12, 1862, Confederate State Department Papers, vol. 15, LC; also in ORUCN, ser. 2, vol. 3:386–90.

49.   Hotze to Benjamin #7, Apr. 25, 1862, Confederate State Department Papers, vol. 54, LC; also in ORUCN, ser. 2, vol. 3:399–401.

50.   Ironically, this letter was not received by Rost; instead it was intercepted by U.S. agents and landed on the desk of President Lincoln. JMM to Rost, Apr. 24, 1862, in Abraham Lincoln Papers, Reel 35, LC.

51.   JMM to Benjamin #13, June 23, 1862, in JMM Papers, Dispatch Book, LC; also in ORUCN, ser. 2, vol. 3:448–49.

52.   For details of those Confederate military campaigns, see three books that, in addition to telling the story of southern armies, include discussions of Confederate diplomacy: Frank Vandiver, *Their Tattered Flags: The Epic of the Confederacy* (New York: Harper and Row, 1970); Thomas, *Confederate Nation*; and Eaton, *History of the Southern Confederacy.*

53.   Unemployment due to the shortage peaked in December. See Frank L. Owsley, *King Cotton Diplomacy,* 136–37.

54.   JMM to Benjamin #13, June 23, 1862, in JMM Papers, Dispatch Book, LC; also in ORUCN, ser. 2, vol. 3:448–49.

55.   In June, Spence wrote to JMM that, even though the tide of opinion was moving favorably, it still was not a good time to push the ministry. He also said that he had advised Lindsay to postpone a motion for recognition that Lindsay intended to introduce in the House of Commons. Spence to JMM, June 3 and 11, 1862, in JMM Papers, vol. 2, LC.

56.   The Confederacy's first secretary of state, Robert Toombs of Georgia, once commented that the duties of the office were so small that the entire department existed under his hat. See Rembert W. Patrick, *Jefferson Davis and His Cabinet* (Baton Rouge: Louisiana State Univ. Press, 1944), 84–85.

57.   Young, "Jefferson Davis," 30.

58.   Benjamin to JMM #1, #2, #3, Apr. 5, 8, 12, 1862, in JMM Papers, vol. 2, LC; also in ORUCN, ser. 2, 3: 373–78, 379–84, 384–86.

59.   JMM complained to Benjamin in May about having received no letters from Richmond, which left a bad impression of the Confederacy on his British acquaintances. He wrote that "constant inquiry is made what I hear from home, and when I answer that I get nothing, a doubt seems implied that the Government hesitates to

commit itself to persistence in the war." JMM to Benjamin #10, in JMM Papers, Dispatch Book, LC; also in ORUCN, ser. 2, vol. 3:420–22.

60.   VMPL, 247.

61.   Benjamin to JMM #2, Apr. 8, 1862, in JMM Papers, vol. 2, LC; also in ORUCN, ser. 2, vol. 3:379–84.

62.   Jefferson Davis, *Rise and Fall* 2:10–11.

63.   Benjamin to JMM #2, Apr. 8, 1862, in JMM Papers, vol. 2, LC; also in ORUCN, ser. 2, vol. 3:379–84.

64.   Despite such statements, however, by that time the Confederacy was contributing to the shortage by destroying cotton in order to increase the diplomatic pressure on Britain and France. See Howard Jones, *Union in Peril*, 130–31.

65.   JMM to Russell, July 7, 1862, in JMM Papers, Dispatch Book, LC; also in ORUCN, ser. 2, vol. 3:495–98.

66.   Great Britain, Parliament, *Hansard's Parliamentary Debates*, 3d ser., vol. 167:1213–14 (June 30, 1862).

67.   Ibid., vol. 167:168–511 (July 18, 1862).

68.   Ibid., vol. 167:168–570 (July 18, 1862).

69.   The entire debate is in the same volume: Great Britain, Parliament, *Hansard's Parliamentary Debates*, 3d ser., vol. 168:511–78 (July 18, 1862).

70.   Slidell wrote that parliament "seems to be as afraid of him [Palmerston] as the urchins of a village school of the birch of their pedagogue." Slidell to JMM, July 11, 1862, in JMM Papers, vol. 2, LC.

71.   JMM to Eliza Chew Mason, July 20, 1862, in Pamela C. Copeland, Mason Family Research File, Main Research File, GHL; also in VMPL, 279–81.

72.   Jefferson Davis to his wife Varina, July 6, 1862, in Rowland, *Jefferson Davis, Constitutionalist* 5:291.

73.   Benjamin to JMM #6, July 19, 1862, in JMM Papers, vol. 2, LC; VMPL, 295–303.

74.   Spence to JMM, July 11, 1862, in JMM Papers, vol. 2, LC.

75.   Benjamin to JMM #6, July 19, 1862, in JMM Papers, vol. 2, LC; VMPL, 295–303.

76.   JMM to Russell, July 17, 1862, in JMM Papers, Dispatch Book, LC; also in ORUCN, ser. 2, vol. 3:498–99.

77.   Russell to JMM, July 24, 1862, in JMM Papers, vol. 3, LC; also in ORUCN, ser. 2, vol. 3:499.

78.   JMM to Russell, July 24, 1862, in JMM Papers, Dispatch Book, LC; also in ORUCN, ser. 2, vol. 3:500.

79.   Russell to JMM, July 31, 1862, in JMM Papers, vol. 3, LC; also in ORUCN, ser. 2, vol. 3:501.

80.   JMM to Russell, Aug. 1, 1862, in JMM Papers, Dispatch Book, LC; also in ORUCN, ser. 2, vol. 3:501–3.

81.   Russell to JMM, Aug. 2, 1862, in JMM Papers, vol. 3, LC; also in ORUCN, ser. 2, vol. 3:503–4.

82.   Hendrick, *Statesmen of the Lost Cause*, 280.

83.   Ephraim Douglass Adams, *Great Britain* 2:27–46, discusses the events of that two-month period in Britain. For the story of Lee's army and the battles of Second Manassas and Sharpsburg, see Dowdey, *Land They Fought For*, 197–221.

84.   David F. Krein, *The Last Palmerston Government: Foreign Policy, Domestic Politics, and the Genius of "Splendid Isolation"* (Ames: Iowa State Univ. Press, 1978), 67.

85.   Kinley J. Brauer, "British Mediation and the American Civil War: A Reconsideration," *Journal of Southern History* 38, no. 1 (1972): 51–54.

86.   Ephraim Douglass Adams, *Great Britain* 2:36–41.

87.   JMM to Slidell, Aug. 3, 1862, in JMM Papers, vol. 3, LC.

88.   Slidell to Benjamin #12, Aug. 24, 1862, Confederate State Department Papers, vol. 55, LC; also in ORUCN, ser. 2, vol. 3:520–21.

89.   Krein, *Last Palmerston Government*, 67–68.

90.   Frank J. Merli and Theodore A. Wilson, "The British Cabinet and the Confederacy: Autumn 1862," *Maryland Historical Magazine* 65, no. 3 (1970): 247–48.

91.   Brauer, "British Mediation," 57.

92.   JMM to Benjamin #17, Sept. 18, 1862, in JMM Papers, Dispatch Book, LC; also in ORUCN, ser. 2, vol. 3:533.

93.   Frank L. Owsley, *King Cotton Diplomacy*, 347–48.

94.   JMM believed that Lincoln's proclamation "was issued under the promptings of their Minister Adams, as the means of warding off recognition." JMM wrote that the document "had little effect . . . and met with general contempt and derision." JMM to Benjamin #20, Nov. 7, 1862, in JMM Papers, Dispatch Book, LC; also in ORUCN, ser. 2, vol. 3:600–601.

95.   Russell, Memorandum, Oct. 13, 1862, in Bourne and Watt, *British Documents on Foreign Affairs,* ser. C, vol. 6:91–96.

96.   Ibid.

97.   Brauer, "British Mediation," 58–60.

98.   JMM to Lord Bath, Sept. 12, 1862, in Mason Family Research File, Main Research File, GHL.

99.   JMM to his son George Mason, Oct. 1, 1862, in VMPL, 342–43.

100.   JMM to Benjamin #23, Dec. 11, 1862, in JMM Papers, Dispatch Book, LC; also in ORUCN, ser. 2, vol. 3:618–19.

101.   Henry Blumenthal, "Confederate Diplomacy: Popular Notions and International Realities," *Journal of Southern History* 32, no. 2 (1966): 166–67. Also see Krein, *Last Palmerston Government,* 74–76; and Merli and Wilson, "British Cabinet and the Confederacy," 259–62.

102.   Howard Jones, *Union in Peril,* 30–32.

103.   Ibid., 34–35 and 126.

104.   Seward had issued those instructions in August, but Adams did not inform Russell of them until then. Merli and Wilson, "British Cabinet and the Confederacy," 259.

105.   Ephraim Douglass Adams, *Great Britain* 2:55.

106.   Brauer, "British Mediation," 62–64.

107.   Lewis's role in preventing British intervention in 1862 is emphasized in Howard Jones, *Union in Peril,* 189–98 and 210–30.

108.   Krein, *Last Palmerston Government,* 72–73.

109.   Russell to Cowley, Nov. 13, 1862, in Bourne and Watt, *British Documents on Foreign Affairs,* ser. C, vol. 6:111–12.

110.   Merli and Wilson, "British Cabinet and the Confederacy," 260–62.

111.   Spence to JMM, Oct. 13, 1862, in JMM Papers, vol. 3, LC.

112.   Throughout the year, JMM dealt with aspects of Confederate purchasing, with October being no exception. See various purchasing agreements and statements, in JMM Papers, vol. 3, LC.

113.   Reported in JMM to Benjamin #19, Nov. 4, 1862, in JMM Papers, Dispatch Book, LC; also in ORUCN, ser. 2, vol. 3:590–93.

114.   JMM to Benjamin (unofficial), Nov. 8, 1862, Confederate State Department Papers, vol. 53, LC; also in ORUCN, ser. 2, vol. 3:602–3.
115.   Slidell to Benjamin #20, Nov. 11, 1862, Confederate State Department Papers, vol. 55, LC; also in ORUCN, ser. 2, vol. 3:603–4.
116.   JMM to Benjamin #20, Nov. 7, 1862, in JMM Papers, Dispatch Book, LC; also in ORUCN, ser. 2, vol. 3:600–601.
117.   JMM to Benjamin #23, Dec. 11, 1862, in JMM Papers, Dispatch Book, LC; also in ORUCN, ser. 2, vol. 3:618–19.
118.   Blumenthal, "Confederate Diplomacy," 159.
119.   Frank L. Owsley, *King Cotton Diplomacy,* 552–53.
120.   Benjamin to JMM #11, Dec. 11, 1862, in JMM Papers, vol. 3, LC; also in ORUCN, ser. 2, vol. 3:619–25.
121.   Jefferson Davis, *Rise and Fall* 1:402.
122.   Benjamin to JMM #9, Oct. 31, 1862, in JMM Papers, vol. 3, LC; also in ORUCN, ser. 2, vol. 3:584–88.
123.   JMM to Russell, Jan. 3, 1863, in JMM Papers, Dispatch Book, LC; also in ORUCN, ser. 2, vol. 3:643–45.
124.   JMM to Eliza Chew Mason, Dec. 28, 1862, in VMPL, 367–69.
125.   On Oct. 1, 1862, JMM wrote to his son, George Mason, "You will have heard how the vandals, whilst in Winchester, desolated our dear home, and that your excellent mother and sisters had, very prudently, abandoned it in advance." He drew comfort "that they are all safe in the southern part of the State, and in the midst of a body of friends, able and willing to guide and protect them." In VMPL, 342–43.
126.   Laura Lee, Diary, Apr. 26, 1862, Item No. 1242–12 WFCHS, Archives Room, HLWV.
127.   JMM to Eliza Chew Mason, Jan. 18, 1863, in VMPL, 371–73.
128.   JMM to Benjamin #27, Jan. 15, 1863, in JMM Papers, Dispatch Book, LC; also in ORUCN, ser. 2, vol. 3:653–54.

Chapter 10. 1862–1865: Mason and Confederate Purchasing, Shipbuilding, and Finance

1.   Jefferson Davis, *Rise and Fall* 1:313–14.
2.   Bulloch to Mallory, Aug. 13, 1861, in ORUCN, ser. 2, vol. 2:83–87.
3.   North to Mallory, Aug. 16, 1861, in ORUCN, ser. 2, vol. 2:87.
4.   The most complete study of the Confederacy's attempts to finance its overseas purchases is Lester, *Confederate Finance.*
5.   John C. Schwab, *The Confederate States of America, 1861–1865: A Financial and Industrial History of the South during the Civil War* (New York: Charles Scribner's Sons, 1901), 169–73. A more recent study of the Confederate economy is Douglas B. Ball, *Financial Failure and Confederate Defeat* (Urbana: Univ. of Illinois Press, 1991).
6.   Charles S. Davis, *Colin J. McRae: Confederate Financial Agent* (Tuscaloosa, Ala.: Confederate Publishing Co., 1961), 49.
7.   Frank L. Owsley, *King Cotton Diplomacy,* 360–61.
8.   Vandiver, *Their Tattered Flags,* 231–33. He also passed along to A. Dudley Mann in Brussels a great deal of both money and correspondence, rather than either being sent directly to Belgium. See, e.g., JMM to Mann, July 1 and Dec. 29, 1862, in JMM Papers, vols. 2 and 4, LC.
9.   Semmes to JMM, Jan. 24, 1862; JMM to Semmes, Feb. 1 and 2, 1862; and JMM to Fraser, Trenholm and Co., Feb. 1, 1862; all in ORUCN, ser. 2, vol. 3:329–

30. Fraser, Trenholm and Co. to JMM, Feb. 19 and 21, 1862, in JMM Papers, vol. 2, LC.

10. The fate of Fraser, Trenholm and Company became so intertwined with that of the Confederacy that the firm had to declare bankruptcy at the end of the war. See Warren F. Spencer, *The Confederate Navy in Europe* (Tuscaloosa: Univ. of Alabama Press, 1983), 6.

11. Fraser, Trenholm and Co. to JMM, June 10, 1862, in JMM Papers, vol. 2, LC.

12. Semmes to JMM, Mar. 14 and 19, and Apr. 28, 1862, in JMM Papers, vol. 2, LC. Secretary of the Navy Stephen R. Mallory earlier had instructed JMM to insure that Semmes had adequate resources at his disposal. Mallory to JMM, Mar. 1, 1862, in JMM Papers, vol. 2, LC; also in ORUCN, ser. 1, vol. 1:670.

13. Bulloch to JMM, May 3, 1862, in JMM Papers, vol. 2, LC.

14. JMM to Benjamin #9, May 2, 1862, JMM Papers, Dispatch Book, LC; also in ORUCN, ser. 2, vol. 3:401–2.

15. Spence to JMM, Apr. 28, 1862, in JMM Papers, vol. 2, LC; also in ORUCN, ser. 2, vol. 3:402–5.

16. Receipt for cotton bonds, Aug. 6, 1862, in JMM Papers, vol. 3, LC.

17. James Galbraith and Edgar P. Stringer to JMM, Sept. 17, 1862; Stringer to JMM, Sept. 23 and Oct. 13, 1862; and Bulloch to JMM, Sept. 15, 1862; all in JMM Papers, vol. 3, LC. The last item is also in ORUCN, ser. 2, vol. 2:268.

18. JMM to Benjamin #16, Sept. 18, 1862, in JMM Papers, Dispatch Book, LC; and JMM to Mallory, Sept. 18, 1862, Confederate States of America, Department of State Papers, vol. 53, LC. Both are also in ORUCN, ser. 2, vol. 3:529–32.

19. Lester, *Confederate Finance,* 19–21; Spencer, *Confederate Navy in Europe,* 86–91.

20. Slidell to JMM, Sept. 26, 1862, in JMM Papers, vol. 3, LC.

21. Slidell to JMM, Oct. 29, Nov. 1, and 4, 1862, in JMM Papers, vol. 3, LC; and Richard I. Lester, "An Aspect of Confederate Finance During the American Civil War: The Erlanger Loan and the Plan of 1864," *Business History* 16, no. 2 (1974): 130.

22. A copy of the contract, dated Oct. 28, 1862, is in JMM Papers, vol. 3, LC.

23. The Richmond government's approval of JMM's actions regarding the Sinclair bonds is expressed in Benjamin to JMM #8, Oct. 28, 1862, in JMM Papers, vol. 3, LC; also in ORUCN, ser. 2, vol. 3:581–82.

24. JMM to Benjamin #19, Nov. 4, 1862, in JMM Papers, Dispatch Book, LC; also in ORUCN, ser. 2, vol. 3:590–93.

25. JMM to Benjamin #22, Dec. 10, 1862, in JMM Papers, Dispatch Book, LC; also in ORUCN, ser. 2, vol. 3:617–18.

26. Spence expressed great distrust of Erlanger, largely because he feared that his own role would be diminished if the loan gained approval. Spence to JMM, Dec. 31, 1862, and Jan. 12, 1863, in JMM Papers, vol. 4, LC.

27. Spence to JMM, Feb. 6, 1863, in JMM Papers, vol. 4, LC.

28. Hudson Strode, *Jefferson Davis: Confederate President* (New York: Harcourt Brace and Co., 1959), 368.

29. Lindsay's plan would not nearly have met Confederate needs, so Jefferson Davis chose the Erlanger proposal. Benjamin wrote to JMM that the president would have rejected that offer out of hand "but for the political considerations indicated by Mr. Slidell, in whose judgement in such matters we are disposed to place a very great confidence." Benjamin to JMM #12, Jan. 15, 1863, in JMM Papers, vol. 4, LC; also in ORUCN, ser. 2, vol. 3:648–51.

30. Lester, *Confederate Finance,* 27–31.

31. Judith Fenner Gentry, "A Confederate Success in Europe: The Erlanger Loan," *Journal of Southern History* 36, no. 2 (1970): 158–60.

32. JMM did not meet personally with Erlanger until late Feb. See Slidell to JMM, Feb. 23 and 24, 1863, in JMM Papers, vol. 4, LC.

33. JMM to Slidell, Jan. 9, 1863, in JMM Papers, vol. 4, LC.

34. Bulloch to JMM, Jan. 5, Jan. 20, and Feb. 4, 1863, all in JMM Papers, vol. 4, LC; also in ORUCN, ser. 2, vol. 2:330–31, 342, and 352.

35. See, e.g., Caleb Huse to JMM, Jan. 31, 1863; and North to JMM, Feb. 3 and 19, 1863, all in JMM Papers, vol. 4, LC. The latter two are also in ORUCN, ser. 2, vol. 2:350–51 and 364.

36. JMM to Slidell, Jan. 28, 1863, in JMM Papers, vol. 4, LC.

37. North to JMM, Feb. 19 and Mar. 4, 1863, both in JMM Papers, vol. 4, LC; also in ORUCN, ser. 2, vol. 2:364 and 370.

38. JMM to North, Feb. 21, 1863, in ORUCN, ser. 2, vol. 2:366.

39. JMM to North, Mar. 18, 1863, in ORUCN, ser. 2, vol. 2:375.

40. Gentry, "Confederate Success," 176–78.

41. JMM to Benjamin #29, Feb. 5, 1863, in JMM Papers, Dispatch Book, LC; also in ORUCN, ser. 2, vol. 3:675–77.

42. JMM to Benjamin #31, Mar. 19, 1863, in JMM Papers, Dispatch Book, LC; also in ORUCN, ser. 2, vol. 3:712–16.

43. JMM to Benjamin #32, Mar. 30, 1863, in JMM Papers, Dispatch Book, LC; also in ORUCN, ser. 2, vol. 3:730–31.

44. Slidell to Benjamin #29, Mar. 21, 1863, in ORUCN, ser. 2, vol. 3:720–21.

45. JMM to Erlanger & Co., Apr. 24, 1863, and JMM to Benjamin (unofficial), Apr. 27, 1863, Confederate States of America, Department of State Papers, vol. 53, LC; also in ORUCN, ser. 2, vol. 3:749 and 751–53.

46. Lester, *Confederate Finance,* 37–40.

47. JMM to Benjamin (unofficial), Apr. 9, 1863, in JMM Papers, vol. 5, LC; also in ORUCN, ser. 2, vol. 3:735–37. That letter was not in JMM's dispatch book, making it unofficial. The ORUCN incorrectly labels it dispatch #33, even though earlier a Mar. 30 letter to Benjamin is corrected labeled #33.

48. Lester, "Aspect of Confederate Finance," 137. JMM labeled the Vicksburg siege the cause of a decrease to par in May, and in September he referred to both Vicksburg and Gettysburg as having "a most depressing effect on the barometer of the stock exchange." JMM to Benjamin #36 and #44, May 11 and Sept. 4, 1863, in JMM Papers, Dispatch Book, LC; also in ORUCN, ser. 2, vol. 3:766 and 890–92.

49. JMM to Benjamin #45, Sept. 5, 1863, in JMM Papers, Dispatch Book, LC; also in ORUCN, ser. 2, vol. 3:896–97.

50. Schwab, *Confederate States,* 35–36.

51. Frank L. Owsley, *King Cotton Diplomacy,* 380.

52. Gentry, "Confederate Success," 170–71.

53. That estimate appears to be more accurate from a financial standpoint and is similar to the number in Ball, *Financial Failure,* 284–85. The Erlanger loan can be called a success when placed within the context of the weakened Confederate economy, which had deteriorated markedly since 1861. The amount of currency in circulation had risen to nearly $700 million; its value had depreciated rapidly, as domestic prices rose in an uncontrolled fashion. All this gave European financial experts an unfavorable impression of the Confederacy. Schwab, *Confederate States,* 165–67.

54. Crenshaw to JMM, Mar. 20, Apr. 27, and June 4, 1863; Sinclair to JMM, Apr. 5, 1863; and Maury to JMM, Apr. 22 and 28, 1863; all in JMM Papers, vol. 5, LC.

55. JMM to North, Mar. 23, 1863, in JMM Papers, vol. 5, LC; also in ORUCN, ser. 2, vol. 2:393.

56. North to JMM, Mar. 30 and Apr. 4, 1863, in JMM Papers, vol. 5, LC; also in ORUCN, ser. 2, vol. 2:397–99.

57. North to JMM, Apr. 16 and 23, 1863, both in JMM Papers, vol. 5, LC; also in ORUCN, ser. 2, vol. 2:404 and 408.

58. JMM to North, Apr. 20, 1863, in JMM Papers, vol. 5, LC; also in ORUCN, ser. 2, vol. 2:405.

59. North to JMM, May 21, 1863; also in ORUCN, ser. 2, vol. 2:426.

60. Ball, *Financial Failure*, 70–78.

61. JMM to Eliza Chew Mason, May 12, 1863, in VMPL, 408–9.

62. JMM to Slidell, May 14, 1863, in JMM Papers, vol. 5, LC; also in ORUCN, ser. 2, vol. 2:422–23.

63. Benjamin to Christopher Memminger, James A. Seddon, and Mallory, Sept. 15, 1863, in ORUCN, ser. 2, vol. 3:896–99.

64. Frank L. Owsley, *King Cotton Diplomacy*, 382–86; Lester, *Confederate Finance*, 48 and 189.

65. Asked by Sinclair for money in July, JMM responded, "I have none under my control," as, since McRae's arrival, "everything pertaining to money . . . must be referred to him." JMM to Sinclair, July 20, 1863, in ORUCN, ser. 2, vol. 2:466.

66. The most thorough study of Confederate shipbuilding in Britain is Merli, *Great Britain and the Confederate Navy*.

67. Frank L. Owsley, *King Cotton Diplomacy*, 402–6.

68. D. P. Crook, *The North, the South, and the Powers, 1861–1865* (New York: John Wiley and Sons, 1974), 258–61. For U.S. protests, see Charles Francis Adams to Lord Russell, Sept. 30 and Oct. 9, 1862, in Bourne and Watt, *British Documents on Foreign Affairs* 6:88 and 90.

69. Mallory to Charles M. Conrad, May 10, 1861, in ORUCN, ser. 2, vol. 2:67–69.

70. For a concise study of the diplomatic and legal maneuvers surrounding those rams, see Wilbur D. Jones, *The Confederate Rams at Birkenhead: A Chapter in Anglo-American Relations* (Tuscaloosa, Ala.: Confederate Publishing Co., 1961).

71. Bulloch to Mallory, Dec. 2, 1862, in ORUCN, ser. 2, vol. 2:306–7.

72. Case and Spencer, *United States and France*, 429–30.

73. Slidell to JMM, Mar. 15, 1863, in JMM Papers, vol. 4, LC.

74. Benjamin to JMM #17, Mar. 27, 1863, in JMM Papers, vol. 5, LC; also in ORUCN, ser. 2, vol. 3:728–29.

75. Spence to JMM, Apr. 10, 1863, in JMM Papers, vol. 5, LC.

76. L. C. Duncan to JMM, Apr. 15, 1863, in JMM Papers, vol. 5, LC.

77. JMM to Benjamin #37, May 16, 1863, in JMM Papers, Dispatch Book, LC; also in ORUCN, ser. 2, vol. 3:772–73.

78. JMM to Benjamin #38, June 4, 1863, in JMM Papers, Dispatch Book, LC; also in ORUCN, ser. 2, vol. 3:782–83.

79. Bulloch to Mallory, June 30, 1863, in ORUCN, ser. 2, vol. 2:444–47.

80. Lucius Q. C. Lamar, Slidell, and JMM to North, in ORUCN, ser. 2, vol. 2:439–40.

81. Merli, *Great Britain and the Confederate Navy*, 89–93.

82. Ephraim Douglass Adams, *Great Britain* 2:136–39.

83. The first letter on the subject from U.S. Minister Charles Francis Adams to Russell was dated July 11. Nine additional letters followed over the next three months: Adams to Russell, July 11 and 25; Aug. 14; Sept. 3, 4, 5, 16, 24, and 29; and Oct. 12,

1863; all in Bourne and Watt, *British Documents on Foreign Affairs* 6:158–59, 162, 164–65, 169–70, 172–73, 185–88, 195–96, and 218.

84.   Russell to JMM, Slidell, and Mann, Feb. 13, 1865, and JMM, Slidell, and Mann to Russell, Feb. 27, 1865, both in JMM Papers, vol. 8, LC; also in ORUCN, ser. 2, vol. 3:1267–70.

85.   After the war, both Bulloch and Jefferson Davis continued to press the case for the legality of constructing ships in Europe. Bulloch wrote that the Confederacy, "in the effort to supply its wants in England . . . acted with due circumspection, and endeavored to conform to the laws of the realm and to the principles of neutrality." Davis also stressed legality, asserting that the ships seized by the British government were "purchased in Great Britain, as a neutral country with strict observance both of the law of nations and the municipal law of Great Britain." See James D. Bulloch, *The Secret Service of the Confederate States in Europe; or, How the Confederate Cruisers Were Equipped* (London: Richard Bentley and Son, 1883), vol. 1:458–59; Jefferson Davis, *Rise and Fall* 2:381.

86.   Frank J. Merli, "Crown versus Cruiser: The Curious Case of the *Alexandra*," *Civil War History* 9, no. 2 (1963): 167–77.

87.   Merli, *Great Britain and the Confederate Navy*, 167–75; Spencer, *Confederate Navy in Europe*, 102–5.

88.   North to JMM, June 26, 1863, in JMM Papers, vol. 6, LC; and JMM to North, June 27, 1863, in ORUCN, ser. 2, vol. 2:443.

89.   Under great pressure from Adams, Lord Russell had decided on that course of action in early September. But not until five weeks of cabinet debate gave him the necessary support within the government did the confiscation occur. See David F. Krein, "Russell's Decision to Detain the Laird Rams," *Civil War History* 22, no. 2 (1976): 158–63; Merli, *Great Britain and the Confederate Navy*, 200–210; Wilbur D. Jones, *Confederate Rams*, 55–58; Spencer, *Confederate Navy in Europe*, 110–11.

90.   Bulloch to Mallory, Oct. 20, 1863, in ORUCN, ser. 2, vol. 2:507–11.

91.   JMM to Benjamin (unofficial), Oct. 19, 1863, in JMM Papers, Dispatch Book, LC; also in ORUCN, ser. 2, vol. 3:934–35.

92.   Benjamin to JMM #30, Aug. 4, 1863, in JMM Papers, vol. 6, LC; also in ORUCN, ser. 2, vol. 3:852.

93.   JMM to Slidell, Sept. 15, 1863, in JMM Papers, vol. 6, LC; also in ORUCN, ser. 2, vol. 2:493.

94.   Slidell to JMM, Sept. 17, 1863, in JMM Papers, vol. 6, LC.

95.   JMM to North, Nov. 27, 1863, in ORUCN, ser. 2, vol. 2:528.

96.   Benjamin to JMM #32, Nov. 13, 1863, in JMM Papers, vol. 6, LC; also in ORUCN, ser. 2, vol. 3:950–51.

97.   Bulloch to Mallory, Oct. 20, 1863, in ORUCN, ser. 2, vol. 2:507–11.

98.   Bulloch to Mallory, Aug. 7, 1863, in ORUCN, ser. 2, vol. 2:476–78.

99.   Crook, *North, South, and Powers*, 327–28.

100.   Case and Spencer, *United States and France*, 462–63.

101.   Frank L. Owsley, *King Cotton Diplomacy*, 423–24.

102.   Bulloch to Mallory, Aug. 5, 1864, in ORUCN, ser. 2, vol. 2:697–98.

103.   Lindsay to JMM, Jan. 8, 1864, in JMM Papers, vol. 6, LC.

104.   Bulloch to Mallory, Feb. 17, 1864, in ORUCN, ser. 2, vol. 2:583–86.

105.   JMM to Benjamin #3 (with his new commission, he numbered his dispatches starting with #1 again), Feb. 18, 1864, in JMM Papers, Dispatch Book, LC; also in ORUCN, ser. 2, vol. 3:1030–31.

106.   JMM to Jefferson Davis, Feb. 19, 1864, in Joseph O. Baylen and William W.

White, "JMM and the Failure of the Confederate Naval Effort in Europe, 1863–1864," *Louisiana Studies* 2, no. 2 (1963): 101–3.

107.   Bulloch to Mallory, Feb. 17, 1864, in ORUCN, ser. 2, vol. 2:583–86.

108.   Jefferson Davis to Russell, Apr. 1864, qtd. in Hudson Strode, *Jefferson Davis: Tragic Hero* (New York: Harcourt Brace and Co., 1964), 27.

109.   Merli, *Great Britain and the Confederate Navy,* 210–12; Spencer, *Confederate Navy in Europe,* 113–16.

110.   Frank L. Owsley, *King Cotton Diplomacy,* 381–82.

111.   Bulloch to Mallory, Jan. 24, 1864, in ORUCN, ser. 2, vol. 2:575–78.

112.   Semmes to JMM, June 21, 1864, in JMM Papers, vol. 7, LC. Brief accounts of the *Alabama*'s sinking are in Merli, *Great Britain and the Confederate Navy,* 94–98; and Spencer, *Confederate Navy in Europe,* 185–91.

113.   For a discussion of the Confederate naval effort in the war's final months, see Spencer, *Confederate Navy in Europe,* 177–207.

114.   Journal of John R. Thompson, Oct. 20, 1864, in John R. Thompson Collection, Box 2, ALUV.

115.   Sinclair to JMM, Jan. 15, 1865, in JMM Papers, vol. 8, LC.

116.   Merli, *Great Britain and the Confederate Navy,* 195–96.

117.   *London Times,* Sept. 7, 1863.

118.   Young, "Jefferson Davis," 43–47.

Chapter 11. 1863: Disappointment, Disillusion, Defeat

1.   JMM to Russell, Jan. 3, 1863, in JMM Papers, Dispatch Book, LC; also in ORUCN, ser. 2, vol. 3:643–45.

2.   Secretary of State Benjamin wrote to propagandist Edwin De Leon that "universal conviction on this side attributes the injustice and unfairness . . . to one cause alone . . . fear of the North." Benjamin to De Leon, Jan. 16, 1863, in ORUCN, ser. 2, vol. 3:657.

3.   Jefferson Davis, *Rise and Fall* 2:376.

4.   Jefferson Davis, speech to the Confederate Congress, Jan. 12, 1863, in Rowland, *Jefferson Davis, Constitutionalist* 5:396–419.

5.   Stephen R. Wise, *Lifeline of the Confederacy,* 221.

6.   Ibid., 227–328, contains 22 detailed appendices that list departures and arrivals for Confederate ports and trace the histories of the individual blockade-running vessels.

7.   Case and Spencer, *United States and France,* 547–55.

8.   James P. Baxter, "The British Government and Neutral Rights, 1861–1865," *American Historical Review* 34, no. 4 (1928): 9–29; James P. Baxter, "Some British Opinions as to Neutral Rights, 1861–1865," *American Journal of International Law* 23, no. 3 (1929): 517–37.

9.   Jefferson Davis, speech to the Confederate Congress, Dec. 7, 1863, in Rowland, *Jefferson Davis: Constitutionalist* 6:93–128.

10.   JMM to Russell, Feb. 16 and 18, 1863, in JMM Papers, Dispatch Book, LC; also in ORUCN, ser. 2, vol. 3:694–97.

11.   Russell to JMM, Feb. 10, 19, and 27, 1863, in JMM Papers, vol. 4, LC; also in ORUCN, ser. 2, vol. 3:688–89, 697, and 703–4.

12.   JMM to Benjamin #27, Jan. 15, 1863, in JMM Papers, Dispatch Book, LC; also in ORUCN, ser. 2, vol. 3:653–54.

13.   JMM, memorandum, Feb. 11, 1863, in VMPL, 388–89. An account of the

evening's festivities, including JMM's speech, appeared in the *London Times,* Feb. 12, 1863.

14.   His calendar did not include activities that would put him in contact with diplomats from other countries. Isolated by the British ministry's refusal to grant diplomatic recognition to the Confederacy, he rarely saw them, and then only briefly, when he attended sessions of Parliament or in other crowded situations that rendered any personal conversation exceedingly difficult.

15.   JMM to Eliza Chew Mason, Jan. 18, 1863, in VMPL, 371–73.

16.   See, e.g., Bulloch to JMM, Jan. 5, Jan. 20, and Feb. 4, 1863, and North to JMM, Feb. 3 and 19, 1863, in JMM Papers, vol. 4, LC; also in ORUCN, ser. 2, vol. 2:330–31, 342, 350–51, 352, and 364.

17.   Benjamin to JMM #8, Oct. 28, 1862, in JMM Papers, vol. 3, LC; also in ORUCN, ser. 2, vol. 3:581–82.

18.   Spence to JMM, Jan. 23, 1863, in JMM Papers, vol. 4, LC.

19.   Spence to JMM, Jan. 19, 1863, in JMM Papers, vol. 4, LC.

20.   Spence to JMM, Jan. 12, 1863, in JMM Papers, vol. 4, LC.

21.   Slidell to JMM, Feb. 15, 1863, in JMM Papers, vol. 4, LC.

22.   Spence to JMM, Feb. 18, 1863, in JMM Papers, vol. 4, LC.

23.   Slidell to JMM, Apr. 5, 1863, in JMM Papers, vol. 5, LC.

24.   Slidell to JMM, May 15, 1863, in JMM Papers, vol. 5, LC.

25.   Spence to JMM, Mar. 14, 1863, in JMM Papers, vol. 4, LC.

26.   Spence to JMM, Apr. 4, 1863, in JMM Papers, vol. 5, LC.

27.   Spence to JMM, July 25, 1863, in JMM Papers, vol. 6, LC.

28.   Frank L. Owsley, *King Cotton Diplomacy,* 383–84.

29.   Spence to JMM, Dec. 7, 1863, in JMM Papers, vol. 6, LC.

30.   In Oct. 1862, Hotze, while not doubting Spence's sincere friendship and devotion to Confederate independence, wrote, "I almost dread the direction his friendship and devotion seem about to take." Hotze to Benjamin #13, Oct. 24, 1862, in ORUCN, ser. 2, vol. 3:565–67.

31.   Hotze to Benjamin #31, Oct. 31, 1863, in ORUCN, ser. 2, vol. 3:944–48.

32.   Benjamin to Hotze #13, Jan. 9, 1864, in ORUCN, ser. 2, vol. 3:993–96.

33.   JMM to Benjamin #30, Feb. 9, 1863, in JMM Papers, Dispatch Book, LC; also in ORUCN, ser. 2, vol. 3:687.

34.   Benjamin to JMM (unofficial), Jan. 15, 1863, in JMM Papers, vol. 4, LC; also in ORUCN, ser. 2, vol. 3:648.

35.   Jefferson Davis to Brown, Jan. 27, 1863, in Rowland, *Jefferson Davis, Constitutionalist* 5:422–23.

36.   Milton to Jefferson Davis, Apr. 15, 1863, in WROR, ser. 4, vol. 2:487–89.

37.   Hotze to Benjamin #19, Mar. 14, 1863, Confederate States of America, Department of State Papers, vol. 53, LC also in ORUCN, ser. 2, vol. 3:710–12.

38.   Great Britain, Parliament, *Hansard's Parliamentary Debates,* 3d ser., vol. 169:581–91 (Feb. 20, 1863) and 170:776–838 (Apr. 27, 1863).

39.   Lord Clanricarde to JMM, Mar. 20, 1863, in JMM Papers, vol. 5, LC.

40.   Gregory to JMM, Mar. 18, 1863, in JMM Papers, vol. 5, LC.

41.   JMM to Slidell, Mar. 20, 1863, in JMM Papers, vol. 5, LC.

42.   Great Britain, Parliament, *Hansard's Parliamentary Debates,* 3d ser., vol. 169:1714–41 (Mar. 23, 1863).

43.   Two excellent articles on the Polish revolt and the American Civil War are John Kutolowski, "The Effect of the Polish Insurrection of 1863 on American Civil War Diplomacy," *Historian* 27, no. 4 (1965): 560–77; and Laurence J. Orzell, "A 'Favor-

able Interval': The Polish Insurrection in Civil War Diplomacy, 1863," *Civil War History* 24, no. 4 (1978): 332–50.

44. Crook, *North, South, and Powers,* 316.

45. Kutolowski, "Effect of the Polish Insurrection," 562.

46. Ibid., 565–71.

47. Slidell to JMM, Mar. 15, 1863, in JMM Papers, vol. 4, LC.

48. Slidell to Benjamin #29, Mar. 21, 1863, in ORUCN, ser. 2, vol. 3:720–21.

49. JMM to Benjamin #32, Mar. 30, 1863, in JMM Papers, Dispatch Book, LC; also in ORUCN, ser. 2, vol. 3:730–31.

50. Hotze to Benjamin #19, Mar. 14, 1863, Confederate States of America, Department of State Papers, vol. 53, LC; also in ORUCN, ser. 2, vol. 3:710–12.

51. Lucius Q. C. Lamar to Benjamin, Mar. 20, 1863, in ORUCN, ser. 2, vol. 3:716–18.

52. Crook, *North, South, and Powers,* 284–86. Relations between the tsar's government and the Lincoln administration became increasingly cordial throughout the Civil War. This was made obvious when the Russian fleet visited a number of U.S. ports in late 1862 and early 1863. See Van Deusen, *William Henry Seward,* 538–39.

53. Kutolowski, "Effect of the Polish Insurrection," 571–73.

54. JMM to Benjamin #31, Mar. 19, 1863, in JMM Papers, Dispatch Book, LC; also in ORUCN, ser. 2, vol. 3:712–16.

55. JMM to Benjamin #34, Apr. 27, 1863, in JMM Papers, Dispatch Book, LC; also in ORUCN, ser. 2, vol. 3:749–51.

56. Conway to JMM, June 10, 1863, in *William and Mary Quarterly* 21, no. 4 (1913): 221.

57. JMM to Conway, June 11, 1863, in *William and Mary Quarterly* 21, no. 4 (1913): 222.

58. JMM to Conway, June 17, 1863, in *William and Mary Quarterly* 21, no. 4 (1913): 223.

59. Benjamin to JMM #14, Feb. 6, 1863, in JMM Papers, vol. 4, LC; also in ORUCN, ser. 2, vol. 3:677–78.

60. Benjamin to JMM #17, Mar. 27, 1863, in JMM Papers, vol. 5, LC; also in ORUCN, ser. 2, vol. 3:728–29.

61. L. C. Duncan to JMM, Mar. 31, 1863, in JMM Papers, vol. 5, LC.

62. Mrs. Hugh Lee, Diary, Mar. 14, 1862, Item No. 1182 WFCHS, Archives Room, HLWV.

63. Ibid., Mar. 18, 1862. Connecticut soldiers even confiscated and sent home a cat and kittens they found at Selma, mistakenly believing them to belong to JMM. Teenager Laura Lee wrote in her diary, "It proves to be Steeles' old cat, and he is highly amused at their mistake." Laura Lee, Diary, Apr. 4, 1862, Item No. 1242-12 WFCHS, Archives Room, HLWV.

64. Cornelia McDonald, *Diary with Reminiscences,* 132. The occupying troops tore the roof off in June 1862, which led McDonald to lament in her diary the loss of "that roof, the shelter of which had never been denied to the homeless, and whose good and gifted owners had never withheld their sympathy from the sad and suffering, or their generous hospitality from any." Ibid., 76.

65. Qtd. in Julia Davis, *Shenandoah,* 186 and 235.

66. Mrs. Hugh Lee, Diary, Jan. 15 and 16, 1863, Item No. 1182 WFCHS, Archives Room, HLWV.

67. JMM to his daughter Virginia, early May 1863, in VMPL, 407–8.

68.   Ibid. Most significant for historians, the family then learned that JMM's pre-war letters were among the possessions destroyed.

69.   He traced a typical day from breakfast to dinner in JMM to Eliza Chew Mason, Apr. 1863, in VMPL, 406–7.

70.   JMM to Eliza Chew Mason, May 12, 1863, in VMPL, 408–9.

71.   Benjamin to JMM #21, Apr. 29, 1863, in JMM Papers, vol. 5, LC; also in ORUCN, ser. 2, vol. 3:753–54.

72.   Frank L. Owsley, *King Cotton Diplomacy,* 495–98.

73.   JMM to Benjamin #38, June 4, 1863, in JMM Papers, Dispatch Book, LC; also in ORUCN, ser. 2, vol. 3:782–83.

74.   JMM to Dowling, June 8, 1863, in ORUCN, ser. 2, vol. 2:436.

75.   Benjamin to JMM #29, July 6, 1863, in JMM Papers, vol. 6, LC; also in ORUCN, ser. 2, vol. 3:836.

76.   JMM to Benjamin #44, Sept. 4, 1863, in JMM Papers, Dispatch Book, LC; also in ORUCN, ser. 2, vol. 3:890–92.

77.   Jefferson Davis to Pope Pius IX, Sept. 23, 1863, and Pope Pius IX to Jefferson Davis, Dec. 3, 1863, in ORUCN, ser. 2, vol. 3:910–11 and 975.

78.   Frank L. Owsley, *King Cotton Diplomacy,* 505–6.

79.   One Confederate sympathizer suggested linking the Polish and American questions together, but JMM and his other advisors said no. See Hilton Kay to JMM, June 13, 1863, in JMM Papers, vol. 5, LC.

80.   The most recent study of what many consider Lee's ultimate triumph is Ernest B. Furgurson, *Chancellorsville, 1863: The Souls of the Brave* (New York: Alfred A. Knopf, 1992).

81.   JMM to Benjamin #37, May 16, 1863, in JMM Papers, Dispatch Book, LC; also in ORUCN, ser. 2, vol. 3:772–73.

82.   Clanricarde to JMM, May 17, 1863, in JMM Papers, vol. 5, LC.

83.   JMM to Benjamin #38, June 4, 1863, in JMM Papers, Dispatch Book, LC; also in ORUCN, ser. 2, vol. 3:782–83.

84.   JMM took the opportunity to do some touring, being quite impressed by Versailles. While at the races, he saw but did not meet Napoleon III. Being a few feet from the emperor for an hour, JMM described the French leader as not having that "grave, almost stolid expression, which his portraits give him." Instead, he had a "dignified" but "easy and almost jaunty air." JMM to Eliza Chew Mason, June 14, 1863, in VMPL, 409–10.

85.   Slidell to JMM, June 15, 1863, in JMM Papers, vol. 5, LC.

86.   Slidell to JMM, June 18, 1863, Confederate States of America, Department of State Papers, vol. 53, LC; also in ORUCN, ser. 2, vol. 3:808.

87.   Slidell to JMM, June 21, 1863, in JMM Papers, vol. 6, LC.

88.   JMM to Benjamin #40, June 20, 1863, in JMM Papers, Dispatch Book, LC; also in ORUCN, ser. 2, vol. 3:809–10.

89.   Lindsay's account of the interview is in JMM Papers, vol. 6, LC; also in VMPL, 419–25.

90.   Great Britain, Parliament, *Hansard's Parliamentary Debates,* 3d ser., vol. 171:1504–6 (June 26, 1863).

91.   JMM to Slidell, June 27, 1863, in JMM Papers, vol. 6, LC.

92.   Slidell to JMM, June 29, 1863, in JMM Papers, vol. 6, LC.

93.   Great Britain, Parliament, *Hansard's Parliamentary Debates,* 3d ser., vol. 171:1719 (June 26, 1863).

94.   Ibid., vol. 171:1771–1841 (June 30, 1863).

95.   Frank L. Owsley, *King Cotton Diplomacy,* 452–54.

96.   Great Britain, Parliament, *Hansard's Parliamentary Debates,* 3d ser., vol. 172:68–73 (July 2, 1863), 554–71 (July 10, 1863), and 661–73 (July 13, 1863).

97.   JMM to Benjamin #41, July 2, 1863, in JMM Papers, Dispatch Book, LC; also in ORUCN, ser. 2, vol. 3:824–27.

98.   JMM to Slidell, July 1, 1863, in JMM Papers, vol. 6, LC.

99.   Slidell to JMM, July 9, 1863, in JMM Papers, vol. 6, LC.

100. Spence to JMM, July 4, 1863, in JMM Papers, vol. 6, LC.

101. JMM to Benjamin #42, July 10, 1863, in JMM Papers, Dispatch Book, LC; also in ORUCN, ser. 2, vol. 3:837–38.

102. The most thorough account of the greatest battle in the history of North America remains Edwin B. Coddington, *The Gettysburg Campaign: A Study in Command* (New York: Charles Scribner's Sons, 1968).

103. Spence to JMM, July 25, 1863, in JMM Papers, vol. 6, LC.

104. Editorials ran the gamut, from predicting a quick collapse of the Confederate government to finding ways to claim the battles as southern victories. For a sample from British newspapers, see Ephraim Douglass Adams, *Great Britain* 2:176–80.

105. Frank L. Owsley, *King Cotton Diplomacy,* 472–74.

106. Benjamin to JMM #16, Feb. 21, 1863, vol. 4, LC; also in ORUCN, ser. 2, vol. 3:698.

107. Benjamin to JMM #24, June 6, 1863, in JMM Papers, vol. 5, LC; also in ORUCN, ser. 2, vol. 3:786–88.

108. JMM to Russell, July 4, 24, and 29, 1863, in JMM Papers, Dispatch Book, LC; also in ORUCN, ser. 2, vol. 3:838–39, 861, and 862.

109. Russell to JMM, Aug. 19, 1863, in JMM Papers, vol. 6, LC; also in ORUCN, ser. 2, vol. 3:892.

110. JMM to Russell, Sept. 4, 1863, in JMM Papers, Dispatch Book, LC; also in ORUCN, ser. 2, vol. 3:892–93.

111. Benjamin to Slidell #25, Oct. 8, 1863, in ORUCN, ser. 2, vol. 3:922–27.

112. Benjamin to JMM #30, Aug. 4, 1863, in JMM Papers, vol. 6, LC; also in ORUCN, ser. 2, vol. 3:852.

113. Frank L. Owsley, *King Cotton Diplomacy,* 488–90.

114. Benjamin to JMM #30, Aug. 4, 1863, in JMM Papers, vol. 6, LC; also in ORUCN, ser. 2, vol. 3:852.

115. Henry Adams to Charles Francis Adams, Jr., Sept. 25, 1863, in Worthington Chauncey Ford, ed., *A Cycle of Adams Letters, 1861–1865* (Boston, Mass.: Houghton Mifflin, 1920), vol. 2:85–88.

116. Charles Francis Adams to his son, Sept. 25, 1863, in Ford, *Cycle of Adams Letters* 2:84–85.

117. Slidell to JMM, Sept. 17, 1863, in JMM Papers, vol. 6, LC.

118. He wrote that both he and Slidell "agreed on the propriety and soundness of the policy embodied in your instructions to terminate this mission." See JMM to Benjamin #46, Sept. 25, 1863, in JMM Papers, Dispatch Book, LC; also in ORUCN, ser. 2, vol. 3:913–14.

119. JMM to Benjamin (unofficial), Oct. 19, 1863, in JMM Papers, Dispatch Book, LC; also in ORUCN, ser. 2, vol. 3:934–35.

120. JMM to Russell, Sept. 21, 1863, in JMM Papers, Dispatch Book, LC; also in ORUCN, ser. 2, vol. 3:904–5.

121. Russell to JMM, Sept. 25, 1863, in JMM Papers, vol. 6, LC; also in ORUCN, ser. 2, vol. 3:935.

122. JMM to Benjamin (unofficial), Oct. 19, 1863, in JMM Papers, Dispatch Book, LC; also in ORUCN, ser. 2, vol. 3:934–35. An inventory of his books taken at the time of his departure for Paris offers insight into his serious legalism. Containing no light reading, the list includes: "Congressional Globe and Appendix, 1856–60; American State Papers; Reports, Secretary of Treasury on the Finances, 1790–1849; Opinions of the Attorney Generals of the United States; Diplomatic Correspondence of the United States, 1783–89; United States Commercial Relations with Foreign Nations; Benton's Thirty Years in the Senate; United States Statutes at Large, 1854–60; Madison Papers and Debates on the Federal Constitution; Reports in Commerce and Navigation, 1857–59; Hickey's Constitution." In JMM Papers, vol. 6, LC.

123. JMM to Jefferson Davis, Oct. 2, 1863, in JMM Papers, vol. 6, LC; also in VMPL, 454–55.

124. JMM to A. Dudley Mann, Nov. 24, 1863, in JMM Papers, vol. 6, LC.

125. JMM to Jefferson Davis, Oct. 2, 1863, in JMM Papers, vol. 6, LC; also in VMPL, 454–55.

126. Spence to JMM, Aug. 6, 1863, in JMM Papers, vol. 6, LC.

127. Spence to JMM, Dec. 7, 1863, in JMM Papers, vol. 6, LC.

128. Spence to JMM, Dec. 17, 1863, in JMM Papers, vol. 6, LC.

129. Southern defeat at Gettysburg overshadowed the earlier victory at Chancellorsville, much as defeat at Chattanooga overshadowed the earlier triumph at Chickamauga.

130. Blumenthal, "Confederate Diplomacy," 159.

131. Frank L. Owsley, *King Cotton Diplomacy,* 549–57.

132. Thomas, *Confederate Nation,* 175–76.

133. Lindsay to JMM, Jan. 1, 1864, in JMM Papers, vol. 6, LC.

134. JMM to Eliza Chew Mason, Jan. 13, 1864, in VMPL, 458–59.

Chapter 12. 1864: Hopes, Fears, and Defiant Determination

1. Jefferson Davis and Benjamin considered JMM "too valuable and useful to be dispensed with." Benjamin to JMM #32, Nov. 13, 1863, in JMM Papers, vol. 6, LC; also in ORUCN, ser. 2, vol. 3:950–51.

2. Benjamin to JMM #34, Jan. 25, 1864, in JMM Papers, vol. 6, LC; also in ORUCN, ser. 2, vol. 3:1009–10.

3. JMM to Benjamin #1, Jan. 25, 1864, in JMM Papers, Dispatch Book, LC; also in ORUCN, ser. 2, vol. 3:1007–9.

4. In her message at the opening of Parliament, Queen Victoria made no mention of the American situation. See JMM to Benjamin #2, Feb. 8, 1864, in JMM Papers, Dispatch Book, LC; also in ORUCN, ser. 2, vol. 3:1020–21.

5. The Polish rebellion continued into August 1864, but after 1863 Britain and France virtually washed their hands of the problem. See Kutolowski, "Effect of the Polish Insurrection," 574–75.

6. René Albrecht-Carrié, *A Diplomatic History of Europe Since the Congress of Vienna,* rev. ed. (New York: Harper and Row, 1973), 127–29.

7. JMM to Benjamin #1, Jan. 25, 1864, in JMM Papers, Dispatch Book, LC; also in ORUCN, ser. 2, vol. 3:1007–9.

8. For a short discussion of the three wars of German unification, see George O. Kent, *Bismarck and His Times* (Carbondale: Southern Illinois Univ. Press, 1978), 45–76.

9. Ephraim Douglass Adams, *Great Britain* 2:202–4.

10. JMM to Benjamin #2, Feb. 8, 1864, in JMM Papers, Dispatch Book, LC; also in ORUCN, ser. 2, vol. 3:1020–21.

11. JMM to Benjamin #5, Mar. 16, 1864, in JMM Papers, Dispatch Book, LC; also in ORUCN, ser. 2, vol. 3:1047–51.

12. JMM to Jefferson Davis, Feb. 19, 1864, in Baylen and William W. White, "James M. Mason and the Failure," 101–3.

13. JMM to Benjamin #2, Feb. 8, 1864, in JMM Papers, Dispatch Book, LC; also in ORUCN, ser. 2, vol. 3:1020–21.

14. JMM to Eliza Chew Mason, Feb. 16, 1864, in VMPL, 464–66.

15. Clanricarde to JMM, Mar. 8, 1864, in JMM Papers, vol. 7, LC.

16. Frank L. Owsley, *King Cotton Diplomacy*, 154–61.

17. Hotze had little patience for Europeans who failed to understand what he saw as the beneficent nature of southern slavery. He clashed verbally and in writing with British supporters of the Confederacy who remained antislavery, while the more diplomatic JMM did not. Hendrick, *Statesmen of the Lost Cause*, 399.

18. Frank L. Owsley, *King Cotton Diplomacy*, 171–77.

19. JMM to Eliza Chew Mason, Feb. 16, 1864, in VMPL, 464–66.

20. Benjamin to JMM #34, Jan. 25, 1864, in JMM Papers, vol. 6, LC; also in ORUCN, ser. 2, vol. 3:1009–10.

21. JMM to Benjamin #5, Mar. 16, 1864, in JMM Papers, Dispatch Book, LC; also in ORUCN, ser. 2, vol. 3:1047–51.

22. JMM to Eliza Chew Mason, Apr. 12, 1864, in VMPL, 491–92.

23. Slidell to Edouard Thouvenel, July 21, 1862, in ORUCN, ser. 2, vol. 3:467–79.

24. See JMM to Eliza Chew Mason, May 12, 1863, in VMPL, 408–9. And see JMM to Benjamin #44, Sept. 4, 1863, in JMM Papers, Dispatch Book, LC; also in ORUCN, ser. 2, vol. 3:890–92.

25. For an account of the diplomacy surrounding French efforts in Mexico, see Alfred Jackson Hanna and Kathryn Abbey Hanna, *Napoleon III and Mexico: American Triumph over Monarchy* (Chapel Hill: Univ. of North Carolina Press, 1971).

26. Allan Nevins, *The War for the Union*, vol. 2: *War Becomes Revolution, 1862–1863* (New York: Charles Scribner's Sons, 1960), 259.

27. For a thorough discussion of the Monroe Doctrine and U.S. policies toward the Mexican adventure, see Dexter Perkins, *The Monroe Doctrine, 1826–1867* (Baltimore, Md.: Johns Hopkins Univ. Press, 1933), 357–548.

28. U.S. diplomats had warned Napoleon III against interfering with Mexican affairs, but their country was unwilling and unable to back up tough talk with any significant action. See Case and Spencer, *United States and France*, 547–48.

29. James Williams to JMM, Jan. 1, 1864, in JMM Papers, vol. 6, LC.

30. James Williams to JMM, Jan. 22, 1864, in JMM Papers, vol. 6, LC.

31. Alfred Hanna and Kathryn Hanna, *Napoleon III and Mexico*, 117.

32. Jefferson Davis, speech to the Confederate Congress, Jan. 12, 1863, in Rowland, *Jefferson Davis, Constitutionalist*, vol. 6:93–128.

33. Slidell to Benjamin #50, Dec. 3, 1863, in ORUCN, ser. 2, vol. 3:968–70.

34. James Williams to JMM, Jan. 22, 1864, in JMM Papers, vol. 6, LC.

35. Slidell to Benjamin #58, Mar. 16, 1864, in ORUCN, ser. 2, vol. 3:1063–65.

36. Mann to Benjamin #80, Mar. 11, 1864, in ORUCN, ser. 2, vol. 3:1057–59.

37. Reacting to the early favorable reports, Jefferson Davis had named Preston "Envoy Extraordinary and Minister Plenipotentiary to the Government of Mexico" in Janu-

ary. See Jefferson Davis to Preston, Jan. 7, 1864, in ORUCN, ser. 2, vol. 3:154–55; and Benjamin to Preston #2, Jan. 7, 1864, in ORUCN, ser. 2, vol. 3:988–90.

38.   James Williams to JMM, Mar. 16, 1864, in Rowland, *Jefferson Davis, Constitutionalist* 6:206.

39.   JMM to Benjamin #5, Mar. 16, 1864, in JMM Papers, Dispatch Book, LC; also in ORUCN, ser. 2, vol. 3:1047–51.

40.   Slidell to JMM, Mar. 13, 1864, in JMM Papers, vol. 7, LC.

41.   JMM to Eliza Chew Mason, Apr. 12, 1864, in VMPL, 491–92.

42.   JMM to Benjamin #7, Apr. 12, 1864, in JMM Papers, Dispatch Book, LC; also in ORUCN, ser. 2, vol. 3:1082–84.

43.   Jefferson Davis, speech to the Confederate Congress, May 2, 1864, in Rowland, *Jefferson Davis, Constitutionalist* 6:239–44.

44.   Benjamin to JMM #37, July 12, 1864, in JMM Papers, vol. 7, LC; also in ORUCN, ser. 2, vol. 3:1171–72.

45.   The statue "presented by English Gentlemen as a tribute of admiration for the soldier and patriot Thomas J. Jackson" still stands on the capitol square in Richmond. See JMM to Benjamin (unofficial) and JMM to Hon. William Smith, Mar. 17, 1864, in ORUCN, ser. 2, vol. 3:1065–66. Governor Smith's acceptance of "the proposed token of a great nation's appreciation of our illustrious son" on behalf of Virginia is in William Smith to JMM, Apr. 28, 1864, in Personal Papers, Acc. #13774, VSL.

46.   Benjamin to JMM #23, May 20, 1863, in JMM Papers, vol. 5, LC; also in ORUCN, ser. 2, vol. 3:773–75.

47.   JMM to Benjamin #2, #4, #7, and #9, Feb. 8 and 18, Apr. 12, and June 9, 1864, all in JMM Papers, Dispatch Book, LC; also in ORUCN, ser. 2, vol. 3:1020–21, 1031–32, 1082–84, and 1144–46.

48.   Benjamin to JMM #35, Apr. 18, 1864, in JMM Papers, vol. 7, LC; also in ORUCN, ser. 2, vol. 3:1093–95.

49.   JMM to Benjamin #10, July 6, 1864, in JMM Papers, Dispatch Book, LC; also in ORUCN, ser. 2, vol. 3:1163–64.

50.   Benjamin to JMM #38, Sept. 20, 1864, in JMM Papers, vol. 7, LC; also in ORUCN, ser. 2, vol. 3:1216–17.

51.   JMM to Benjamin #9, June 9, 1864, in JMM Papers, Dispatch Book, LC; also in ORUCN, ser. 2, vol. 3:1144–46.

52.   On Grant's strategic campaign plans for 1864, see McPherson, *Battle Cry of Freedom,* 718–24 and 742–43.

53.   Jefferson Davis, *Rise and Fall* 2:526.

54.   Benjamin to JMM #35, Apr. 18, 1864, in JMM Papers, vol. 7, LC; also in ORUCN, ser. 2, vol. 3:1093–95.

55.   JMM to Benjamin #9, June 9, 1864, in JMM Papers, Dispatch Book, LC; also in ORUCN, ser. 2, vol. 3:1144–46.

56.   Clanricarde to JMM, May 1, 1864, in JMM Papers, vol. 7, LC.

57.   Lindsay to JMM, May 10, 1864, in JMM Papers, vol. 7, LC.

58.   Palmerston had become a bit more flexible because he wanted Lindsay and other friends of the Confederacy to support his policy on the situation in Schleswig-Holstein. See Ephraim Douglass Adams, *Great Britain* 2:210; Baylen and William W. White, "James M. Mason and the Failure," 100–101.

59.   Lindsay to JMM, May 27, 1864, in JMM Papers, vol. 7, LC.

60.   JMM to Lindsay, May 29, 1864, in JMM Papers, vol. 7, LC.

61.   Lindsay to JMM, May 30, 1864, in JMM Papers, vol. 7, LC.

62. Spence to JMM, May 31, 1864, in JMM Papers, vol. 7, LC.

63. JMM to Benjamin #8, June 1, 1864, in JMM Papers, Dispatch Book, LC; also in ORUCN, ser. 2, vol. 3:1136–39.

64. JMM to Eliza Chew Mason, June 2, 1864, in VMPL, 502–3.

65. See Lindsay remarks in the House of Commons, May 31, 1864, in Great Britain, Parliament, *Hansard's Parliamentary Debates,* 3d ser., vol. 175:912. And see JMM to Benjamin #9, June 9, 1864, in JMM Papers, Dispatch Book, LC; also in ORUCN, ser. 2, vol. 3:1144–46.

66. JMM to Eliza Chew Mason, June 2, 1864, in VMPL, 502–3.

67. JMM to Eliza Chew Mason, June 11, 1864, in VMPL, 503–4.

68. JMM to Benjamin #11, July 8, 1864, in JMM Papers, Dispatch Book, LC; also in ORUCN, ser. 2, vol. 3:1168–69.

69. Ephraim Douglass Adams, *Great Britain* 2:214.

70. JMM to Benjamin (unofficial), July 14, 1864, in JMM Papers, Dispatch Book, LC; also in ORUCN, ser. 2, vol. 3:1173–74.

71. JMM to Slidell, July 16, 1864, in JMM Papers, vol. 7, LC.

72. Slidell to JMM, July 17, 1864, in JMM Papers, vol. 7, LC.

73. JMM to Benjamin #12, Aug. 4, 1864, in JMM Papers, Dispatch Book, LC; also in ORUCN, ser. 2, vol. 3:1183–84.

74. Spence to JMM, July 18, 1864, in JMM Papers, vol. 7, LC.

75. JMM to Benjamin #12, Aug. 4, 1864, in JMM Papers, Dispatch Book, LC; also in ORUCN, ser. 2, vol. 3:1183–84.

76. Journal of John R. Thompson, Aug. 4–Nov. 4, 1864, in John R. Thompson Collection, Box 2, ALUV.

77. JMM to Benjamin (unofficial), Sept. 18, 1864, Confederate States of America, Department of State Papers, vol. 53, LC.

78. JMM learned of the Canadian talks and reports of northern weariness, in Clement C. Clay and James P. Holcombe to JMM, July 18, 1864, in JMM Papers, vol. 7, LC.

79. Benjamin to JMM (circular), Aug. 25, 1864, in JMM Papers, vol. 7, LC; also in ORUCN, ser. 2, vol. 3:1190–94.

80. JMM to Eliza Chew Mason, Sept. 19, 1864, in VMPL, 511–12.

81. Thompson to his wife, Sept. 20, 1864, in John R. Thompson Collection, Box 2, ALUV.

82. JMM to Eliza Chew Mason, Sept. 19, 1864, in VMPL, 511–12.

83. JMM to his son George Mason, Sept. 21, 1864, in VMPL, 512–14.

84. Benjamin to JMM #38, Sept. 20, 1864, in JMM Papers, vol. 7, LC; also in ORUCN, ser. 2, vol. 3:1216–17.

85. "Manifesto of the Confederate Congress," June 14, 1864, qtd. in Benjamin to JMM (circular), Aug. 25, 1864, in JMM Papers, vol. 7, LC; also in ORUCN, ser. 2, vol. 3:1190–94.

86. JMM to Slidell, Oct. 12, 1864; Slidell to Mann, Oct. 13, 1864; and JMM to Mann, Oct. 14, 1864; all in JMM Papers, vol. 7, LC.

87. JMM to Mann, Nov. 3, 1864, in JMM Papers, vol. 7, LC.

88. JMM to Benjamin #14, Nov. 10, 1864, in JMM Papers, Dispatch Book, LC; also in ORUCN, ser. 2, vol. 3:1230–33.

89. Russell to JMM, Slidell, and Mann, Nov. 25, 1864, in JMM Papers, vol. 7, LC; also in ORUCN, ser. 2, vol. 3:1246.

90. JMM to Benjamin #15, Dec. 16, 1864, in JMM Papers, Dispatch Book, LC; also in ORUCN, ser. 2, vol. 3:1250–51.

91. Ephraim Douglass Adams, *Great Britain* 2:241.

92. Jefferson Davis, speech to the Confederate Congress, Nov. 7, 1864, in Rowland, *Jefferson Davis, Constitutionalist* 6:384–98.

93. Benjamin to Slidell #44 , Dec. 27, 1864, and Benjamin to JMM #39, Dec. 30, 1864, in JMM Papers, vol. 8, LC; also in ORUCN, ser. 2, vol. 3:1253–57.

94. Patrick, *Jefferson Davis and His Cabinet,* 188.

95. Benjamin to Slidell #44, Dec. 27, 1864, and Benjamin to JMM #39, Dec. 30, 1864, both in JMM Papers, vol. 8, LC; also in ORUCN, ser. 2, vol. 3:1253–57.

96. JMM to Benjamin #17, Jan. 21, 1865, in JMM Papers, Dispatch Book, LC; also in ORUCN, ser. 2, vol. 3:1257–58.

97. He also predicted that warnings issued in the German states regarding U.S. "frauds practiced on Emigrants to force them, on arrival, into the army" would "have the effect of deterring emigration for the present." See JMM to Benjamin (unofficial), Nov. 29, 1864, in Confederate States of America, Department of State Papers, vol. 53, LC.

98. JMM to Benjamin #16, Jan. 12, 1865, in JMM Papers, Dispatch Book, LC; also in ORUCN, ser. 2, vol. 3:1057–58.

99. JMM, Jr., to his father, Dec. 30, 1864, in Pamela C. Copeland, Mason Family Research File, Main Research File, GHL.

100. Ibid.

Chapter 13. 1865–1866: From Diplomat to Exile

1. JMM to Benjamin #17, Jan. 21, 1865, in JMM Papers, Dispatch Book, LC; also in ORUCN, ser. 2, vol. 3:1270–71.

2. Ibid.

3. A. Coolidge to JMM, Dec. 15, 1864, in VMPL, 531–32.

4. JMM to Coolidge, Jan. 25, 1865, in VMPL, 532–39.

5. Ibid.

6. JMM to Benjamin #18, Feb. [6], 1865, in JMM Papers, Dispatch Book, LC; also in ORUCN, ser. 2, vol. 3:1260.

7. Slidell to JMM, Feb. 3, 1865, in JMM Papers, vol. 8, LC.

8. Russell to JMM, Slidell, and Mann, Feb. 13, 1865, in JMM Papers, vol. 8, LC; also in ORUCN, ser. 2, vol. 3:1267–69.

9. Slidell to JMM, Feb. 14, 1865, in JMM Papers, vol. 8, LC.

10. Frank L. Owsley, *King Cotton Diplomacy,* 536–37.

11. JMM to Benjamin #19, Mar. 31, 1865, in JMM Papers, Dispatch Book, LC; also in ORUCN, ser. 2, vol. 3:1266–67.

12. JMM, Slidell, and Mann to Russell, Feb. 27, 1865, in JMM Papers, vol. 8, LC; also in ORUCN, ser. 2, vol. 3:1269–70.

13. Slidell to JMM, Mar. 6, 1865, in JMM Papers, vol. 8, LC.

14. JMM to Mann, Mar. 15, 1865, in JMM Papers, vol. 8, LC.

15. JMM, memorandum on his conversation with Lord Palmerston, Mar. 14, 1865, enclosed with JMM to Benjamin #20, Mar. 31, 1865, in JMM Papers, Dispatch Book, LC; also in ORUCN, ser. 2, vol. 3:1272–76.

16. JMM to Benjamin #20, Mar. 31, 1865, in JMM Papers, Dispatch Book, LC; also in ORUCN, ser. 2, vol. 3:1270–71.

17. JMM, memorandum on his conversation with Lord Donoughmore, Mar. 26, 1865, enclosed with JMM to Benjamin #20, Mar. 31, 1865, in JMM Papers, Dispatch Book, LC; also in ORUCN, ser. 2, vol. 3:1276–77.

18.   JMM to Mann, Mar. 15, 1865, in JMM Papers, vol. 8, LC.

19.   JMM to Benjamin #20, Mar. 31, 1865, in JMM Papers, Dispatch Book, LC; also in ORUCN, ser. 2, vol. 3:1270–71.

20.   George M. Henry to Jefferson Davis, Feb. 25, 1865, in Rowland, *Jefferson Davis, Constitutionalist* 6:484–87.

21.   JMM to Eliza Chew Mason, Mar. 25, 1865, in VMPL, 568–70.

22.   For a full account of the Confederate government's evacuation and flight from the federal armies, see Burke Davis, *The Long Surrender* (New York: Random House, 1985), 19–131.

23.   Jefferson Davis, *Rise and Fall* 2:696–97.

24.   Hampton to Jefferson Davis, Apr. 19, 1865, in Rowland, *Jefferson Davis, Constitutionalist* 6:552–53.

25.   Burke Davis, *Long Surrender,* 135–48.

26.   Jefferson Davis to J. D. Shaw, Mar. 22, 1865, in Rowland, *Jefferson Davis, Constitutionalist* 6:518–19.

27.   JMM to Mann, Apr. 23, 1865, in JMM Papers, vol. 8, LC.

28.   JMM to Slidell, Apr. 23, 1865, in JMM Papers, vol. 8, LC.

29.   Slidell to JMM, Apr. 26, 1865, in JMM Papers, vol. 8, LC.

30.   JMM to Slidell, Apr. 29, 1865, in JMM Papers, vol. 8, LC.

31.   Ibid.

32.   On the floor of the U.S. Senate, the plebeian Johnson often had clashed rhetorically with the patrician JMM. Memories of such clashes no doubt informed the Virginian's expectations regarding the new president's actions toward the South.

33.   Innumerable studies of Lincoln's assassination have offered various grand conspiracy theories. Most were debunked thoroughly by William Hanchett, *The Lincoln Murder Conspiracies* (Urbana: Univ. of Illinois Press, 1983). A more recent book, William A. Tidwell, with James O. Hall and David Winfred Gaddy, *Come Retribution: The Confederate Secret Service and the Assassination of Lincoln* (Jackson: Univ. Press of Mississippi, 1988), discusses the Confederate government's involvement in espionage. Despite the provocative title, the authors produce no conclusive evidence to link Richmond to the assassination.

34.   Stanton to Adams, Apr. 15, 1865, in WROR, ser. 1, vol. 46:784–85.

35.   JMM to the editor of the *London Index,* Apr. 27, 1865, in VMPL, 565–67.

36.   Ibid.

37.   JMM to Shaftesbury, Apr. 28, 1865, in JMM Papers, vol. 8, LC. See also JMM to A. J. Beresford Hope, Apr. 26, 1865, in JMM Papers, Special Collections Department, William R. Perkins Library, Duke Univ., Durham, N.C.

38.   JMM to Benjamin #21, May 1, 1865, in JMM Papers, Dispatch Book, LC; also in ORUCN, ser. 2, vol. 3:1277.

39.   JMM to Mann, May 25, 1865, in JMM Papers, vol. 8, LC.

40.   John W. Cowell to JMM, May 31, 1865, in JMM Papers, vol. 8, LC.

41.   France and Britain's coordination in revoking those rights is discussed in Case and Spencer, *United States and France,* 579–85, and in Ephraim Douglass Adams, *Great Britain* 2:265–69.

42.   The subject came up for discussion in both houses of Parliament on May 15. But Palmerston and Russell refused to act with undue haste. See Great Britain, Parliament, *Hansard's Parliamentary Debates,* 3d ser., vol. 179:286–91 and 296–97 (both, May 15, 1865).

43.   That caused the ministry's withdrawal of Confederate belligerent rights to come

under criticism in the House of Lords. See Great Britain, Parliament, *Hansard's Parliamentary Debates,* 3d ser., vol. 180:1–6 (June 12, 1865); Ephraim Douglass Adams, *Great Britain* 2:267–68.

44. JMM to Eliza Chew Mason, June 7, 1865, in VMPL, 570–71.

45. Spence suggested that Eliza and the girls join JMM in England instead. See Spence to JMM, June 16, 1865, in JMM Papers, vol. 8, LC.

46. JMM to Eliza Chew Mason, June 14, 1865, in VMPL, 571.

47. Bulloch, *Secret Service of the Confederate States* 2:155–56.

48. JMM to Bulloch, June 13, 1865, in Bulloch, *Secret Service of the Confederate States* 2:156–57.

49. Bulloch to James Waddell, June 19, 1865, in JMM Papers, vol. 8, LC; also in ORUCN, ser. 2, vol. 2:811–12.

50. Bulloch to JMM, June 19, 1865, in JMM Papers, vol. 8, LC; also in ORUCN, ser. 1, vol. 3:775.

51. JMM to Russell, June 20 and 26, 1865, in JMM Papers, vol. 8, LC; also in ORUCN, ser. 1, vol. 3:777–78.

52. Bulloch, *Secret Service of the Confederate States* 2:162–63.

53. Jefferson Davis, *A Short History of the Confederate States of America* (New York: Belford Co., 1890), 319.

54. For examples in which JMM blamed European power politics for the lack of diplomatic recognition, see JMM to Benjamin #32, Mar. 30, 1863, and JMM to Benjamin #5, Mar. 16, 1864, both in JMM Papers, Dispatch Book, LC; also in ORUCN, ser. 2, vol. 3:730–31 and 1047–51.

55. Blumenthal, "Confederate Diplomacy," 166–67.

56. JMM to O'Conor, June 19, 1865, in JMM Papers, vol. 8, LC. Imprisoned at Fort Monroe in Hampton Roads, Va., Jefferson Davis had written a personal acceptance of the offer, but U.S. officials insisted that the letter be rewritten and refused O'Conor's attempts to see the Confederate leader. See Robert McElroy, *Jefferson Davis the Unreal and the Real* (New York: Harper and Brothers, 1937), vol. 2:536–39.

57. McRae to JMM, June 20, 1865, in JMM Papers, vol. 8, LC; see Charles S. Davis, *Colin J. McRae,* 81–82.

58. JMM to O'Conor, July 29, 1865, in JMM Papers, vol. 8, LC.

59. O'Conor to JMM, July 9, 1865, in JMM Papers, vol. 8, LC.

60. JMM, "What Is to Be the Future of the South?" (memorandum), July 1865, in JMM Papers, vol. 8, LC; also in VMPL, 575–77.

61. Ibid.

62. Slidell wrote that he could not "stomach the word *pardon* or *amnesty.*" Neither could Mason. Slidell to JMM, July 26, 1865, in JMM Papers, vol. 8, LC.

63. JMM to Eliza Chew Mason, Aug. 9, 1865, in VMPL, 572.

64. Benjamin's escape from federal authorities reads like a James Bond novel, complete with intrigue, disguises, near-captures, and brushes with death. See Eli N. Evans, *Judah P. Benjamin: The Jewish Confederate* (New York: Free Press, 1988), 294–321; Robert Douthat Meade, *Judah P. Benjamin: Confederate Statesman* (London: Oxford Univ. Press, 1943), 319–25.

65. JMM to Eliza Chew Mason, Aug. 16, 1865, in VMPL, 572.

66. JMM to Eliza Chew Mason, Aug. 17, 1865, in VMPL, 572.

67. JMM to Eliza Chew Mason, Aug. 23, 1865, in VMPL, 572–73.

68. JMM to daughter Virginia Mason, Sept. 23, 1865, in VMPL, 573–74.

69. JMM to his daughters, Oct. [27], 1865, in VMPL, 574–75.

70. JMM to his daughters, Oct. 24, 1865, in VMPL, 574.

71. Bulloch to JMM, Sept. 28, 1865, in JMM Papers, vol. 8, LC.

72. JMM to Mann, Sept. 3, 1865, in JMM Papers, vol. 8, LC. The trio arranged for the disbursement of money in the remaining Confederate bank accounts to the various commissioners and agents for expenses and services rendered, an action that JMM had to defend to U.S. authorities who claimed that the funds had become federal property after Richmond's surrender. See JMM to General Walker, Nov. 8, 1865, in JMM Papers, vol. 8, LC.

73. O'Conor to JMM, Aug. 16, Sept. 6, Oct. 9, and Dec. 26, 1865, in JMM Papers, vol. 8, LC. The first and last letters are excerpted in McElroy, *Jefferson Davis the Unreal and the Real* 2:547–48 and 552–53.

74. A vast number of monographs on Reconstruction exists, but the most recent comprehensive treatment of the subject is Eric Foner, *Reconstruction: America's Unfinished Revolution, 1863–1877* (New York: Harper and Row, 1988).

75. JMM to his daughters, Oct. [27], 1865, in VMPL, 574–75.

76. JMM to his daughters, Nov. 23, 1865, in VMPL, 575.

77. Spence to JMM, Oct. 4, 1865. in JMM Papers, vol. 8, LC.

78. JMM to Eliza Chew Mason, Jan. 18, 1866, in VMPL, 577–79. Because of his peculiar status, the U.S. consulate could not help him and sent him to the Lord Mayor's office.

79. Charles Wells Russell to Margaret Watkins Gaines, Nov. 29, 1865, in Charles Wells Russell Papers, Mss2R 9122a 1, VHS.

80. JMM to Eliza Chew Mason, Jan. 18, 1866, in VMPL, 577–79.

81. JMM to his daughters, Nov. 23, 1865, in VMPL, 575.

82. JMM to Eliza Chew Mason, Mar. 15 and 22, 1866, in VMPL, 579–81.

83. JMM to Eliza Chew Mason, Apr. 12, 1866, in VMPL, 584.

84. JMM to daughter Virginia Mason, Apr. 5, 1866, in VMPL, 581–83.

85. JMM to Eliza Chew Mason, Apr. 12, 1866, in VMPL, 584.

86. JMM to daughter Virginia Mason, Apr. 5, 1866, in VMPL, 581–83.

87. JMM to Eliza Chew Mason, Apr. 26, 1866, in VMPL, 585; JMM to Corcoran, Apr. 21, 1866, in Corcoran Papers, vol. 15, LC.

88. JMM to Eliza Chew Mason, Apr. 26, 1866, in VMPL, 585.

89. JMM to daughter Virginia Mason, Apr. 5, 1866, in VMPL, 581–83.

Chapter 14. 1866–1871: Virginia Homecoming

1. VMPL, 586.

2. JMM to Eliza Chew Mason, Aug. 9 and 16, 1865, in VMPL, 572.

3. VMPL, 586.

4. JMM to McRae, June 22, 1866, qtd. in Charles S. Davis, *Colin J. McRae*, 82.

5. For recent discussions of Jefferson Davis's imprisonment, see Burke Davis, *Long Surrender*, 173–223; and William C. Davis, *Jefferson Davis: The Man and His Hour* (New York: Harper Collins, 1991), 640–57.

6. The letter ended on a more personal note, with Benjamin asking JMM to send "a photograph of yourself" to "your truly attached friend." Benjamin to JMM, Oct. 25, 1866, in JMM Papers, ALUV.

7. JMM to Corcoran, Nov. 13, 1866, in Corcoran Papers, vol. 16, LC.

8. JMM to Mrs. Thomas H. Ellis, Nov. 12, 1866, in Elizabeth Byrd Nicholas Collection, Mss1 1N5156a, Reel 68, VHS.

9. JMM, handwritten documents regarding the suit for debts against his property in Winchester, Va., Mar. 30 and June 8, 1867, in JMM Papers, ALUV.

10. *Winchester Times,* July 3, 1867.

11. Robert Steel acquired the property and sold it to Judge Edward Pendleton in 1872. Judge Pendleton erected his dwelling on the site of the original Mason home. That building on Amherst Street, bearing the famous name "Selma," still stands, surrounded by ancient trees that undoubtedly stood there when the Masons called the spot home. See Garland R. Quarles, *The Story of One Hundred Old Homes in Winchester, Virginia* (Winchester, Va.: Prepared for Farmers and Merchants National Bank, 1967), 11; and Quarles, *Some Worthy Lives,* 173.

12. VMPL, 587.

13. JMM to Jefferson Davis, May 14, 1867, in Rowland, *Jefferson Davis, Constitutionalist* 7:104.

14. VMPL, 587.

15. JMM to Jefferson Davis, May 14, 1867, in Rowland, *Jefferson Davis, Constitutionalist* 7:104.

16. Qtd. in William C. Davis, *Jefferson Davis: The Man and His Hour,* 658.

17. JMM to Jefferson Davis, June 7, 17, and 28, 1867, in Rowland, *Jefferson Davis, Constitutionalist* 7:111, 115, and 116.

18. JMM to Jefferson Davis, Aug. 12, 1867, in Rowland, *Jefferson Davis, Constitutionalist* 7:125.

19. Benjamin to JMM, May 29, 1867, in JMM Papers, ALUV.

20. JMM to Corcoran, Mar. 24, 1868, in Corcoran Papers, vol. 17, LC.

21. JMM to Jefferson Davis, June 13, 1868, in Rowland, *Jefferson Davis, Constitutionalist* 7:241.

22. John Hope Franklin, *Reconstruction after the Civil War* (Chicago: Univ. of Chicago Press, 1961), 83.

23. JMM to Corcoran, Mar. 24, 1868, in Corcoran Papers, vol. 17, LC.

24. Ibid.

25. JMM to Jefferson Davis, June 13, 1868, in Rowland, *Jefferson Davis, Constitutionalist* 7:241.

26. JMM to Corcoran, Oct. 19, 1868, in Corcoran Papers, vol. 17, LC.

27. Qtd. in VMPL, 589.

28. JMM to Corcoran, Oct. 19, 1868, in Corcoran Papers, vol. 17, LC.

29. Written at Niagara, the document is entitled "The Last Will and Testament of the Subscriber JMM of Virginia in the late United States of America—now in exile in Canada because he loved Virginia, and detested the enemies." Mason Last Will and Testament, May 26, 1868, in Mason Family Papers, GHL.

30. Qtd. in VMPL, 590.

31. JMM to Corcoran, Apr. 27, 1869, in Corcoran Papers, vol. 17, LC.

32. VMPL, 590.

33. JMM to Robert M. T. Hunter, Oct. 15, 1869, in Papers of R. M. T. Hunter, Hunter-Garnett Collection, Box 39, ALUV.

34. VMPL, 591.

35. JMM to Hunter, Oct. 15, 1869, in Papers of R. M. T. Hunter, Hunter-Garnett Collection, Box 39, ALUV.

36. Clarens still stands on Quaker Lane, in what is now downtown Alexandria. See Somerville, "Confederacy's Special Commissioner," 24 and 28–29.

37. VMPL, 591.

38. Somerville, "Confederacy's Special Commissioner," 28.

39. JMM to Hunter, Oct. 15, 1869, in Papers of R. M. T. Hunter, Hunter-Garnett Collection, Box 39, ALUV.

40. Hunter to JMM, Oct. 16, 1869, in VMPL, 592–93.

41. Cooper teased JMM for having shucked less corn than he, with his own unblistered hands, had shucked. VMPL, 591–92.

42. JMM to Corcoran, Oct. 22, 1869, in Corcoran Papers, vol. 18, LC.

43. Somerville, "Confederacy's Special Commissioner," 29.

44. See, e.g., JMM to Corcoran, Mar. 28 and Apr. 9, 1870, in Corcoran Papers, vol. 18, LC.

45. Robert E. Lee to JMM, Mar. 3, 1870, in Robert E. Lee Papers, MSSC-L51-C-738, VHS.

46. Jefferson Davis to JMM, June 11, 1870, in VMPL, 593–95.

47. Although disappointed that JMM could not travel with him, Jefferson Davis did spend some time at Clarens before sailing in August.

48. JMM to Jefferson Davis, June 16, 1870, in Rowland, *Jefferson Davis, Constitutionalist* 7:272.

49. Jefferson Davis to JMM, June 11, 1870, in VMPL, 593–95.

50. JMM to Jefferson Davis, June 16, 1870, in Rowland, *Jefferson Davis, Constitutionalist* 7:272.

51. JMM pointed out that his failing eyesight made an honest opponent an absolute necessity, because he had "to trust his adversary to tell me the throws." See JMM to Corcoran, July 12, 1870, in Corcoran Papers, vol. 18, LC.

52. Virginia Mason to Corcoran, Nov. 18, 1870, in Corcoran Papers, vol. 18, LC.

53. JMM to Corcoran, Nov. 21, 1870, in Corcoran Papers, vol. 18, LC.

54. JMM to Hunter, Jan. 31, 1871, Papers of R. M. T. Hunter, Hunter-Garnett Collection, Box 41, ALUV.

55. Benjamin to JMM, Feb. 8, 1871, in JMM Papers, ALUV.

56. Hunter to JMM, Feb. 14, 1871, Launcelot Minor Blackford Papers, ALUV.

57. JMM to Hunter, Jan. 31, 1871, Papers of R. M. T. Hunter, Hunter-Garnett Collection, Box 41, ALUV.

58. Benjamin responded to a Jan. 24 letter from JMM by updating his old colleague on European diplomatic and military affairs, as well as on the death of Slidell's wife. See Benjamin to JMM, Feb. 8, 1871, in JMM Papers, ALUV.

59. Hunter to JMM, Sept. 19, 1870, in VMPL, 595–97; and JMM to Hunter, Jan. 31, 1871, in Papers of R. M. T. Hunter, Hunter-Garnett Collection, Box 41, ALUV.

60. Hunter to JMM, Feb. 14, 1871, in Launcelot Minor Blackford Papers, ALUV.

61. Emily Virginia Mason to "My dear Harriet," Mar. 31, 1871, in Harrison Family Papers, Mss1 H2485 g 15–32, VHS.

62. VMPL, 603.

63. Ida Mason (daughter of JMM) to "My dear Harriet," May 15, 1871, in Harrison Family Papers, Mss1 H2485 g 15–32, VHS.

64. Qtd. in VMPL, 603.

65. Ida Mason to "My dear Harriet," May 15, 1871, in Harrison Family Papers, Mss1 H2485 g 15–32, VHS.

66. Lucy Ambler (granddaughter of JMM) to "My dear Cousin," Apr. 29, 1871, in Harrison Family Papers, Mss1 H2485 g 15–32, VHS.

67. Ibid.

68. Ida Mason to "My dear Harriet," May 15, 1871, in Harrison Family Papers, Mss1 H2485 g 15–32, VHS.

69. Lucy Ambler to "My dear Cousin," Apr. 29, 1871, in Harrison Family Papers, Mss1 H2485 g 15–32, VHS.

70. *Alexandria Gazette* and *Virginia Advertiser,* both May 1, 1871.

71.   Ida Mason to "My dear Harriet," May 15, 1871, in Harrison Family Papers, Mss1 H2485 g 15–32, VHS.

72.   Also buried in the family's section of the Christ Church Episcopal Cemetery on Wilkes Lane in Alexandria are JMM's mother and father, three of his daughters, a brother, a sister, and a number of cousins and grandchildren.

73.   *Richmond Enquirer,* May 10, 1871, rpt. in Henry A. Wise, "James Murray Mason," 186–92.

◆◆◆ Bibliography ◆◆◆

I. Manuscripts

Alderman Library, University of Virginia, Charlottesville, Virginia:
    Manuscripts Department
        Launcelot Minor Blackford Papers
        William McCreary Burwell Papers, 4400-B
        Cooper Family Papers, 8610
        Papers of Alexander Galt, Jr., and His Family
        Hubard Family Papers
        Papers of R. M. T. Hunter, Hunter-Garnett Collection
        James Murray Mason Papers
        John Mason Papers, 5036
        Socrates Maupin Papers, 2769
        McGregor Collection—Madison-Todd Papers
        Thomas Jefferson Randolph Papers, 8937-B
        John R. Thompson Collection
Boston Public Library, Boston, Massachusetts:
    Manuscripts
        James Murray Mason Papers
Gunston Hall Library, Lorton, Virginia:
        Pamela C. Copeland, Mason Family Research File, Main Research File
        Mason Family Papers, 1664–1897
Handley Library, Winchester, Virginia:
    Archives Room
        Harriet H. Griffith, Diary, Item No. 1179 WFCHS

Mrs. Hugh Lee, Diary, Item No. 1182 WFCHS
Laura Lee, Diary, Item No. 1242-12 WFCHS
Frederick County Personal Property Tax Books, 1821–1850
United States Census, Slave Schedules, Frederick County, Sept. 3, 1860
Library of Congress, Washington, D.C.:
Manuscripts Division
Confederate States of America, Department of State Papers
W. W. Corcoran Papers
Jefferson Davis and Family Papers
Abraham Lincoln Papers
William Learned Marcy Papers
James Murray Mason Papers
Franklin Pierce Papers
William Cabell Rives Papers
John Tyler Papers
Massachusetts Historical Society, Boston, Massachusetts:
George Bancroft Papers
J. H. Clifford Papers
Samuel G. Howe Papers
Miscellaneous Papers
Norcross Papers
Robert C. Winthrop Papers
National Archives, Washington, D.C.:
Manuscripts
RG 46 Records of the United States Senate
Microfilm Series
M-179 Miscellaneous Letters of the Department of State, 1789–1906
M-1196 Records of the Senate Committee That Investigated John Brown's
Raid at Harpers Ferry, Virginia, in 1859
New-York Historical Society, New York City:
Manuscripts Department
Miscellaneous Manuscripts—James Murray Mason
William R. Perkins Library, Duke University, Durham, North Carolina:
Special Collections Department
Jefferson Davis Papers
James Murray Mason Papers
Pierpont Morgan Library, New York, New York:
Autographs
Miscellaneous Americans
Virginia Historical Society, Richmond, Virginia:
Manuscripts
William Garnett Chisholm Collection
Harrison Family Papers
Robert E. Lee Papers
James Murray Mason Papers
Elizabeth Byrd Nicholas Collection
Paulus Powell Papers
Charles Wells Russell Papers
William Selden Papers
Virginia Governor, 1830–1834 (John Floyd) Papers

Virginia State Library and Archives, Richmond, Virginia:
  Archives and Records Division
        Custis-Lee-Mason Papers, Acc. #20975, Items 54–63
        Executive Branch, Governor's Office, Letters Received
        Mason Family Papers, 1756–1877
        Personal Papers

II. Printed Primary Sources

Ambler, Charles H., ed. *Correspondence of Robert M. T. Hunter, 1826–1876.* American Historical Association Annual Report, 1916, vol. 2. Washington, D.C.: AHA, 1918.

Bourne, Kenneth, and D. Cameron Watt, eds. *British Documents on Foreign Affairs: Reports and Papers from the Foreign Office Confidential Print: Part I, From the Mid-Nineteenth Century to the First World War.* Volumes 5, 6, and 7: *The Civil War Years.* Series C, North America, 1837–1914. 15 vols. Bethesda, Md.: University Publications of America, 1986.

Calendar of Virginia State Papers and Other Manuscripts, from Jan. 1, 1836, to Apr. 15, 1869, Preserved in the Capitol at Richmond, Arranged, Edited, and Printed under the Authority and Direction of H. W. Flournoy, Secretary of the Commonwealth and State Librarian. 11 vols. Richmond, Virginia, 1893.

Chittenden, L. E., ed. *Report of the Debates and Proceedings of the Peace Convention Held at Washington, D.C., Feb. 1861.* 1861. Rpt. New York: Da Capo Press, 1971.

Confederate States of America. Congress. *Journal of the Congress of the Confederate States of America, 1861–1865.* 7 vols. Washington, D.C.: U.S. Government Printing Office, 1904–5.

Farrand, Max, ed. *The Records of the Federal Convention of 1787.* 4 vols. Rpt. New Haven, Connecticut: Yale University Press, 1966.

Ford, Worthington Chauncey, ed. *A Cycle of Adams Letters, 1861–1865.* 2 vols. Boston, Massachusetts: Houghton Mifflin Company, 1920.

Giles, William Branch, comp. *Political Miscellanies.* Richmond, Virginia, 1829.

Great Britain, Parliament. *Hansard's Parliamentary Debates,* 3d ser. London, 1862–65.

Manning, William R., ed. *The Diplomatic Correspondence of the United States: Inter-American Affairs, 1831–1860.* 12 vols. Washington, D.C.: Carnegie Endowment for International Peace, 1932–39.

McPherson, Edward, ed. *The Political History of the United States of America during the Great Rebellion: 1860–1865.* Rpt. New York: Da Capo Press, 1972.

Monroe, Haskell M., Jr.; James T. McIntosh; Lynda Lasswell Crist; Mary Seaton Dix; and Kenneth H. Williams, eds. *The Papers of Jefferson Davis.* 8 vols. to date. Baton Rouge: Louisiana State University Press, 1971–95.

Moore, John B., ed. *The Works of James Buchanan: Comprising His Speeches, State Papers, and Private Correspondences,* 12 vols. Rpt. New York: Antiquarian Press Ltd., 1960.

Official Records of the Union and Confederate Navies in the War of the Rebellion. 31 vols. Washington, D.C.: U.S. Government Printing Office, 1894–1927.

Proceedings and Debates of the Virginia State Convention of 1829–30: To Which Are Subjoined, the New Constitution and the Votes of the People. 2 vols. Richmond, Virginia: Printed by S. Shepherd and Co., for Ritchie & Cook, 1830. Rpt. New York: Da Capo Press, 1971.

Reese, George H., ed. *Journals and Papers of the Virginia State Convention of 1861.* 4 vols. Richmond, Va., 1965.

Richardson, James D., ed. *A Compilation of the Messages and Papers of the Presidents, 1789–1908.* 11 vols. New York: Bureau of National Literature and Art, 1896–1910.

————. *The Messages and Papers of Jefferson Davis and the Confederacy, Including Diplomatic Correspondence: 1861–1865.* 2 vols. New edition. New York: Chelsea House–Robert Hector Publishers, 1966.

Rowland, Dunbar, ed. *Jefferson Davis, Constitutionalist: His Letters, Papers, and Speeches.* 10 vols. Jackson: Printed for the Mississippi Department of Archives and History, 1923.

Spence, James. *The American Union: Its Effect on National Character and Policy, with an Inquiry into Secession as a Constitutional Right, and the Causes of Disruption.* London: Richard Bentley, New Burlington Street, Publisher in Ordinary to Her Majesty, 1862.

Strode, Hudson, ed. *Jefferson Davis: Private Letters, 1823–1889.* New York: Harcourt, Brace and World, 1966.

U.S. Congress. *Congressional Globe.* Washington, D.C., 1834–73.

————. Senate. *Journal of the Executive Proceedings of the Senate of the United States of America, 1789–1861.* 11 vols. Washington, D.C., 1828–87.

————. Senate. Select Committee on the Harpers Ferry Invasion. *Mass Violence in America: Invasion at Harpers Ferry* (Journal of the Select Committee Appointed to Inquire into the Facts Attending the Late Invasion and Seizure of the U.S. Armory at Harpers Ferry, Virginia). Rpt. New York: Arno Press and the *New York Times*, 1969.

The War of the Rebellion: A Compilation of the Official Records of the Union and Confederate Armies. 128 vols. Washington, D.C.: U.S. Government Printing Office, 1880–1901.

III. Memoirs and Biographies

Adams, Charles Francis, Jr. *1835–1915: An Autobiography.* Boston: Houghton Mifflin Company, 1916.

Bulloch, James D. *The Secret Service of the Confederate States in Europe; or, How the Confederate Cruisers Were Equipped.* 2 vols. London: Richard Bentley and Son, 1883.

Chesnut, Mary Boykin. *A Diary from Dixie, as Written by Mary Boykin Chesnut, . . .* Edited by Isabella D. Martin and Myrta Lockett Avary. New York: Appleton Company, 1905.

Davis, Charles S. *Colin McRae: Confederate Financial Agent.* Tuscaloosa, Alabama: Confederate Publishing Company, 1961.

Davis, Jefferson. *The Rise and Fall of the Confederate Government.* 2 vols. New York: Belford Company, 1881.

————. *A Short History of the Confederate States of America.* New York: Belford Company, 1890.

Davis, Varina. *Jefferson Davis, Ex-President of the Confederate States of America: A Memoir by His Wife.* 2 vols. New York: Belford Company, 1890.

Davis, William C. *Jefferson Davis: The Man and His Hour.* New York: Harper Collins Publishers, 1991.

Durkin, Joseph T. *Stephen R. Mallory: Confederate Navy Chief.* Chapel Hill: University of North Carolina Press, 1954.

Eaton, Clement. *Jefferson Davis.* New York: Free Press, 1977.

Evans, Eli N. *Judah P. Benjamin: The Jewish Confederate.* New York: Free Press, 1988.

Kent, George O. *Bismarck and His Times.* Carbondale: Southern Illinois University Press, 1978.

Leonard, Cynthia Miller, comp. *The General Assembly of Virginia, July 30, 1619, to Jan. 11, 1978: A Bicentennial Register of Members.* Richmond: Published for the General Assembly of Virginia by the Virginia State Library, 1978.

Mason, Virginia. *The Public Life and Diplomatic Correspondence of James M. Mason, with Some Personal History by Virginia Mason (His Daughter).* New York: Neale Publishing Company, 1906.

McElroy, Robert. *Jefferson Davis the Unreal and the Real.* 2 vols. New York: Harper and Brothers Publishers, 1937.

Meade, Robert Douthat. *Judah P. Benjamin: Confederate Statesman.* London: Oxford University Press, 1943.

Moran, Benjamin. *The Journal of Benjamin Moran, 1857–1865.* Edited by Sarah A. Wallace and Frances E. Gillespie. 2 vols. Chicago: University of Chicago Press, 1949.

Nichols, Roy F. *Franklin Pierce: Young Hickory of the Granite Hills.* Revised edition. Philadelphia: University of Pennsylvania Press, 1958.

Niven, John. *John C. Calhoun and the Price of Union.* Baton Rouge: Louisiana State University Press, 1988.

Parrish, William E. *David Rice Atchison of Missouri: Border Politician.* Columbia: University of Missouri Press, 1961.

Peterson, Merrill D. *The Great Triumvirate: Webster, Clay, and Calhoun.* Oxford, England: Oxford University Press, 1987.

Quarles, Garland R. *Some Worthy Lives: Mini-Biographies of Winchester and Frederick County.* Winchester, Virginia: Winchester–Frederick County Historical Society, 1988.

Rutland, Robert. *George Mason: Reluctant Statesman.* Charlottesville: University Press of Virginia, 1961.

Scarborough, William Kauffman, ed. *The Diary of Edmund Ruffin.* 3 vols. Baton Rouge: Louisiana State University Press, 1972.

Sears, Louis Martin. *John Slidell.* Durham, North Carolina: Duke University Press, 1925.

Spencer, Ivor D. *The Victor and the Spoils: A Life of William L. Marcy.* Providence, Rhode Island: Brown University Press, 1959.

Strode, Hudson. *Jefferson Davis: American Patriot.* New York: Harcourt Brace and Company, 1955.

———. *Jefferson Davis: Confederate President.* New York: Harcourt Brace and Company, 1959.

———. *Jefferson Davis: Tragic Hero.* New York: Harcourt Brace and Company, 1964.

Van Deusen, Glyndon G. *William Henry Seward.* New York: Oxford University Press, 1967.

Walpole, Spencer. *The Life of Lord John Russell.* 2 vols. London: Longmans, Green and Company, 1889.

Wiltse, Charles Maurice. *John C. Calhoun.* 3 vols. Indianapolis, Indiana: Bobbs-Merrill, 1944–51.

Wise, Henry A. "James Murray Mason." *Southern Historical Society Papers* 25 (1897): 186–92.

IV. Secondary Accounts: Books

Adams, Ephraim Douglass. Great Britain and the American Civil War. 2 vols. New York: Longmans, Green and Company, 1925.

Albrecht-Carrié, René. *A Diplomatic History of Europe since the Congress of Vienna.* Revised edition. New York: Harper and Row Publishers, 1973.

Bailey, Thomas A. *A Diplomatic History of the American People.* 10th ed. Englewood Cliffs, New Jersey: Prentice-Hall, 1980.

Balace, Francis. *La Belgique et la guerre de sécession: 1861–1865.* 2 vols. Paris: Société d'édition "Les Belles Lettres," 1979.

Ball, Douglas B. *Financial Failure and Confederate Defeat.* Urbana: University of Illinois Press, 1991.

Barney, William L. *Battleground for the Union: The Era of the Civil War and Reconstruction, 1848–1877.* Englewood Cliffs, New Jersey: Prentice-Hall, 1990.

———. *The Road to Secession: A New Perspective on the Old South.* New York: Praeger, 1972.

Beard, Charles A., and Mary R. Beard. The Rise of American Civilization. 2 vols. New York: Macmillan, 1927.

Bemis, Samuel Flagg. *John Quincy Adams and the Foundations of American Foreign Policy.* New York: Alfred A. Knopf, 1949.

———, ed. *The American Secretaries of State and Their Diplomacy.* 10 vols. New York: Alfred A. Knopf, 1928.

Blassingame, John W. *The Slave Community: Plantation Life in the Antebellum South.* Oxford, England: Oxford University Press, 1972.

Blumenthal, Henry. *A Reappraisal of Franco-American Relations: 1830–1871.* Chapel Hill: University of North Carolina Press, 1959.

Bonham, Milledge L. *The British Consuls in the Confederacy.* New York: Columbia University Press, 1911.

Burns, Richard Dean, ed. *Guide to American Foreign Relations since 1700.* Santa Barbara, California: ABC-Clio, for the Society for Historians of American Foreign Relations, 1983.

Callahan, James Morton. *Diplomatic History of the Confederacy.* Baltimore, Maryland: Johns Hopkins University Press, 1901. Rpt. New York: Frederick Ungar Publishing Company, 1964.

Campbell, Stanley W. *The Slave Catchers: Enforcement of the Fugitive Slave Law, 1850–1860.* Chapel Hill: University of North Carolina Press, 1968.

Carpenter, Jesse. *The South as a Conscious Minority, 1789–1861.* New York: New York University Press, 1930.

Case, Lynn M., and Warren F. Spencer. *The United States and France: Civil War Diplomacy.* Philadelphia: University of Pennsylvania Press, 1970.

Coddington, Edwin B. *The Gettysburg Campaign: A Study in Command.* New York: Charles Scribner's Sons, 1968.

Connor, Seymour V., and Odie B. Faulk. *North America Divided: The Mexican War, 1846–1848.* New York: Oxford University Press, 1971.

Cooper, William J., Jr. *The South and the Politics of Slavery, 1828–1856.* Baton Rouge: Louisiana State University Press, 1978.

Copeland, Pamela C., and Richard K. MacMaster. *The Five George Masons: Patriots and Planters of Virginia and Maryland.* Charlottesville: Published for the Board of Regents of Gunston Hall by the University Press of Virginia, 1975.

Coulter, E. Merton. *The Confederate States of America, 1861–1865.* Baton Rouge: Louisiana State University Press, 1950.

Craven, Avery. *The Coming of the Civil War.* Chicago: University of Chicago Press, 1942.

———. *Edmund Ruffin, Southerner: A Study in Secession.* Baton Rouge: Louisiana State University Press, 1932.

———. *The Growth of Southern Nationalism, 1848–1861.* Baton Rouge: Louisiana State University Press, 1953.

Crawford, Martin. *The Anglo-American Crisis of the Mid-Nineteenth Century: 'The Times' and America, 1850–1862.* Athens: University of Georgia Press, 1987.

Crofts, Daniel W. *Reluctant Confederates: Upper South Unionists in the Secession Crisis.* Chapel Hill: University of North Carolina Press, 1989.

Crook, D. P. *The North, the South, and the Powers, 1861–1865.* New York: John Wiley and Sons, 1974.

Crozier, William A., ed. *Virginia Heraldica, Being a Registry of Virginia Gentry Entitled to Coat Armor with Genealogical Notes of the Families.* New York: Virginia County Record Series, 1908. Rpt. Baltimore, Maryland: Genealogical Publishing Company, 1965.

Cullop, Charles P. *Confederate Propaganda in Europe, 1861–1865.* Coral Gables, Florida: University of Miami Press, 1969.

Davis, Burke. *The Long Surrender.* New York: Random House, 1985.

Davis, Julia. *The Shenandoah.* New York: Farrar and Rinehart, 1945.

Davis, William C. *"A Government of Our Own:" The Making of the Confederacy.* New York: Free Press, 1994.

Donald, Davis Herbert. *Charles Sumner and the Coming of the Civil War.* New York: Alfred A. Knopf, 1960.

———. *Lincoln Reconsidered: Essays on the Civil War Era.* 2d ed. New York: Vintage Books of Random House, 1956.

Dowdey, Clifford. *Experiment in Rebellion.* Garden City, New York: Doubleday and Company, 1946.

———. *The Land They Fought For: The Story of the South as the Confederacy, 1832–1865.* Garden City, New York: Doubleday and Company, 1955.

Dowty, Alan. *The Limits of American Isolation: The United States and the Crimean War.* New York: New York University Press, 1971.

Dumond, Dwight Lowell. *The Secession Movement, 1860–1861.* New York: Century Press, 1931.

Eaton, Clement. *A History of the Southern Confederacy.* New York: Free Press, 1954.

Ellison, Mary. *Support for Secession: Lancashire and the American Civil War.* Chicago: University of Chicago Press, 1972.

Ettinger, Amos A. *The Mission to Spain of Pierre Soulé, 1853–1855: A Study in the Cuban Diplomacy of the United States.* New Haven, Connecticut: Yale University Press, 1932.

Fehrenbacher, Don E. *The Dred Scott Case: Its Significance in American Law and Politics.* Oxford, England: Oxford University Press, 1978.

———. *The South and Three Sectional Crises.* Baton Rouge: Louisiana State University Press, 1978.

Ferris, Norman B. *Desperate Diplomacy: William Henry Seward's Foreign Policy, 1861.* Knoxville: University of Tennessee Press, 1976.

———. *The 'Trent' Affair: A Diplomatic Crisis.* Knoxville: University of Tennessee Press, 1977.

Filler, Louis. *The Crusade Against Slavery: 1830–1860.* New York: Harper and Brothers, 1960.

Finkelman, Paul, ed. *His Soul Goes Marching On: Responses to John Brown and the Harpers Ferry Raid.* Charlottesville: University Press of Virginia, 1995.

Foner, Eric. *Free Soil, Free Labor, Free Men: The Ideology of the Republican Party before the Civil War.* Oxford, England: Oxford University Press, 1970.

———. *Reconstruction: America's Unfinished Revolution, 1863–1877.* New York: Harper and Row, 1988.

Franklin, John Hope. *Reconstruction after the Civil War.* Chicago: University of Chicago Press, 1961.

Freehling, Alison Goodyear. *Drift Toward Dissolution: The Virginia Slavery Debate of 1831–1832.* Baton Rouge: Louisiana State University Press, 1982.

Freehling, William W. *Prelude to Civil War: The Nullification Controversy in South Carolina, 1816–1836.* New York: Harper and Row, 1965.

———. *The Road to Disunion: Secessionists at Bay, 1776–1854.* London: Oxford University Press, 1990.

Furgurson, Ernest B. *Chancellorsville, 1863: The Souls of the Brave.* New York: Alfred A. Knopf, 1992.

Graebner, Norman A. *Empire on the Pacific: A Study in American Continental Expansion.* New York: Ronald Press, 1955; rpt. Santa Barbara, California: ABC-Clio, 1983.

Hamilton, Holman. *Prologue to Conflict: The Crisis and Compromise of 1850.* Lexington: University of Kentucky Press, 1964.

Hammond, Bray. *Banks and Politics in America from the Revolution to the Civil War.* Princeton, New Jersey: Princeton University Press, 1957.

Hanchett, William. *The Lincoln Murder Conspiracies.* Urbana: University of Illinois Press, 1983.

Hanna, Alfred Jackson, and Kathryn Abbey Hanna. *Napoleon III and Mexico: American Triumph over Monarchy.* Chapel Hill: University of North Carolina Press, 1971.

Hendrick, Burton J. *Statesmen of the Lost Cause: Jefferson Davis and His Cabinet.* New York: Literary Guild of America, 1939.

Hendrickson, Robert. *Sumter: The First Day of the Civil War.* Chelsea, Michigan: Scarborough House, 1990.

Holt, Michael F. *The Political Crisis of the 1850s.* New York: John Wiley and Sons, 1978.

Horsman, Reginald. *Race and Manifest Destiny: The Origins of American Racial Anglo-Saxonism.* Cambridge, Massachusetts: Harvard University Press, 1981.

Huston, James L. *The Panic of 1857 and the Coming of the Civil War.* Baton Rouge: Louisiana State University Press, 1987.

Jaffa, Harry V. *Crisis of the House Divided: An Interpretation of the Issues in the Lincoln-Douglas Debates.* Chicago: University of Chicago Press, 1959.

Jenkins, Brian. *Britain and the War for the Union.* 2 vols. Montreal, Canada: McGill-Queen's University Press, 1974 and 1980.

Johnson, Ludwell H. *Division and Reunion: America, 1848–1877.* New York: John Wiley and Sons, 1978.

Jones, Howard. *Mutiny on the 'Amistad': The Saga of a Slave Revolt and Its Impact* on

American Abolition, Law, and Diplomacy. Oxford, England: Oxford University Press, 1987.

———. *Union in Peril: The Crisis over British Intervention in the Civil War.* Chapel Hill: University of North Carolina Press, 1992.

Jones, Wilbur D. *The Confederate Rams at Birkenhead: A Chapter in Anglo-American Relations.* Tuscaloosa, Alabama: Confederate Publishing Company, 1961.

Jordan, Donaldson, and Edwin J. Pratt. *Europe and the American Civil War.* Boston: Houghton Mifflin Company, 1931.

Kaestle, Carl F. *Pillars of the Republic: Common Schools and American Society, 1780–1860.* New York: Hill and Wang, 1983.

Kaminski, John P., and Richard Leffler, eds. *Federalists and Anti-Federalists: The Debate over the Ratification of the Constitution.* Madison, Wisconsin: Madison House, 1989.

Krein, David F. *The Last Palmerston Government: Foreign Policy, Domestic Politics, and the Genius of "Splendid Isolation."* Ames: Iowa State University Press, 1978.

Lester, Richard I. *Confederate Finance and Purchasing in Great Britain.* Charlottesville: University Press of Virginia, 1975.

McCormick, Richard P. *The Second American Party System: Party Formation in the Jacksonian Era.* Chapel Hill: University of North Carolina Press, 1966.

McDonald, Cornelia. *A Diary with Reminiscences of the War and Refugee Life in the Shenandoah Valley, 1860–1865.* Annotated and supplemented by Hunter McDonald. Nashville, Tennessee: Cullom and Ghertner, Co., 1934.

McGrane, Reginald Charles. *The Panic of 1837: Some Financial Problems of the Jacksonian Era.* Chicago: University of Chicago Press, 1924.

McPherson, James M. *Abraham Lincoln and the Second American Revolution.* Oxford, England: Oxford University Press, 1991.

———. *Battle Cry of Freedom: The Civil War Era.* New York: Ballantine Books, 1988.

May, Robert E. *The Southern Dream of a Caribbean Empire: 1854–1861.* Baton Rouge, Louisiana: Louisiana State University Press, 1973.

Merk, Frederick. *Manifest Destiny and Mission in American History.* New York: Vintage Books of Random House, 1963.

Merli, Frank J. *Great Britain and the Confederate Navy.* Bloomington: Indiana University Press, 1970.

Morgan, Edmund S. *American Slavery, American Freedom: The Ordeal of Colonial Virginia.* New York: W. W. Norton and Company, 1975.

Nevins, Allan. *The Emergence of Lincoln.* 2 vols. New York: Charles Scribner's Sons, 1950.

———. *Ordeal of the Union.* 2 vols. New York: Charles Scribner's Sons, 1947.

———. *The War for the Union.* 4 vols. New York: Charles Scribner's Sons, 1959–71.

Nichols, Roy F. *The Democratic Machine, 1850–1854.* 1923. Rpt. New York: AMS Press, 1967.

———. *The Disruption of American Democracy.* New York: Free Press, 1948.

Oates, Stephen B. *To Purge the Land with Blood: A Biography of John Brown.* New York: Harper and Row, 1970.

Owsley, Frank L. *King Cotton Diplomacy: Foreign Relations of the Confederate States of America.* Chicago: University of Chicago Press, 1931. Revised by Harriet C. Owsley, 1959.

Patrick, Rembert W. *Jefferson Davis and His Cabinet.* Baton Rouge: Louisiana State University Press, 1944.

Perkins, Dexter. *The Monroe Doctrine, 1826–1867.* Baltimore, Maryland: Johns Hopkins University Press, 1933.

Peterson, Merrill D., ed. *Democracy, Liberty, and Property: The State Constitutional Conventions of the 1820s.* New York: Bobbs-Merrill, 1966.

Pletcher, David M. *The Diplomacy of Annexation: Texas, Oregon, and the Mexican War.* Columbia: University of Missouri Press, 1973.

Potter, David M. *The Impending Crisis, 1848–1861.* Edited and completed by Don E. Fehrenbacher. New York: Harper and Row, 1976.

———. *Lincoln and His Party in the Secession Crisis.* New Haven, Connecticut: Yale University Press, 1942.

———. *The South and the Sectional Conflict.* Baton Rouge: Louisiana State University Press, 1968.

Quarles, Garland R. *The Story of One Hundred Old Homes in Winchester, Virginia.* Winchester, Virginia: Prepared for Farmers and Merchants National Bank, 1967.

Rable, George. *The Confederate Republic: A Revolution Against Politics.* Chapel Hill: University of North Carolina Press, 1994.

Rawley, James A. *Race and Politics: "Bleeding Kansas" and the Coming of the Civil War.* Philadelphia, Pennsylvania: J. B. Lippincott, 1969.

Renehan, Edward J., Jr. *The Secret Six: The True Tale of the Men Who Conspired with John Brown.* New York: Crown Publishers, 1995.

Richards, Leonard L. *The Life and Times of Congressman John Quincy Adams.* Oxford, England: Oxford University Press, 1986.

Schwab, John C. *The Confederate States of America, 1861–1865: A Financial and Industrial History of the South during the Civil War.* New York: Charles Scribner's Sons, 1901.

Sewell, Richard H. *A House Divided: Sectionalism and Civil War, 1848–1865.* Baltimore, Maryland: Johns Hopkins University Press, 1988.

Shanks, Henry T. *The Secession Movement in Virginia, 1847–1861.* Richmond, Virginia: Garrett and Massie Publishers, 1934.

Smith, Elbert B. *The Death of Slavery: The United States, 1837–1865.* Chicago: University of Chicago Press, 1967.

———. *The Presidency of James Buchanan.* Lawrence: University Press of Kansas, 1975.

Spencer, Warren F. *The Confederate Navy in Europe.* Tuscaloosa: University of Alabama Press, 1983.

Stampp, Kenneth M. *America in 1857: A Nation on the Brink.* Oxford, England: Oxford University Press, 1990.

———. *And the War Came: The North and the Secession Crisis.* Baton Rouge: Louisiana State University Press, 1950.

———. *The Imperiled Union: Essays on the Background of the Civil War.* Oxford, England: Oxford University Press, 1980.

Stern, Philip Van Doren. *When the Guns Roared: World Aspects of the American Civil War.* Garden City, New York: Doubleday and Company, 1965.

Swanberg, W. A. *First Blood: The Story of Fort Sumter.* New York: Charles Scribner's Sons, 1957.

Sydnor, Charles S. *American Revolutionaries in the Making: Political Practices in Washington's Virginia.* New York: Free Press, 1965.

Taylor, William R. *Cavalier and Yankee: The Old South and American National Character.* New York: George Braziller, 1961.

Temin, Peter. *The Jacksonian Economy.* New York: W. W. Norton and Company, 1969.

Thomas, Emory M. *The Confederacy as a Revolutionary Experience.* Englewood Cliffs,

New Jersey: Prentice-Hall, 1971. Rpt. Columbia: University of South Carolina Press, 1991.

———. *The Confederate Nation: 1861–1865*. New York: Harper and Row, 1979.

Tidwell, William A., with James O. Hall and David Winfred Gaddy. *Come Retribution: The Confederate Secret Service and the Assassination of Lincoln*. Jackson: University Press of Mississippi, 1988.

Vandiver, Frank E. *Jefferson Davis and the Confederate State: An Inaugural Lecture Delivered before the University of Oxford on 26 Feb. 1964*. Oxford, England: Clarendon Press, 1964.

———. *Their Tattered Flags: The Epic of the Confederacy*. New York: Harper and Row, 1970.

Ward, A. W., and G. P. Gooch, eds. *The Cambridge History of British Foreign Policy: 1783–1919*. 3 vols. Cambridge, England: Cambridge University Press, 1922–23.

Warren, Gordon H. *Fountain of Discontent: The Trent Affair and Freedom of the Seas*. Boston, Massachusetts: Northeastern University Press, 1981.

Weinberg, Albert K. *Manifest Destiny: A Study of National Expansionism in American History*. Baltimore, Maryland: Johns Hopkins University Press, 1935.

Wharton, Anne Hollingworth. *Social Life in the Early Republic, with Numerous Reproductions of Portraits, Miniatures and Residences*. Philadelphia, Pennsylvania: J. B. Lippincott, 1902.

White, Leonard D. *The Jacksonians: A Study in Administrative History, 1829–1861*. New York: Free Press, 1954.

———. *The Jeffersonians: A Study in Administrative History, 1801–1829*. New York: Free Press, 1951.

Willson, Beckles. *John Slidell and the Confederates in Paris, 1862–1865*. New York: Minton and Balch, 1932.

Wise, Stephen R. *Lifeline of the Confederacy: Blockade Running during the Civil War*. Columbia: University of South Carolina Press, 1988.

Wolff, Gerald W. *The Kansas-Nebraska Bill: Party, Section, and the Coming of the Civil War*. New York: Revisionist Press, 1977.

Wooster, Ralph A. *Politicians, Planters, and Plain Folk: Courthouse and Statehouse in the Upper South: 1850–1860*. Knoxville: University of Tennessee Press, 1975.

Wyatt-Brown, Bertram. *Southern Honor: Ethics and Behavior in the Old South*. Oxford, England: Oxford University Press, 1982.

———. *Yankee Saints and Southern Sinners*. Baton Rouge: Louisiana State University Press, 1985.

Yearns, Wilfred Buck. *The Confederate Congress*. Athens: University of Georgia Press, 1960.

V. Secondary Accounts: Articles

Baxter, James P. "The British Government and Neutral Rights, 1861–1865." *American Historical Review* 34, no. 4 (1928): 9–29.

———. "Some British Opinions as to Neutral Rights, 1861–1865." *American Journal of International Law* 23, no. 3 (1929): 517–37.

Baylen, Joseph O., and William W. White. "James M. Mason and the Failure of the Confederate Naval Effort in Europe, 1863–1864." *Louisiana Studies* 2, no. 2 (1963): 98–108.

Blumenthal, Henry. "Confederate Diplomacy: Popular Notions and International Realities." *Journal of Southern History* 32, no. 2 (1966): 151–71.

Brady, Eugene A. "A Reconsideration of the Lancashire 'Cotton Famine'." *Agricultural History* 37, no. 3 (1963): 156–62.

Brauer, Kinley J. "British Mediation and the American Civil War: A Reconsideration." *Journal of Southern History* 38, no. 1 (1972): 49–64.

———. "The Slavery Problem in the Diplomacy of the American Civil War." *Pacific Historical Review* 46, no. 3 (1977): 439–69.

———. "The United States and British Imperial Expansion, 1815–60." *Diplomatic History* 12, no. 1 (1988): 19–37.

Eaton, Clement. "Henry A. Wise and the Fire Eaters of 1856." *Mississippi Valley Historical Review* 21, no. 4 (1935): 495–512.

Gentry, Judith Fenner. "A Confederate Success in Europe: The Erlanger Loan." *Journal of Southern History* 36, no. 2 (1970): 157–88.

Gienapp, William E. "The Crime Against Sumner: The Caning of Charles Sumner and the Rise of the Republican Party." *Civil War History* 25, no. 3 (1979): 218–45.

Harrison, Royden. "British Labour and the Confederacy." *International Review of Social History* 2, no. 1 (1957): 78–105.

Hernon, Joseph M., Jr. "British Sympathies in the American Civil War: A Reconsideration." *Journal of Southern History* 33, no. 3 (1967): 356–67.

Hitchcock, William S. "Southern Moderates and Secession: Senator Robert M. T. Hunter's Call for Union." *Journal of American History* 59, no. 4 (1973): 871–84.

Hodder, Frank H. "The Authorship of the Compromise of 1850." *Mississippi Valley Historical Review* 22, no. 3 (1936): 525–36.

Jones, Horace P. "Southern Opinion on the Crimean War." *Journal of Mississippi History* 29, no. 2 (1967): 95–117.

Jones, Wilbur D. "The British Conservatives and the American Civil War." *American Historical Review* 58, no. 3 (1953): 527–43.

Krein, David F. "Russell's Decision to Detain the Laird Rams." *Civil War History* 22, no. 2 (1976): 158–63.

Kutolowski, John. "The Effect of the Polish Insurrection of 1863 on American Civil War Diplomacy." *Historian* 27, no. 4 (1965): 560–77.

Landry, Harral E. "Slavery and the Slave Trade in Atlantic Diplomacy, 1850–1861." *Journal of Southern History* 27, no. 2 (1961): 184–207.

Lester, Richard I. "An Aspect of Confederate Finance During the American Civil War: The Erlanger Loan and the Plan of 1864." *Business History* 16, no. 2 (1974): 130–44.

McKivigan, John R. "James Redpath, John Brown, and Abolitionist Advocacy of Slave Insurrection." *Civil War History* 37, no. 4 (1991): 293–313.

McWhiney, Grady. "Jefferson Davis and the Art of War." *Civil War History* 21, no. 2 (1975): 101–12.

Mering, John V. "The Slave-State Constitutional Unionists and the Politics of Consensus." *Journal of Southern History* 43, no. 3 (1977): 395–410.

Merli, Frank J. "Crown versus Cruiser: The Curious Case of the Alexandra." *Civil War History* 9, no. 2 (1963): 167–77.

Merli, Frank J., and Theodore A. Wilson. "The British Cabinet and the Confederacy: Autumn 1862." *Maryland Historical Magazine* 65, no. 3 (1970): 239–62.

Nichols, Roy F. "The Kansas-Nebraska Act: A Century of Historiography." *Mississippi Valley Historical Review* 43, no. 2 (1956): 187–212.

Orzell, Laurence J. "A 'Favorable Interval': The Polish Insurrection in Civil War Diplomacy, 1863." *Civil War History* 24, no. 4 (1978): 332–50.

Roberts, William P. "James Dunwoody Bulloch and the Confederate Navy." *North Carolina Historical Review* 24, no. 3 (1947): 315–66.

Russel, Robert Royal. "The Issues in the Congressional Struggle Over the Kansas-Nebraska Bill, 1854." *Journal of Southern History* 29, no. 2 (1963): 187–210.

Sears, Louis M. "A Confederate Diplomat at the Court of Napoleon III." *American Historical Review* 26, no. 2 (1921): 255–81.

Somerville, Mollie. "The Confederacy's Special Commissioner to Great Britain." *Virginia Record* 90 (Sept. 1968): 24–29.

———. "General John Mason of Analostan Island." *Iron Worker* 26, no. 2 (Spring 1962): 3–11.

Stanard, W. G. "Abstracts of Virginia Land Patents." *Virginia Magazine of History and Biography* 1 (1893): 87–88.

Sutherland, Keith A. "The Senate Investigates Harpers Ferry." *Prologue* 8 Winter (1976): 192–207.

Urban, C. Stanley. "The Africanization of the Cuba Scare, 1853–1855." *Hispanic American Historical Review* 37, no. 1 (1957): 29–45.

Walmsley, James Elliott. "The Change of Secession Sentiment in Virginia in 1861." *American Historical Review* 31, no. 1 (1925): 82–101.

Webster, Sidney. "Mr. Marcy, the Cuban Question, and the Ostend Manifesto." *Political Science Quarterly* 8, no. 1 (1893): 1–32.

William and Mary Quarterly 21, no. 4 (1913): 221–23.

Wolff, Gerald W. "Party and Section: The Senate and the Kansas-Nebraska Bill." *Civil War History* 18, no. 4 (1972): 332–50.

VI. Newspapers

Alexandria Gazette and Virginia Advertiser
Boston Evening Transcript
Boston Post
London Times
New York Herald
New York Times
Richmond (Va.) Enquirer
Richmond (Va.) Examiner
Richmond (Va.) Whig
Washington Constitution
Washington Herald
Washington National Intelligencer
Washington Union
Winchester (Va.) Times
Winchester Virginian

VII. Dissertations and Theses

Bugg, James L., Jr. "The Political Career of James Murray Mason: The Legislative Phase." Ph.D. dissertation, University of Virginia, 1950.

Case, Walter M. "James M. Mason, Confederate Diplomat." M.A. thesis, Stanford University, 1915.

Dugan, Ethel. "John Slidell, Confederate Diplomat to France." M.A. thesis, Stanford University, 1915.

Hix, Evelyn. "James M. Mason, Confederate Commissioner to England: 1862–1865."
    M.A. thesis, University of Alabama, 1944.
Olson, Magne B. "The Evolution of a Senate Institution: The Committee on Foreign
    Relations to 1861." Ph.D. dissertation, University of Minnesota, 1971.
Stegmaier, Mark J. "The U.S. Senate in the Sectional Crisis, 1846–1861: A Roll-Call
    Voting Analysis." Ph.D. dissertation, University of California at Santa Barbara,
    1975.
Todd, Herbert H. "The Building of a Confederate States Navy in Europe." Ph.D.
    dissertation, Vanderbilt University, 1941.
Turner, Ammon B. "James M. Mason and the Confederate States Mission to En-
    gland." M.A. thesis, University of Chicago, 1932.
Young, Robert W. "Jefferson Davis and Confederate Foreign Policy." M.A. thesis,
    University of Maryland, 1987.

♦♦♦ Index ♦♦♦

Senator James Murray Mason was designed and typeset on a Macintosh computer
system using PageMaker software. The text and titles are set in Galliard. This book was
designed and composed by Kim Scarbrough and was printed and bound by Thomson-
Shore, Inc. The recycled paper used in this book is designed for an effective life of at
least three hundred years.